Architecture in Vienna

A publication of the
Stadtplanung Wien, Magistratsabteilung 18
and Magistratsabteilung 19, and
the Architektur Zentrum Wien

Planned and Edited by
August Sarnitz

With Contributions by
Renate Banik-Schweitzer
August Sarnitz
Dietmar Steiner
Siegfried Mattl

 SpringerWienNewYork

Impressum

"Architecture in Vienna" was conceived in 1996 by the City Councillor Dr. Hannes Swoboda, and published during the period of office of deputy Mayor and City Councillor Dr. Bernhard Görg.

A publication of the
Stadtplanung Wien,
Magistratsabteilung 18,
Magistratsabteilung 19,
and the Architektur Zentrum Wien

Planned and Edited by
August Sarnitz

Selection of Buildings
Friedrich Achleitner, Otto Kapfinger, Harald Niebauer, Dieter Pal,
August Sarnitz, Dietmar Steiner

Special Adviser
Arnold Klotz

Essays by
Renate Banik-Schweitzer
August Sarnitz
Dietmar Steiner
Siegfried Mattl

Copy-Editing
Susan and Katia Siegle

Descriptions and Data of the Selected Buildings
August Sarnitz, Ruth Hanisch

Translations into English
Ramesh Kumar Biswas
David Gogarty
Nita Tandon

Colour photographs
Georg Riha

Black and white photographs
Margherita Spiluttini, Robert Kiermayer, Mischa Erben, Gerald Zugmann, Atelier Hollein,
Werner Kaligofsky

Printed in Austria

Graphic design
August Sarnitz

Cover design
Haller and Haller

Cover photo
Georg Riha

Cartography - district maps
© Freytag & Berndt

Printing
Adolf Holzhausens Nfg., A - 1070 Wien

Printed on acid-free and chlorine-free bleached paper

SPIN: 10674063

ISBN 3-211-83111-8 Springer-Verlag Wien New York

Contents

Architecture in Vienna

Presented here are 500 buildings, which, on account of their representative character, give the city its identity. 2000 years of Viennese history lie before the reader, approximately one-third of the buildings described dating from the Middle Ages to 1918, the end of the Habsburg monarchy. The remaining two-thirds cover the architecture of the inter-war years up to the present period, with particular emphasis being laid on the building of the last two decades.

The topography of a place is its most important feature, its structure and character developing from it. The buildings are thus presented topographically because, as the specific layers have piled up over the ages, it is at each particular location that the historical, political, economic and social structure is to be seen at its densest: the city as a "compact package".

Vienna is a city of contrasts, a place where things intersect, with multicultural as well as traditional aspects, and a deep skepticism shown towards change. It is a magical city with an extensive history and multifarious strata, and its architecture reflects all these varied influences, generating a heterogenous and multifaceted art of building.

Each building has been allotted a topographical index number corresponding to the 23 districts into which Vienna is divided. The first number indicates the district in which the object is located, the second, in bold type, the object itself (e.g. St. Stephen´s Cathedral 1. 1. = 1st district, number 1; Schönbrunn Palace 13. 3. = 13th district, number 3), and a whole page is allocated to buildings of outstanding significance. Each building is introduced by a short description, with accompanying photos and plans, other objects of interest being mentioned at the end of each section. Beneath the address of each building is both information on its accessibility by public transport, and whether it is open to the public.

The buildings are indicated on 14 folding maps by the corresponding index numbers, enabling each to be found quickly and, on walks, to be located easily within the individual topographical setting.

Four essays present the architecture of the city in its historical and socio-cultural context: an urban history of Vienna is followed by an architectural history of 20th century Viennese architecture; a short article on housing in the city from a social-economic standpoint is accompanied, at the end of the guide, by a socio-historical survey of Vienna´s contemporary history.

Each object is chronologically listed in the appendix, which also cites the architects and planners. Personal tips and special routes devised by well-known Viennese architects bring the icons of the city´s architecture to life, and the colour photographs will, it is hoped, help send the urban wanderer, joyfully off, eyes open to the glories of Viennese architecture.

Vienna
Development of the city

Vienna is over 2000 years old, thanks to its strategic position. This latter fact has also meant that its architectural history up to the second Turkish siege of 1683 is purely a history of the fortified first district. The city lies at the point where different regions and cultures intersect, which is why it was, up to the end of the seventeenth century, a permanently embattled border fortress city. The continuity of urban form, however, only goes back to about 100 a.d., when the Roman garrison of Vindobona was built as part of the frontier fortifications against the barbarians from the north. After the fall of the Western Roman Empire in 500 a.d., the region was invaded by the Huns, Avars and Slavs. The tenth century saw Vienna as part of a Magyar Empire extending far into the West, but soon after, once the Magyars had been forced back, the city became a borderland outpost on the south- eastern flank of the German Empire. The Babenbergs, of Frankish stock, were invested with the new border province, and when, in 1137, they moved their seat from Klosterneuburg to Vienna, the latter was made their residence. For almost 600 years, Vienna functioned both as a border city and capital.

The City of Vienna had difficulty in asserting itself in this new constellation. The security and independence needed for it to develop of its own accord and exert an interregional influence, as had been achieved for example by more autonomous towns such as Augsburg and Nuremberg, were lacking. In terms of production, financial power and size of population, these cities outstripped Vienna in the Middle Ages. This was triggered off by local entrepreneurs there engaging in long-distance trade and organizing a putting-out system among local craftsmen, establishing at the same time a financial apparatus. Such a grouping could never develop in Vienna, on the one hand because the influence of the princes was too great, on the other, because the Viennese patriciate lived mainly off ground rents - the only export product being the wine from the vineyards in the environs of the city, which enabled such a good living to be made that there was no need for any kind of risky involvement in long- distance trade. When, in 1221, the princes bestowed on Vienna the staple right, in essence an additional rent in the form of a trade margin on foreign goods, any incentive there may have been for Viennese merchants to risk more died a natural death. Certain Viennese merchant families did, it is true, accumulate enormous wealth on occasion, but an independent trading tradition in the city did not become established.

The inherent weakness of a Viennese commerce based on the staple right finally came to light at the beginning of the sixteenth century, when the Habsburg emperor Maximilian I., greatly in debt to those Southern German trading families such as the Fuggers of Augsburg, was forced to allow free access to Vienna, and lift the staple right. The fate of an independent Viennese wholesale trade was therefore sealed. From then on, wholesalers in the city were always "foreigners". In the field of finance, the position was similar. Although a Viennese burgher council had been given the right by the princes to mint, it was the Jews that dominated the money- lending business. Even when the latter were driven out of Vienna for the first time in 1420/21, and those remaining burnt to death, the Viennese townspeople were neither successful in making up for the lost revenue in taxes nor in getting themselves established in the money- lending business. The mentality of the Viennese patriciate as men of private means, and the concentration of the city's craftsmen on local trade, were effectively encouraged by the princes, who concerned themselves primarily with activities that would increase their own power. The continuing position as a frontier fortress contributed to the prevailing self-preoccupation and lack of outwardness displayed by the Viennese townspeople.

The location of the Roman garrison, of which the outlines (Salzgries, Rotgasse, Kramergasse, Graben, Naglergasse, Tiefer Graben) and main thoroughfares (Wipplingerstraße and Marc-Aurel-Strasse - Tuchlauben) can still be clearly recognized today in the ground-plan of the inner-city, was ideally chosen. It was on a plateau, protected on three sides by waterways: the Danube (the Danube canal of today) to the north, the river Wien to the east, and the small Ottakring river to the west. An old Roman land route, today's Herrengasse, touched on the fortress to the south. That the garrison has left its mark to this day (in contrast to the Roman civitas near to St. Marx) is due to the fact that the fortifications (wall, moat) remained more or less intact, even surviving the battles during the era of the barbarian invasions.

It was protected by these fortifications that the first settlement in the early Middle Ages became established in the vicinity of the Berghof. When the Babenbergs assumed control of the city in 1137, the eastern part of the Roman fort was already repopulated. South of the Berghof lay the Hohe Markt, in those days the city's main market, and adjoining this again to the south was a wik, a merchant settlement. Vienna already had three churches within its walls: on the northern edge was the main church, the Ruprechtskirche, the oldest of Vienna's churches and the only one to have retained its original form; on the southern boundary, the Peterskirche and to the north of the almost empty western half of the fortress, the church of Maria am Gestade.

The Babenbergs, as town lords, had their castle built adjacent to the civilian settlement in the western half of the garrison in the square Am Hof. In 1194, again within the Roman wall near to Seitenstettengasse, the first ghetto came into being for the Jews, who served as master minters to the princes. Everyone else who wished to settle in the area had to reside outside the wall. Affected were the foreign long-distance traders, who settled along Bäckerstrasse, the Schottenkloster, founded in 1155 on the very land it stands on today, and even the ecclesiastical head of the city, the Bishop of Passau, who had the Romanesque church of St. Stephen built directly outside the fortress wall just where the Gothic cathedral, Vienna's landmark, stands today.

This exclusion from the residence and the City within the Roman wall did not last for long. When the English king Richard Lionheart, returning from the Third Crusade, was taken prisoner near to Vienna, the Babenbergs demanded such a high ransom that they were able, in 1200, to have a new town wall built from the proceeds. This was to encircle the city until 1857 when the fortifications finally came down. At the time it was built, there were still large expanses of barren land within the new ring made by the wall, and these were gradually filled in with churches, monasteries and collegiate courts, mostly on the periphery. The City spread out from its core, and initially filled the area of the Roman garrison. In the course of this development, the ghetto was removed to Judenplatz. Once the Roman wall was demolished, the City spread across the intervallum (the building up of the southern edge of Naglergasse and the strip of land between Rot- and Kramergasse and Rotenturmstrasse), and then expanded along the new main thoroughfare Kärntnerstrasse - Rotenturmstrasse. The Neue Markt, which was later to outstrip the Hohe Markt, provided the link between the new quarters on both sides of Kärtnerstraße.

This gradual expansion was probably the reason why the street layout in the heart of the city continued to orientate itself on that of the Roman era. The new intersection Naglergasse/ Graben/ Singerstrasse - Kärntnerstrasse/ Rotenturmstrasse is only a shift parallel to the old Roman junction Wipplingerstrasse - Tuchlauben. Most of the minor streets of the old part of the city orientate themselves on this junction, the only exception to this orthogonal street plan being Herrengasse, nevertheless an old Roman road too. It is the closely-knit street plan that indicates the earlier age of the part of the city within the Roman wall compared with the areas of expansion.

After the Babenberg line had died out in 1246, the city was conquered by Ottocar Pryzemysl, and, from 1251-1276, Vienna was part of the Moravian Empire of the Pryzemysl line. Ottocar had the fortress moved from the square Am Hof to its present site (Amalientrakt) on the city wall. This relocation was probably also conducive to the spread of the City in a southernly direction.The Habsburgs, who assumed control of the city in 1282, left the fortress where it was and, in 1365, also had the new Gothic cathedral of St.

Ecclesiastical building
Nobleman's palace
University
Hofburg
Burgher's house
City buildin

Historical city plan of Vienna, city centre, based on the plan by M. Bonfacius Wolmuet, 1547.
Design: R. Banik-Schweitzer

Stephen erected on the same site as the Romanesque church, which was demolished. As legitimate rulers, they were set on spatial continuity. The location of the secular and ecclesiastical centre of power was irrevocably established. The university, founded in 1365, fared slightly differently, but it was still only in the 19th century that it was relocated on the Ringstrasse.

The Habsburgs, who were also German emperors, did not reside permanently in Vienna, but the city nevertheless fell under their influence, be it only indirectly. An example of this is the above-mentioned lifting of the staple right by Maximilian I., but the civil liberties enjoyed by the citizens were first quashed when his grandson, Emperor Ferdinand I. transferred the residence of the Austrian line of the Habsburgs to Vienna in 1533. Shortly prior to this, in 1529, the city had been successful in thwarting the first Turkish siege, during which the suburbs, just in the process of being built, were completely destroyed. It was subsequently that Ferdinand I. established the political, administrative and infrastructural basis in Vienna for the conquest of Hungary and the foundation of an eastern central European empire.

The first step was to give the city new fortifications, but it was not a question this time of providing more space for development as it had been when the Babenberg walls were built, but of turning the existing city into a practically unconquerable stronghold. The new city wall was erected directly round that of the Babenbergs, in front of it a wide moat, adjoining which was a broad strip of land over 100 metres wide left vacant in order to give the city's defenders a free field of fire. As a result the stronghold of Vienna was completely isolated from the suburbs.

It was just when the city was being confined to the circumference it had had since the Middle Ages that its population rapidly increased. With the transfer of the residence to Vienna came the court, the court nobility, the civil servants of the centralized administration and the court craftsmen. Even though all the reserves of building land were made use of, and an extra storey added to existing houses, the city was unable to absorb such an influx. The so-called "Hofquartierspflicht" was therefore introduced in 1566, whereby house owners were compelled to rent apartments out to the court nobility, court personnel and civil servants. Even though a rental system had already existed, it now became the predominant legal form of building utilisation.

Bonifaz Wolmuet''s city plan of 1547 shows Vienna at the outset of its development as seat of an absolutist ruler. The most noticeable structural change compared to the late Middle Ages was the formation of the noble quarter between Herrengasse and the southern city wall adjoining the Hofburg. Several of the centralized administration buildings were also already in existence. (The Austrian chancellery and armory in the vicinity of the Hofburg, and the Salt Office, for practical reasons close to the bank of the Danube). Church property had but little increased, the centre of the City continued to be in the area of the former Roman garrison, and round the quarter where the foreign merchants resided. The street plan had hardly changed either. In addition to the large irregular episcopal complexes, various other types of building were to be seen; the house arranged round an inner court represented by the palaces of the nobility, and the residence of the patrician or the wealthy merchant; the house with two wings extending to the rear inhabited by those living off wine-growing, and the small house on a narrow plot inhabited by the craftsman and tradesperson.

Just when it seemed that Vienna was equipped to deal with any external threat and enjoying a period of internal peace, a new source of conflict appeared on the horizon - the rise of Protestantism. This new doctrine had spread so rapidly, and become so established among the landowning aristocracy and the townspeople of Vienna that for a period of approximately 100 years, Vienna could be described as a Protestant city. Protestantism was considered such a threat because it not only caused the old antagonism between prince and burgher to reappear but was also linked with economic and cultural modernisation. During the short period that Emperor Maximilian II., the pacifist, humanist and "crypto-Protestant", held power (1564-1576), it seemed as if Vienna was going to take the decisive step towards modernisation, putting the Aristotelian conception of the world behind it forever. Outstanding Protestant humanists and scientists were summoned to Maximilian's court, among them the most famous botanist of the time, Carolus Clusius (Charles de l' Ecluse from Amiens), who advised the emperor on the layout of the gardens at Neugebäude palace, and brought hitherto unknown plants to Vienna (the chestnut, lilac and tulips). Maximilian II. left but few traces within the fortified city itself, the Stallburg being the most important. Nevertheless, several of the outstanding structures that set new spatial foci in the environs of the stronghold Vienna were due to him: he not only had the Neugebäude built, the largest profane Renaissance building north of the Alps, but also had the Prater transformed into an imperial hunting-ground, thus ensuring a building-ban that was to last for 200 years. At the end of the main avenue, which his father Ferdinand I. had had laid out, Maximilian had the "Grünes Lusthaus" (Pleasure-House) erected in 1566. Finally, it was he who bought the land on which the palace of Schönbrunn was later to be built.

Maximilian's untimely death was, however, to put an end to these modernizing experiments. His son and successor Emperor Rudolph II. retreated to Prague and his cabinets of curiosities. The humanists and scientists left Vienna. Neugebäude remained unfinished and fell into decay. The Jesuits, the strongest pillars of the Counter Reformation, were called to Vienna. The Protestant nobility and citizens were expelled, their property confiscated and partly transferred to the Jesuits. Finally, in 1623, the University of Vienna was entrusted to the Jesuits, and the Jesuit church built next to the university building. The triumph of scholasticism over the beginnings of modern science was complete.

Around 1580 began the so-called "monastery offensive", during which 50 burghers' houses were demolished to make way for the foundation of 9 new monasteries in the old part of the city. With the increase of centralization, the number of administrative buildings also rose, and it was the townspeople's houses again that were affected. In the course of this reconstruction plots were combined, but the street plan nevertheless remained unaltered.

The thwarting of the second Turkish siege in 1683 which again caused the total devastation of the suburbs, revolutionized Vienna's strategic position. The subsequent expulsion of the Turks from Hungary not only resulted in the Habsburg monarchy becoming a great power, but also relieved Vienna of its role as a frontier outpost, drew it into the secure centre of the new state, and allowed for permanent growth on land beyond the fortifications, which were left standing.

Now at last thoughts could turn towards the country's internal development, and, in accordance with the then fashionable views, mercantilistic principles were applied. This entailed an improvement in transport facilities, and the development of an export-orientated production. With Vienna as centre, Emperor Charles VI. had a network of so-called "commercial roads" laid out, based on the existing main road system (Praterstrasse, Rennweg, Triesterstrasse, Mariahilferstrasse). When it came to developing an export industry for the likes of Vienna, textile manufacture in the form of silk weaving was chiefly considered. As no such tradition existed in the city, specialists were called in from Lombardy, Switzerland, France and Southern Germany, and settled in the rebuilt suburbs.

It was the absolutist state and the nobility that particularly profited from this new constellation. The latter had played a prominent part in pushing back the Turks, thereby amassing great wealth, particularly the commander in chief, Prince Eugene of Savoy. A veritable building boom hit the city and its suburbs. There was a big increase both in the number of residences for the nobility as well as public buildings, whereas church ownership stagnated, and property belonging to burghers declined. Once again, rebuilding was rendered possible by joining plots of land whereas the street network again remained untouched.

Major structural changes took place by contrast in the suburbs, which, in 1704, were also provided with fortifications, the so-called Linienwall, as protection against marauders. After the repeated devastation, it was not in the suburbs a question of converting existing buildings, but of extending the city, of turning areas hitherto used for agricultural purposes, into building land. Within a very short space of time, the vineyards, for example, in the south of Vienna had to make way for the summer palaces of Prince Eugene, Prince Schwarzenberg and Counts Starhemberg and Czernin. A factor making the area an attractive choice was of course the imperial summer residence Favorita, erected there in 1642 (the Theresianum of today).

The only other summer palace of similar size still in existence is in the northern part of the city, namely the Liechtenstein palace. It is an excellent example of the way urban development functioned at the time. In contrast to other rulers, the Habsburgs had never possessed large areas of land in their capital, nor had they been ground landlords on a large scale. Inherent in the feudal system was the right and duty of landowners to develop an area. The biggest landowners therefore in the Vienna region were neither the ruling family, nor the nobility, but ecclesiastical institutions, particularly the monastery of Klosterneuburg, which controlled the whole northern area of Vienna, followed by the Schottenstift, which owned land in several western suburbs beyond the Viennese toll barriers. Within the Linienwall itself, there were only small pockets of land owned by the nobility. Among these were the Liechtenstein possessions in the triangle between the Danube (the canal), Währingerbach, and the Linienwall. The Princes of Liechtenstein possessed their own water supply and could therefore run a brewery. Adjoining their summer palace, built between 1691 and 1706, they had the Lichtental estate laid out to the north from 1699 to house their employees and the tradesmen who had been forced out of the city. On Joseph Nagel's city plan of 1770/80, the ensemble, including the summer palace, brewery, personnel estate, with the hospital and orphanage, which were added later, has the air of a country estate, a haven in the midst of still mainly agricultural land.

This rag rug-like pattern of development is a clear indication of the fact that in Vienna it was not one but several developers who were at work simultaneously. Whereas the aim of the Liechtensteins and the monastery of Klosterneuburg in developing their land was to gain ground-rents from the agricultural production (cultivation), the Schottenstift was more interested in the rental income from its buildings. As a result of the increase in residences for the nobility, and buildings for central government institutions in the city itself, the middle-class tradesmen were increasingly being pushed out, not to mention the immigrants involved in the production of luxury goods. For this class, the Schottenstift developed the land it owned in Schottenfeld, providing it with a regular large-grid network of streets, enclosing deep plots of building land, and ideal for the erection of houses with long wings extending to the rear and a narrow frontage. This type of building derived from the winegrower's house, which was, in the Middle Ages, also to be found in the inner city area. It was also ideal for commercial production. In its first stage of development, Schottenfeld possessed neither a centre nor square nor stretches of green. It was seemingly planned uniquely as a commercial area with a view to making the highest profits possible. The Schottenstift was right in its calculation; the area became the manufacturing centre of Vienna, and made on occasion such high profits that it came to be called the "Brillantengrund".

With the exception of the Karlskirche, it was, in contrast to the higher nobility, only beyond the Linienwall that the imperial family set new architectural foci, namely Schönbrunn Palace, particularly encouraged by Maria Theresia, and the Augarten, developed by her son, co-Regent and heir, Emperor Joseph II. As though the deeply religious empress was subtley getting her own back on the apostate Maximilian II., she had parts taken from Neugebäude and used as spoils in Schönbrunn. In no less subtle a manner, Joseph II., the next unpopular reformer within the family, vindicated the memory of his ancestor by extending the axis of the main avenue of the Prater to the Augarten, and setting an architectural focus at each end, the Augarten portal, and, in place of the "pleasure-house", the one that is still standing there today, the Lusthaus. This 5.5 kilometre-long avenue is the most splendid axis Vienna possesses. Unfortunately, most of its effect was already lost in 1859 when the overhead railway line was built to cross over the Praterstern. None of the later imperial buildings ever reached the symbolic status of Schönbrunn, which was seen as a challenge to Versailles after Austria had not only defeated the Turks but also their ally, the French. The Augarten, for example, could never have had such pretensions.

As state assignments increased and became more varied, there was an acute demand for space on which to erect public buildings. The inner-city could in no way continue to fulfil such a need, even when some land had been gained by Joseph II.'s dissolution of the monasteries in 1782. This was nevertheless inadequate by far for large buildings such as army barracks or hospitals. The locations chosen for military barracks were often situated for strategic reasons on arterial roads, and on the outer edge of the glacis (Alser Kaserne, Court Stables and the later Stiftskaserne, Getreidemarktkaserne, Heumarktkaserne but also the Reiterkaserne next to the Augarten). Although the case was different with hospitals, these too were built on the outer edge of the glacis (Allgemeines Krankenhaus, Nepomukspital/Landstrasse). Of importance here were probably proximity to the city and good traffic communications. The glacis moreover was in state hands, surrounded by wasteland, making the cost of land acquisition more attractive.

With the exception of the Danube marshes, Vienna's large spatial configurations are circular. Pre-determined by the fan-shaped network of waterways flowing from the Vienna Woods, responded to in turn by the star-shaped network of land routes, this circular form is consolidated by the Babenberg wall of 1200, and the new fortifications with the glacis erected in the 16th century. In the Middle Ages, it was above all the large monastic complexes that lay in a circle on the inner-side of the city wall. As not all were dissolved, and some converted for official use, this very first ring of public buildings still exists. The second came into existence, as already mentioned, at the beginning of the 18th century on the outer edge of the glacis. This development continued in the 19th century as building sites near to the city centre for public buildings became increasingly rare. In addition to the buildings already named, the first half of the 19th century saw the addition of the Landesgericht, the Militärgeographisches Institut, the Chemie Institut on the Heumarkt, the Technische Hochschule, the Hauptmünzamt, and the Hauptzollamt. It was after mid-century, and with a consistent symbolism, that the sequence of public buildings was laid out in the Ringstrasse zone between these two series of official buildings. However, in front of the inner ring is a succession of buildings erected during the Gründerzeit so that the Ringstrasse itself is solely lined with buildings dating from the Gründerzeit. By contrast, on the above-mentioned second ring, buildings from the Baroque and Classicistic periods stand facing those of the Gründerzeit. In the suburbs themselves, official state buildings are extremely rare.

Around the turn of the 19th century, a new form of development made its appearance. It was only suitable for small areas, which again had to be under single ownership. In this case, the usual grid development became subordinate to a central rectangular square with built-up corners that did not primarily function as a market square, but as a public space. The most interesting experiment using this model was undertaken by the Schottenstift when it came to developing Breitenfeld in 1802. Here, the model was duplicated by using two squares, Bennoplatz and Albertplatz. The former was planned to become the spiritual centre of the new community; Albertplatz with its community centre and school became the secular centre. The example of Breitenfeld, however, made it obvious that this kind of development was unsuitable for larger areas on account of the monotony of repetition.

The beginning of the industrial era made necessary a new infrastructure. The Wiener Neustadt canal had been built very late between 1795-1803 although it would have been more appropriate in the mercantilist era, and was already made obsolete in the 1830's by the advent of the first railways. However, it did still prove itself useful by the fact that the line connecting the North and South Railway Stations could be conducted along its drained bed and led at low cost through the urban zone. All the other railway lines end at the Linienwall. This rail connection introduced a new structural element into the urban fabric. Whereas the main railway lines like the major land routes take a radial approach to the city, additionally consolidating the star pattern, the junction line runs at a tangent in a long drawn-out S-shaped bend past an area that was in those days already densely built up.

Hand in hand with the new mobility brought about by the railway went a revolutionary change in the organization of production, and the spatial structural changes thus extended far beyond those brought about by the railway. On the principle that productivity could be increased by the division of labour, the temporal and spatial spheres of the individual's life were reorganized in such a way that many people were now grouped together doing the same job at the same time and in the same place. This called for, among other things, the development of new types of building. The factory, the purely residential building, the station, the department store, the museum, and different varieties of administrative building, for example, the bank, were added to the already familiar types such as city-hall, church, school, hospital, military barracks and prison. The German planning theoretician Reinhard Baumeister had already pointed out in 1874 that a functional homogenization was not limited to individual buildings, but tended to spread over whole districts. Already at this stage, one could observe the formation of the city as central business district, and the crystallization of industrial and purely residential areas.

Whereas commercial enterprises had during the mercantilist era mainly become established in Schottenfeld and the valley of the River Wien because water was required for driving power and means of production, the modern industrial enterprises, in particular the engineering industry that had expanded with the advent of railway engineering, were set up along the railway lines. The same was true of the gasworks established in the 1840's, which needed coal delivered by rail for the production of illuminating gas. This had a serious effect on the distribution of the population in the urban areas, as large-scale public transport was still non-existent. Whereas up to this point, tradespeople or the domestic worker in the textile industry had settled in the inner and outer suburbs along the Wien valley, it was now particularly Brigittenau and Favoriten that became the working-class districts of modern factory-based industry.

This zoning of the functions living and working, produced not only the factory but also the purely residential building. In Vienna this took the form of two basic types of apartment building, both in a middle-class and working-class version, the latter known as the "Gangküchenhaus" (accommodation with the kitchen on the corridor).

The liberal revolution of 1848 swept the feudal system away at last. Vienna had very quickly to catch up on its economic backwardness, but had not the resources to do so alone. Managers and engineers therefore came from England and Germany, Jewish and Calvinist bankers from Germany and Switzerland, building technicians from Italy, and architects from Germany, Switzerland and Denmark. Together with the Jewish and Greek wholesalers, the textile magnates from Lower Austria, Bohemia and Moravia, and a good number of liberal-minded senior civil servants, university professors, lawyers and journalists, they formed the new liberal upper middle-class that found its home round the Ringstrasse. The homogenous building structure of the Ringstrasse zone, unusual for Vienna, was primarily the result of the fact that the entire building land was in state hands, and that therefore one single institution had control, and this was then an exception, over such a large expanse of land.

In addition to the badly needed specialists from the more highly developed parts of

Europe, masses of unqualified immigrants from Bohemia, Moravia and Galicia came to Vienna as well in search of work, now that the feudal ties had been abolished. Their fate was ignored until their standard of living had become so catastrophic that the more affluent section of the population saw its health endangered too. As a result the sewerage system in the central urban area was improved, and the first pipeline supplying mountain spring water to the middle-class districts constructed. The question of where the masses were to be housed was left to private building activity on the periphery. Nonetheless, with the disappearance of feudal ground landlords, a new development model had to be found. Consequently, private firms with an organizational structure ranging from a single-run business to a stock company, took over the developer role, consisting of the purchase and consolidation of plots of land, their partitioning, and the sale of the new lots to interested parties. Control over development as a whole and the establishment of an superimposed infrastructure was transferred to the public sector, primarily to the newly constituted municipal authorities. They were committed to drawing up regulatory plans ie. for the street network, but were not in a position to decree when, or indeed whether, the area was to be built upon. Nevertheless, this procedure led to a more systematic connection of the different development areas. The rag rug-character of the feudal age was replaced by the homogenous pattern of a bourgeois society slowly moving towards egalitarianism. Every hierarchical tendency, still noticeable in the Josephine-Classicistic pattern of development, was discarded. Each building block was basically considered equal; squares and stretches of green were made possible by the omission of whole blocks, the costs of which had usually to be borne by the public sector.

Vienna's topography and the shape the city had taken in over 1000 years of development, hardly allowed for any other conception of development than that of concentric expansion. Already in 1857, when a competition for the first Ringstrasse was held, F. Stache put forward the proposal for Vienna to be enclosed by 5 circumferential roads (Ringstrasse, Lastenstrasse, Vorstadtring, Linienwall and Aussenring).

This proposal was followed in principle, but at the same time a serious structural stumbling-block became apparent. It was particularly the chronic lack of capital in Austria that made structural changes in built-up areas practically impossible. Infrastructural projects on a larger scale could therefore only be undertaken on plots of land that were still vacant, or on land that had become available through the demolition of large building complexes (e.g. the so-called "barracks transactions" from 1890 onwards). That such plots of land would become available could nevertheless not be foreseen, making the inclusion of such land in infrastructural network planning impossible. It could therefore be assumed that the project of the third ring would come to nothing on account of the densely built-up inner suburbs. However, the Linienwall fulfilled the first-mentioned prerequisite. Around the middle of the 19th century this boundary wall was just as obsolete from the military point of view as were the fortifications encircling the centre of the city. With these it had one or two characteristics in common, such as the 190-metre wide zone on which building was banned, on land in the outer suburbs. There the so-called Gürtelstrasse, 80-metres wide, was laid out in the 1860's, while the Linienwall itself was left standing as it represented an ideal control point for urban tolls and consumption taxes levied on those entering from the outer suburbs. Similar to Berlin during the boom of 1867-73, stock companies had become involved on a large-scale in Vienna in urban development, which they hoped to foster by the construction of fast city railway systems. Within a very short space of time, over 20 projects were ready for submission. None were realized as, after the stock-exchange crash of 1873, private funding was out of the question, but the more ingenious among those who had submitted a project, among them a consortium in which Otto Wagner was involved, had from the outset, planned for the lines to cut through the available spare land particularly along the banks of the river Wien and the Danube canal, and along the Linienwall. When the outer suburbs were incorporated into the city in 1890, and the infrastructural problems that had accumulated were to be solved by a large-scale project in which the State as the main financier was to play a major part, it was exactly according to this cheapest version that the metropolitan railway system was constructed under the artistic directorship of Otto Wagner . The circle-ring structure was thus further consolidated. Only the Wien valley line, however, provided the hoped-for stimulus to development, as Hietzing's rapid growth soon illustrated. Public awareness of the Gürtel as a spatial configuration found its expression in the fact that it was chosen as the location for a church-building programme aimed at the rechristianization of the workers from the suburbs.

From 1890 to the First World War, Vienna experienced yet another period of strong expansion, albeit again with foreign help, when it became the most important foreign location for the German electrical industry. More significant than the number of jobs created, was their more modern social character. Technical employees and specialists had never before been so highly qualified, and for the first time a larger number of jobs in industry were available to women too. This growing group of employees swelled by the service sector, which, within the empire was largest in Vienna anyway, increased purchasing power thus encouraging the spread of new trading structures as exemplified by the department store.

City development accelerated too, and was no longer limited to the demolition and rebuilding of single buildings. In the vicinity of St. Stephen's it included whole building blocks, bringing about some modifications of the street network. Two new department stores appeared opposite the main portal of the cathedral, several others in Kärntner- and Rotenturmstrasse. The largest department stores, however, did not go up in the centre of the city but along Mariahilferstrasse, the main shopping street.

The "Strassenhof" as exemplified by Brahmsplatz and Altplatz among others, was a new form of development for larger plots in densely built-up areas. It was both representative and exemplified an optimal use of space using existing types of residential building. In areas marked out for urban expansion, larger projects were again planned by financially powerful developers, an example being an industrial and residential area located where nowadays the Grossfeldsiedlung stands, financed by a bank consortium.

Apart from a few reform projects involving apartment blocks that reverted to the collegiate church court of the Baroque and Classicist period as a model, no new types of residential building that would be more humane but less profitable were developed for the sole reason that the state budget was dependent on tax from rents, in the final analysis therefore on the rentability of the Viennese apartment buildings. This is less an indication of the backwardness of Vienna than that of the rest of the country, whose economic position did not offer any other tax base.

As far as its development was concerned, Vienna lagged behind other western metropolises around 1910, but was the empire's most modern city by far. Its infrastructure was planned for a metropolis of 4 million inhabitants, the underground was on the point of being built, and it was then that Otto Wagner presented his model plan for the "infinitely expandable city", comprising an extendable net of semi-autonomous districts. He resolutely rejected the green belt created in 1905, the last large ring-shaped spatial configuration, as an obstacle to growth.

Vienna was more radically affected by the outcome of the First World War than any other large city. Its economic ties were severed, it ceased to function as imperial residence, the old elite with the exception of the bureaucrats were stripped of power, and the capital of the new and shrunken state, was, after the introduction of universal suffrage, now governed by the Social-Democrats; all against a backdrop of world-wide economic change and the approaching international economic crisis. In face of this seemingly hopeless situation, the Social-Democrats responded by introducing a plan of reform aimed at replacing the capitalistic model, considered as failed, by the gradual socialization of all spheres of life. Since control over the production sector was unattainable despite its weak position, the desired changes were attempted in the cultural, social, and housing fields. Red Vienna, which had become a federal state in its own right, financed its house-building programme out of general taxes and the taxes on luxury articles. This programme was basically a new urban development model. The garden city, which, in its continental European version in any case only boiled down to functional and social segregation was rejected although the necessary new infrastructure would have made it too expensive anyway. Even the private and cooperative settlers' movement was only half-heartedly supported.

Instead the decision was made to build in the time-tested block and street-grid form. This made projects ranging from the superblock to in-filling possible and for optimal use to be made of the existing infrastructure. The "New City" grew within the framework of the old, in its gaps and on its fringes, but with a new internal structure that provided the residents with a communal life in the collective bathing facilities, washhouses, kindergartens, spaces of green, shops (co-op) and the recreational sport, health and educational amenities. The "New Vienna" can be interpreted as a subversionary reflection of the Wagner model, in that the "New City", superimposed on the old, formed a network of autonomous cells more representative of the new society.

In the inter-war years, Austrian society was deeply divided into two camps, Conservative and Social-Democratic. The socio-political experiment of Red Vienna had only served to exacerbate the division. In 1934, the Conservative camp brought the experiment to an end by force, and in the authoritarian Corporate State, the housing programme was abandoned forthwith. Urban development was confined to investment in the technical infrastructure as a job creation scheme (Höhenstrasse, Reichsbrücke), to small-scale reconstruction projects in the city centre (the opening-up of Operngasse), to the building of several family asylums offering a minimal standard of living, to the subsidization of settlements for the unemployed on supplementary income and to that of single family homes on the periphery. On assuming power in 1938, the Nazis had extensive plans for Vienna, but these remained purely theoretical. 80.000 previously Jewish apartments were "arianized", and just as many destroyed towards the end of the Second World War, which also left Vienna with six monstrous flak towers, an unfortunately indestructible symbol of war.

After the war ended and democracy was restored, Vienna found itself once again administered by the Social-Democrats. But society had changed; a direct continuation of the inter-war development model was no longer possible. So-called Fordism gained ground in the developed industrial nations the world over, based on mass production, and mass consumption, mostly state-subsidized. Its spatial equivalent was to be found in the "planned and spacious city" (R. Rainer), ie. in the functionalistic city model for a broad new middle-class that divided the city up into various functional zones linked with each other by the motorcar. There was no place in this model for the small-scale functional mix, and the traditional block-grid-scheme. Development now for residential areas took the form of free-standing rows of buildings in large monofunctional layouts. Within other functional areas too, the individual building was replaced by the large-scale: the factory was succeeded by the industrial zone, the department store by the shopping centre, and the scattered recreational and sporting facilities by the recreational or theme park.

In order to keep the cost of land acquisition as low as possible, the new large functional units emerged on the periphery, well outside the built-up areas (industrial zones in Auhof, Strebersdorf, Liesing; large residential complexes such as Grossfeldsiedlung, Trabrennengründe, Alt-Erlaa, Am Schöpfwerk, Wienerflur; the shopping centres Donauzentrum and Shopping City Süd, the latter the largest shopping centre in Europe and beyond the city boundary; recreational parks Donaupark, Oberlaa, Donauinsel, Wienerberg, Laaerberg).

The transportation network had to be extended in order to connect these new sites with each other and with the city centre. Priority was given to road building. A city motorway network gradually emerged partly taking in existing roads (Gürtel) and leading

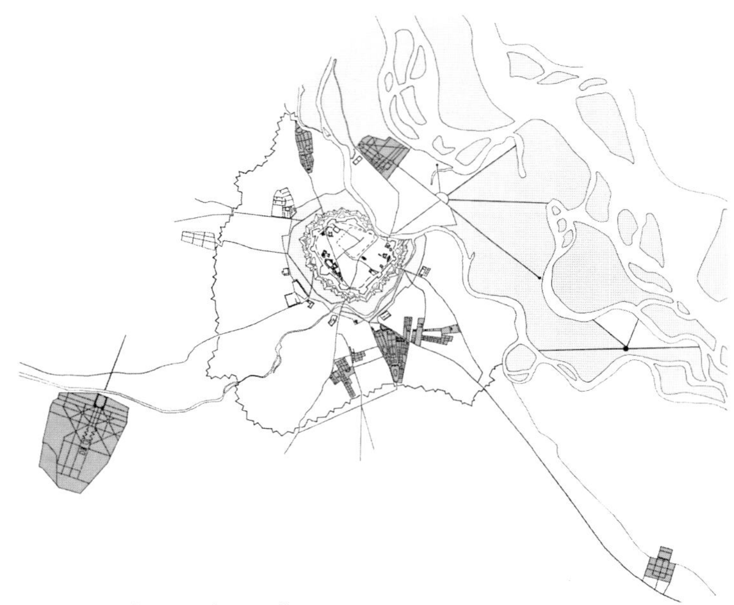

Vienna 1770/80 (by Joseph Nagel)
Circular spatial elements: fortifications, Glacis, Linienwall
Linear spatial elements: Danube (marshes), axis Augarten – Praterstern – Lusthaus
Scattered spatial elements: imperial and noble (garden-) palace (dark grey)
no scale

Vienna at the end of the 19th century
Circular spatial elements: Ringstrasse zone, Gürtel, suburban line, areas of green (Vienna woods, Schönbrunn, Laaerberg, main cemetery/Neugebäude)
Linear spatial elements: Danube (marshes) with axis Augarten – Praterstern – Lusthaus, industrial area along the railway
no scale

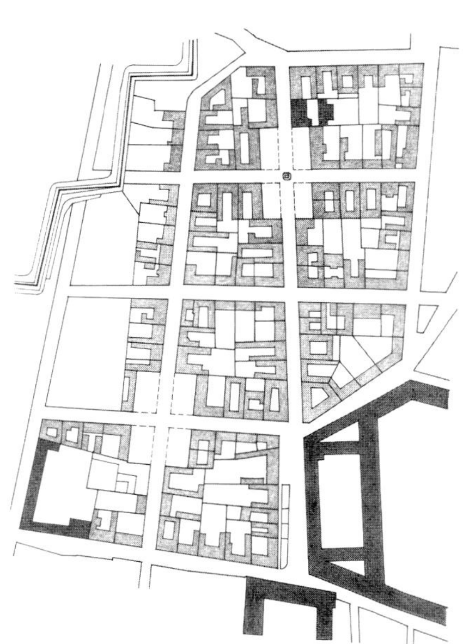

Type of development 1st half 19th century
(Albert- and Bennoplatz)
Drawing: R. Banik-Schweitzer
no scale

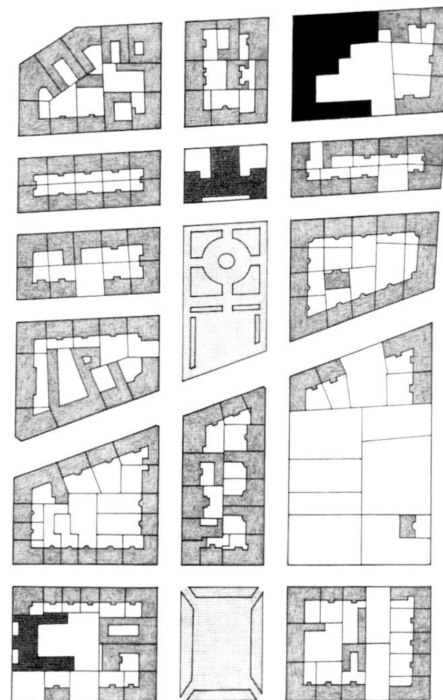

Type of development 2nd half 19th century
(Favoriten)
Drawing: R. Banik-Schweitzer
no scale

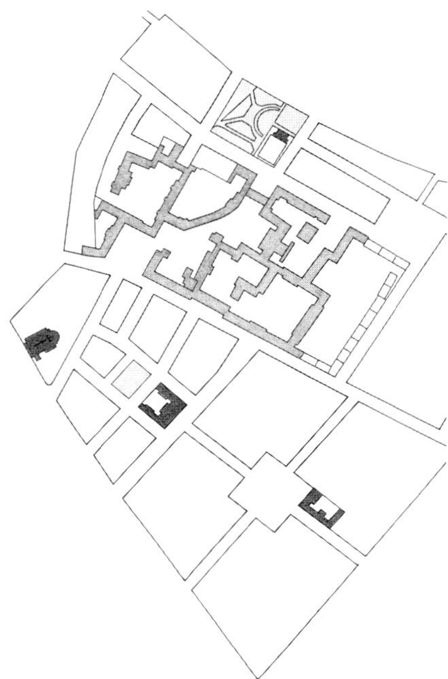

Type of development 1st half 20th century
Municipal superblock
(Rabenhof)
Drawing: R. Banik-Schweitzer
no scale

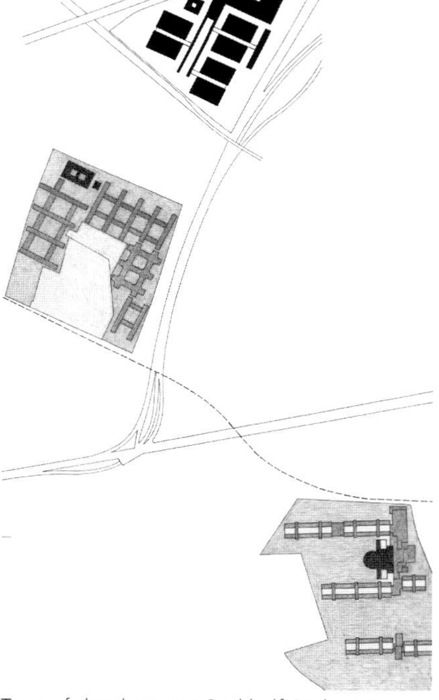

Type of development 2nd half 20th century
(residential park Alt-Erlaa, housing estate Am Schöpfwerk, industrial area)
Drawing: R. Banik-Schweitzer
no scale

new stretches where possible through still unbuilt-on land (Donauuferautobahn). The so-called "Südosttangente" became the main artery of this new network, its name exactly describing its route and function. Austria's busiest road, it serves to connect the urban development area on the left bank of the Danube with the central part of the city on the right bank. The main line of the fast suburban railway also runs at a tangent due to the fact that the north-, south-bound, and junction lines that had fallen into disuse when the Iron Curtain went up, could now be made use of. Following suit, Vienna was also provided with its underground system, plans for which had already been put forward in 1914. It serves above all the densely built urban area, and the city-centre.

Changes in the high-density urban area took place less obtrusively, and tended to follow the usual pattern. War damage had been sporadic and had not affected whole areas. Reconstruction within the framework of the block-grid-scheme and continued use of the existing infrastructure therefore seemed natural. The process of urban renewal that succeeded the post-war rebuilding followed the same pattern of piecemeal reconstruction. Wide-scale redevelopment was out of the question because of the continuing lack of capital. The large housing developments on the periphery were primarily for those who had entered the new middle-class, and therefore did not develop the social problems of the dormitory suburbs on the periphery of many a Western European capital. The new buildings in the dense urban area on the whole provided housing for the higher-income groups both in districts near to the centre, and in the outlying middle-class districts. These were able to maintain their social standards, even improving on them in some cases, whereas the working-class districts of the Gründerzeit beyond the Gürtel gradually became the catchment area for the socially-deprived on account of the house owners neglecting to renovate. Due to the fact that up to the Eighties the entire housing programme lay in the hands of building corporations that were only allowed to build apartments, the practice of piecemeal urban renewal in most cases showed a lack of urban design of quality.

The changes in society that have since taken place could break this pattern. Globalization and the new flexibility in the economy have put an end to Fordism and its architectural counterpart, the functionalistic urban model. There is no longer room in the centres of the Old World for mass production using conventional technology. The crossing of state boundaries by multi-national corporations has knocked the bottom out of national or local regulations laid down to safeguard standardized ways of life. The implications for cities is that they no longer have to defend their position within a national economy, but on a global scale in competition with others of comparable type. This in turn calls for the development of an independent, unmistakable profile; for a city such as Vienna, time and again dependent on external help, lacking an entrepreneurial tradition of its own, a difficult undertaking.

On an urban level, these transformations in society have put an end for the time being to comprehensive development concepts. Flexible intervention in parts of the urban fabric could, in the sphere of urban development, correspond to the growing economic flexibility, and by the remixing of existing structural elements and the introduction of new ones, provide the built form with varying specific requirements. The superstructure over the former Franz-Josef Station, or the "Second City" on the left bank of the Danube, where the jettisoned Expo 1995 would have been located, can be interpreted as experiments in this direction. Were the concept of the "Second City" to be a success, it would represent a radical break with the tenacious circle-ring tradition so typical of urban development in Vienna, and, by means of the intersection Danube-"Twin Cities" (linked by the axis Praterstrasse-Lassallestrasse-Reichsbrücke-Wagramerstrasse), create a new spatial configuration.

Twentieth century Viennese architecture

Vienna is inseparably linked with the term "metropolis". Since the Baroque era a large city among the European Capitals, it had, in the 19th century, serving as it did as centre of the Imperial and Royal Austro-Hungarian dual monarchy, become one of the first metropolises in Europe alongside London, Paris and Naples. As a phenomenon of urban communal living the metropolis was a result of the nineteenth century industrial revolution. Architects such as Otto Wagner believed it to be the greatest architectural challenge of modern architecture in that the architect was called upon to find solutions to new assignments in the fields of industry, transport, housing and social amenities. Industrial production had made many things possible, and architects were often led to the false assumption that the metropolis too was a calculable product. The entire 20th century is a commentary on the "metropolis", on the attempt to transform a great mass of buildings into an orderly system and give them an urban structure.

Around the turn of the century, two diametrically opposed theories on city planning that were of the greatest relevance for an interpretation of what indeed was urban, were developed by Camillo Sitte (Der Städte-Bau nach seinen künstlerischen Grundsätzen, City Planning according to its Artistic Principles, 1901), and Otto Wagner (Die Großstadt, Metropolis, 1911). Sitte's example (for Vienna) of urban regulation along artistic lines shows a theatre-like composition of every kind of building style, a sentimental journey through southern Italy, where public squares function as the hub of urban life. In contrast, Wagner's sober and rational study of the metropolis is based on the real needs of the same, on the realities of our time. For him, Vienna was a laboratory for his experiments and pet urban utopia in one. His architecture included all aspects of contemporary life, the urban railway, municipal housing schemes, business premises, buildings for social and cultural institutions as well as churches. As a result, Otto Wagner's pupils, working later as architects for Vienna City Council, were very much to leave their stamp on the architectural scene of the Twenties and Thirties.

With the inscription over the portal of the Secession in 1896 "To the Age its Art, to Art its Freedom", (quotation after Ludwig Hevesi), Josef Olbrich left his personal definition of what was the artistic credo of a whole generation. There could not have been a shorter and more precise renunciation of the Pan-European historicism and eclecticism that had taken possession of Vienna and other European cities. Architects and artists sought to liberate themselves from the conventions of the 19th century, first in the "Wiener Werkstätte" and successively in the Werkbund movement.

This liberation from the historical intellectual world of the fin de siècle revolved round such themes as realism and utopia, aesthetics and ethics. Otto Wagner's critical realism served not only as the basis for his concepts of urban planning but also for his individual buildings. With his city railway system (1894-1900) - the largest construction in Vienna - Wagner combined technical innovation with the formal language of the artist-architect to form a metaphor of the flourishing metropolis. The speed of the urban railway train is equated with a city perpetually in motion: men in motion, money in motion, goods in motion, thoughts in motion.

Some years after the urban railway had been completed, transportation in general was dealt with as a special subject in Otto Wagner's "Special School" at the Academy of Fine Arts in Vienna, the course being completed by architectural design projects on airports for airships. The work of Christof Stumpf (Airport, 1904) and Friedrich Pindt (Airport, 1912), gives an insight into the wonderful world of fantasy displayed by the Wagner pupils, a world already anticipating in thought an aspect of Italian Futurism and the città nuova. The art historian, Otto Graf, pointed out these ideas of Wagner and the Wagner School over 30 years ago. Certain buildings by Wagner can be counted among the high-tech icons of the turn of the century. The glass and steel architecture of the Postal Savings Bank (1903-10) represents built architectural theory: the walk-over glass floor and the glass roof construction suspended from steel cables changed the spatial conceptions of the whole era.

Almost simultaneously, Josef Hoffmann brought about an aesthetic revolution with his sanatorium Westend in Purkersdorf just outside Vienna. According to Eduard Sekler, Hoffmann's masterpiece is "in its clarity and disposition, in the logical consistency of its formal execution, and above all in the utter simplicity of its cubistic forms, for 1904 just as epoch-making as Frank Lloyd Wright's Larkin Building in Buffalo, and Mackintosh's Scotland Street School in Glasgow". With his middle-class villas in the Vienna districts of Döbling and Grinzing, Hoffmann was able to realize his aesthetic visions of an everyday culture ennobled by art and crafts.

The dualism of aesthetics and ethics in the architecture of the Modern Movement in Vienna was often compared to that of Josef Hoffmann and Adolf Loos: Hoffmann's strong creative urge no doubt contributed towards this opinion just as Loos strengthened his theoretical position by his moralizing comments on architecture. The Goldman and Salatsch building (1909-11) on Michaelerplatz can be considered the best example of this stance, and it was here that the cosmopolite Adolf Loos was able to put into practice the experience he had gained in London and the United States, making clear at the same time his opposition to the Vienna Secession and Art Nouveau.

Within a very short space of time, and in relative proximity to each other, three different architectural icons of the Viennese Modern Movement were built, each well able to bear comparison on an international level. Remarkable in the case of all three buildings is the heterogeneous approach to architecture, which can be seen as synonymous for the entire 20th century architectural debate in Vienna.

It was thus not a revolutionary course but an evolutionary one that led in Vienna to the freedom of art. The critical moment in the development of architecture in the city (Otto Wagner's "realism") did not lead to an acceptance of a dogmatic Modernism, but to that specific Viennese Modernism for which Adolf Loos and Josef Frank are responsible. Unambiguity was not, and is not, always seen in Vienna as clarity, but often as an inadmissable simplification of complex structures. This is also evident in the handling of a centuries-old, multi-cultural situation, in which the element of "tradition" was firmly rooted (Adolf Loos). It also manifests itself in the historical permanence of urban structures, which, in the centre of Vienna, go back to before 1683.

The development of Austrian architecture of the Twenties and Thirties was influenced and determined in the main by external, socio-economic forces outside the architectural sphere. The strains of the First Republic had a fatal effect on the cultural situation in Austria: cosmopolitan fin de siècle Vienna, with its close intellectual, cultural, political and economic ties with the other metropolises in Europe, became a city of social deprivation. This situation was exacerbated by the international economic crisis of 1929. The Thirties were therefore dominated by "economic crisis", "emigration" and "Austrofascism". It was against this complex background that the remarkable and highly rated municipal housing projects came into being, the parameters of which primarily reflected the socio-political realities of the time. In contrast to the pre-1918 era when much-heeded international impulses went out from Vienna and Austria (Viennese Jugendstil, the Secession, Otto Wagner and the Wagner School), the essential impulses in architectural theory were, in the First Republic, limited to just a few single architects: Adolf Loos, Lois Welzenbacher, Ernst Plischke and Josef Frank.

In the eyes of the internationally relevant publications on classical modern architecture, Viennese architecture was too ambivalent and not "modern" enough. The great achievements of Red Vienna (1919-1933) were determined by the pragmatic reforms of the Social Democrats, but the aesthetic paragons did not correspond to the radical ideological concept. The traditional monumentality of the large housing complexes mostly planned by Wagner pupils such as Karl Ehn, Hubert Gessner, Rudolf Perco among others did not conform to the iconography of the Modern Movement.

Vienna's inter-war council housing is first and foremost an achievement and a result of Social-Democratic urban policy, and must be seen within the framework of the entire Socialist commitment: in the period from 1918 to 1934 Vienna with the Social Democratic Party represented the world's largest political party organization of the time. The city was regarded as the testing-ground for the feasibility of Social-Democratic ideals. In addition to the policies followed in education, culture and employment, housing policy represented that essential field which, by dint of its complementary function with regards to the working world in general, made private identity possible. It was primarily through the functioning "communal" amenities within the housing estates themselves that the municipal housing schemes of the Vienna City Council achieved their quality: through the communal kindergartens and areas for communal sport and leisure activities.

Prerequisite to this great transformation was the housing tax introduced in 1923 by Vienna City Council, a special purpose tax, which in the following years made the Vienna council housing programme possible. Private house building had, after the end of the First World War in 1918, practically come to a standstill. Between 1923 and 1933 the Vienna City Council had approximately 65.000 apartments built.

The economic situation meant that the single family home played little part in residential building as a whole, but it was just in this field that houses of particular quality were built; the Stonborough-Wittgenstein house, Vienna (1926-28), which the philosopher Ludwig Wittgenstein, together with Paul Engelmann, built for his sister; the Moller house, Vienna (1927-28) built by Adolf Loos; the Dos Santos house, Vienna (1930) by Felix Augenfeld, as well as the Beer house in Hietzing, Vienna (1929-31) by Josef Frank (together with Oskar Wlach), to mention just a few. Varied as these single-family houses are as regards their architecture, what they do have in common is the tradition of the middle-class and upper-middle-class residence, in which the distinctive cultural conventions are reflected. Spatial planning, an architectural concept of Adolf Loos, whereby the individual rooms were designed to have varying heights within the rigid limitations of the cube, found special expression in the Moller house.

Rationalization was one of the most important catchwords of modern architecture, its parameter one-dimensionality achieved by a reduction of material in the repetitive elements of a building. Rationalization and mass production were therefore the twin concepts of Modernism, which thus directed itself against diversity and heterogeneity. The unambiguity of rationalization is inconsistent with cultural differentiation, and it was this incompatibility that was felt by certain Viennese architects when it came to adopting the rationality of the new way of building. The reservations of Adolf Loos and Josef Frank towards the International Style are well known, just as are the attacks made by Rudolph Schindler on functionalism and the International Style. Seen from an Austrian angle, this modification of international functionalism had many facets, represented by such names as Ernst Plischke, Franz Singer, Friedl Dicker, Ernst Lichtblau and others. The Austrian Werkbund exhibitions can be seen as a yardstick by which Austrian "internationalism" can be measured.

The second Werkbund exhibition in the form of the Werkbundsiedlung (Vienna 1932) was representative of "inter-European thought", with parallel "siedlung" projects taking place almost simultaneously in Stuttgart, Zürich, Prague and Budapest. Taking part in the Vienna Werkbundsiedlung were, among others, the following architects: Adolf Loos, Clemens Holzmeister, André Lucart, Ernst Lichtblau, Hugo Häring, Oswald Haerdtl, Ernst Plischke, Eugen Wachberger, Richard Neutra, Arthur Grünberger as well as Josef Hoffmann.

Summing up, it can be said of both these Werkbund exhibitions that they were a fateful sign of a change in trend: cultural policy and artistic developments had become so ambivalent in Austria by 1930, that from 1933 onwards, the Modern movement was finally deprived of its right to exist on the pretext that it lacked "native quality".

From February 1934 the advance of Austrofascism led to Austria becoming increasingly provincial. A result of this new ideology was that international contacts were also limited, thus enabling Nazi ideology to spread. The 1938-45 period in Austria could be described as the era of "monumental architecture". Building activity constantly declined during these years, the most important projects nevertheless not being planned for Vienna, but for Linz and Salzburg. These architectural monuments, however, were designed by German architects such as Albert Speer - a clear indication of political hegemony.

The year 1938 has become a symbol for a change in the Austrian constitutional and cultural policy spheres that affected every aspect of the individual's public and private life.

When one attempts nowadays to offer an interpretation of the effects emigration from Vienna had on culture, it can be said for the field of architecture that practically the entire artistic avant-garde was compelled to leave the country involuntarily: Felix Augenfeld, Rudolf Baufeld, Josef F. Dex, Ernst Egli, Herbert Eichholzer, Josef Frank, Jacques Groag, Fritz Gross, Otto Rudolf Hellwig, Heinrich Kulka, Ernst Lichtblau, Walter Loos, Ernst Anton Plischke, Egon Riss, Otto Schönthal, Stephan Simon, Franz Singer, Margarethe Schütte-Lihotzky, Walter Sobotka, Hans Adolf Vetter, Oskar Wlach, Liane Zimbler, geb. Fischer, Wilhelm Baumgarten, Artur Berger, Walter Eichberg, Martin Eisler, Ernst Leslie Fooks (until 1946 Fuchs), Fred Forbát (until1915 Alfred Füchsl), Paul Theodore Frankl, Ernst von Gotthilf, Viktor Guen (actually Grünbaum), Rudolf Hönigsfeld, Fritz Janeba, Leopold Kleiner, Fritz Michael Müller, Emanuel Neubrunn, Kurt Popper, Alfred Preis, Harry Seidler, as well as Hans Vetter, and others.

Rebuilding in all central European cities after 1945 was marked by the attempt to establish a symbiosis between the reconstruction of damaged cultural and political monuments and the establishment of a modern contemporary architecture. Reconstruction in Vienna was marked by the renovation of the city's architectural symbols such as St. Stephen's cathedral, the State Opera, the Burgtheater, Parliament and the Stock Exchange as well as the new West- and South Railway Stations, the Opernringhof, the Ringturm, the Stadthalle and the Gänsehäufl, Vienna's open-air swimming pool on the Old Danube. These public and semi-public buildings enabled positions for a new identity to be taken up that were to contribute towards a new definition of urbanism, adding to the traditional look of the city. Further, an active housing policy was pursued in the form of the Vienna "Schnellbauprogramm" (Franz Schuster), the achievements of which are primarily to be judged by the pure number of buildings erected. The promise of the Modern Movement remained just as unfulfilled in postwar Vienna as it had been before the war. The foundation for the crisis of Modernism in the Sixties was thus indirectly laid in the reconstruction period, for it was this that brought about a change whereby the organization behind building concentrated on purely operative mechanisms, the ideological parameters being sacrificed to a logic of procedure alone. Detached from its socio-cultural background of the Socialist movement, Modernism had lost its ideological prerequisites, which, through the industrial and rational production of apartments and social educational facilities such as kindergartens, day-care centers for children, schools, libraries and sportsgrounds, had given it its legitimacy in the eyes of a large section of the population. The debate on the quality of architecture was therefore made obsolete, what counted was the sheer number of buildings erected; reflection on the art of building was non-existent.

It is in this context that the reactions in Vienna calling for a new architectural debate are to be seen. On the theoretical level Roland Rainer contributed to the discussion with his publications "Städtebauliche Prosa" and "Ebenerdiges Wohnen", an articulation of his concept of "low density building". Further discussion on modern art and architecture took place in the "Galerie nächst St. Stefan" where Otto Mauer had established a forum for cultural debate and where artists such as Josef Mikl, Arik Brauer,

Arnulf Rainer, Oswald Oberhuber and Fritz Wotruba met, as well as the architects Johann Georg Gsteu, Josef Lackner, Rudolf Schwarz and Ottokar Uhl. With their declaration, "Alle sind Architekten, Alles ist Architektur", Hans Hollein and Walter Pichler presented a total concept of architecture, and further enriched the post-functional architectural debate by the terms "symbol", "ritual" and "myth".

It was those very architects, who, in the Sixties, emancipating themselves from the Academy of Fine Arts, and in particular the master classes of Clemens Holzmeister and Lois Welzenbacher, became representative of Viennese architecture: Gustav Peichl, Hans Hollein, Wilhelm Holzbauer, Johannes Spalt, Friedrich Achleitner, Ottokar Uhl, Friedrich Kurrent, Anton Schweighofer and Johann Georg Gsteu. BAU, a journal under the editorship of Peichl, Hollein, Oberhuber and Pichler provided a vital forum for the architectural discourse, not only helping to establish the first international contacts but also providing a platform for a critical dialogue with the "heterogeneous" Vienna Modernist Movement. It was here too that the critical stance towards late-modernism developed.

Almost parallel to these first international developments within the Viennese architectural circles was the growing number of architectural groups and collectives. Names such as Haus-Rucker-Co, Coop Himmelblau and Missing Link are representative of the sudden eruption in the architecture of the Seventies. Here, almost automatically, the work of groups took precedence over that of individuals because the social aspect of architecture was seen as inherent. Whereas Coop Himmelblau dissociated themselves from the Viennese architecture of the past, Missing Link (Otto Kapfinger and Adolf Krischanitz) and the Igirien trio (Werner Appelt, Eberhard Kneissl, Elsa Prochazka) attempted in their work to critically reflect upon just this architecture by superimposing and confronting in a phenomenological sense, and, arguing that there is beauty in monotony, integrating commercial and everyday aesthetics into their projects. Hermann Czech worked in much the same way, seeing the dialogue between the past and daily life as an integral part of his architecture. To quote Dietmar Steiner, "Viennese architecture of the Seventies was concerned with writing, drawing and projecting ... the large projects were built by anonymous offices, whose sole qualifications amounted to their members moving about at ease in political and society circles".

At the time of the oil crisis (1973) and the onset of the international debate on Postmodernism, the younger Viennese architects had already made their position doubly clear: a reflective attitude towards the past, and a critical one towards an unbroken belief in progress. With the exhibitions "Austrian New Wave" at the Institute of Architecture and Urban Studies, New York in 1980 (Missing Link, Adolf Krischanitz and Otto Kapfinger, Rob Krier, Hermann Czech, Heinz Tesar, Heinz Frank, Igirien), and "Versuche zur Baukunst" in the Vienna "Künstlerhaus" in 1985 (Alessandro Alvera, Luigi Blau, Roland Hagmüller, Otto Häuselmayr, Dimitris Manikas, Boris Podrecca) further internationalization of young Austrian architecture was achieved. In small, almost inconspicuous projects, the theoretical foundations for the 80's and 90's had thus been laid.

The new Vienna "Gründerzeit" from the mid-Eighties under Mayor Helmut Zilk opened political,urban and cultural doors. As regards architecture, it was those architects who, for many years already, had indirectly represented Vienna on an international level, among them Hans Hollein and Coop Himmelblau, who were now invited to plan public buildings. At the same time the city's urban development plan (STEP) took on form and, after several years of preparation was adopted in 1984 by the Vienna City Council. It was divided into the sections "Political Principles", "Spatial Development Concept" and "Main Thematic Assignments". Vienna's "School Building Programme 2000", initiated by the then city councillor Hannes Swoboda, can be taken as an example of the latter. School building is, for dynamic urban development of quality of great significance as leitmotif for representative and modern public architecture. The sheer number of over 50 new school buildings, including the conversion projects, would justify talking about a new era in Viennese school building, and the quality of the completed projects testifies to the fact that here first-rate architecture is to be found. In the last decade, the real contribution to the art of building has been the actual act of building itself.

The last ten years have seen a younger generation of architects become active in Vienna, and it is these very architects who have established a new relationship with the Modern Movement, offering despite their differences, a new interpretation, in the sense of a second Modernist Movement, of the qualities of "unexploited" Modernism. The following, mainly active in the fields of social housing and shop design, belong among others to this group: Ablinger/Vedral, ARTEC: Bettina Götz/Richard Manahl, Maria Auböck, Karin Bily, BKK-2 (Christoph Lammerhuber, Axel Linemayr, Franz Sumnitsch, Florian Wallnöfer, Johann Winter, Evelyn Wurster), Margarethe Cufer, Elke Delugan-Meissl/Roman Delugan, Georg Driendl, Eichinger oder Knechtl, Irmgard Frank, Henke/Scheieck, Heidecker/Neuhauser, Paul Katzberger, Martin Kohlbauer, Rüdiger Lainer, Lautner/Scheifinger/Szedenik/Schindler, Michael Loudon, Reinberg/Treberspurg, Raith, August Sarnitz and Franziska Ullmann.

Remarkable about late twentieth century Viennese architecture is its high quality design starting out from a heterogenous base. Embedded as this architecture is in a historical consciousness, the ensuing dialectical position offers a spectrum that has made it a much discussed cultural phenomenon.

Residential building in Vienna

Housing is the true substance of any city, giving a place its structure, atmosphere and life. The representative public buildings, the monuments and the vantage points are to be seen on the picture postcards, but Vienna and probably every other city in the world can only be understood by carefully scrutinizing the way the population is housed.

Vienna's residential buildings are for several reasons unique, firstly on account of the fabric itself, with the majority of apartments dating from before the First World War. An obstinate old city it is too, for the damage caused by the Second World War, approximately 85.000 apartments, did not lead to the large-scale construction of a "new city", but was made good solely by means of the structure-saving programme of "reconstruction". Even the wave of modernization that swept across Europe in the Sixties and Seventies took place in Vienna only piecemeal. What instead did very quickly become fashionable in those years was a strategy of low-key, substance-saving urban renewal. As a result, during the last couple of decades, thousands of single apartments have been renovated, improved upon, and their standard raised, leaving the structure and substance of the buildings themselves intact.

Another important reason for the city of Vienna's competence in the housing field is the proven sense of "public responsibility", political policy still today. It was initiated still in imperial times by the then Christian-Social municipal administration, but was introduced on a large scale by the Social-Democrats at the beginning of the Twenties in the form of extensive council housing projects. Vienna's City Council is today, with approximately 250.000 apartments, one of the biggest landlords in the world; a singular role for a municipality and city administration, but one that can be historically explained. The court in the former imperial city of Vienna possessed the special right to make use of apartments in burghers' houses for civil servants and protégés. The only exceptions to this so-called "Hofquartierspflicht" were the large landownerships and the "collegiate courts" of the church and monasteries. This formed the basis for that particularly Viennese tendency to believe that an apartment was not to be had on the open market, but was conferred by "those above" as a reward for good behaviour. After the collapse of the empire, this role the court played of conferring the right of residence was adapted so-to-speak by the ruling Social-Democrats in their large municipal housing projects.

Between 1923 and 1934 the "Red Vienna" of the First Republic had altogether 64.000 apartments built within the municipal housing scheme, creating at the same time, an environment that provided both culture and amenities (washhouses, bathing facilities, libraries, kindergartens, etc.). These residential courts and gigantic housing blocks of the First Republic were practically towns within a town. Here a definite decision was made on the part of the city administration in favour of urban types of residence consisting of multi-storey housing estates of rented apartments and extensive inner areas of green. It was a definite decision against the type of building proposed by the garden city movement, and only a few siedlungen with gardens came into being despite such well-known architects as Adolf Loos and Josef Frank championing the idea. The housing programme of "Red Vienna" was as far as the architecture and urban planning were concerned pragmatic, using the Gründerzeit infrastructure that was in any case equipped to take further growth in the metropolis. (Otto Wagner's plan for the metropolis of Vienna was after all designed for a population of 4 million). Conventional building methods were opted for, with the aim of boosting employment figures, but there were no declared aims with regard to form and style. Important were the inclusion of large areas of free space, a compactness of street frontage, and a wide range of infrastructural facilities. A typological innovation with historic roots was the establishment of the "courts" and "superblocks".

It was only at the beginning of the Thirties that the aims of Modernism and the garden city movement could be realized in exemplary fashion by Josef Frank with the

Vienna Werkbundsiedlung. Residential building declined dramatically in the Austrofascist (1934-38) and Nazi (1938-45) periods, both leaving hardly a trace of note in the urban fabric. The so-called reconstruction after1945 was at the outset characterized by deep social commitment, and an annual averge of 5000 new apartments was soon achieved.Architecturally and typologically, however, the Biedermeier-like regional style of the Nazi period was continued. It was in the Fifties, due to Franz Schuster in particular, that conceptions of optimized and flexible ground-plans, fast construction programmes and spacious building partly achieved a breakthrough, but the "Modern Movement that had been expelled" was not recalled; innovative beginnings were hampered by continuing bureaucracy.

From the Sixties onwards, large urban expansion projects were undertaken along the lines of Roland Rainer's Urban Development Plan of 1961, without, however, adopting his housing philosophy of the garden city and dense low building. On the whole, the industrially produced large panel wall system was the method chosen, fast and high was the order of the day, the development of systems themselves being neglected in the process. An annual rate of approximately 15.000 apartments was achieved in this period - architecture rendered anonymous. The Seventies began with the re-discovery of the "urban", with demands for compact urban building subsequently taking the form of megastructures. The debates that took place on architecture and urban planning led to projects such as "Wohnpark Alt-Erlaa", modernistic residential hills or the housing project "Am Schöpfwerk", an attempt at a new interpretation of the Vienna court principle and the superblocks of the Twenties.Parallel to the erection of these megastructures on the periphery, the endangered traditional urban fabric was being rediscovered. After all, of those cities with a population of over a million, Vienna still has the highest percentage of apartments over 80 years old.

Thus the Eighties began with a radical change in thought on urban housing policy. Dominating the debate were slogans such as "urban renewal, not urban expansion", and the opinion that the need was not for more apartments, but for quality. Postmodernism and the rediscovery of urban life, of living in one's own "quarter", were additional aspects.

The last large housing estate of the Seventies, the building on the Wienerberg, already followed the concept of low construction and half-open courts. Building assignments were divided up into small units, and assigned to different architects. The Vienna City Council itself increasingly withdrew from its role of municipal developer, transferring the task of social housing to cooperatives and building corporations. A particular form of monopolism became established in 1984: the Vienna municipal land allocation and city restoration Fund (Bodenbereitstellungs- und Stadterneuerungsfonds) gained control of all plots designated for subsidized public housing, re-selling them to developers. This not only enabled land prices for social housing to be kept under control as there was in effect only one potential buyer, but, through regulations for utilization and plot prices, for an important control mechanism to be established.

It was in close proximity to the Fund that at the beginning of the 80's a conservative group of developers with connections to the Austrian People's Party (ÖVP) came into being, coordinated by an association calling itself "Werkstatt Wien" (initially GWV). New self-imposed standards of quality were set for social housing in Vienna, up to this point dominated by the Vienna City Council, and developers with ties to the Austrian Social Democratic Party (SPÖ). Many exemplary infilling projects and small siedlungen were realized by well-known architects, who had previously not had access to the close system of social housing. Viennese housing projects thus became recognized internationally as notable examples of new and committed architecture.

The Viennese housing projects of this period were altogether marked by an inquiring and calm spirit. They offered an enormous opportunity for innovative architecture, but were nevertheless based on the premise of a stagnating population.

The situation changed dramatically when, at the end of the Eighties, the Iron Curtain began to crumble. For the first time since the Twenties, after 60 years of stagnating development and a shrinking population, the city began to grow, and a new urban development plan was drawn up. The city reeled into the euphoric planning of large-scale and committed development projects. Demand exploded, the small, fine piecemeal projects of the 80's no longer an answer to what was now required. Nevertheless, in part adventurous and interesting new beginnings in urban planning were followed by rather conventional residential buildings. As in the Seventies, the old machinery again began to work towards mastering the now new "big number". Developers and administration aimed at achieving an annual turnover of approximately 10.000 apartments, a debate on what the new era demanded in terms of quality being secondary. The only prerequisite of urban expansion was now a mythicized "density", so that the appropriate infrastructure could be provided. A small house with a garden was what in fact a now mobile population dreamed of, a dream that was fulfilled in the unplanned land surrounding Vienna.

With the exception of a few single examples, the important social and political-economic boom in social housing at the beginning of the Nineties did not really make the most of the opportunity given as far as conception and content were concerned. From the mid-Nineties, the pendulum once again swung in the other direction. It was now political policy to more or less halt immigration, bringing with it a reduction in the nominal need for housing. More attention is once again to be given to urban renewal in the built-up areas, and attempts be made to reduce the cost of social housing by making commissions given to developers subject to competition. New ideas and concepts in the field of social housing going beyond this are currently not in sight. The City Council of Vienna, the big landlaord, the pioneer of municipal commitment in the housing of its citizens is contenting itself with the social achievement of the hereditary rent law with state-controlled rents, and biding its time. And when all is said and done, the glorious age of Viennese social housing is certainly an accomplishment that can be drawn on.

Colour plates by Georg Riha

St. Stephen's Cathedral (1230), general view, index-no. 1.-**1**

St. Stephen's Cathedral (1230), interior view, index no. 1.-**1**

The New Haas-House (1985), general view, index no. 1.-**3**

The New Haas-House (1985), interior view, index no. 1.-**3**

Retti Candle Shop (1964), interior, index no. 1.-**11**

Loos House (1909), interior staircase, index no. 1.-**15**

Loos House (1909),interir view, mezzanine, index nro. 1.-**15**

National Library (1723–26), interior view, index no. 1.-**16**

Palmery Burggarten (1899), aerial view, index no. 1.-**17**

Palmery Burggarten (1899), interior detail, index no. 1.-**17**

The Jewish Museum of Vienna (1995), interior view, index no. 1.-**27**

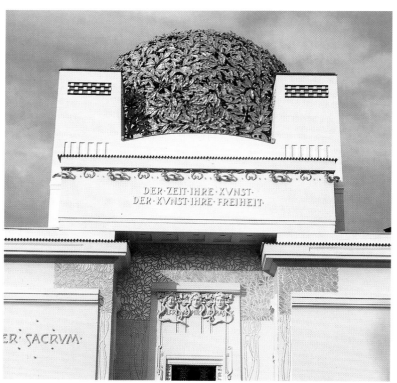

Secession (1897), main facade (detail), index no. 1.-**35**

Secession (1897), interior view, index no. 1.-**35**

Zacherl House (1903), foyer, index no. 1.-**70**

Zacherl House (1903), staircase, index no. 1.-**70**

Former Länderbank (1882), former banking hall, index no. 1.-**73**

Synagogue (1824), interior view, index no. 1.-**82**

Postal Savings Bank (1903), facade (detail), index no. 1.-**88**

Postal Savings Bank (1903), interior view, banking hall, index no. 1.-**88**

MAK-Café (1989), interior view, index no. 1.-**91**

Lassallestraße Office Complex (1989), interior view, atrium, index no. 2.-**6**

Lassallestraße Office Complex (1989), interior view, atrium, index no. 2.-**6**

Rehersal stage of the Burgtheater (1993), entrance, index no. 3.-**8**

Stonborough-Wittgenstein House (1926), foyer, index no. 3.-**12**

Portois & Fix Residential and Commercial Building (1899), facade (detail), index no. 3.-**15**

Karlskirche (1715), interior view, index no. 4.-**3**

Former depot for stage-sets (1875), interior view, index no. 6.-**1**

Bank, Favoriten (1975), interior view, index no. 10.-**2**

Absberggasse secondary school (1994), interior view, recreation area, index no. 10.-**5**

Amalienbad (1923), indoor swimming pool, index no. 10.-**8**

Skywa-Primavesi villa (1913), view from the garden, index no. 13.-**10**

The house of Roland Rainer (1968), interior-exterior view, index no. 13.-**11**

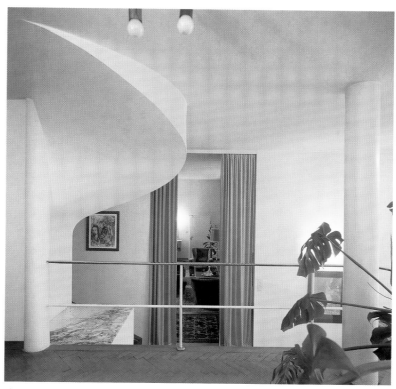

The Beer House (1929), interior view, index no. 13.-**12**

The Steiner House (1910), view from the road, index no. 13.-**18**

The Steiner House (1910), living room, as in 1997, index no. 13.-**18**

Werkbundsiedlung (1930), aerial view, index no. 13.-**23**

Matznergasse residential home (1993), inner courtyard, index no. 14.-**3**

Kinkplatz secondary school (1994), gymnasiums, interior view, index no. 14.-**6**

Steinhof Church (1905), interior view, index no. 14.-**9**

Heilig-Geist-Church (1910), interior view, index no. 16.-**3**

Frauenfelderstraße residential building (1991), index no. 17.-**2**

Karl-Marx-Hof and Svoboda-Hof (1926), general view, index no. 19.-**25**

Office building (1990), inner courtyard, index no. 20.-**6**

Friedrich-Engels-Platz housing estate (1930), general view, index no. 20.-**4**

Bank branch (1971), banking hall, index no. 21.-**1**

Frauen-Werk-Stadt (1994), inner courtyard, index no. 21.-**18**

Wagramerstraße high-rise (1994), facade (detail), index no. 22.-**4**

Pilotengasse siedlung (1989), view from the garden, index no. 22.-**24**

Underground station U 6 (1990), staircase (detail), index no. 23.-**1**

Brunner Straße housing estate (1986), street facade, index no. 23.-**4**

Purkersdorf sanatorium (1904), main facade, index no. S. D.-**1**

Architecture in Vienna

How to use the maps and index numbers

Each building has been allotted a topographical index number, chosen to correspond to the 23 districts into which Vienna is divided. The first number indicates the district in which the object is to be found, the second, in bold type, the object itself (e.g. St. Stephan's Cathedral 1.1.= 1st District, number 1; Schönbrunn Palace: 13.3. = 13th District, number 3). Given underneath the address of each building is both information on whether it is on a public transport route and if so, which, and whether it is open to the public. (Public transportation: Suburban train (Schnellbahn) with the appropriate line; U= Underground (U-Bahn) with the appropriate line; Tram (Strassenbahn) with the appropriate line; Bus (Bus) with the appropriate number. The nearest stop to the building in question is given in brackets.) Each building is introduced by a brief description, and accompanied by photos and plans.

Buildings worth visiting – Suggestions by Viennese architects

1st District:

Friedrich Achleitner:
- Augustinerkirche, Index no. 1.-**18**
- Kärntner Bar, Index no. 1.-**26**
- Kleines Café, Index no. 1.-**42**

Maria Auböck:
- Kornhäusel Turm, Index no. 1.-**82**

Luigi Blau
- Scheinkuppel (illusionistic cupola) by Andrea Pozzo in the Universitätskirche, dated 1705, Index no. 1.-**86**
- A walk from the Börse to the Staatsoper along the Ringstrasse - including a visit to the Reichsratssaal in the Parliament building by Theophil Hansen (1847-83), Index no. 1.-**29**, 1.-**63**, 1.-**71**

Coop Himmelblau:
- St. Stephen's Cathedral, Index no. 1.-**1**
- Kärntner Bar, Index no. 1.-**26**

Margarethe Cufer:
- Palais Equitable, Index no. 1.-**2**

Hermann Czech:
- Prunksaal of the Nationalbibliothek (National Library), Index no. 1.-**16**

Heidulf Gerngroß:
- A walk along the Ringstrasse (with a running commentary)

Otto Graf (Kunsthistoriker):
- Hofbibliothek (Imperial Library), Index no. 1.-**16**
- Staatsoper (State Opera House), Index no. 1.-**29**

Hans Hollein:
- Nationalbibliothek (particularly the Prunksaal), Index no. 1.-**16**
- Postsparkasse (Postal Savings Bank), Index no. 1.-**88**
- Haas-House, Index no. 1.-**3**
- Kärntner Bar, Index no. 1.-**26**
- Falkestrasse loft adaptation, Index no. 1.-**92**

Wilhelm Holzbauer:
- Courtyard in Palais Equitable, Majolica tile-cladding, Index no. 1.-**2**
- Artaria House, Index no. 1.-**13**

Martin Kohlbauer:
- Herrengasse high-rise, Index no. 1.-**49**

Adolf Krischanitz:
- Stadtbahn stations, Index no. 1.-**36**

Gustav Peichl:
- Kärntner Bar, Index no. 1.-**26**

Boris Podrecca:
- Maria am Gestade Church, Index no. 1.-**67**
- Zacherl-House, Index no. 1.-**70**
- Kärntner Bar, Index no. 1.-**26**

Elsa Prochazka:
- Synagogue, Index no. 1.-**82**

Roland Rainer:
- Maria am Gestade Church, Index no. 1.-**67**
- Kärntner Bar, Index no. 1.-**26**

August Sarnitz:
- Postsparkasse (interior), Index no. 1.-**88**
- Tower of St. Stephen's Cathedral, Index no. 1.-**1**

Margherita Spiluttini (architecture photographer):
- Kornhäusel Tower, Index no. 1.-**82**

Dietmar Steiner:
- Augustinerkirche (St. Augustine's Church), Index no. 1.-**18**

Heinz Tesar:
- Zacherl-House (vestibule and stairwell), Index no. 1.-**70**
- Gate to the Garden (in the Museum of Applied Arts), Index no. 1.-**91**

Franziska Ullmann:
- St. Stephen's Cathedral, Index no. 1.-**1**

Manfred Wehdorn:
- Ringstrasse (as an Austrian variation of French urban planning)
- Hofburg (Redoutentrakt), Index no. 1.-**16**

1.-**1** | *Hans von Prachatitz, Hans Puchspaum et al.*

St. Stephen's Cathedral 1230

Stephansplatz
Access: Open to public
Public transportation: U1, U3 (Stephansplatz)

Now the symbol of the topographical centre of Vienna, St. Stephen's Cathedral symbolised its political and spiritual centre for centuries. Commissioned by the ruling house and the bourgeoisie, the cathedral was originally located outside the city. The main entrance area (Riesentor, Heidentürme and gallery) still remains of its original Romanesque construction (1230/40–1263). The high Gothic Albertine choir hall was added on to the Romanesque nave and side-aisles between 1304–40, which were in turn replaced by a raised, windowless Gothic nave between 1359–1440. The south tower (completed in 1433 by Hans Prachatitz) is the hallmark of the cathedral and a prominent feature of the city. Although work was begun on the north tower, it was never completed.

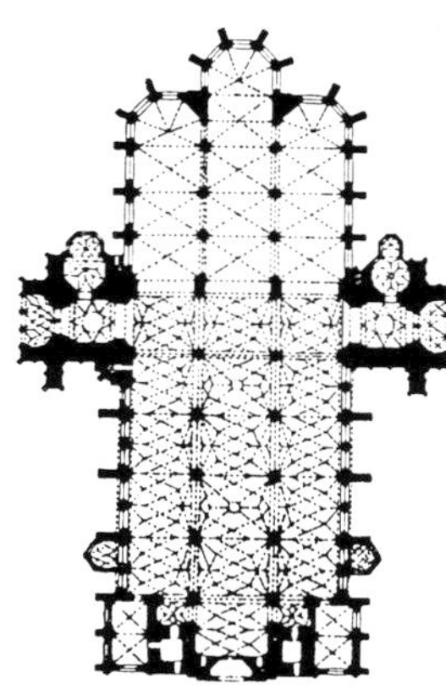

1.-**2** | *Andreas Streit*

Palais Equitable 1887

Stock im Eisen Platz 3-4
Access: Not open to public
Public transportation: U1, U3 (Stephansplatz)

This building, constructed for a New York insurance company, replaced five older houses. Its setback partially created the same urban problem that was to preoccupy Hans Hollein during the building of the Haas House. In contrast to Otto Wagner, who was influenced by the American office buildings while designing the nearby Anker House, Streit reintroduced the vocabulary of the beaux-arts tradition. The stairwell is one of the most beautiful examples of Viennese Historicism.

Opposite St. Stephen's Cathedral – in the most central location in Vienna – Hans Hollein designed an exclusive shopping centre with offices and restaurants. The form of the house was partially determined by topographical considerations – the break caused by the bay extending over several floors was intended to demarcate the Stock im Eisen Platz and St. Stephen's Square. The five-storey high atrium opens above to a shallow glass dome with artificial lighting. The opulent decor in rich materials is an attempt to ennoble the mundanity of the commercial world. Within the context of Viennese architectural discussion it is comparable to the house on Michaelerplatz by Adolf Loos.

Neues Haas-Haus (The New Haas House) 1985

Stock im Eisen Platz 4
Access: Open to public
Public transportation: U1, U3 (Stephansplatz)

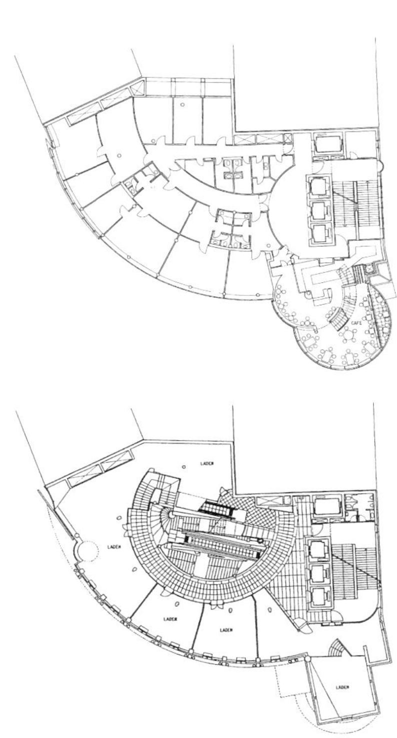

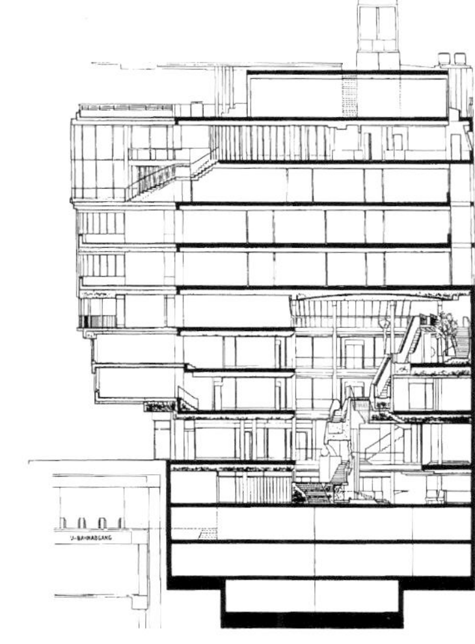

Otto Wagner

Anker House
1894

The insurance company "Der Anker" commissioned Otto Wagner to build a residential and commercial building on the Graben. Though two buildings were initially planned, a larger version of the house "Zum Anker" was finally preferred. The building permit was granted on 22nd December 1894 (ref. Otto Graf). It is noteworthy for the metropolitan approach reflected in the two-storeyed commercial zone and in the glazed superstructure intended as a photographer's studio.

Graben 10, Spiegelgasse 2
Access: Not open to public
Public transportation: U1, U3 (Stephansplatz)

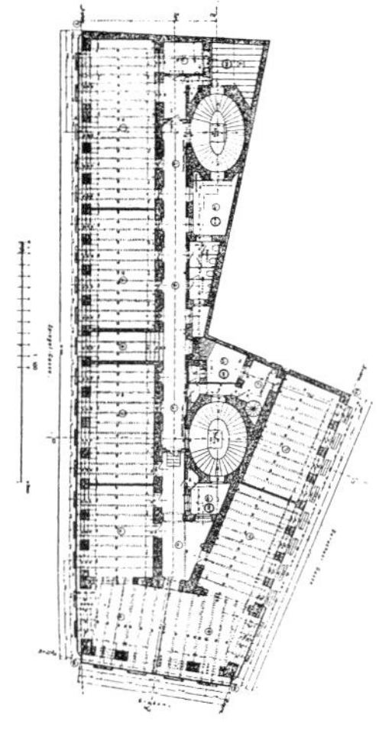

1.-5

Rudolf Krauß

Trattnerhof
1911

The architectural history of this house with its residential and commercial facilities is relatively complicated. The complex was planned as a closed structure with access through several courtyards. This initial conception was ultimately altered and the building was divided in order to create a passageway between Dorotheergasse and Bauernmarkt via the Graben. Its internal framework of reinforced concrete allowed a free structuring of the ground plan for the apartments.

Graben 29-29a,
Trattnergasse
Access: Not open to public
Public transportation: U1, U3 (Stephansplatz)

Hans Hollein

1.-**6**

The metaphor (gold vein – jeweller) underlies the architecture of Hollein and thematizes the dualism in design between technical grid and naturalistic free-form. This small jeweller's shop is replete with symbolism, offering the viewer different levels of interpretation. The interior decoration is opulent, resembling the inside of a jewellery box.

Schullin Jewellers I (now Deutsch Jewellers) 1972

Graben 21
Access: Business hours
Public transportation: U1, U3 (Stephansplatz)

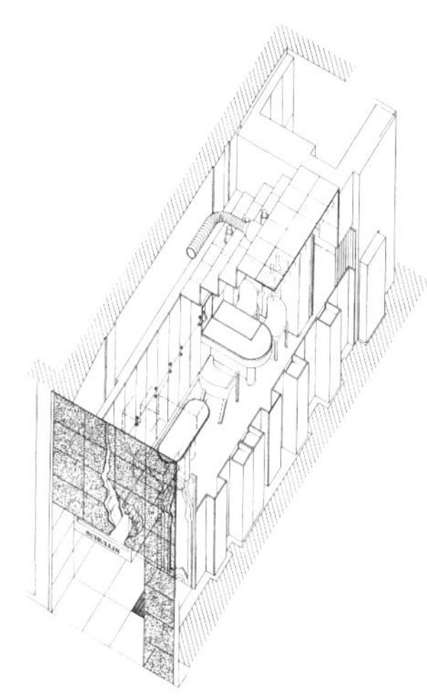

Elsa Prochazka

1.-**7**

This little bookshop, in close proximity to St. Stephen's Cathedral, was meant primarily for religious books. Unfortunately, its prime location has led it away from its original intention and it has increasingly taken on the characteristics of a souvenir shop. Prochazka received the prize awarded by the public in the Loos Prize Competition for Architecture in 1994, for her sensitive refurbishment of the old premises. The architectonic design of the shelves stylised them into a theme in itself.

Bibelwerk Bookshop 1991

Singerstrasse 7
Access: Business hours
Public transportation: U1 (Stephansplatz)

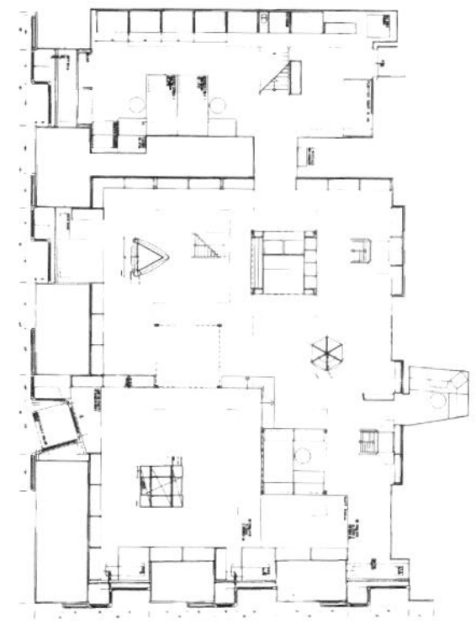

1.-**8** | *Gabriele Montani, Johann Lukas von Hildebrandt*

Peterskirche (St. Peter's Church) 1702

Petersplatz
Access: Open to public
Public transportation: U1, U3 (Stephansplatz)

St. Peter's was constructed on the site of one of the oldest churches of Vienna at the beginning of the 18th century. It was built according to the plans of Gabriele Montani, which were revised by Johann Lukas von Hildebrandt. It is not exactly in alignment with the construction line of the Graben, but stands somewhat recessed. The impression of being "cramped" into the small square is heightened by the "folded" façade. The trompe l'oeil architecture inside the choir dome is attributed to Antonio Galli-Bibiena.

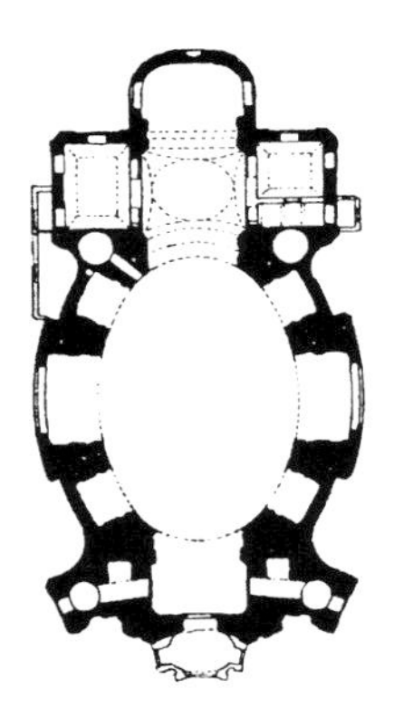

1.-**9** | *Johann B. Fischer v. Erlach, L. Burnacini, P. Strudel*

Pestsäule (Plague Column) 1682

Graben
Access: Open to public
Public transportation: U2, U3 (Stephansplatz)

This votive pillar was erected in fulfilment of a pledge by Leopold I, made in the hope of exorcising the plague of 1679. It was constructed by Ludovico Burnacini and Paul Strudel, according to the plans of Johann B. Fischer von Erlach. The reason for its erection forms the main theme of the sculptures – the praying Leopold I, the group of figures "Faith Conquers the Plague" and the portrayal of the Holy Trinity. The votive construction is typical of the High Baroque's attempt to merge architecture and sculpture.

The shop was designed by Adolf Loos between 1910 and 1913 for the men's tailor Knize, who catered for an international clientele. The atmosphere of an exclusive London club is not purely coincidental, for Adolf Loos after all considered men's clothing from London the only suitable attire for gentlemen. The minimally scaled façade in no way reveals the generous designing of the shop's interior. In addition to a small sales area on the ground floor there is a two-storeyed hall on the floor above, as well as an enfilade of display rooms. The furnishings of the shop and the storage rooms are all custom made, like a well-fitted suit. The premises were extended by Paolo Piva in 1993.

Knize Gentlemen's Outfitters 1910

Graben 13
Access: Business hours
Public transportation: U1, U3 (Stephansplatz)

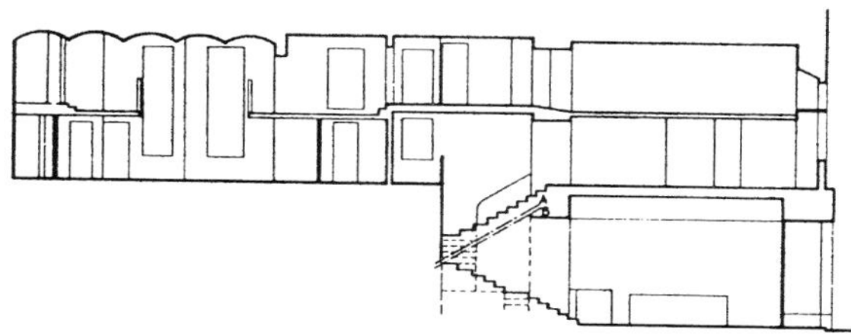

Retti Candle Shop
1964

Kohlmarkt 8-10
Access: Business hours
Public transportation: U1, U3 (Stephansplatz)

This candle store is a symbol of Viennese commercial architecture and a manifesto for Hans Hollein's architecture. He created a complex spatial sequence within a restricted space. An octagonal room creates an almost spiritual atmosphere that is reflected into infinity by the use of alternating mirrored surfaces. The deliberate "cutting out" of the aluminium portal creates iconographical associations with light and candle.

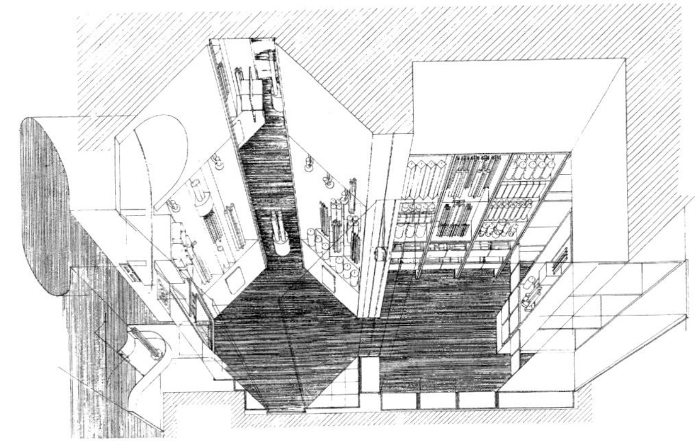

Schullin Jewellers II
1981

Hans Hollein built a second, larger jeweller's shop for Schullin and Sons ten years after he had built the first. Contrary to the former theme of the "gold vein", the emphasis here is more on the "sacred" and "mystic" qualities of jewellery. The arched form above the entrance can be associated with a blade, weapon or ornament. The "play" between real and apparently real materials is brought to perfection in the interior.

Kohlmarkt 7
Access: Business hours
Public transportation: U1, U3 (Stephansplatz)

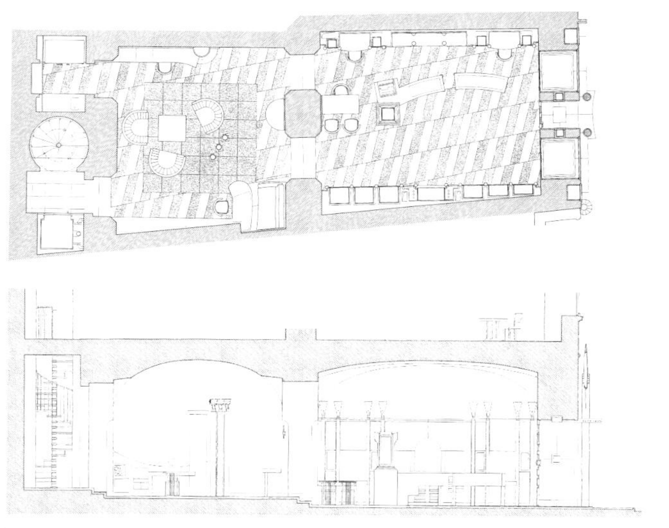

1.-**13**

Max Fabiani

Artaria House
1900

Kohlmarkt 9
Only shops open to public
Public transportation: U1, U3 (Stephansplatz)

The Artaria Publishing House building almost seems to herald the "impending disaster" that its contemporaries were to face in the form of Loos' Michaelerhaus, which was to be built in its immediate vicinity somewhat later. The setback from the building line of Kohlmarkt creates a court-like extension that is enclosed above by the projecting cornice. The form of the cornice is also adopted in the bay windows and gives still more systematic uniformity to the façade of the upper floors. The circulation in the interior reflects Fabiani's assured handling of a difficult site.

1.-**14**

Antonio Beduzzi, Ernest Koch

Michaelerkirche (St. Michael's Church)
1220

Michaelerplatz
Access: Open to public
Public transportation: U1, U3 (Stephansplatz)

The centuries of construction this former royal parish and Barnabite church underwent is evident in its appearance. The walls of the nave with their late Romanesque pilaster arcades, to which a choir dating back to the 14th century is attached, still remain of the original Romanesque construction. In 1792 Ernest Koch incorporated Classicist norms into the façade, providing a backdrop to the baroque portal by Antonio Beduzzi with its group of angels by Lorenzo Matielli (1724/25). In 1991–92 Hans Hollein exposed a circular site on Michaelerplatz that revealed a 2000 year cross-section of Viennese architecture to the field of urban archaeology.

Looshaus (Loos House) (formerly Goldman & Salatsch tailoring company) 1909

Michaelerplatz 3
Access: Ground floor open to public during business hours
Public transportation: U1, U3 (Stephansplatz)

Fierce controversy and a tug-of-war with the building authorities gave the Loos House controversial fame even before its completion (1909–11). Its location directly opposite the Hofburg Palace was largely responsible for the ferocity of this conflict. Apart from the provocative "nakedness" of the residential floors, Loos' first major Viennese project boasts of an innovative reinforced concrete construction, clever and functional conception of space and an exquisite choice of materials.

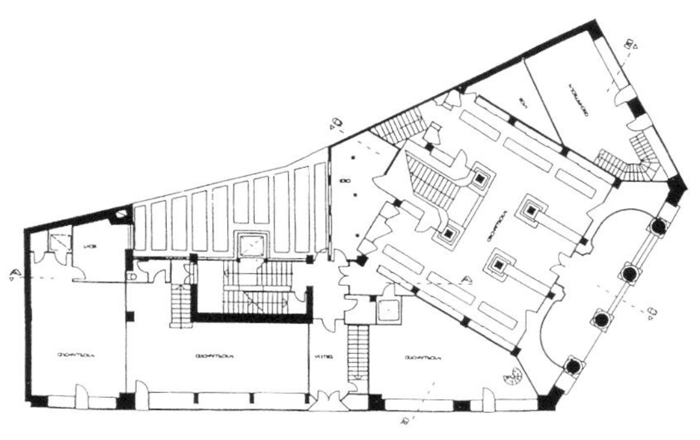

1.-16 | *J.-N. Jadot de Ville-Issey, J. L. v. Hildebrandt,*

Hofburg
1279

Hofburg, Heldenplatz
Access: Opening hours
Public transportation: Tram lines 1and 2 (Burgring)

The Hofburg Palace is a complex that grew steadily from the 13th century onwards, undergoing major changes between the 16th and 19th centuries. The Schweizerhof with its entrance to the Imperial Treasury (newly fitted by K. Mang and E. Mang-Frimmel in 1986/87) formed the core of the medieval castle, to which the Stallburg (1558–65), the Amalienburg (Pietro Ferrabosco, 1575–1611) and the Leopoldinischer Trakt (1660–66) were loosely attached in the 16th century. Major steps towards a consolidation of this open structure were undertaken in the 18th century with the construction of the Reichskanzleitrakt (Johann von Hildebrandt and Josef E. Fischer von Erlach, 1723–30) and the Winterreitschule (Josef E. Fischer von Erlach, 1729–35). Similarly, the originally free-

1 Schweizerhof (1279 onwards) (entrance to Imperial Treasury, refurbished in 1986-87)
2 Burgkapelle (Imperial Chapel)
3 Amalienburg (1575 onwards)
4 Stallburg (Neue Galerie, or New Gallery) (1558 onwards)
5 Leopoldinischer Trakt (1547 onwards) (Leopoldine Wing)
6 Nationalbibliothek (1723–26) (National Library)
7 Redoutensäle
8 Reichskanzleitrakt (1723) (Imperial Chancellery Wing)
9 Winterreitschule (1729–35) (Winter Riding School)
10 Michaelertrakt (1889–93) (Imperial Apartments)
11 Äußeres Burgtor (Outer Castle Gateway) (1821 onwards)
12 Heldenplatz
13 Neue Burg (1869–73) (New Hofburg including the Ephesos Museum, Arms Collection, Collection of Musical Instruments)
14 Wintergarten (1899) (Conservatory)
15 Museum für Völkerkunde (Ethnological Museum)

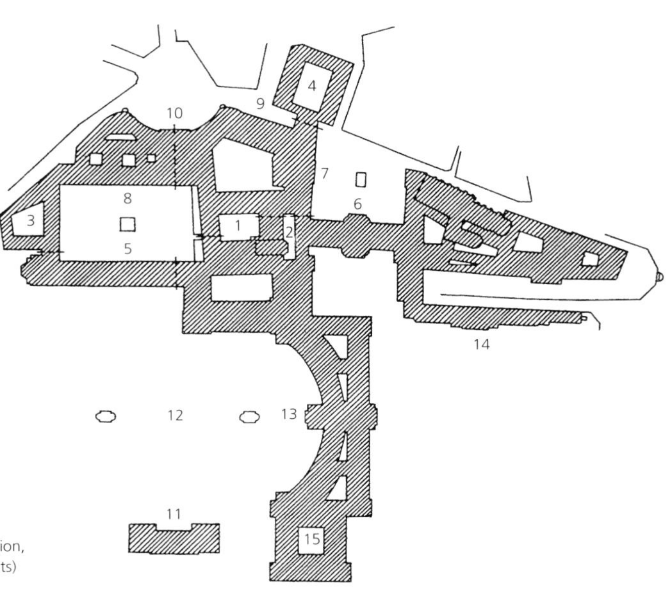

standing Hofbibliothek, built by Johann B. Fischer von Erlach (now the Nationalbibliothek), was also incorporated into the complex through the construction of the Redoutensäle (Nicholas Jadot de Ville-Issey, 1744–48) and a unified reorganisation of the façade (1767) to form a homogeneous structure. At the beginning of the 19th century Luigi Cagnola and Peter Nobile expanded the constructed area of the castle by building the Burgtor (1821–24), which was connected to the Neue Hofburg by Gottfried Semper and Carl Hasenauer between 1881–1913. Although Josef E. Fischer von Erlach designed the Michaelertrakt, it was completed much later by Ferdinand Kirschner between 1889 and 1893.

1.-**17** *Friedrich Ohmann*

Palmenhaus Burggarten (Palmery) 1899

Burggarten
Access: Open to public
Public transportation: U1 (Karlsplatz)

Designed in 1899 the Palmery, also known as the "Neuer Wintergarten", was built between 1901 and 1906. It is a pioneering achievement in the field of steel and glass construction. "Through the use of huge stonework bays Ohmann was able to react to the massive stonework of the Neue Hofburg's façade, while the copper tetrahedron roofs 'hail' the Nationalbibliothek" (Friedrich Achleitner). A poetic shrine of palms – sensual and emotional, it is a remnant of the fin de siècle. The Palmery is currently undergoing extensive renovation.

1.-**18** *Dietrich L. v. Pirn, Johann F. H. v. Hohenberg*

Augustinerkirche (St. Augustine's Church) 1330

Augustinerstrasse by 3
Access: Open to public
Public transportation: U1, U4 (Karlsplatz)

Both the church building and cloister have a close architectural affinity to the imperial Hofburg. The church was built by the Bavarian architect Dietrich Ladtner von Pirn as a three-aisled hall church between 1330 and 1339. The interior, which had been completely transformed to Baroque, was restored to its Gothic form by Johann Ferdinand Hetzendorf von Hohenberg in the 18th century. A memorial to Archduchess Marie Christine, the wife of Albert von Sachsen-Teschen (the founder of the nearby Albertina Graphic Collection) can be found within. It was erected in 1798–1805 by the Italian sculptor Antonio Canova.

Art History and Natural History Museums 1871

Burgring 5 and 7
Access: Opening hours
Public transportation: Tram lines 1and 2 (Burgring)

Both buildings were originally conceived as partial extensions of the Hofburg, stretching over the Ringstrasse, connecting the imperial stables with the palace. Apart from the two state museums, only one of the two concave wings of the New Hofburg was ultimately built. The entire complex, which marks both the beginning and the end of the grand Ringstrasse, was punctuated by two triumphal arches. The intention was to create an "eye catcher", while also including it in the imperial sphere of influence. The interior of both museums is by Hasenauer, whereas the exterior was designed by Semper. Renowned artists such as Hans Makart and the young Gustav Klimt were responsible for the decoration in the interior of the Art History Museum.

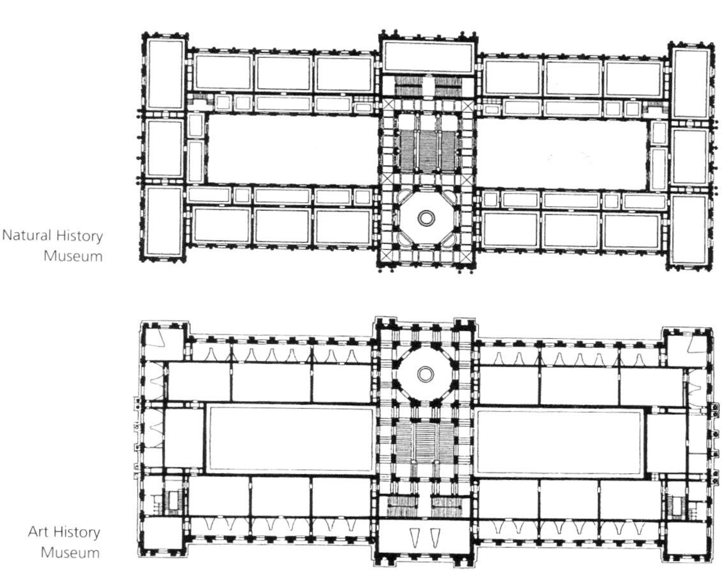

Natural History Museum

Art History Museum

1.-20 | *Johann Ferdinand Hetzendorf von Hohenberg*

Palais Pallavicini
1783

Josefsplatz 5
Access: Not open to public
Public transportation: U1, U3 (Stephansplatz)

Like the Loos House on the nearby Michaelerplatz, this building too provoked fierce discussion; it too was criticised as being too plain and not stately enough for its location so near the Hofburg. Sculptural embellishments such as the statues by Franz Anton Zauner were added later to "enhance" the façade. The statue of Leopold II facing the palace is also by the same artist.

1.-21 | *Louis von Montoyer, Josef Kornhäusel*

Albertina
1745

Augustinerstrasse 1
Access: Opening hours
Public transportation: U1, U4 (Karlsplatz)

Originally located on the ramparts of a former city wall, this classicist building affords a good insight into the city planning of the period prior to the construction of the Ringstrasse. The construction of the palace incorporated the building that had already stood upon the site, as well as parts of the Augustine cloister. It was built by Louis von Montoyer for Albert Casimir von Sachsen-Teschen, whose collection forms the basis for the present Albertina Graphics Collection. The interior was extended and adapted by Josef Kornhäusel. The reconstruction now taking place by Steinmayr and Mascher is planned to create additional space for the graphics collection. In addition to this collection, the Albertina also houses the Austrian Film Museum.

Giovanni P. Tencala, Johann B. Fischer von Erlach 1.-**22**

Palais Lobkowitz
1685

The city palace of Count Dietrichstein was presumably built by Giovanni Pietro Tencala between 1685–87. He arranged the façade by creating a weave of flat surfaces in a style common to Early Baroque. Johann B. Fischer von Erlach gave the building a High Baroque appearance with a monumental attic zone above the flat central bay. The palace, which was a meeting place in the 19th century, for those interested in culture was also where Beethoven's "Eroica" premiered to an intimate circle in 1803. It has housed the Austrian Theatre Museum (designed by K. Mang and E. Mang Frimmel) since 1991.

Lobkowitzplatz 2
Access: Opening hours
Public transportation: U1, U4 (Karlsplatz)

Georg Raphael Donner 1.-**23**

Donnerbrunnen
(The Donner Fountain)
1737

The river gods Traun, Enns, March and Ybbs idle around the brink of the basin. The lead moulds of the figures (the originals are in the Austrian Baroque Museum in the Lower Belvedere) and the dynamic inclusion of the environs make this fountain unique in Vienna. While the structure of the fountain and the figure of "Providentia" belong to the outdated Augsburg fountain style, the elongated figures are typical of the late Donner. It is one of the most beautiful fountains of Vienna.

Neuer Markt
Access: Open to public
Public transportation: U1 (Stephansplatz)

1.-**24**

Coop Himmelblau

Reiss-Bar
1977

An early work of the architects Wolf D. Prix and Helmut Swiczinsky, who practise under the name "Coop Himmelblau". During the 80s they made notable contributions towards the Austrian discourse on Deconstructi-vism. The idea for the Reiss-Bar arose from the fictive necessity to provide space for 66 people and from the 48 cm. wide "rip" in the wall, which became a metaphor for the architecture.

Marco-d'Aviano-Gasse 1
Access: Open to public
Public transportation: U1, U4 (Karlsplatz)

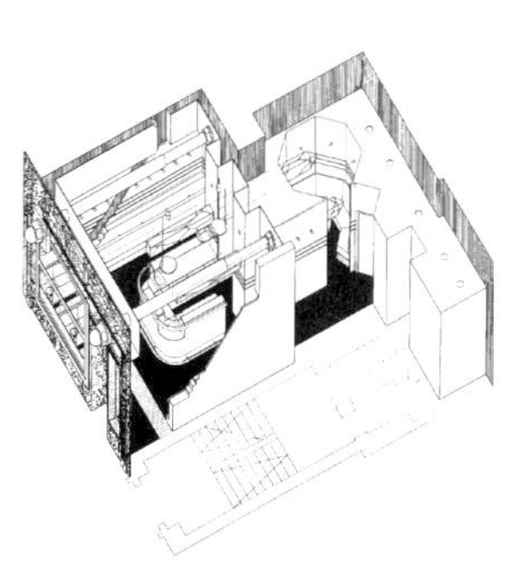

1.-**25**

Hans Hollein

CM Boutique
1966

A modular shop, consisting of a single room and planned to the minutest detail. The 60s world of plastics has been "frozen" here for the modern customer. Similar to the Retti Candle Shop (Hollein, 1964), its façade has been designed as a form of beacon that is scaled to be effective not only along the entire length of the street but also from close-up.

Tegetthoffstrasse 3
Access: Business hours
Public transportation: U1, U4 (Karlsplatz)

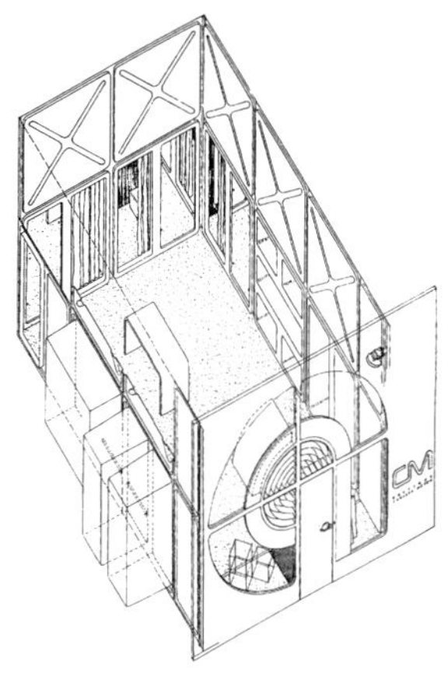

Kärntner-Bar (Loos-Bar) 1908

A contribution towards the "Introduction of Occidental culture in Austria" Loos' experiences in America found somewhat nostalgic expression in the case of this small, private assignment. The façade is impressive in its unorthodox combination of rich marble and its coloured glass signboard. The interior, in turn, is impressive for its extreme economy of space. After decades of neglect, this early work of Loos had to be reconstructed by Hermann Czech and Burkhardt Rukschcio (1985, 1989).

Kärntner Durchgang
Access: Business hours
Public transportation: U1, U3 (Stephansplatz)

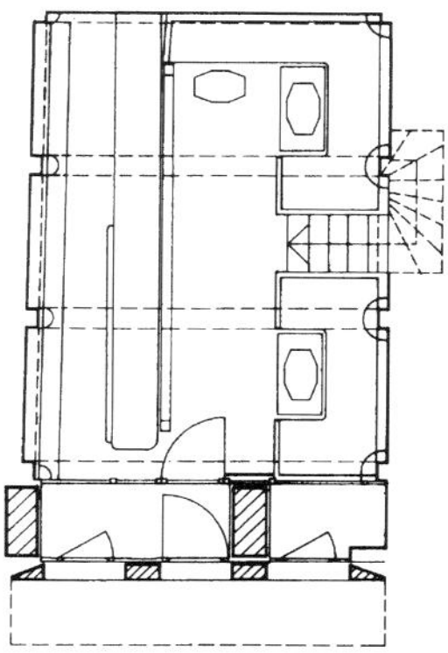

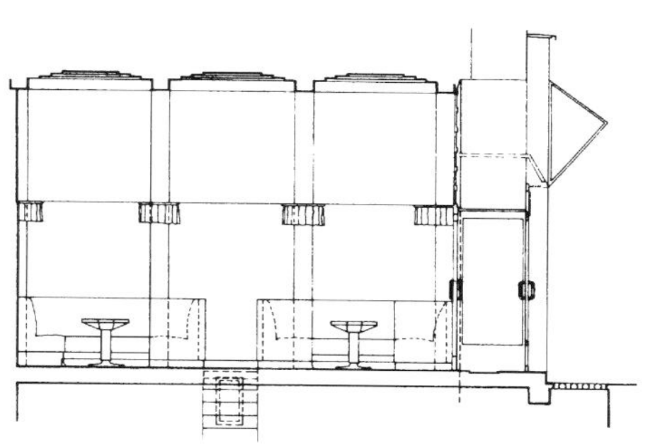

1.-**27** | ***Renovated by Eichinger oder Knechtl / Franz Sam***

The Jewish Museum of Vienna 1995

Dorotheergasse 11, Palais Eskeles
Access: Business hours
Public transportation: U1 (Stephansplatz)

The Eskeles Palace has housed the Jewish Museum of Vienna since 1993. After its temporary conversion by Martin Kohlbauer in 1993 for the museum's opening, Eichinger oder Knechtl adapted the entire building. They gave it a "cupola", a parabolic glass roof, which covers the entire courtyard and serves as its new atrium. Since the palace is a protected monument, its interior had to be partially preserved despite conflicts with the museum's requirements.

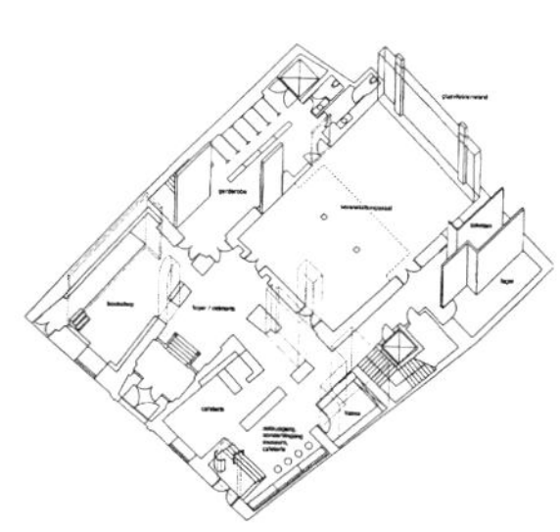

1.-**28** | ***Ludwig Förster and Theophil von Hansen***

Palais Todesco 1861

Kärntner Strasse 51, Walfischgasse 2, Mahlerstrasse 1
Access: Not open to public
Public transportation: U1, U4, tram lines 1 and 2 (Karlsplatz)

The palace was constructed by Ludwig Förster and Theophil von Hansen for the banker Eduard Todesco. In the architectural context of the city it belongs to the same style as the Staatsoper, as do the Heinrich-Hof (also by Theophil von Hansen), destroyed during the Second World-War, and the Schey von Koromla Palace (Julius Romano and August Schwendenwein). The neo-Renaissance palace, with its generous layout and remarkable glazed-in inner courtyard, was a meeting place for the Viennese theatre scene. It served as the seat of the Austrian People's Party between 1947 and 1995 and was completely renovated and restored in 1997.

Staatsoper (State Opera House) 1861

Opernring 2
Access: Open to public
Public transportation: Tram lines 1and 2, U1 (Karlsplatz)

This principal work of E. v. d. Nüll and A. S. v. Sicardsburg, in the style of "Romantic Historicism", was amongst the first monumental constructions to be built along the newly-laid Ringstrasse. While E. v. d. Nüll was responsible for the artistic design, A. S. v. Sicardsburg was responsible for the structural framework, in the tradition of the division between architect and engineer. It suffered heavy damage during the Second World War, and was rebuilt in 1946–55 by Erich Boltenstern, who made considerable alterations to its interior. Hermann Czech designed the winter-glazing of the loggia in 1991–1994, as well as a bookstore on the ground floor.

Loggia with winter glazing

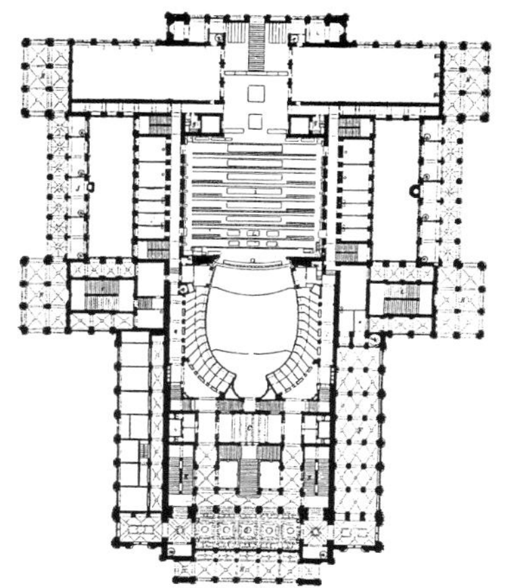

1.-**30** *Wilhelm Holzbauer et al.*

The Ringstrasse Galleries 1993

Kärntner Ring 5–13
Access: Open to public
Public transportation: Tram lines 1and 2, U1 (Karlsplatz)

The "Ringstrassen Galleries" represent one of the largest complexes of new buildings on the noble Viennese boulevard. Approximately 18,000 m² of office space, 12,000 m² of commercial space and 4,000 m² of penthouse apartments, as well as a 205 room luxury hotel lend it an urban flair. A steel bridge, designed by Holzbauer, connects the building with the newly renovated Palais Corso. Opulent materials such as natural stone, brass and chrome were used in order to furnish the multi-levelled shopping arcade with an ambience of luxury. It is a shoppers' paradise with cosmopolitan ambitions.

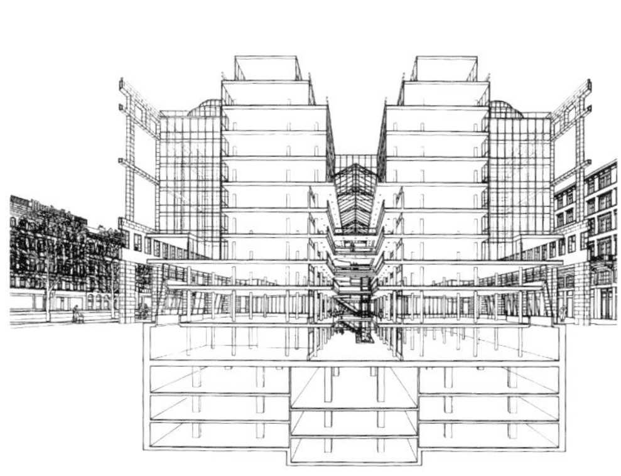

1.-**31** *Theophil von Hansen*

Akademie der bildenden Künste (Academy of Fine Arts) 1871

Schillerplatz 3
Access: Open to public
Public transportation: U1, tram lines 1and 2 (Karlsplatz)

The Academy of Fine Arts is the oldest state school of art in Austria. The clearly organised building with its tower-like corner elevations is certainly one of Hansen's principal works. It stands a short distance away from the Ringstrasse, separated from it by a square. The independent structure of the aula within the single courtyard of the academy makes the internal organisation of the building clearly visible. On the side facing Makartgasse, Josef Hoffmann erected a monument to Otto Wagner, the most celebrated holder of the Academy's chair of architecture.

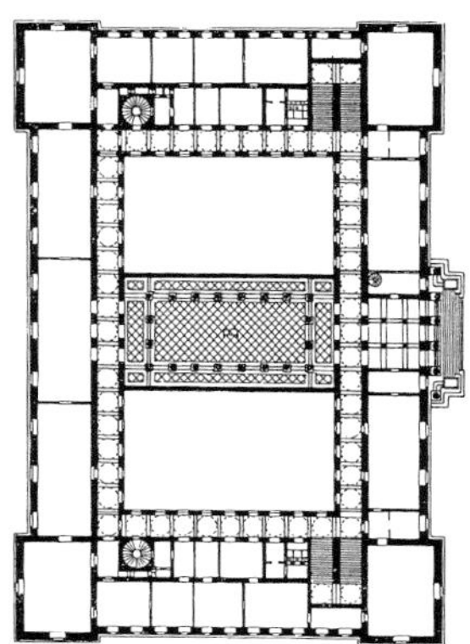

Böhler-House
1956

Elisabethstrasse 12
Access: Not open to public
Public transportation: U1, U4 (Karlsplatz)

The "Böhler-House" was conceived as an extension of the Gründerzeit house located further west, which is the reason why a main flight of steps was not planned for the annexe. The glass curtain-wall façade not only refers to the steel-production of the Böhler works, but was at that time perceived as one of the first signs of life of a young generation of Austrian architects. In its specific Austrian context, it is comparable to the Museum of the Twentieth Century by Karl Schwanzer. The building itself is based on a functional ground-plan for offices, with the general administrative offices occupying the top floor. The house is now classified as a historical monument.

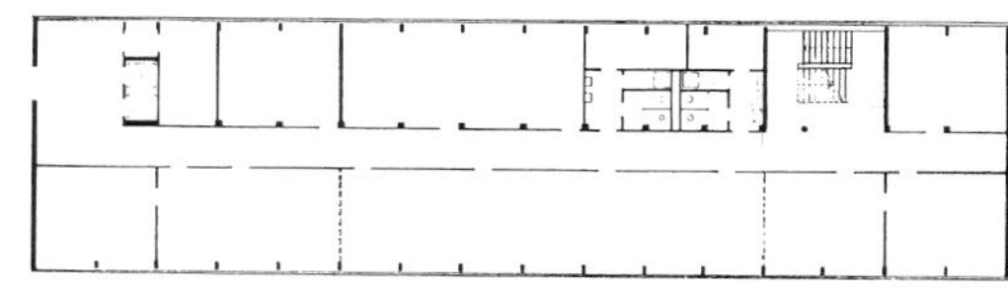

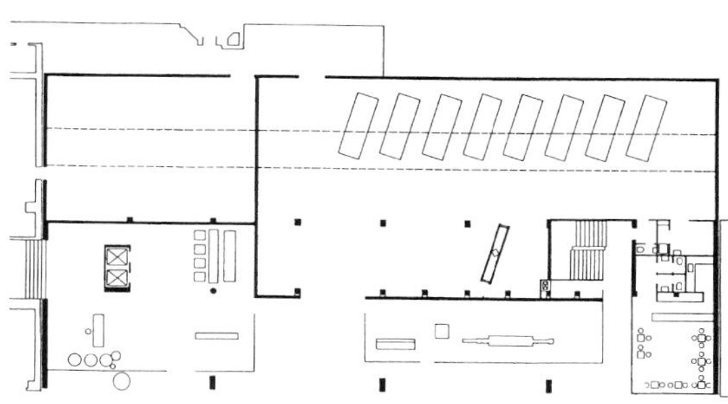

1.-**33** *Gustav Peichl, Roland Rainer*

Akademiehof Karlsplatz 1991

The new Akademiehof is situated next to the Secession and the Academy of Fine Arts. On the occasion of the Academy's 300th anniversary, the City of Vienna presented the site to the Academy as a gift. Roland Rainer and Gustav Peichl developed a multi-functional building with an urban flair. It contains an arcade on the ground floor and shops, exhibition rooms, offices and apartments on the top two floors. The diverse functions of the building are clearly reflected in its façade.

Getreidemarkt 2–4
Access: Museum and ground floor open to public
Transportation: U1, U4 (Karlsplatz)

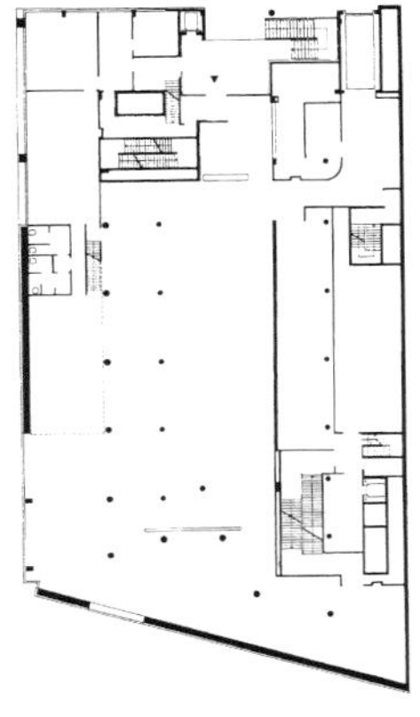

1.-**34** *Oswald Haerdtl*

Historisches Museum der Stadt Wien (Museum of Viennese History) 1954

The Museum of Viennese History is situated on Karlsplatz on a site specified as a museum location by Otto Wagner. In a nation-wide competition in 1953, Oswald Haerdtl was awarded the project for the museum over the other contestants, including Clemens Holzmeister, Lois Welzenbacher and Roland Rainer. The simple cube, however, has not been able to provide the appropriate urban setting for the Karlskirche by Fischer von Erlach, situated further south.

Karlsplatz, Maderstraße
Access: Open to public
Public transportation: U1, U4 (Karlsplatz)

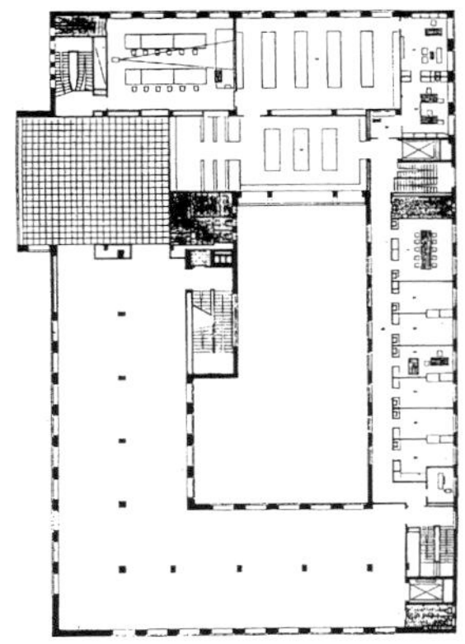

Secession 1897

The Vienna Secession was founded in 1897 and was modelled on the Münchner Künstlervereinigung (Artists' Association of Munich). Its purpose was to unify all new, avant-garde trends in art, and introduce them to a wider public by means of an exhibition building. Olbrich solved the task by splitting the volumina into a main building and a simple hall. Classical interpretations pervade the design of the Secession, arising from the inspiration Olbrich gained from the Segesta Temple. He nevertheless achieves a sensitive balance in the use of these abstract, rational (cube, square and circle) and mimetic, mystical (ivy, snakes) elements. It was renovated and altered by Adolf Krischanitz between 1982 and 1986.

Friedrichstraße 12
Access: Open to public
Public transportation: U1, U4 (Karlsplatz)

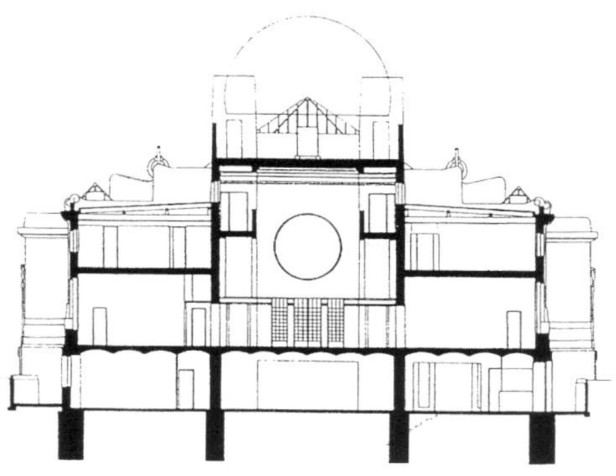

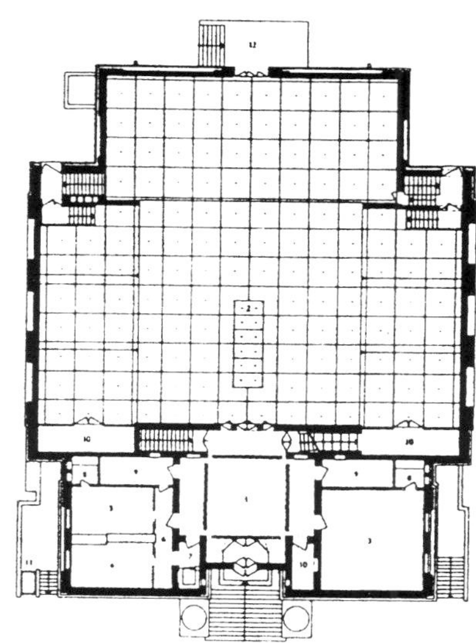

The Stadtbahn and Suburban Lines 1896

Access: Open to public
Public transportation: U4, U6, suburban train (Schnellbahn) 45

On unanimous recommendation of the "Viennese Fine Arts Society", the public transportation "commission" (formed in 1892) appointed Otto Wagner to an advisory position on 25th April 1894. He was made responsible for the artistic elements in the construction of the Viennese city railway (Stadtbahn). Consisting of 30 stations and stops, this network of approximately 45 km. of tracks – including the Suburban Line (1895–1896), Danube Canal-Wiental (Wien Valley) line (1896–1900), Gürtellinie (1895–1897) and the 2nd district lines (1899, later demolished) - was designed by Otto Wagner and can be called the city's largest structure. Wagner drew more than 2,000 plans with precise specifications for the Stadtbahn: the stations were to be rendered,

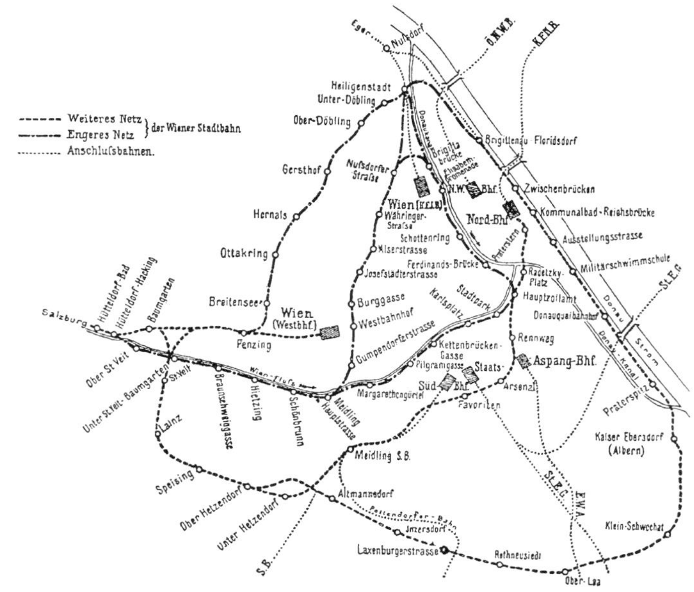

while the viaducts and bridges were to be brickwork and iron respectively. From the perspective of its technical, functional and urban design, the Stadtbahn is one of the most complex structures of Vienna and a landmark of the city. Extensive changes have been made to it in the process of expanding the underground system (see 1.-**79**).

Musikvereinsgebäude (Music Association Building) 1866

Bösendorferstrasse 12,
Canovagasse, Karlsplatz
Access: Open during concerts
Public transportation: U1, U4 (Karlsplatz)

The annual, world-wide broadcast of the New Year's Concert performed by the Viennese Philharmonic has made the main Music Association Hall in Theophil Hansen's Musikvereinsgebäude the most prominent concert hall in the world. The hall forms the core of the building and is noticeable on the exterior through the protruding central nave. The construction of the clerestory, in particular, is of captivating lightness. Since the building is at 90 degrees to the Künstlerhaus (built 1865–1868, according to plans by Andreas Streit, Eduard von der Nüll, August Sicard von Sicardsburg), the open space in front of it remains undefined and ambiguous.

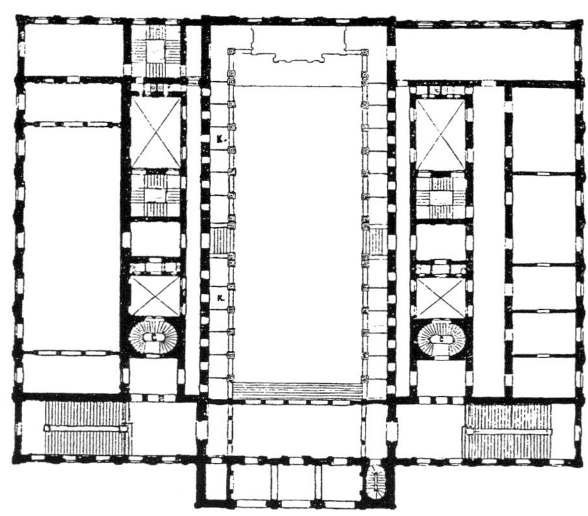

Town Palace of Prince Eugene (now the Ministry of Finance) 1695

The town Palace of Prince Eugene, who also commissioned the Belvedere palace, was essentially designed by Johann B. Fischer von Erlach. Built along seven axes, the centre of the palace was later expanded by Hildebrandt along another five axes on either side, in complete conformity with Fischer's façade. Emphasised by the annexes, the well-balanced rhythmic façade fits perfectly into the narrow street. The staircase, with atlantes by the sculptor Giovanni Giuliani, marks the apex of Fischer's interior planning. The palace now serves as the seat of the Ministry of Finance.

Himmelpfortgasse 8
Access: Not open to public
Public transportation: U1, U3 (Stephansplatz)

Edmund Hoke 1.-**39**

Slavik Gallery 1990

A semantic approach to the theme of a jeweller's shop would involve a number of cultural references. Especially in the tradition of Viennese architecture, the result would be anticipated even as such a process was being considered. Edmund Hoke's design of the gallery, however, displays an analogy to the precision of jewellery-making: the mobile, high-tech showcases (constructed by Thomas Hoke) are superb workmanship per se. Hanging from rails fixed onto the ceiling, the showcases generate additional space that lends the small gallery considerable transparency.

Himmelpfortgasse 17
Access: Open to public
Public transportation: Tram lines 1and 2 (Weihburggasse)

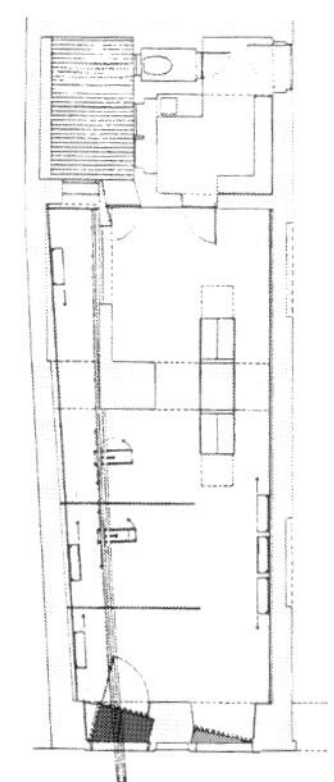

1.-**40** | *Ferdinand Fellner, Hermann Helmer, Luigi Blau*

Ronacher
1887, (1991)

Seilerstätte 9
Access: Opening hours: Open to public
Public transportation: Tram lines 1and 2 (Weihburggasse)

The Ronacher is one of the numerous establishments built in the 19th century that represented the "Light Muse" of entertainment culture. Realised along the plans of the theatre architects Ferdinand Fellner and Hermann Helmer, it was the first German language variety theatre. The Ronacher lay in disuse for years until in 1991 an assessment was made as to how it could be put to use.
The "deconstructivist" project by Coop Himmelblau, with its plans for disrupting the historical substance, was rejected in favour of a "gentle renovation" by Luigi Blau, who also commissioned Nancy Spero for the mural paintings in the lobby.

1.-**41** | *Bonaventura Daum*

Franziskanerkirche (Francíscan Church) 1603

Franziskanerplatz
Access: Open to public
Public transportation: U1, U3 (Stephansplatz)

One of the few Renaissance churches of Vienna, it is built more in the Italian than the southern German style. The tapering windows and ceiling are in fact reminiscent of Gothic architecture. The Franciscan monk Bonaventura Daum was presumably responsible for the planning of this extraordinary church. In 1742, the original main entrance was covered over by a canopy. The high altar by Andrea Pozzo unifies architectural elements with trompe l'oeil mural paintings.

Kleines Café
1970

The two statements by Hermann Czech – "Architecture is background" and "Architecture should not irritate. The customer is not to notice it; it could always have been so" – are fundamental to understanding the architecture of the Kleines Café. Representing new developments in commonplace architecture at the beginning of the 70s, Czech achieved an architectural density and quality that used historical references, parallel mirror arrangements and varying room levels to create an atmosphere of "age". The construction of the café was accomplished in several stages (1970, 1974, 1985).

Franziskanerplatz 3
Access: Open to public
Public transportation: U1, U3 (Stephansplatz)

(1970)

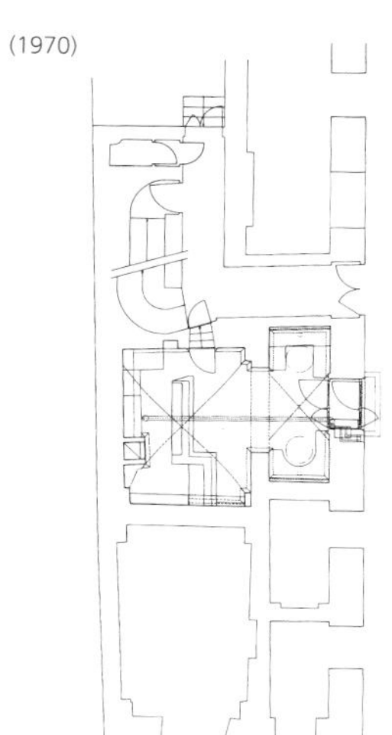

(1985)

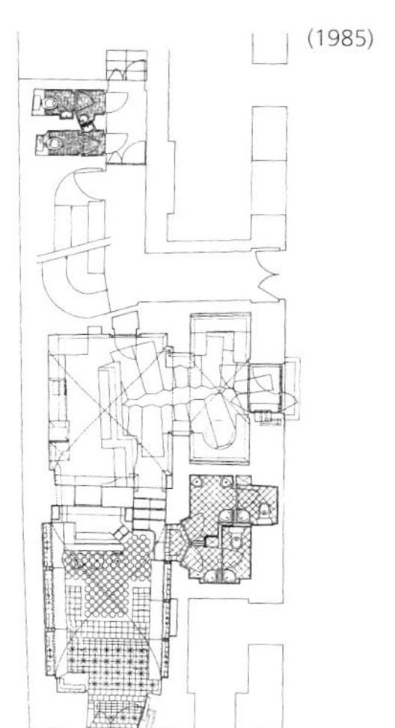

1.-**43** | ***Oskar Laske***

Engel-Apotheke (Engel Pharmacy) 1901

Bognergasse 9
Access: During business hours
Public transportation: U1, U3 (Stephansplatz)

The Engel Pharmacy was built on this narrow site by Oskar Laske, a student of Otto Wagner, who later dedicated himself exclusively to painting (his works are on exhibit at the Österreichische Galerie in the Belvedere). Laske concentrated the painted, secessionist decor on the lower shop levels, while arranging the upper floors far more sparingly in the style of Otto Wagner. The original fittings of the pharmacy have been maintained to this day.

1.-**44** | ***Carlo Antonio Carlone***

Alte Jesuitenkirche (Old Jesuit Church) 1386

Am Hof
Access: Open to public
Public transportation: U3 (Herrengasse)

In the 14th century the chapel of the Babenberg Residence was converted into a three-aisled hall church. Commissioned by Eleonore of Portugal, the spectacular façade was begun in 1662, probably according to plans by Carlo Antonio Carlone. Consisting of a balcony between two residential wings, the front of the building forms a bridge between the profane/public and ecclesiastical spheres. As such, it has been used equally for state and religious ceremonies.

Anton Ospel

1.-**45**

Following the first Turkish siege of Vienna, a new building complex was constructed in 1529 for the storage of civic weapon supplies. Extensive alterations during 1731–32 resulted in the gabled façade which, with its French or Spanish overtones, is almost unique in Viennese architectural typology. Although the sculptures titled "Constantia" and "Fortitudo" by Domenico Mattielli refer to the motto of Karl VI, they apply equally well to the fire brigade headquarters now housed within.

Bürgerliches Zeughaus (Civic Arsenal) (now the Fire Brigade Headquarters) 1731

Am Hof 10
Access: Not open to public
Public transportation: U3 (Herrengasse)

Heinrich von Ferstel

1.-**46**

On the irregular site formerly occupied by a baroque palace, Ferstel built a complex building as the seat of the Austro-Hungarian National Bank. A noteworthy feature is the opulent public arcade in the style of the Italian and French passageways, which connects the Freyung with Herrengasse and gives the building an international and metropolitan flair. The palace houses the famous Café Central, which was a favourite rendezvous for the Viennese art scene of the fin de siècle.

Palais Ferstel (formerly the Austro-Hungarian National Bank) 1856

Herrengasse 14, Freyung 2
Access: Only the passage
Public transportation: U3 (Herrengasse)

1.-**47**

Domenico Martinelli

Palais Harrach
1690

Freyung 3
Access: Opening hours
Public transportation: U2 (Schottentor)

From outside, the appearance of the palace is marked by the numerous renovations it has undergone. The façade, built according to plans by Domenico Martinelli, was completely altered in the mid 19th century. After being damaged by a bomb blast, the original baroque façade was reconstructed between 1948–52. The palace has been used for diverse purposes since its thorough renovation by the architect Manfred Wehdorn in the 1990s. Part of it serves as exhibition space for the Art History Museum.

1.-**48**

Johann Lukas von Hildebrandt

Palais Kinsky (formerly Palais Daun)
1713

Freyung 4
Access: Not open to public
Public transportation: U2 (Schottentor)

Johann Lukas von Hildebrandt erected this important baroque town palace for Wirich Philipp Laurenz von und zu Daun. The façade, consisting of large flat surfaces, is given life by the tension between its additive partitioning and the formation of the central protruding bay. Rather than being sculpted, the bay is only suggested through tapered, ornamental pilasters that contrast with the canonical ones on either side. The entire arrangement of the façade culminates in the sculpted main portal.

Hochhaus Herrengasse (Herrengasse High-rise) 1931

The "residential tower" was built in response to the homing projects of "Red Vienna", which were undisputed even by the conservatives. It was financed by the Austrian Credit Institute's funds for residential housing. The over nine-storey high block ends at one corner in a sixteen-storey residential tower, which was the only high-rise built in Vienna during the interwar period. By terracing the top floors of the tower, the architects succeeded in weaving it almost invisibly into the streetscape. Although the procedure is not entirely consistent, it presents an ingenious solution that was one of the most interesting architectural accomplishments in Vienna during the 1930s.

Herrengasse 6–8, Fahnengasse 2, Wallnerstrasse 5–7
Access: Not open to public
Public transportation: U3 (Herrengasse)

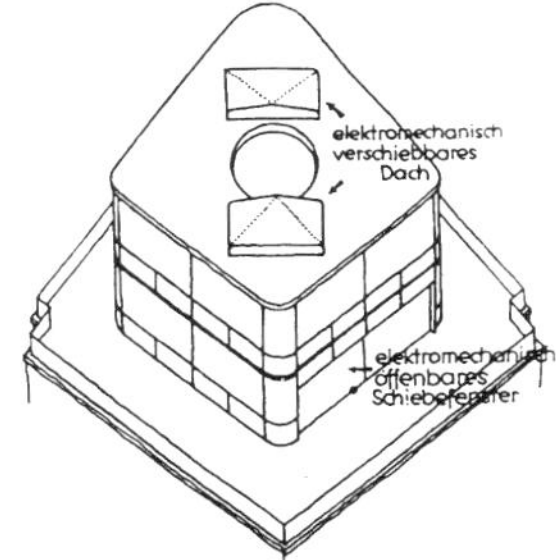

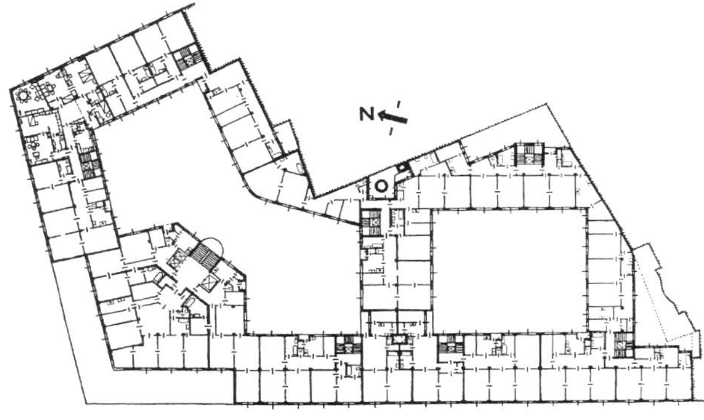

1.-**50** **|** ***Josef Kornhäusel***

Schottenhof
1826

Freyung 6, Schottengasse 2, Helferstorferstrasse
Access: Partially open to public
Public transportation: U2 (Schottentor)

Josef Kornhäusel modified this medieval monastery between 1826 and 1832, giving it a uniform appearance and structure in a subdued, classicist style that also harmonised with 17th century church architecture. He replaced the Gothic cloister with a new convent, and the offices with a residential building. Kornhäusel also undertook the interior furnishing of the cloister, the most notable result of which is the library. The museum of the Schottenstift was recently refurbished and is again open to the public.

1.-**51** **|** ***Johann B. Fischer von Erlach***

Palais Batthyány-Schönborn
1698

Renngasse 4
Access: Not open to public
Public transportation: U3 (Herrengasse)

Johann B. Fischer von Erlach incorporated existing structures into the construction of the palace. Plans for alterations proposed by Johann Lukas von Hildebrandt were not realised. Notable features of the building are the large arrangement of pilasters, an eccentric central portal, the entrance hall and the double staircase.

Alois Pichl

1.-**52**

Construction of this massive classicist building by Alois Pichl was begun in 1837 and incorporated elements of older structures. The closed, cubic structure is dominated by the colossal order of the central protruding bay, which is primarily designed to be viewed from the Freyung. The second main façade on Minoritenplatz, on the other hand, displays an arrangement of flat pilasters. It has served as an office building since St. Pölten's election as the new capital of Lower Austria.

Parliament Building of Lower Austria
1832

Herrengasse 13,
Minoritenplatz 7
Access: Not open to public
Public transportation: U3 (Herrengasse)

Luigi Blau

1.-**53**

The spatial conception of the teashop interprets the traditionally Viennese use of space with oriental elements in the style of Josef Frank. Blau created an exotic atmosphere by employing simple architectural elements, an effect that is enhanced by the craftsmanship of the interior. The shop has been slightly altered since its construction.

Demmer's Teashop
1981

Mölkerbastei 3
Access: Business hours
Public transportation: U2, tram lines 1and 2 (Schottentor)

1.-54 | *Heinrich von Ferstel*

University
1873

Dr.-Karl-Lueger-Ring 1
Access: Open to public
Public transportation: U2, tram lines 1and 2 (Schottentor)

After Prague, the University of Vienna is the oldest German-language university. For a long time it was located within the Jesuit College in the inner city. In the course of the Ringstrasse development it was relocated to the new, generously scaled building by Heinrich von Ferstel. The large, massively built block stands at a significant point on the Ringstrasse Its outer side extends all the way to the open area in front of the Votivkirche. The sudden and dramatic change in scale, which began with the construction of the buildings along the Ringstrasse, becomes apparent in contrast to the minutely divisioned baroque constructions of the remaining bastion across the Ring.

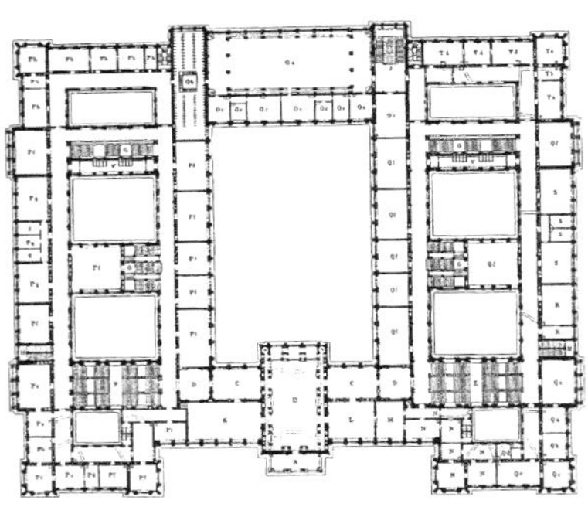

1.-55 | *Walter Stelzhammer*

Office Refurbishment of ÖBV (The Civil Service Insurance Company)
1995

Grillparzerstrasse 14
Access: By appointment (entrance hall)
Public transportation: U2 (Rathaus)

This typical Gründerzeit construction was built by Wilhelm Stiassny in 1881. It is a fine example of the complete, modern and intelligent renovation of an old structure; in the process the attic was extended and the inner courtyard covered over. The spectacular effect of the 23m high courtyard is heightened by the massive pillared construction (90 x 90 cm). The concept for the lighting was designed by Dieter Bartenbach. The sunlight can be steered far down into the courtyard, where prisms break it up, speckling the walls with the colours of the spectrum.

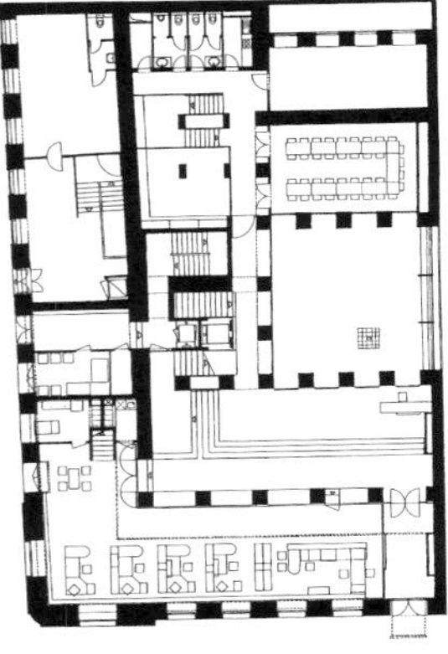

Ensembles
1535

The Mölkerbastei has been chosen to represent many similar baroque ensembles still in existence. Built as the Schottenbastei in 1535, it was largely destroyed during the expansion of the city in the 19th century. Though segmented, the structure still reveals the urban scale of the baroque city. The ensemble consists of: the "Pasqualati House", erected in 1797 (Mölkerbastei 8); "Melkerhof", rebuilt in 1769–74 (Schottenbastei 3); the "Mölkerbastei House", built at the beginning of the 19th century (Mölkerbastei 10). The ensembles in Judenplatz and Schönlaterngasse are also worth visiting.

Mölkerbastei, Mölkersteig, Schreyvogelgasse, Schottengasse
Access: Open to public
Public transportation: U2 (Schottentor)

1.-**57**

Johann Lukas von Hildebrandt

Chancellery 1717

Ballhausplatz 2
Access: Not open to public
Public transportation: U3 (Herrengasse)

This "secret State-Chancellery" was constructed by Johann Lukas von Hildebrandt in the immediate vicinity of the Hofburg. It was modified for the first time by Nikolaus Pacassi in 1766 and underwent a further extension at the beginning of the 19th century. In spite of these changes, the main façade with its sculpturally formed portal still conforms to Hildebrandt's original design. The building is the seat of the Austrian chancellor and the government, which also uses it to hold its cabinet meetings.

1.-**58**

Johann Ferdinand Hetzendorf von Hohenberg

Minoritenkirche (Minorite Church) 1339

Minoritenplatz
Access: Open to public
Public transportation: U3 (Herrengasse)

This light hall church was attached to a somewhat older choir between 1340 and 1400. The central portal with its tympanum follows French models and dates back to approximately 1350. Johann Ferdinand Hetzendorf von Hohenberg drastically changed the medieval building in the 18th century. He pulled down the Ludwig Choir and reverted the interior to its original form by removing the baroque alterations that had been made to it. The sacristy and arcades were built as late as 1902–09.

Oswald Haertdl

1.-**59**

Josef Hoffmann's student Oswald Haerdtl built the Volksgarten in a style "characteristic" of the 50s, based on preliminary plans from 1948. The concept was to incorporate a partially destroyed colonnade by the architect Peter Nobile (1823). The conservatory, with its tropical vegetation and ambience of marble, mirrors and rare wood veneer, has became popular in Viennese clubbing circles in the 1990s.

Volksgarten 1954

Volksgarten
Access: Opening hours
Public transportation: Tram lines 1, 2, U3 (Dr.-Karl-Renner-Ring)

Peter Nobile, Friedrich Ohmann, Oswald Haertdl

1.-**60**

In contrast to the Burggarten, the Volksgarten was laid out in 1819–23 as a green zone for the city and was open to the public. The famous concerts of Josef Lanner and the Strauss family took place here in the "Cortisches Kaffeehaus", built by Peter Nobile in 1823. The café was altered by Oswald Haerdtl in 1954–58. Almost at the same time as the café, Peter Nobile also built the Theseus Temple where the Theseus Group by Antonio Canova was originally exhibited (now on exhibit in the stairwell of the Art History Museum). As with the constructions along the Wien river in the Stadtpark, Friedrich Ohmann's intention was to create a picturesque ambience for the monument of the Empress Elisabeth. The seated figure of the empress is by Hans Bitterlich.

Volksgarten, Theseus Temple and Monument to the Empress Elisabeth 1819 (1904)

Volksgarten
Access: Open to public
Public transportation: Tram lines 1and 2 (Parlament), U3 (Herrengasse)

1.-61 — *Otto Wagner*

Stadiongasse Apartment Building 1882

Stadiongasse 10, Stadiongasse 6–8
Access: Not open to public
Public transportation: U2 (Rathaus)

The building permit for this house (Stadiongasse 6–8), which was built by Otto Wagner who also lived there for a while, was granted on 7th June 1882. In Wagner's own words "A simple, practical ground plan thus emerged from a more than 1500 m^2 site ... The monolithic pillars of the vestibule were thus made of Untersberg marble, the steps of Karst marble, the large corridor windows of iron and the wall lamps of brass. The façade is very simple ... the emphasis is on the large scale, larger window elements and simple yet clear motifs."

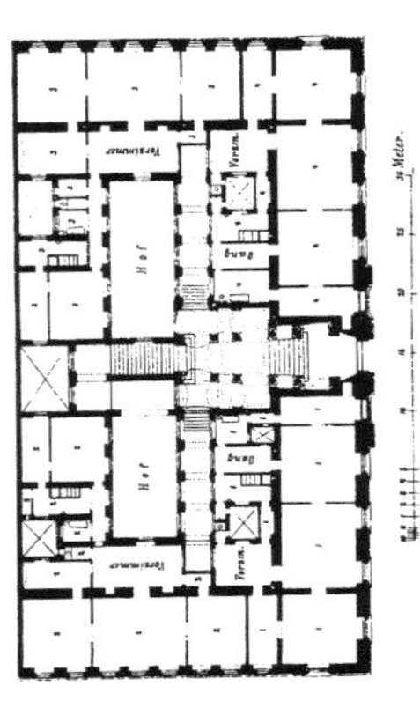

1.-62 — *Friedrich von Schmidt*

Rathaus (City Hall) 1872

Rathausplatz 1, Felderstrasse, Friedrich-Schmidt-Platz
Access: Open to public
Public transportation: Tram lines 1and 2 (Rathausplatz)

Despite its "Gothic" appearance, the Rathaus is actually an admixture of styles due to its rusticated basement level. Influenced by medieval Dutch architecture, it seems somewhat out of place within the city, particularly since very few secular Gothic structures still exist. Friedrich von Schmidt was the main proponent of the Gothic style in Austria, and had acquired precise knowledge of this epoch as head architect of the Stephansdom.

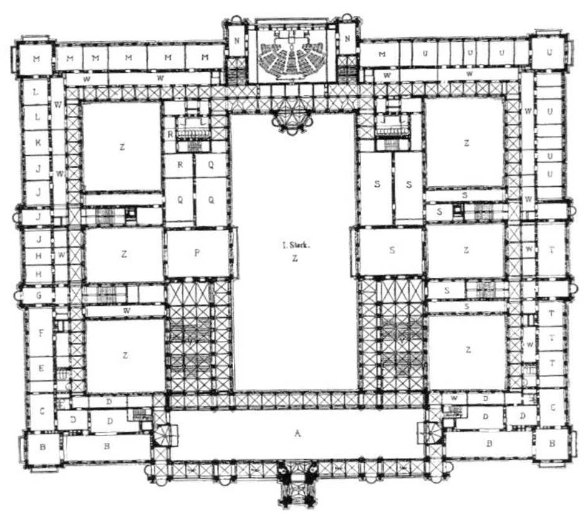

The choice of classical antique forms for the construction of the parliament building was deliberate. The reference to Greek democracies was an allusion to the long tradition of a form of government that was as yet relatively new to Austria. The decision, however, had its roots in the more widespread Classicist movement. The building is the seat of both the Upper and Lower Houses – the highest legislative bodies in Austria. The building was severely damaged during the Second World War and was renovated by Eugen Wörle and Max Fellerer in 1955–1956.

Parliament
1871

Dr.-Karl-Renner-Ring 3
Access: By appointment
Public transportation: Tram lines 1and 2 (Parlament)

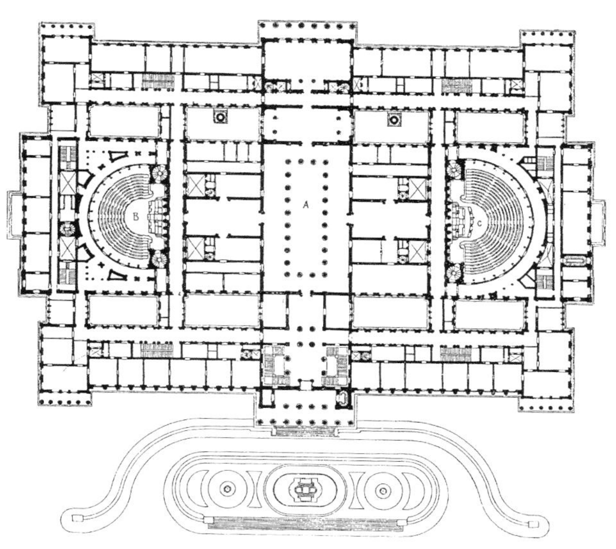

1.-**64** | ***Gottfried Semper, Carl von Hasenauer***

Burgtheater
1874

Dr.-Karl-Lueger-Ring 2
Access: Open to public
Public transportation: Tram lines 1and 2 (Burgtheater)

The Burgtheater was built as a replacement for the old Hoftheater (Imperial Theatre) on Michaelerplatz. While building it, Gottfried Semper adhered to his plans for the Dresden Opera House. The convex central protruding bay is compact and includes both the foyes and the access staircases, with the auditorium clearly and recognisably laid out behind. Both side wings are connected to the galleries more for reasons of urban planning than from any real necessity.

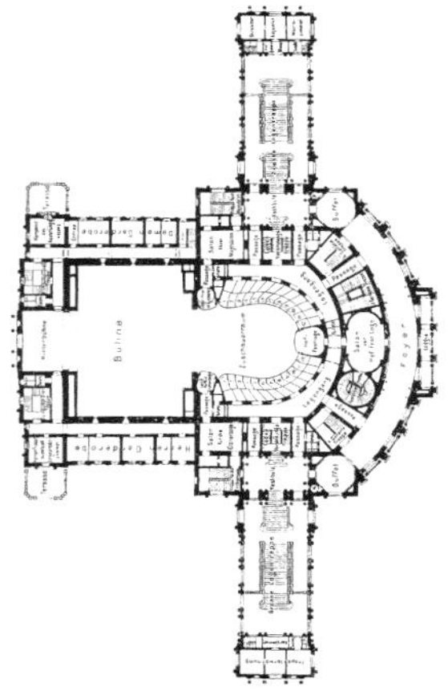

1.-**65** | ***Domenico Martinelli, Gabriel de Gabriele***

Palais Liechtenstein
1694

Bankgasse 9
Access. Not open to public
Public transportation: Tram lines 1and 2 (Burgtheater)

Dominik Graf Kaunitz commissioned this palace to be built according to plans by Domenico Martinelli. It was, however, only completed under Johann Adam von Liechtenstein following several alterations by Gabriel de Gabriele. Grouped around a square courtyard, the building has two imposing portals – one opening out to Bankgasse and the other to Minoritenplatz. The sculptural ornamentation is partially by Giovanni Giuliani. The interior was later furnished in a neo-Rococo style by P. H. Devigny, with contributions by Michael Thonet, the inventor of the renowned bentwood furniture.

Theophil von Hansen

1.-**66**

Palais Epstein (now the Education Authority Building) 1868

Theophil Hansen built this city palace for the ennobled banker Gustav R. von Epstein. The development along the Ringstrasse gave the aspiring upper middle classes a welcome opportunity to flaunt their new wealth. They were now in a position to compete with the aristocrats, who were in many cases far less wealthy. The neo-Renaissance palace, which has been owned by the state since 1902, was the seat of the Higher Administrative Court until 1922. It housed the Soviet Command between 1945–55, after which it was handed over to the Education Authority.

Dr.-Karl-Renner-Ring 1
Access: Not open to public
Public transportation: Tram lines 1and 2, U3 (Dr.-Karl-Renner-Ring)

Michael Knab, Friedrich von Klinkowström

1.-**67**

Maria am Gestade 1343

The church with its tall, narrow façade reacts to the surrounding city development and to its terrain, which slopes down towards an arm of the Danube. The Romanesque church that had previously stood here was replaced by a new construction in the 14th and 15th centuries. The constraints of the terrain resulted in a slight shift in the axis between nave and choir. Built upon a heptagonal ground-plan and concluded by an intricate tracery cap, the tower was completed in 1430, it can be considered one of the most remarkable Gothic churches of Vienna.

Salvatorgasse, Am Gestade
Access: Open to public
Public transportation: U1, U4 (Schwedenplatz)

1.-68

Josef Hackhofer

Hohe Brücke (High Bridge) 1903

Wipplingerstrasse,
Tiefer Graben
Access: Open to public
Public transportation: U2 (Schottentor)

Ever since the 13th century a bridge has existed over the low-lying Tiefer Graben at its intersection with Wipplingerstrasse. With the construction of the Hohe Brücke, Josef Hackhofer created one of the most spectacular urban elements of the inner city. By completely panelling the bridge, the Viennese bridge-builder gave the construction a definite architectural character that conforms with the other buildings around it and, seen from the perspective of the Tiefer Graben, gives it a gate-like appearance. (Statics by Karl Christl)

1.-69

Eichinger oder Knechtl

Wrenkh Café and Restaurant 1989

Bauernmarkt 10
Access: Open to public
Public transportation: U1, U3 (Stephansplatz)

This café initiated a new genre of reduced aesthetics. On the one hand it affirms the simplicity and informality of everyday life, while celebrating the commonplace through precision of form and calculated lighting on the other. It is an aestheticization of the fifties, for the generation of the 50s.

Zacherl House
1903

Friedrich Achleitner describes the Zacherlhaus as "probably ... the most important building of the Wagner School." It is a perfect example of how rampant the theme "cladding" was in this school around 1900. Plecnik used a fixed framework into which he inserted panels of polished granite, whose rhythmic arrangement also serves to structure the façade. He used the difficult shape of the site by taking the façade in a sweeping curve towards the Brandstätte, thus concealing the rigid grid of reinforced concrete supports that form the structural framework of the building. The atlantes on the top floor are by Franz Metzner.

Brandstätte 6,
Wildpretmarkt 2–4
Access: Not open to public
Public transportation: U1, U3 (Stephansplatz)

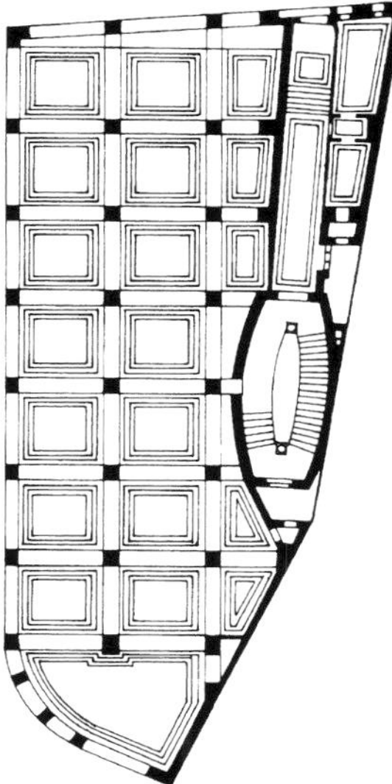

1.-**71** | ***Theophil von Hansen***

Börse (Vienna Stock Exchange) 1871

Schottenring 16
Access: By appointment
Public transportation: U2, tram lines 1and 2 (Schottentor)

Founded in 1771, the Vienna Stock Exchange was relocated several times until it was given a permanent home in this building on the Ringstrasse, built by Theophil von Hansen. The central bay and the higher corner bays result in it being one of the most sculpturally composed constructions along the Ringstrasse, making it stand out from the more uniform residential development around it. The banking hall burnt down completely in the 1950s and was reconstructed by Erich Boltenstern.

1.-**72** | ***Coop Himmelblau***

Baumann Studio 1985

Börseplatz 3
Access: By appointment
Public transportation: U2, tram lines 1and 2 (Schottentor)

The 5 metre high studio opens up onto the street through three windows. "The dynamic staging (Coop: the field of tension arising between surfaces that open up the space and transversally interwoven lines) creates the impression of space being sucked in from the street, to be deformed within and then flattened against the wall" (Friedrich Achleitner). The refurbishment of this studio is a kind of architectural manifesto of the 80's.

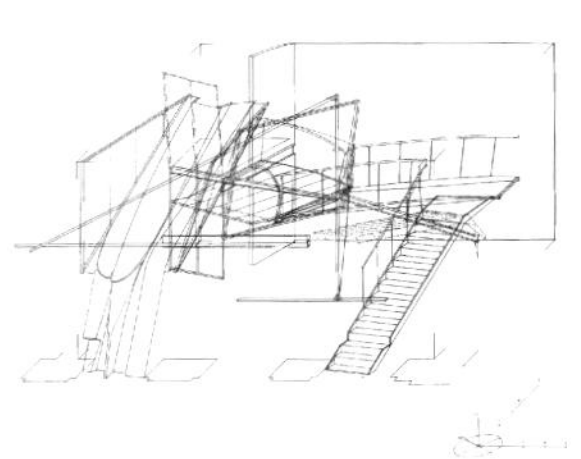

Länderbank (former)
1882

This construction by Otto Wagner was the first modern office building (banking institute) in Vienna. The ground plan, the cross-section and the courtyard façade show the revolutionary character of the structure. Glass floors, glass ceilings, light separation walls and a radical, reduced façade along the courtyard emphasize this character. The street front reveals little of this architectural jewel, while a visit inside is to experience a spatial symphony. It currently houses public administration offices.

Hohenstaufengasse 3
Access: Not open to public
Public transportation: U2 (Schottentor)

1.-**74**

Otto Wagner

Schottenring Apartment Building 1877

Schottenring 23
Access: Not open to public
Public transportation: Tram lines 1, 2 (Schottenring)

Otto Wagner received permission to build this house on 25th July 1877. Built for his own use, this structure is an extravagant construction in keeping with its prominent location on the Schottenring. The row of windows on the 3rd floor, as well as the design of the façade, are particularly noteworthy. Wagner himself occupied the apartment on the first floor from approximately 1878 to 1882.

1.-**75**

Erich Boltenstern

Ringturm (Ring Tower) 1953

Schottenring 30
Access: Not open to public
Public transportation: U2 (Schottenring)

At the time of the competition for the development along the Danube Canal in 1949, the high-rise was still a valid theme for urban innovation. The "Ringturm" can be considered an "eyewitness" to the discussions revolving around this topic. The ensemble along the Ringstrasse did not have the same significance after the Second World War as it does today. The approximately 60 metre high tower represents the restrained modern architecture typical of administration buildings of the 50s in Vienna. Modifications on the ground (1995–98) and top floors (1993, 1994) are by Boris Podrecca. A branch of the Austrian Tourist Agency on the ground floor is by Hans Hollein (1977). The façade of the building was renovated in 1996 (Arch. Vana).

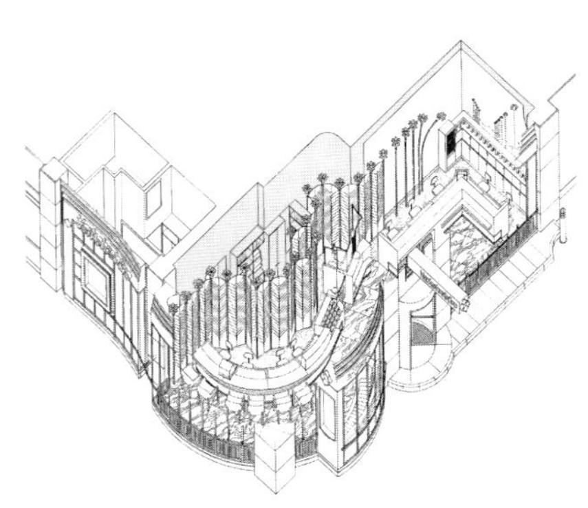

One of the few high-tech buildings in the city, the Juridicum stands just a few minutes' walk away from the old main building of the University of Vienna. The building occupies a whole Gründerzeit block and is striking for its intelligent construction. In order to create an open, undivided space on the ground floor, the entire building was suspended from four 9 metre high steel framings, which in turn rest on four reinforced concrete shafts. The suspension pillars were filled with water for fire-prevention. The Juridicum is an exceptional structure that is unique in the inner city.

Juridicum (Faculty of Law, University of Vienna)
1968

Schottenbastei 10–16
Access: Open to public
Public transportation: U2, tram lines 1and 2 (Schottentor)

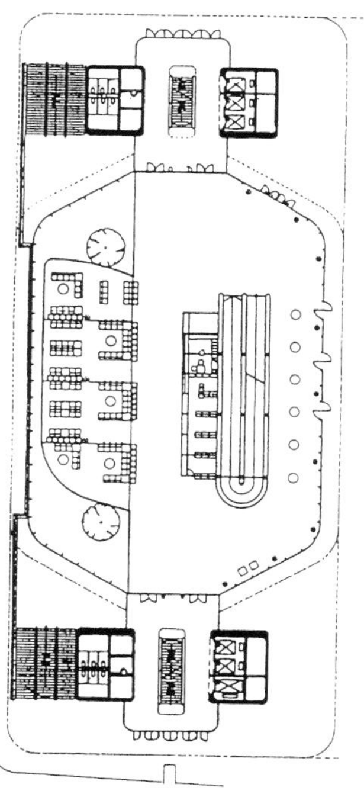

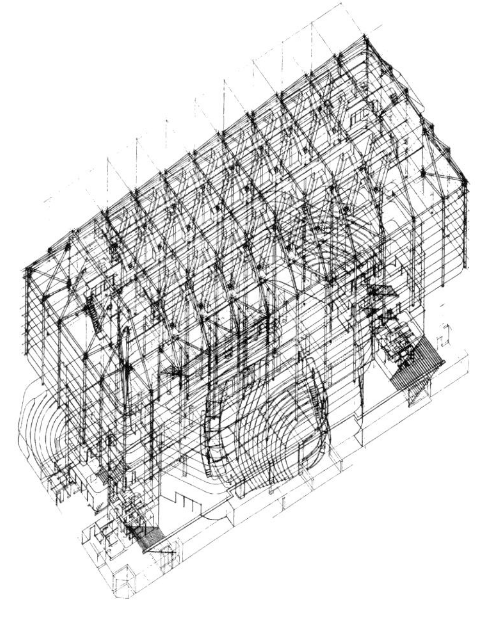

1.-**77**

St. Ruprecht's Church
1161

According to a legend, the core structure was built in the 8th century and was extended in several phases up to the 15th century. The purely Romanesque elements on the exterior make the church unique in the cityscape of Vienna. The west tower, which was added between 1130 and 1170, gives it the appearance of a country church. It is dedicated to the "salt serf" Ruprecht, since the harbour for ships carrying salt was located below the site.

Ruprechtsplatz
Access: Open to public
Public transportation: U1, U4 (Schwedenplatz)

1.-**78**

Hermann Czech

Salzamt Bar and Restaurant
1981

Hermann Czech was commissioned to build his third restaurant opposite St. Ruprecht, the oldest church in Vienna. His client was the same family for whom he had also built the Kleines Café and the Wunderbar. This established his reputation as the "master of interiors". A bar takes up the front area, as in France, while the dining area occupies the rear. The tactile quality of the wooden furniture, mirrored window niches and a visible ventilation system demonstrate that even precise planning should convey an element of the unintentional.

Ruprechtsplatz 1
Access: Open to public
Public transportation: U1, U4 (Schwedenplatz)

Schottenring – Underground Station 1971

Schottenring, Franz-Josefs-Kai
Access: Open to public
Public transportation: U2 (Schottenring)

A competition for the architectural design of the Vienna Underground was held in 1970. Since both the technical and the construction outlines were clearly defined, the task was limited to the "panelling" of the interior and a functional navigation system using colour codes. In the Semperian sense, therefore, it simply amounted to the "cladding" of an underground transportation system. The first lines to be introduced were U1 and U4. The latter was to incorporate Wagner's Stadtbahn network. Further extensions of the system are the U2, U3 and the still incomplete U6.

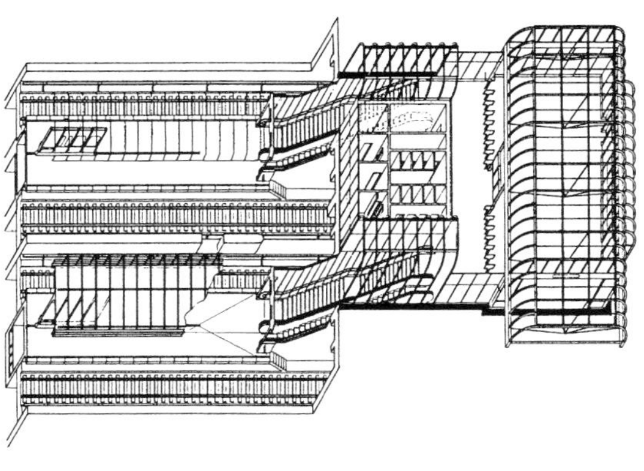

1.-**80** | *Eichinger oder Knechtl*

Ron con Soda
1994

Rabensteig 5
Access: Open to public
Public transportation: U1, U4 (Schwedenplatz)

Several "architectural manifestos of Vienna" in the form of bar-restaurants lie within a few minutes' walk of each other. One of the newest is Ron con Soda by Gregor Eichinger and Christian Knechtl. The interpretation of a bar that reflects the "zeitgeist" takes into regard a calculated randomness and an heterogeneous mix of materials. A flight of stairs leads up to a second bar – aptly called "First Floor" – on the floor above, for which Eichinger oder Knechtl used materials from the former Mounier Bar on Kärntnerstrasse.

1.-**81** | *Helmut Richter, Heidulf Gerngroß*

Kiang Restaurant
1984

Rotgasse 8
Access: Open to public
Public transportation: U1, U4 (Schwedenplatz)

In the atmosphere of change that accompanied the Viennese architecture of the 80s, Kiang was proof that private clients can show courage by commissioning experimental architecture. It demonstrated that in Vienna the tradition of cafés and restaurants was still fertile ground for architecture. Kiang bears no relationship either in its semantics or in its design to a Chinese restaurant or a cosy Viennese tavern.

Seitenstettenhof Synagogue 1824

Seitenstettengasse 2–4
Access: By appointment
Public transportation: U1, U4 (Schwedenplatz)

In keeping with a law imposed by Josef II regarding non-Catholic religious buildings, it is not readily identifiable as a synagogue when viewed from outside. Its concealed location, however, also prevented it from being destroyed during the "Reichskristallnacht". The ambulatory is built along the walls of the oval central hall covered by a cupola, which rests on monumental pillars that also support the ladies' galleries. The interior fittings were destroyed by the Nazis and were reconstructed and completely restored by Otto Niedermoser in 1963. Adjacent to the synagogue is the Seitenstettenhof, built by Josef Kornhäusel in 1825.

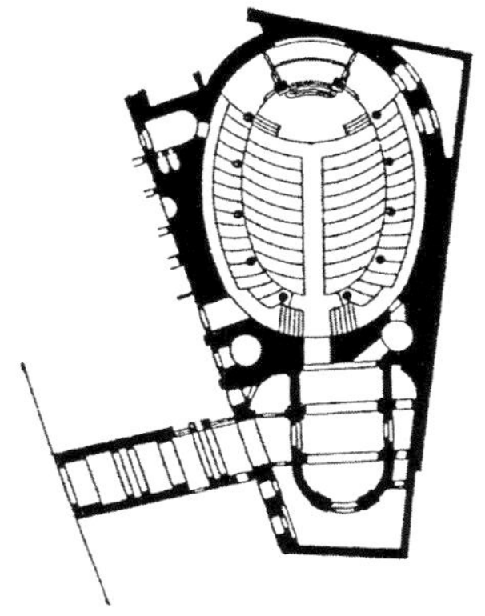

1.-**83** *Theophil von Hansen*

Greek Orthodox Church
1858

Fleischmarkt 13
Access: Not open to public
Public transportation: U1, U4 (Schwedenplatz)

The area around Fleischmarkt was densely settled by Greeks, who had had a church of their own since the 18th century. Theophil von Hansen added a Byzantine entrance hall to the original structure. His preference for sensual and varied surfaces is evident in the interior design of the hall. Although the Byzantine reference is particularly apt to a Greek Orthodox Church, it was a common style in sacred architecture of the Historicist period in Vienna.

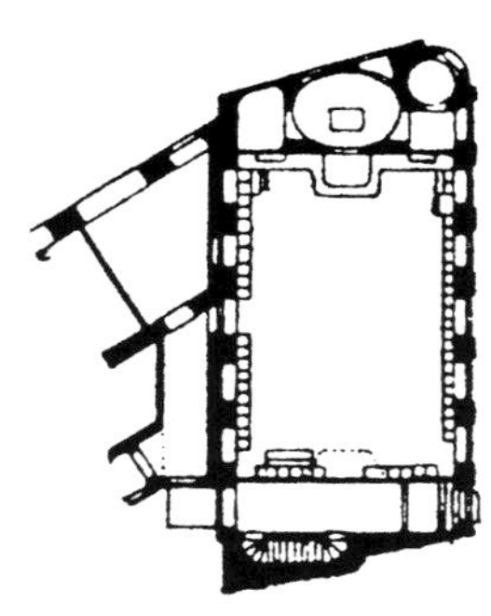

1.-**84** *Hermann Czech*

Wunderbar
1975

Schönlaterngasse 8
Access: Open to public
Public transportation: U3, tram lines 1and 2 (Stubentor)

This is Hermann Czech's second "coffee-house-manifesto" after the "Kleines Café" (1970), which was commissioned by the same client. At a time in Vienna when there was an enormous demand for bars and restaurants in the inner city, the Wunderbar was indeed a small wonder. The pleasant bar has aged with style over the years. "What remains is a bar, barring the wonder" (Friedrich Achleitner).

The Viennese apartments of famous composers count among the gems of Austrian culture. "I wanted neither to reconstruct past conditions nor to convert the apartments into tiny museums. A memorial is a place that cannot be confused with another. Unlike a museum, something very specific took place here. And in contrast to a museum, it is imbued with a most intimate atmosphere. This was an important consideration while renovating the apartment of a musician" (Prochazka).

„Figarohaus" Wolfgang Amadeus Mozart Gedenkstätte 1992

Domgasse 5
Access: During business hours
Public transportation: U1 (Stephansplatz)

Beethoven Gedenkstätte, "Pasqualatihaus":
1010, Mölkerbastei 8
Johann-Strauß-Gedenkstätte:
1020, Praterstrasse 54
Schubert-Gedenkstätte "Sterbewohnung"
1040, Kettenbrückengasse 6
Haydn-Gedenkstätte with the Brahms-room:
1060, Haydngasse 19
Schubert-Gedenkstätte "Geburtshaus" with the Stifter-rooms:
1090, Nußdorfer Strasse 54
Beethoven-Gedenkstätte "Eroicahaus":
1190, Döblinger Hauptstrasse 92
Beethoven-Gedenkstätte "Heiligenstädter Testament":
1190, Probusgasse 6

1.-**86** | ***Andrea Pozzo***

Jesuit Church (University Church) 1626

Ignaz-Seipel-Platz
Access: Open to public
Public transportation: U3 (Stubentor)

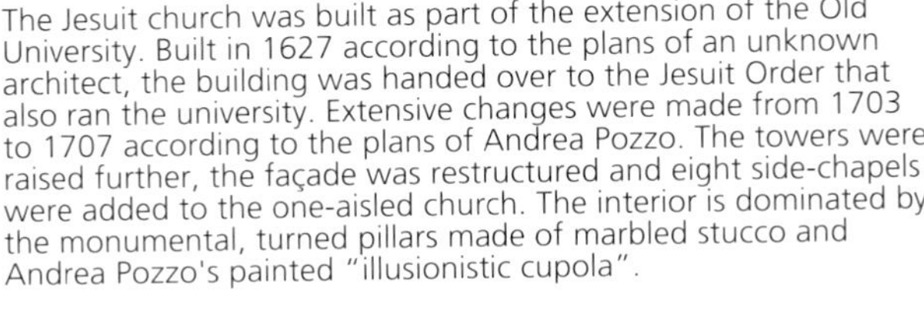

The Jesuit church was built as part of the extension of the Old University. Built in 1627 according to the plans of an unknown architect, the building was handed over to the Jesuit Order that also ran the university. Extensive changes were made from 1703 to 1707 according to the plans of Andrea Pozzo. The towers were raised further, the façade was restructured and eight side-chapels were added to the one-aisled church. The interior is dominated by the monumental, turned pillars made of marbled stucco and Andrea Pozzo's painted "illusionistic cupola".

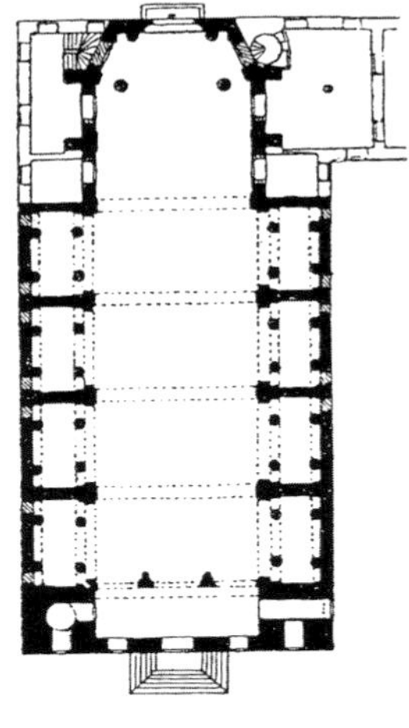

1.-**87** | ***Jean-Nicolas Jadot de Ville-Issey***

Academy of the Sciences (formerly the aula of the university) 1753

Dr.-Ignaz-Seipel-Platz 2
Access: By appointment
Public transportation: U3 (Stubentor)

This building, constructed by the French architect Jean-Nicolas Jadot de Ville-Issey, testifies to a shift in the paradigms of Austrian architecture, which had begun to show more French than Italian influence. Enhanced by its location between two small streets, the sculptural details contrast well with the flatter façade of the Jesuit church that forms the other main accent in the composition of the square.

Postsparkasse (Postal Savings Bank) 1903

Otto Wagner won the contract for the Postsparkasse in an architectural competition in 1903. It was completed in two phases (1903–10 and 1910–12). The Postal Savings Bank is one of the landmarks of Viennese architecture and, alongside St. Leopold's Church at Steinhof, can be considered Otto Wagner's masterpiece in every respect. The glass floor and suspended steel and glass construction of the transaction hall have strongly influenced 20th century architecture. The poetical-rational design of the façade is very convincing. The well-preserved conference room can be visited by prior arrangement.

Georg-Coch-Platz 2
Access: Ground floor and banking hall open to public
Public transportation: U3 (Stubentor)

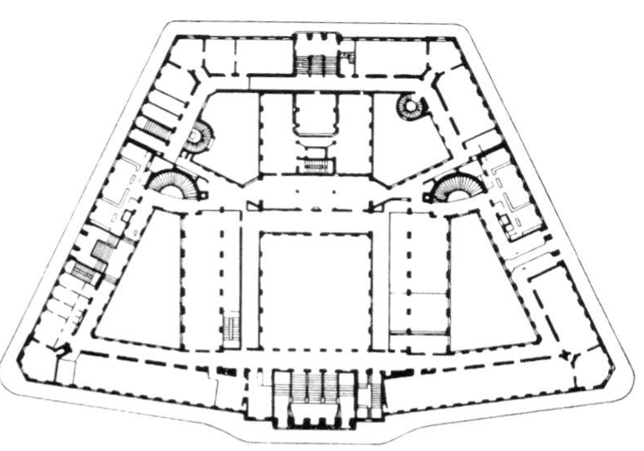

1.-**89**

Adolf Krischanitz, Heinz Neumann

General Post Office 1994

The General Post Office at the Fleischmarkt is located within a Benedictine monastery that was secularized at the end of the 18th century. The new banking hall was placed in the former cloisters under a new glass roof. Krischanitz refers to various geometric systems in the design. The entire block was completely rebuilt according to plans by Heinz Neumann.

Fleischmarkt 19
Access: Open to public
Public transportation: U1, U4 (Schwedenplatz)

1.-**90**

Max Fabiani

Urania 1909

Fabiani chose a path that was contrary to that of most of his colleagues. On the one hand he adhered to Wagner's concept of a separation between framework and decorative cladding – even going far beyond it, as in some aspects of his façade for the residential and office building Portois & Fix. On the other, however, he returned to the use of historicist details in the arrangement of the façade. Brilliantly organized in the interior, the Urania is also a significant structure in the context of city-planning. It houses an institution for adult education and an adjoining observatory. Although its façade is historicist in design, the architectural task and its spatial interpretation have been most innovatively executed.

Uraniastrasse 1
Access: Partially open to public
Public transportation: U1, U4 (Schwedenplatz)

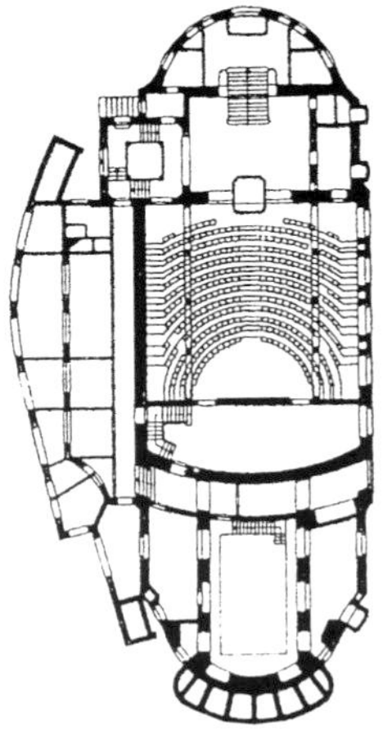

University and Museum of Applied Arts 1867

Towards the end of the 19th century, the building of a museum of art with an affiliated arts and crafts school was part of the attempt to coordinate art with industry. Ferstel's brick building was extended in 1907 by Ludwig Baumann. The interventions by various artists and architects are a commentary on the historical content: the terraced plateau in the MAK (Museum of Applied Art) by Peter Noever, the connecting tract by Sepp Müller, the café by Hermann Czech (1991), the gate to the garden by Walter Pichler and the gate to the Ring by Site (an artist group). The exhibition rooms were arranged by international and Austrian artists. The University of Applied Arts was expanded by Karl Schwanzer and Eugen Wörle between 1960 and 1965.

Stubenring 5
Access: Open to public
Public transportation: U3, tram lines 1and 2 (Stubentor)

1.-**92** | *Coop Himmelblau / Wolf Prix and Helmut Swiczinsky*

Falkestrasse loft adaptation 1987

It is one of the most widely publicized loft adaptations in the city and is internationally acclaimed as Vienna's contribution to deconstructivist architecture. The interior creates the impression of a hyper-subjective spatial composition. In the main (conference) room with the winged structure on the roof, the light changes the view of the city almost every hour. It is full of ambience and displays a very Viennese attitude towards architecture.

Falkestrasse 6
Access: Not open to public
Public transportation: U3, tram lines 1, 2 (Stubentor)

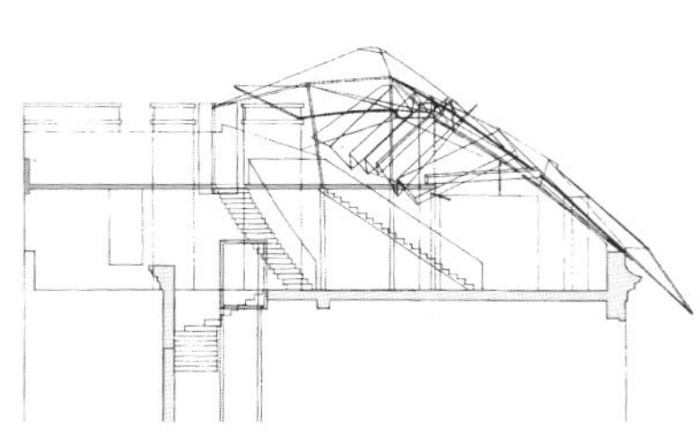

1.-**93** | *Theophil von Hansen*

Palace of the Grand and German Master of the Teutonic Order, the Archduke Wilhelm1864

The building was constructed by Theophil von Hansen as a private palace for Archduke Wilhelm. Soon after its completion, however, the Grand Master sold it to the Order of the Teutonic Knights. The generously scaled neo-Renaissance building blends well into the stately style of the development along the Ringstrasse. A striking feature is the prominent design of the bel étage that indicates the owner's residence through the façade. The building now serves as the OPEC headquarters.

Parkring 8
Access: Not open to public
Public transportation: Tram lines 1and 2 (Weihburggasse)

Stadtpark, the Wien River Constructions 1903 (1985)

Stadtpark
Access: Open to public
Public transportation: U4 (Stadtpark)

The point at which the Wien river enters the Stadtpark, as well as its embankments within the park were designed by Friedrich Ohmann. Built in a sensual baroque style (1903–07), they are in a diametral line with the adjacent Stadtbahn station, built by his colleague Otto Wagner. However, Ohmann was unable to complete the entire layout. The romantic embankments correspond with the historicist concept of the Stadtpark. In 1985–87, Hermann Czech built a new bridge connecting the two banks, replacing the older wooden footbridge. Suspended from two steel arches, it broadens in the middle of the river to a platform providing a vantage point for the entire length of the embankment.

Hermann Czech, Alfred Pauser: Stadtpark footbridge, 1985

Friedrich Ohmann, Josef Hackhofer: Zollamt (Customs Office) footbridge 1903

Supplementary Recommendations

1.**95s**	Lichtforum Wien Hans Hollein	1995 Jasomirgottstrasse 3-5
1.**96s**	Altmann & Kühne Josef Hoffmann and Oswald Haerdtl	1932 Graben 30
1.**97s**	Tromayer Gallery Anna-Lülja Praun	1983 Dorotheergasse 7
1.**98s**	Dorotheergasse Gallery Luigi Blau	1970 Dorotheergasse 14
1.**99s**	Wahliss Arcade Coop Himmelblau Wolf Prix and Helmut Swiczinsky	1985 Kärntnerstrasse 17
1.**100s**	Glass Galerie Maria Auböck, Janos Karasz	1992 Spiegelgasse 12
1.**101s**	Helmut Lang Boutique Gustav Pichelmann	1996 Seilergasse 6
1.**102s**	Tuchlaubenhof Ernst Spielmann, Alfred Teller	1912 Tuchlauben 7–7a
1.**103s**	Manz Booksellers Adolf Loos	1912 Kohlmarkt 16
1.**104s**	Böhmische Hofkanzlei (Bohemian Royal Chancellery) (currently: Constitutional and Administrative Courts) Johann Bernhard Fischer von Erlach	1708 Wipplingerstrasse 7, Judenplatz 11
1.**105s**	Vermählungsbrunnen (Josefs-Brunnen) (Wedding Fountain, or Josef's Fountain) Josef Emanuel Fischer von Erlach	1729 Hoher Markt
1.**106s**	Alois Hauser Apartments Alois Hauser	1874 Hohenstaufengasse 9
1.**107s**	Café Prückel Oswald Haerdtl	1955 Stubenring 24
1.**108s**	Haus der Magnesitwerke (House of the Magnesite Works) Erich Boltenstern	1951 Schubertring 10–12
1.**109s**	Dominikanerkirche (Dominican Church) Antonio Canevale et al.	1626 Postgasse 4
1.**110s**	Studentenkapelle (Student's Chapel) Ebendorferstraße Ottokar Uhl	1956 Ebendorferstrasse 8
1.**111s**	Unger & Klein Wine Store Eichinger oder Knechtl	1994 Gölsdorfgasse 2
1.**112s**	Kunstforum (Art Forum) Bank Austria Gustav Peichl	1988
1.**113s**	"Zum Römertor" Heinrich Schmid, Hermann Aichinger	1934 Lichtensteg 2
1.**114s**	Kix Bar Oskar Putz	1988 Bäckerstrasse 4

Buildings worth visiting – Suggestions by Viennese architects

2nd District:

Margarethe Cufer:
Lusthaus (the Pleasure House) in the Prater, index no. 2.-**11**

Martin Kohlbauer:
Trabrennverein (Trotting Race Association), index no. 2.-**5**

Carl Pruscha:
City planning. Stroll along the "water" (Danube Canal and Wien river)

Wolfdietrich Ziesel:
Riesenrad (Giant Ferris Wheel), index no. 2.-**4**
Stadium – Ernst Happel Stadium, index no. 2.-**8**

3rd District:

Elsa Prochazka:
Wittgenstein House, index no. 3.-**12**

Marta Schreieck:
Wittgenstein House, index no. 3.-**12**

2.-**1**

Otto Wagner

Schützenhaus
1906

The lockhouse "Staustufe Kaiserbad" was necessary in order to convert the Danube Canal into a trading and winter port. Three further locks were planned originally, but only one of these was completed. The form of this conspicuous structure, partially covered with coloured tiles, was determined by its functional requirements. The lock has not been in operation for a long time and the equipment of the lockhouse has been dismantled.

Obere Donaustrasse 26
Access: Not open to public
Public transportation: Tram lines 1, 2 (Salztorbrücke)

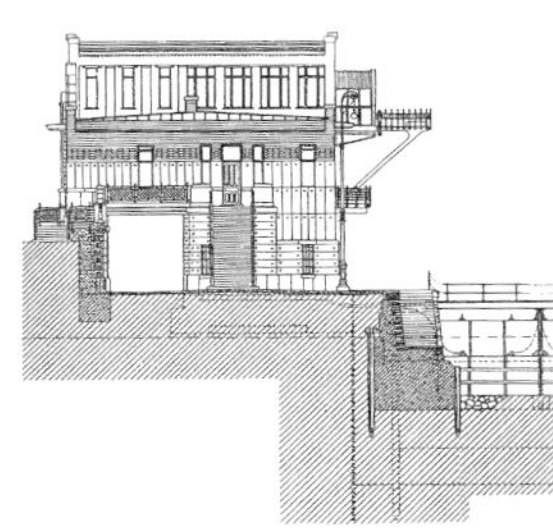

2.-**2**

Hubert Gessner

Augarten Bridge
1928

In the design of this functional construction, Gessner was able to bring into play his talent for formulating clear large-scale forms that are effective in a metropolitan setting. This is a characteristic of his work, visible in the design of his residential buildings as well. The burden of the seven continuous steel girders is borne with only minimal contact with the ground. In addition to the sweeping gesture of the bridge, Gessner refuses to abandon effectively placed details. Examples of these are the pylons on the bridgeheads and details scaled to human dimensions.

Untere Augartenstrasse, Josefs-Kai, Danube Canal
Access: Open to public
Public transportation: U2, U4 (Schottenring)

Flaktürme (Flak Towers), the Augarten flak tower 1942

Augarten
Access: Not open to public
Public transportation: Tram line 31 (Gaussplatz)

The towers, built all over Vienna by the anti-aircraft command ("flak") during the Second World War, form definite disruptions in the framework of the city. The sturdy reinforced concrete construction (with up to 5 metre thick walls) has resisted repeated attempts to remove these municipal blemishes. The towers were coupled together in pairs – one would serve to illuminate the airspace while the other stationed the ordnance. The towers also served as bomb shelters. They have meanwhile become the best "functioning" anti-war memorials of the city, without the necessity for contrived semantic encoding. The tower on Gumpendorferstrasse has been converted into an aquarium ("Haus des Meeres").

Groundplans of the Augarten Flak Tower

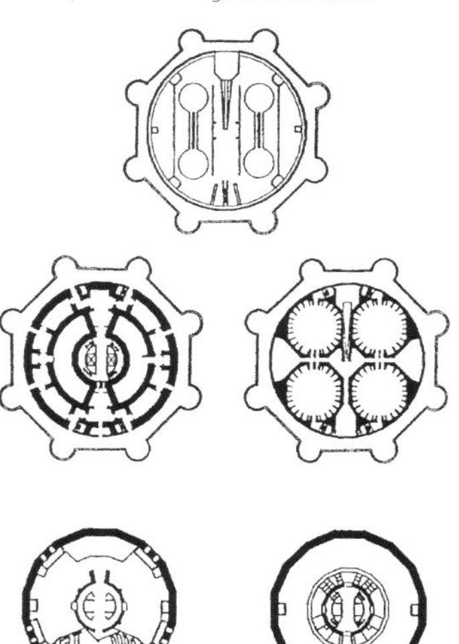

2.-**4**

Walter B. Basset, Hitchins (engineer)

Riesenrad (Giant Ferris Wheel) 1896

Volksprater
Access: Open to public
Public transportation: U1 (Praterstern)

A few hard facts regarding the myth: the Ferris wheel was constructed on the occasion of the 50th anniversary of the coronation of Emperor Franz Joseph. It weighs 430 tonnes, has an overall height of 64.75 metres, consists of 120 flexible spokes and since the Second World War carries only 15 instead of the original 30 wagons. The Viennese landmark was not unique however; the engineer Walter B. Basset of Watermouth had already constructed "Gigantic Wheels" in London and Blackpool.

2.-**5**

Emil Hoppe, Marcel Kammerer, Otto Schönthal

Krieau Trotting Race Association 1910

Prater, Trabrennstrasse, Südportalstrasse
Access: Open to public
Public transportation: Bus 82A (Messegelände, Südportal)

The trotting race course lay along one of the axes of the World Fair grounds, between the rotunda and the buildings nowadays housing studios for sculptors. The establishment was founded as early as the 19th century, but a substantial part of the construction was conducted after 1910 by the consortium Schönthal, Hoppe, Kammerer. All three were students of Otto Wagner, whose constructional ideas found expression in the design of the grandstand. The unusual nature of the assignment facilitated the use of exposed iron and concrete.

Lassallestrasse Office Complex, Bank Austria I and II, OMV, IBM 1989

Holzbauer's construction along Lassallestrasse is the prelude to a complete revivification of the area around the Northern Railway Station. The three administration buildings for IBM, the OMV-Administration and Bank Austria Centre resulted in a dense cluster of contemporary structures. Holzbauer's large-scale and metropolitan construction responds not only to the urban context (Praterstern), but also to the necessity to organize the buildings through generous multi-storeyed inner spaces and atria.

Lasallestrasse 5, Praterstern
Access: By appointment
Public transportation: U1 (Praterstern)

Neue Welt Kindergarten 1994

Aspernallee 2
Access: Not open to public
Public transportation: U3, bus 77A (Lusthaus)

A kindergarten can be seen as a pedagogical shell for little children. In contrast to the usual juvenile kitsch, the Neue Welt kindergarten has clear and well-proportioned rooms, remarkable for their precisely positioned windows. The furniture is individually designed to the scale of children. Materials such as exposed concrete, wooden floors and glass have been used in the construction of the building. Colour has been applied to create spatial depth rather than to serve a merely decorative function.

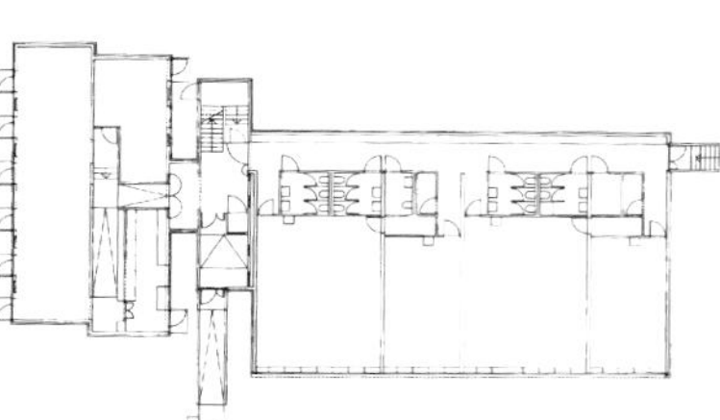

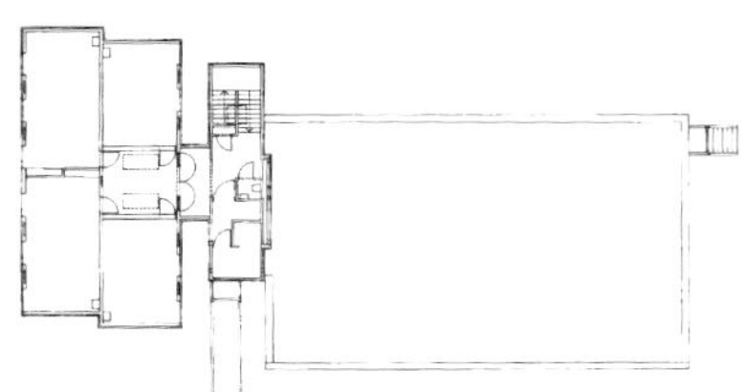

Prater Stadium, Ernst Happel Stadium 1929, 1956, 1985

Prater, Meiereistrasse
Access: By appointment
Public transportation: Buses 80B, 83A (Ernst-Happel Stadium)

The former Prater Stadium was opened in 1931 for the "Arbeiter-olympiade" (Workers' Olympics), in which more than 4,000 people participated. The stadium was expanded by Theodor Schöll to a capacity of 92,708 persons between 1956 and 1959, but was reduced to 72,110 six years later. The largest stadium in Austria, it was restored in 1985-86 and was fully roofed over according to a technique patented by Erich Frantl, Hofstätter, Zemler and Raunicher. This technique was preferred to a partial covering of the stadium, since it had proved to be even more economical than the latter. Sweeping in approximately 50 metres towards the centre of the stadium, the elliptical roof is one of the largest in the world (277 by 223 metres). The stadium took 10 months to build and can currently hold an audience of up to 60,000.

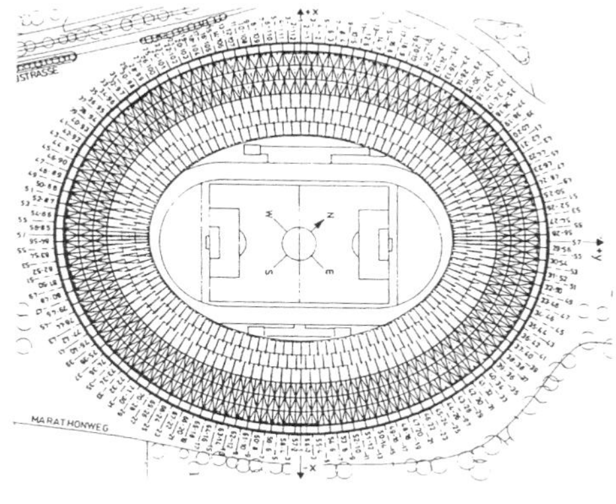

2.-9 | *Carl v. Hasenauer, Adolf Feszty, Anton and Josef Drexler*

Freudenau Racecourse 1885

Prater
Access: Open to public
Public transportation: Bus 77A (Freudenau Rennplatz)

Horse races were among the oldest and most distinguished attractions of the Viennese Prater. The racecourse itself was founded in 1862. Carl von Hasenauer and Adolf Feszty erected a delicately formed cast-iron structure that was walled-in at the rear. Following a fire, Anton and Josef Drexler rebuilt the tribune, stables and admininistration wing in 1885–87. As in the theatres, concert halls and opera houses, the tribune also contained an Imperial Loge, which was glazed much later. The viewing stands underwent a complete renovation in 1982–87.

2.-10 | *A. Wimmer, H. Schwarz, G. Hansjakob, T. Hansjakob*

Freudenau Hydroelectric Plant 1988 (1998)

Praterspitzstrasse, Kraftwerk
Access: Not open to public
Public transportation: Bus 80B (Freudenauer Hafenbrücke)

The Freudenau power plant has a colourful history. The project was awarded to "Team 3c" (Albert Wimmer, Herwig Schwarz and Gottfried & Toni Hansjakob) after a competition, but work was stalled until the conclusion of a public-opinion poll in 1991. The artificial island that arose from the morphology of the river (800 m. long, 60 m. wide) is squeezed in between the power station and the sluices. The island forms the site for the control house, which is accessed over a bridge suspended from four steel pylons.

Prater
1403

Covering more than 6 million square metres, the Prater is one of the largest recreational areas of Vienna. It includes the Volksprater, the Messegelände (Convention Grounds), the landscaped park along the Hauptallee, Freudenau and Krieau, as well as other areas of green. The name "Prater" was given to it in 1403, although documents prove its existence as far back as 1162. It was originally the hunting preserve of the Habsburgs and was opened to the public in 1766. The four and a half kilometer long Hauptallee leads to the "Lusthaus" (Pleasure House), built by Isidor Canevale in 1781–83.

Praterstern, Prater Hauptallee
Access: Open to public
Public transportation: Bus 77A (Lusthaus)

3.-**1**

Artur Perotti, Günther Domenig

Bank Austria Customer Service Centre 1992

Vordere Zollamtstrasse 13
Access: Open to public
Public transportation: U3, U4, tram line O (Landstrasse Wien Mitte)

The former main building of the "Zentralsparkasse der Gemeinde Wien" (Central Savings Bank of Vienna) was built in 1962–65 around a reinforced concrete framework, according to plans by Artur Perotti. Günther Domenig later discarded the entire asbestos during his restructuring of the building. He also transformed the former inner courtyard into an airy atrium, which enabled a completely new sequence together with the banking hall on the ground floor. Ecologically friendly materials were consciously selected to show the bank's commitment to its customers. The frontage presents a clever solution to the problem of insulation created by glass façades.

3.-**2**

Paul Sprenger

Hauptmünzamt (Central Mint) 1835

Am Heumarkt 1
Access: Not open to public
Public transportation: U4 (Stadtpark)

The cubical construction with its simply arranged façade is typical for the functional architecture of Austrian government buildings constructed in the first half of the 19th century. In this case the closed appearance is also appropriate to the function of the building, which is the stamping and storage of coins. The Central Mint is one of the masterpieces of the independent phase of Austrian Classicism. This period, however short, had a significant influence on the first generation of Viennese Modernism, which also included Otto Wagner.

Helmut Richter 3.-**3**

Kiang III
1997

With the full support of his client, Helmut Richter further developed the concepts of Kiang I (1984) in his construction of the new Kiang III. Whereas Kiang I can be seen as a "breaking away" from the post-modern concepts of the time, Kiang III can be considered a refined étude of Richter's stand on architecture. The design of the interior is more subdued and homogeneous in its choice of materials, with the glass and the light-coloured surfaces serving as a background for the Chinese and Japanese dishes. When the glass doors facing the street are opened out during summer, the guests become participants in the theatre of everyday urban life.

Landstrasser Hauptstrasse 50, Rochusmarkt
Access: Business hours
Public transportation: U3 (Rochusgasse)

Siegfried C. Drach, Alexander Osterberger 3.-**4**

Neulinggasse
Apartment Building
1935

Modenaplatz is the only urban middle-class ensemble in Vienna that saw (almost) uninterrupted development during the 1920s and 1930s. At the same time it displays a consistently high standard, even though none of Vienna's "star architects" were involved in the construction. House number 10 is a good example of the quality that even the so-called "normal constructions" could achieve in the 1930s.

Neulinggasse 50, Am Modenapark 10
Access: Not open to public
Public transportation: Bus 4A (Am Modenapark)

3.-**5**

Otto Wagner

Rennweg Apartment Houses 1890

Rennweg 1, 3, 5
Access: Not open to public
Public transportation: Tram line 71 (Unteres Belvedere)

Extremely important from the perspective of town-planning, the Rennweg apartment houses are a series of three separate residential blocks that Otto Wagner constructed from 1890 onwards. The corner building Rennweg 1, the Wagner apartment building (Rennweg 3, now the Yugoslavian Embassy) and the corner building on Auenbruggergasse were planned as a single unit. However, Wagner's own palatial residence was designed particularly lavishly. The composer Gustav Mahler once resided in the building on Auenbruggergasse.

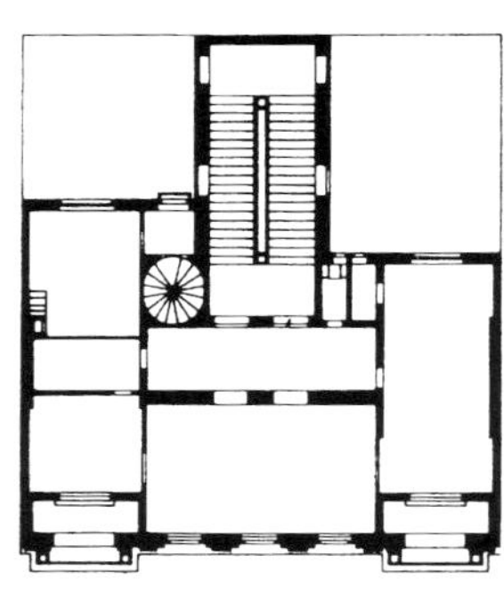

3.-**6**

J. L. v. Hildebrandt, J. B. and J. E. Fischer v. Erlach et al.

Palais Schwarzenberg 1697, (1716–18), 1722, 1751, 1928

Rennweg 2
Access: During public events
Public transportation: Tram line D (Gusshausstrasse)

This garden palace was an impressive prelude to Johann Lukas von Hildebrandt's constructions in Vienna. The generous cour d'honneur with its central pavilion and low side wings faces the inner city. After the still incomplete palace was sold to Prince Adam of Schwarzenberg, the Fischers undertook the task of finishing the construction. The riding school and orangery were built according to the plans of Andrea Altomonte (1751). Together with the Belvedere, it provides a good example of the "baroque garden city" on the perimeter of the fortifications. The administration building was adapted to house the Swiss Embassy by C. Schmidt in 1928. The restaurant in the basement was designed by Hermann Czech between 1982–84.

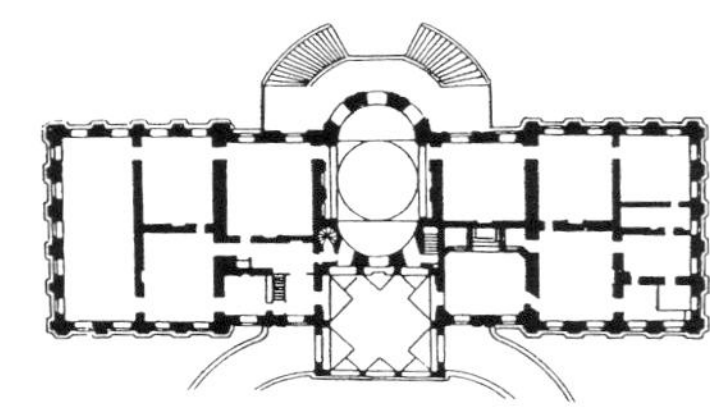

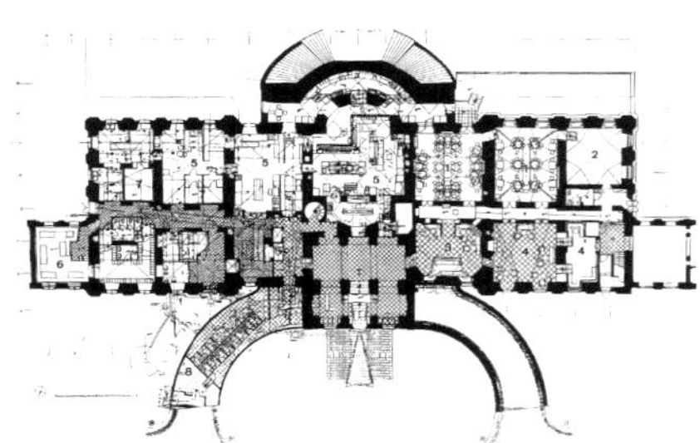

Restaurant renovation, H. Czech

Belvedere
1700

The Belvedere – the suburban residence of Prince Eugen of Savoy – lies on the sloping grounds of the former outskirts of Vienna. Johann Lukas von Hildebrandt used the lie of the land to his own advantage by creating a striking ambience. The Lower Belvedere (the palace wing facing the city) with its cour d'honneur forms a prelude to this baroque ensemble. Continued over the multi-terraced park, it culminates in the moulded construction of the Upper Belvedere. The renovation, restoration and adaptation for the museums that both buildings now house was conducted by the architect Sepp Frank (1992–1997).

Rennweg 6, Prinz-Eugen-Strasse 27, Landstrasser Gürtel
Access: Open to public
Public transportation: Tram line D (Schloss Belvedere)

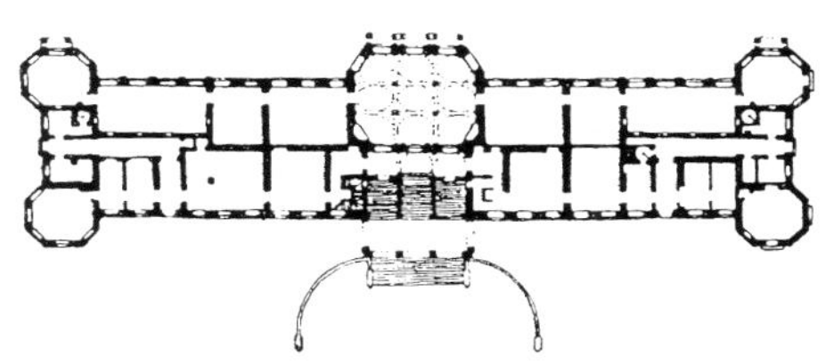

Arsenal 1849
Heeresgeschichtliches Museum (Museum of Military History) 1852

Arsenalstrasse, Ghegastrasse
Access: During opening hours
Public transportation: Tram line D, bus 69A (Arsenal)

After the revolution of 1848, Emperor Franz Joseph decided to quell further civil unrest by building numerous barracks within the city confines. The Arsenal was conceived as a both barracks and museum (symbolic representation of the power of the State). Brickwork facing and sculptural details paraphrase medieval Italian and Islamic-Byzantine standards respectively. In addition to the Heeresgeschichtliches Museum by Hansen, the former garrison headquarters by Sicardsburg and von der Nüll and the Maria vom Siege Chapel by C. Rösner are particularly striking structures. The structure has been extended since the 1950s by the addition of annexes. These include, for example, the stage-set workshops of the state theatres (E. Boltenstern and R. Weinlich, 1959–1963), the telecommunications administration building (F. Pfeffer, 1961–1964), the Central Telecommunications Building with its direct transmission tower (K. Eckel, 1973–1978) and the rehearsal stage of the Burgtheater (G. Peichl, 1993–1995).

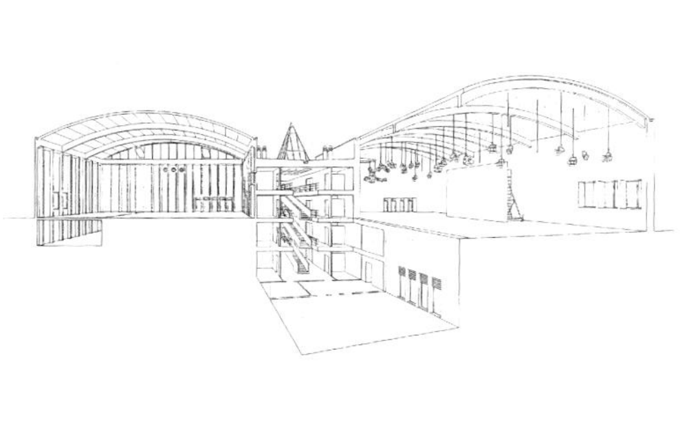

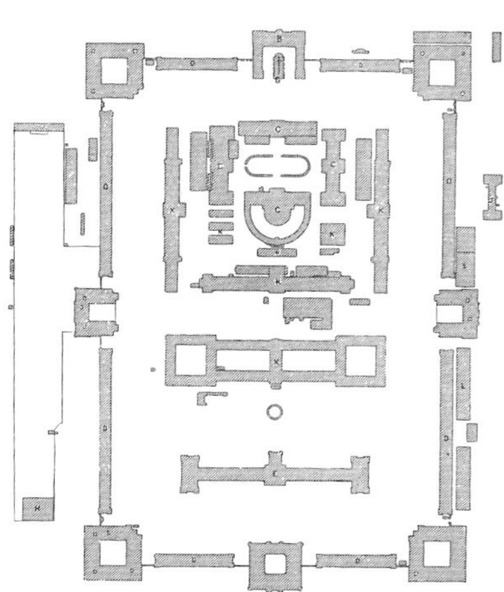

Museum des 20. Jahrhunderts (Museum of the 20th Century) 1959

Schweizergarten
Access: During opening hours
Public transportation: Tram line D (Südbahnhof)

A rare example of permanent pavilion-architecture, the structure was originally used as the Austria House at the World Fair in Brussels (1958). The pavilion was altered for its role as museum by enclosing its ground floor and roofing over the courtyard. The precise workmanship of the steel construction has resulted in an outstanding structure of international standard.

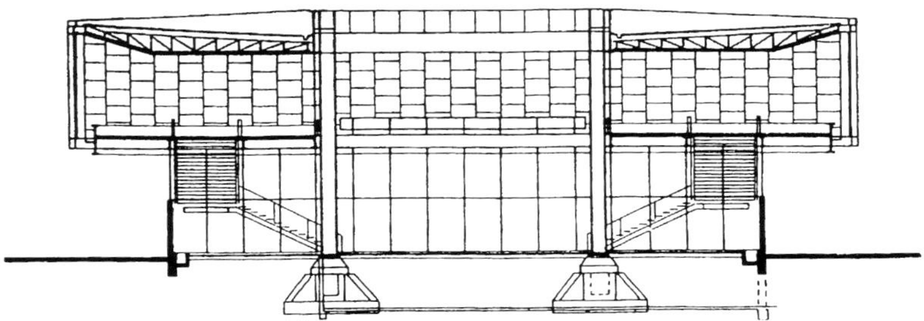

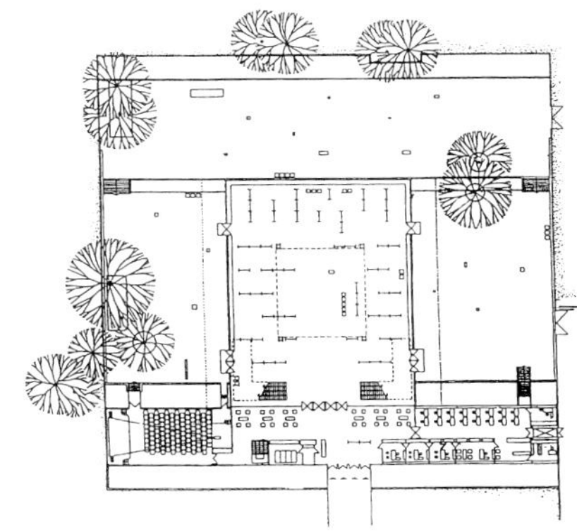

3.-**10** | ***Peter Gerl***

Sünnhof
1823

Landstrasser Hauptstrasse 28, Ungargasse 13
Access: Public passageway
Public transportation: U3 (Rochusgasse)

The original 18th century building was remodelled by Peter Gerl, who also gave it a new façade. The complex provides a passage between the Landstrasser Hauptstrasse and Ungargasse. The four-storeyed construction is proof of the increasing density of development in the outlying areas in the first half of the 19th century. It was a metropolitan extension into the as yet small-scale, suburban structure of the district.

3.-**11** | ***Louis Montoyer, Joseph Meissl Jr.***

Palais Rasumovsky (now the Federal Geological Institute)
1803, 1814

Rasumovskygasse 23-25
Access: By appointment
Public transportation: U3 (Rochusgasse)

Unlike its present location between several small streets, this impressive and sculpturally well designed palace once lay in an extensive English park. Montoyer divided the façade of the closed, cubical structure with the help of a monumental columned foyer, which is repeated in more modest dimensions on the free-standing narrow end. The palace now houses the Federal Geological Institute, with a paleontological collection and a comprehensive library on geology.

Stonborough-Wittgenstein House (now the Bulgarian Cultural Association) 1926

Kundmanngasse 19
Access: By appointment
Public transportation: U3 (Rochusgasse)

The fame of the co-architect Ludwig Wittgenstein clouds the fact that this building is actually an outstanding architectural achievement. Despite being a product of the architectural climate created by Adolf Loos, it does not blindly follow its precepts. The general design of the building is by Paul Engelmann, who was both a student of Loos and a friend of Wittgenstein. The further development and refinement of the plans was carried out by Wittgenstein himself. Natural materials were rejected in favour of iron, glass, concrete and marble stucco for the appointment of the interior. This radical reduction in the use of materials reflects the simple exterior, which is structured entirely through the arrangement of the windows. The design of the interior space is far less revolutionary in nature.

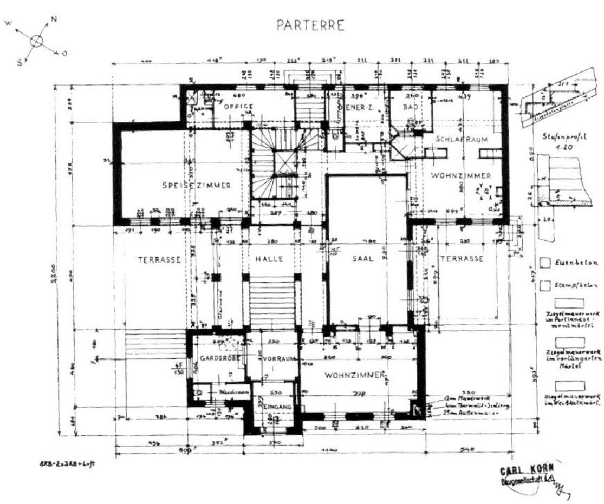

3.-**13** | *Josef Engelhart, Josef Plečnik*

Karl-Borromäus Fountain (Lueger-Fountain) 1904

Karl-Borromäus-Platz
Access: Open to public
Public transportation: U3 (Rochusgasse)

The fountain was constructed on the occasion of the 60th birthday of the Viennese mayor Karl Lueger. The project had already been underway before Josef Plecnik was drawn into it by the sculptor and painter Josef Engelhart. The structure is well integrated into its confined location, both from the perspective of its form as well as its dimensions. The combination of the fountain's circular form and oval border creates sickle-shaped open areas that allow the arrangement of a "minimal park".

3.-**14** | *Hermann Czech*

Petrusgasse Apartment Building 1985

Petrusgasse 4
Access: Not open to public
Public transportation: Bus 74A (Petrusgasse)

Unobtrusiveness and normality have been raised to a principle in this residential building. If architecture is background (Czech), then this structure is the transformation of an architectural stance. Seen within the framework of post-modern architecture of the 80s, this is a liveable-in house with a clear ground plan, sensibly designed oriels and no aesthetic distortions.

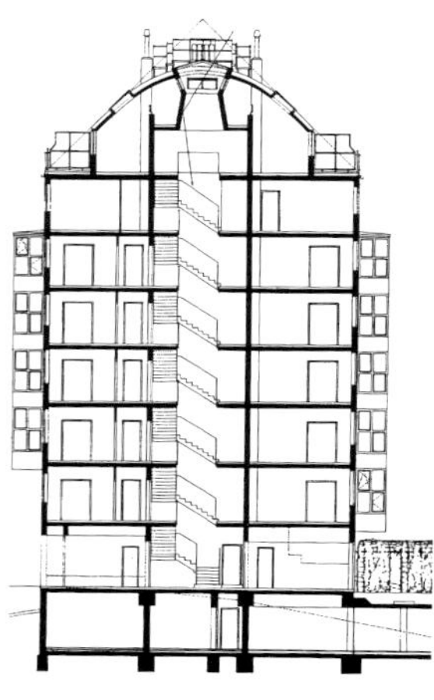

Portois & Fix Residential and Commercial Building 1899

Ungargasse 59–61
Access: Only the shops may be visited
Public transportation: Tram line O (Neulinggasse)

With this construction, Fabiani proved himself to be an audacious pupil of Otto Wagner, not only adopting the teachings of his Master but indeed attempting to outdo them. Built shortly after Wagner's majolica house on the Wienzeile, this commercial building surpasses the rational concept of the former, at least in the design of the façade. The tile cladding does not create a uniformly ornamental façade; the pattern emerges from alternating pieces of different colours. The serially arranged axes of the windows and the rhythmic organisation of the lower floors can in principle be endlessly continued at random. Insensitive renovation, particularly of the lower floors, fortunately did no real harm to the building.

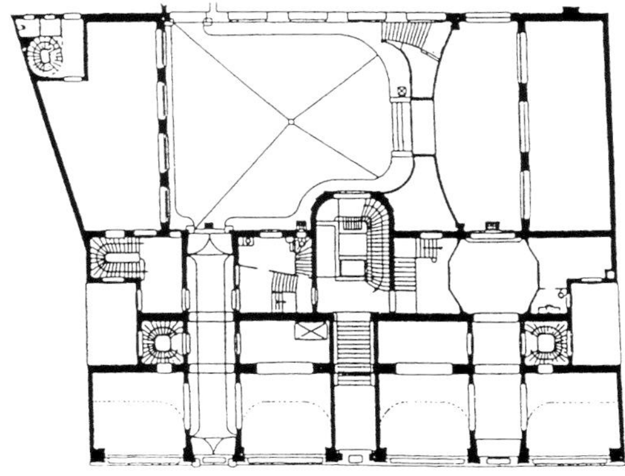

3.-**16** | *Walter Sobotka*

Klopsteinplatz Apartment Block 1927

A very sober municipal housing project that renounces any ornamentation whatsoever. The windows and sharply carved out loggias form the arrangement of the façade. The organisation of the building results from a layering of several spatial elements. This unsentimental attitude makes it an exception in the social-democratic housing programme.

Klopsteinplatz 6,
Schrottgasse 10-12
Access: Not open to public
Public transportation: Bus 77A (Rabengasse)

3.-**17** | *Architektengruppe Rennweg*

Rennweg Residential Park 1994

The residential park has been built on the site of a former barracks near the inner city. It is an attempt to link with the traditional qualities of the municipal residential buildings of the inter-war period. 437 apartments, shops and offices emerged between Oberzellergasse, Rennweg and Landstrasser Hauptstrasse. Following the lines of social housing, a number of details were standardized, with the result that despite the numerous architects who were involved in the project, the entire development displays very little individuality of design. The buildings by Roland Rainer, Nehrer and Medek as well as Anton Schweighofer are worthy of note. Architektengruppe Rennweg consists of: Atelier 4; Bramhas, Waclawek & Karrer; Marschalek & Ladstätter with Bert Gantar; Nehrer & Medek; Neumann & Steiner; Perotti & Greifeneder; Puchhammer & Wawrik; Roland Rainer; Udo Schrittwieser; Anton Schweighofer.

Landstrasser Hauptstrasse 148
Access: Not open to public
Public transportation: Bus 74A (Petrusgasse)

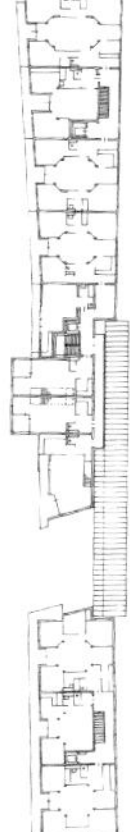

Raben-Hof
1925

Difficulties regarding property-ownership and topographical factors led the architects to decide against an axial court. The decision was made in favour of developing an elongated structure flexibly around large open spaces. None of the court-like structures is really closed. The variegated character of the development is emphasised by the details and the use of diverse materials. As is the case with most large complexes of this kind, the Raben-Hof also had ancillary services and educational facilities.

Baumgasse, Rabengasse, Hainburger Strasse, Lustgasse, St. Nikolaus-Platz
Access: Only open areas
Public transportation: U3 (Kardinal-Nagl-Platz)

LAGEPLAN.

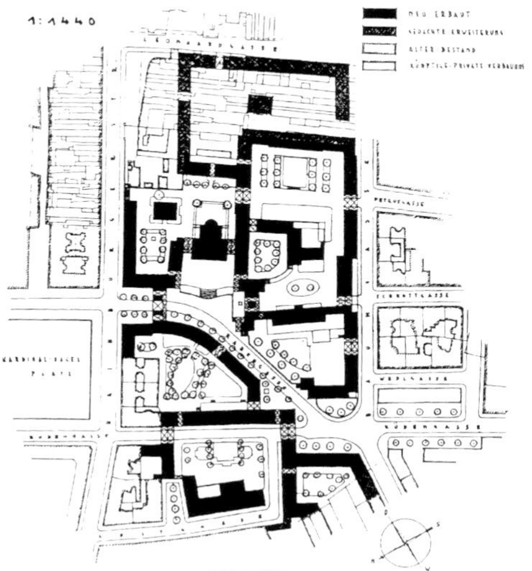

Hundertwasserhaus
1982

Löwengasse 41–43
Access: Only souvenir shop
Public transportation: Tram line N (Löwengasse)

Hundertwasser has seen the straight line as a betrayal of human individuality ever since his "Verschimmelungs-manifesto" (Manifesto of Moulding) of 1958. With the decoration of a council building in Löwengasse, Hundertwasser achieved enormous publicity that is justified neither by its typology nor by the proclaimed ecological considerations in its construction. He decorated the district heating plant and the chimney of the Vienna Public Utilities, located on Spittelauer Lände in the 9th district in a similar manner.

Supplementary Recommendations

2.**12s**	Kai 302 housing complex Albert Wimmer	1995 Handelskai 302–304
2.**13s**	Johann-Nepomuk Church Carl Rösner	1841 Praterstrasse 45
3.**20s**	Hoffmann Apartment Building Josef Kornhäusel, Anton Hoppe	1833 Beatrixgasse 20
3.**21s**	Radetzkyplatz Bank Branch Luigi Blau	1984 Radetzkyplatz
3.**22s**	German Embassy Rolf Gutbrod	1963 Metternichgasse 3
3.**23s**	Residential building Günther Oberhofer	1992 Kardinal Nagl Platz 5–7
3.**24s**	Shopping Mall Ernst Hoffmann	1992 Landstrasser Hauptstrasse 71
3.**25s**	Barichgasse Office Building Peter Schweger & Partner mit Iwan Zelenka	1989 Barichgasse 38–42/Ungargasse 59–61
3.**26s**	Hoffmann-La Roche Georg Lippert	1960 Gürtel/Jaquingasse

Buildings worth visiting – Suggestions by Viennese architects

4th District:

Coop Himmelblau:
Karlskirche, index no. 4.-**3**

Eichinger oder Knechtl:
Exhibition building and tower at Karlsplatz (Josef Hoffmann) – not yet built

Wilhelm Holzbauer:
Palais Starhemberg-Schönburg, index no. 4.-**8s**

Elsa Prochazka:
Kunsthalle, index no. 4.-**2**

6th District:

Wolfdietrich Ziesel:
Stadtbahn bridges, index no. 1.-**36**

7th District:

Martin Kohlbauer:
House with public thoroughfare on Lerchenfelderstrasse 13

9th District:

Margherita Spiluttini (architecture photographer):
Narrenturm (Fools' Tower), index no. 9.-**7**

4.-**1**

Imperial Building Authority, J. S. v. Leytenbach, P. v. Nobile

Technical University of Vienna 1816

Karlsplatz 13
Access: Open to public
Public transportation: U1, U2, U4 (Karlsplatz)

Erected in phases during the 19th century, the complex is built asymmetrically around four inner courtyards. Construction on the main wing facing Karlsplatz was begun in 1819. Its sparing instrumentation makes it a typical example of the style propagated by the Imperial Building Authority in the first half of the century. The assembly hall, furnished according to the plans by Peter Nobile, is worthy of note. The wing along the Karlsgasse was built between 1905 and 1906 by Carl König, who held the chair for architecture in the same institution. Renovation and adaptation of the building were conducted by Hans Puchhammer.

4.-**2**

Adolf Krischanitz

Kunsthalle Wien 1992

Karlsplatz, Treitlstrasse 2
Access: Open to public
Public transportation: U1, U2, U4 (Karlsplatz)

Located directly on Karlsplatz, the Kunsthalle is a provisional exhibition hall that remains in operation all year round. The steel construction consists of 16 frames which rest on individual concrete foundations. It supports a 9 m. high exhibition hall that is 54 m. in length and 17.7 m. in width. The hall is dissected by a "pipe", which was intended to be a communicative element making the public more aware of both the park and the exhibition hall. It was, however, closed at the very outset.

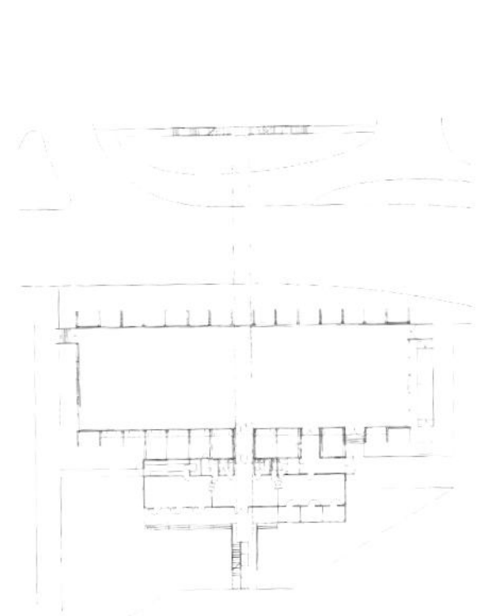

Karlskirche
1715, (1722–39)

An edifice as imprese, dedicated by Charles VI to his patron Saint Charles Borromeo in gratitude for the end of the plague. The two monumental pillars, with their references to antiquity and Rome, allegorize not only the pillars of Solomon's Temple but also the personal motto of Charles: "Constantia and Fortitudo". The intricacy of the interior unfolds in layers. A graduated construction (silhouette-effect), the Church has an oval main hall (longitudinal axis) with annexes and an altar, built along plans by Fischer, with theatrically planned lighting. The dome fresco is by the Austrian painter Johann Michael Rottmayr. It is today difficult to imagine the church as it must have been originally – it once lay in a suburban green belt, along the banks of a river.

Karlsplatz
Access: Open to public
Public transportation: U1, U2, U4 (Karlsplatz)

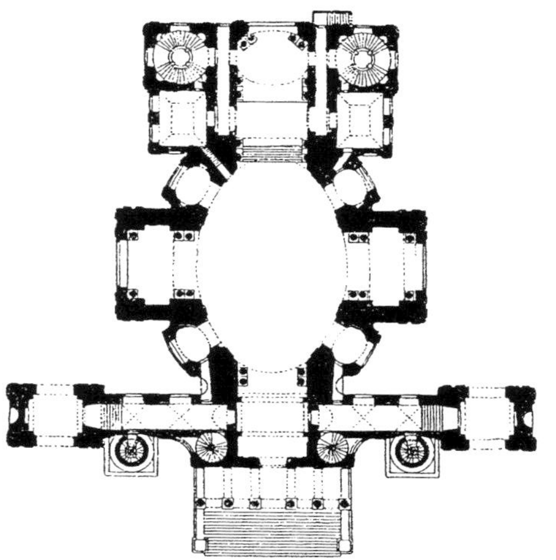

4.-**4** | *Josef Kornhäusel*

The Dittmann Apartment Block 1831

Resselgasse 3–5,
Wiedner Hauptstrasse 3
Access: Not open to public
Public transportation: U1, U2, U4 (Karlsplatz)

The former "House to the Golden Ox" is a large residential block of the late Biedermeier period. Behind the façade, with its flat central bay and the original gate to the building, there is a U-shaped "Pavlatch" courtyard. The Pavlatch is a Viennese peculiarity, whereby the apartments are accessed through a projecting – often glazed – wooden construction.

4.-**5** | *C. Holzmeister, H. Schmid, H. Aichinger; G. Peichl*

Funkhaus: Broadcasting Studios for Vienna and Lower Austria 1935

Argentinierstrasse 30a
Access: Not open to public
Public transportation: U1 (Taubstummengasse)

The building of the studios followed Clemens Holzmeister's revisions of the original plans by Schmid and Aichinger. Both the eminent political significance of the new medium, as well as the contractual obligation to balance functional with publicly accessible representative architecture, are reflected in its construction. Holzmeister's interventions focused mainly on increasing its monument-al appearance and on decorating the entrance area. The layout of the construction follows the ground plan suggested by Schmid and Aichinger. The studio was damaged by bombs during the Second World War and was extended further in 1979–83 by Gustav Peichl, who paid special attention to the previously neglected courtyard.

Andras Pálffy, Christian Jabornegg, Georg Schönfeld

4.-**6**

The architects transformed this space, belonging to a life insurance company, into a new exhibition hall and art centre through their extremely precise architectural modifications. The most significant constructional element is the visible reinforced-concrete construction, which serves to form a new spatial sequence. The light comes in through the ceiling and is reflected into the interior by means of a deflection system that filters out direct sunlight.

EA Generali Foundation 1992

Wiedner Hauptstrasse 15
Access: Business hours
Public transportation: Tram lines 62 and 65 (Paulanergasse)

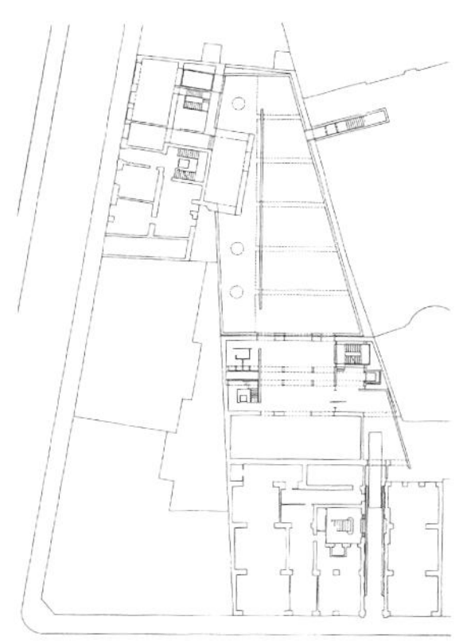

Giovanni Battista Carlone, Tencala, Pacassi, Schlöss

4.-**7**

In 1615 work was begun on the conversion of a 14th century Meierhof with sprawling gardens into a pleasure palace for Emperor Matthias. The Turkish invasions later on in the century caused heavy damage to the palace, the so-called "Favorita", which was then altered and rebuilt according to the plans by Giovanni Pietro Tencala. It was then extended in the 18th century by Nikolaus Pacassi. Since its conversion into a Jesuit college in the 18th century, the palace has been used for educational purposes. It now houses the Diplomatic Academy and a secondary school. The building was last renovated by Erich Schlöss.

Theresian Academy 1615

Favoritenstrasse 11
Access: Not open to public
Public transportation: U1 (Taubstummengasse)

5.-**1**

Josef Plečnik

Steggasse Apartment Building
1901

Rechte Wienzeile 68,
Steggasse 1
Access: Not open to public
Public transportation: U4 (Kettenbrückengasse)

In this twin residential block in the tradition of Otto Wagner, Plečnik actually put into three-dimensional form the volume that Wagner had often only implied through architectural details. The two close-set towers are of unequal heights and can be thus identified as autonomous structures. The exterior of the building reflects the organisation of the interior and emphasizes – particularly through the dominating ornamental cornices and corner balconies – the free-standing construction of the building.

5.-**2**

Hubert and Franz Gessner

Vorwärts – Printers and Publishers
1907

Rechte Wienzeile 97
Access: Not open to public
Public transportation: U4 (Kettenbrückengasse)

Socialist sentimentality, expressed at the highest architectural level, was the forte of the Gessner brothers, who incorporated it into the building programme of "Red" Vienna. The dynamism suggested in the name of the publishing house (which means "forwards") actually finds expression in the architecture without the details expressing too clear a message. The building suffers from the ingratiating post-modernity of the adjoining hotel of which it is now a part.

G. Lautner, P. Scheifinger, R. Szedenik, C. Schindler

5.-**3**

Both the residential buildings, Victor-Christ-Gasse 15–17 (built in 1991) and Zentagasse 46 (built in 1994), stand in close proximity to each other. They display a wide spectrum of options available under the existing building laws for corner sites. The curved building (the boundary of the site is basically defined by a two-storeyed pergola), recessed on Victor-Christ-Gasse allows an opening on to the Gründerzeit street profile. A glazed pergola soundproofs the Zentagasse building, and this, together with the bright colouring behind the glass, has resulted in a striking solution for a corner site.

Zentagasse
1994

Zentagasse 46
Access: Not open to public
Public transportation: Bus 59A (Castelligasse)

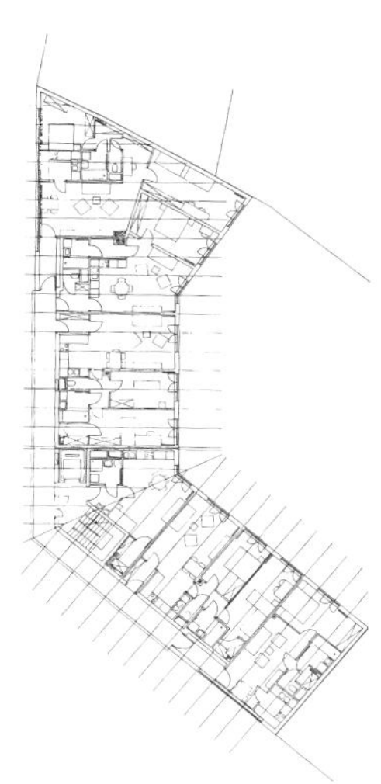

Fritz Judtmann, Egon Riss

5.-**4**

One of the most radical architectural solutions of Vienna City Council's housing programme. The horizontal division created by masonry bonds and balconies is superimposed by "vertical stripes" of the glazed verandas. The façade possesses the harmony of a chequered pattern.

Diehlgasse Appartment Building
1928

Brandmayergasse,
Diehlgasse 20–26
Access: Not open to public
Public transportation: Tram line 18 (Arbeitergasse)

5.-**5**

Hermann Stiegholzer, Herbert Kastinger

Labour Exchange for the Metal and Timber Industries
1928

Embelgasse 2–4,
Siebenbrunnenfeldgasse,
Obere Amtshausgasse 5–7
Access: Not open to public
Public transportation: U4, bus 12A
(Siebenbrunnenfeldgasse)

The monolithic monumentality of the structure can also be read as a didactic message. While being an expression of the social drama of unemployment, it also has the soothing presence of the protecting power of the State. The building block is divided into two on the exterior while the generous circulation in the interior expedites administrative procedures.

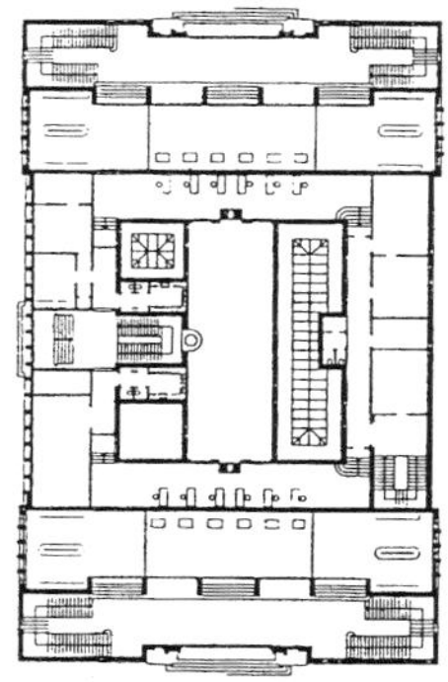

5.-**6**

Rudolf Schwarz

St. Florian Parish Church
1961

Wiedner Hauptstrasse 97-99
Access: Open to public
Public transportation: Tram lines 62 and 65
(Laurenzgasse)

The rebuilding of the parish church St. Florian is a piece of Vienna's urban and church building history. One of the reasons for its construction was that the baroque Floriani Church which stood in the middle of Wiedner Hauptstrasse, was demolished in order to facilitate the flow of traffic. It was built after the architect Rudolf Schwarz won an international competition in 1957, and was of great relevance to the architectural discourse in Vienna.

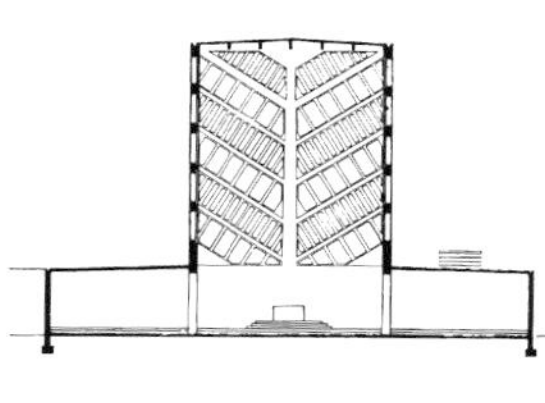

Reumannhof
1924

Most epithets associated with council housing in Vienna apply to the Reumannhof. The definition of the Gürtel as the "Ringstrasse of the proletariat" was coined upon the erection of this building. Josef Frank was right in calling the monumental 478-apartment building "the residential palace of the working classes". The present castellated form only emerged in the course of an alteration to its building plans. It was originally designed as a multi-storeyed building opening onto several courtyards.

Margaretengürtel 100–110, Siebenbrunnengasse, Brandmayergasse
Access: Only open areas
Public transportation: Tram lines 6, 18 (Eichenstrasse)

Heinz Tesar 5.-**8**

Einsiedlergasse Apartment Building
1981

The two residential buildings by Tesar were constructed one after the other and create a new and outstanding street front. His architectural vocabulary on the side facing the street is reduced and refers to the Viennese architecture (Reduced Expressionism) of the inter-war period. On the side facing the courtyard the veranda becomes the central theme. The building presents an exquisite example of housing in Vienna today.

Einsiedlergasse 13
Access: Not open to public
Public transportation: Bus 14A (Reinprechtstorferstrasse)

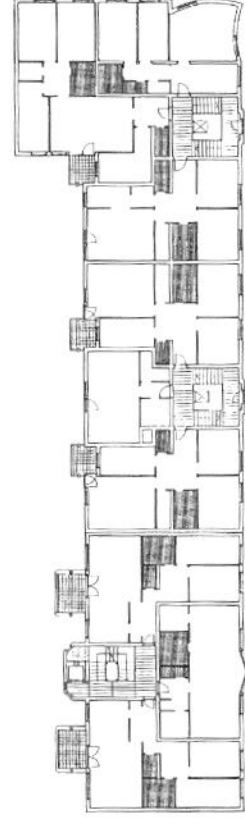

Depot for Backdrop and Decorations of the Court Theatres (Currently Studios of the Academy of Fine Arts) 1875,1993

Lehargasse 6–8
Access: Open to public
Public transportation: U2 (Babenbergerstrasse)

Gottfried Semper's depot for stage sets is a brickwork construction, the kind usually seen in industrial buildings of the time. The façade is formed by rounded, arched windows on the ground area and large, rectangular, iron-mullioned windows on the upper floors. Semper developed a totally untypological structure on an irregularly shaped site, and its many-storeyed hall facilitated the delivery and transport of large stage sets. The building is a good example of how site and task constrictions can lead to innovative architecture. After extensive restoration and adaptation by Carl Pruscha (1993–96) it now houses painting studios of the Academy of Fine Arts.

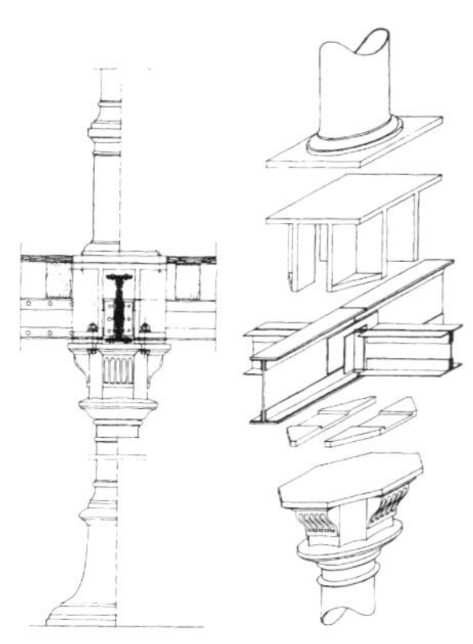

Wienzeile Houses
1898

This sequence of three buildings was beautifully composed to form a unique urban street-corner. One house is completely clad with glazed ceramics (majolica tiles) and the other two façades are rendered. The clear ground plan and the installation of a lift make these houses exemplary of modern urban life-style. Wagner himself lived in Köstlergasse 3, where his famous glass bathtub was also installed.

Linke Wienzeile 40, Linke Wienzeile 38/Köstlergasse 1, Köstlergasse 3
Access: Not open to public
Public transportation: U4 (Kettenbrückengasse)

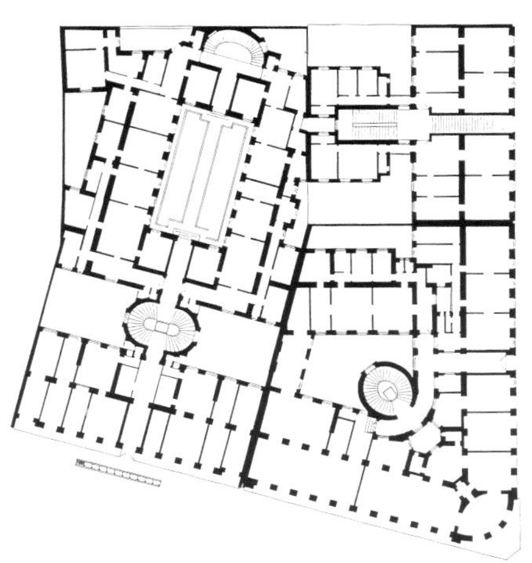

6.-**3** | *Josef Reymund sr., Franz Jäger*

Theatre on the Wien 1797

Linke Wienzeile 6,
Milöckergasse, Lehárgasse
Access: Opening hours
Public transportation: U1, U2, U4 (Karlsplatz)

The name "on the Wien" derives from its location, which is now incomprehensible. At the time of its construction the theatre was on the banks of the still exposed River Wien. The oldest part of the complex was built on a very narrow plot for the director Emanuel Schikaneder in 1800/1801. In 1902 the former foyer was replaced by a new entrance wing, built along the Wienzeile by the theatre-architects Ferdinand Fellner and Hermann Helmer. The building was adapted in the 60s to the new requirements by Otto Niedermoser. Between 1979 and 1982 he also recessed the simplified façade.

6.-**4** | *Ludwig Förster, Theophil von Hansen*

Evangelical Church (Gustav-Adolf Church) 1846

Gumpendorferstrasse next to 129
Access: Open to public
Public transportation: Bus 57A (Sonnenuhrgasse)

Built according to the plans by Ludwig Förster and Theophil von Hansen, this was the first Evangelical church to be erected outside the inner city. Both architects subsequently became well established in the field of sacred architecture. The decoration of the building is Islamic-Byzantine in style, which was to become synonymous with non-Catholic sacred architecture in the following decades. Although the form itself is classicist in its simplicity, the decor anticipates the flexibility of Historicism in adapting to the building task.

Linke Wienzeile Apartment Building 1991

Built as a team effort, this house is a serious reflection on the theme of the artist as architect. Margarethe Cufer was responsible for the architectural planning and Oswald Oberhuber for the artistic elements in the architectural design. The result was a typologically well defined building with a lively and sophisticated façade without a naive prettification of the architecture. The parapets of varying heights and the diverse formats for the windows set a personal stamp on one of the most important main roads of Vienna.

Esterházygasse 2, Linke Wienzeile 96
Access: Not open to public
Public transportation: U4 (Pilgramgasse)

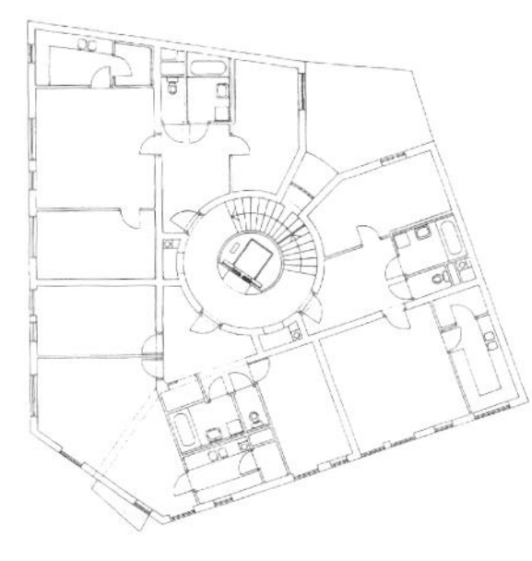

7.-**1** | *Laurids and Manfred Ortner*

Museumsquartier (Museum Quarter) 1988

Museumsplatz
Access: Open to public
Public transportation: U2, U3 (Volkstheater)

"This prize-winning competition entry by Laurids and Manfred Ortner has successfully woven together the urban patterns of the imperial centre with those of the neighbouring middle-class quarter. They have thus suggested a structure that would mean an exciting vitalization, circulation and opening up of the quarter." (Dietmar Steiner)
The premises of the former imperial stables (Fischer von Erlach, 1721–1723) will in future house the Museum of Modern Art, the Leopold Museum and the Kunsthalle. It is presently occupied by the Vienna Architecture Centre and the Childrens' Museum.

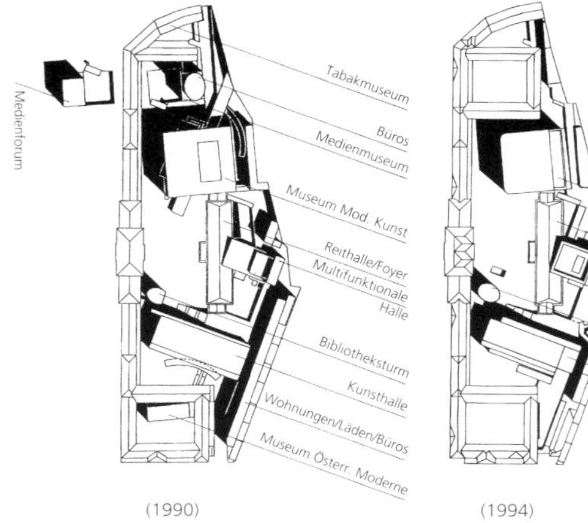

(1990) (1994)

7.-**2** | *Ferdinand Fellner and Hermann Helmer*

Volkstheater 1887

Neustiftgasse 1
Access: Open to public
Public transportation: U2, U3 (Volkstheater)

The building activity of the theatre specialists Fellner and Helmer within the Danube Monarchy is legendary. They built practically every theatre for the imperial and royal lands, even using some of the plans several times over. The oblique façade of the Volkstheater is conspicuous because it does not correspond with the longitudinal development of the building. The reason for this becomes clear when one views it in relation to the imperial stables with which it is aligned. Seen in this context, the Volkstheater is one of those historical buildings that were built along the baroque style of the Hofburg, as were the Natural History and Art History Museums.

Johann B. Fischer von Erlach

7.-**3**

At the time it was built, this garden palace was located on the edge of the city and faced the defensive wall. Johann B. Fischer von Erlach's generous design grouped the buildings around numerous inner courtyards. The street and garden façades are built at a right angle to each other. The side facing the street is dominated by a pronounced central bay of colossal magnitude that is paraphrased on a smaller scale in the façade overlooking the garden. The former garden palace now houses the Ministry of Justice.

Trautson Palace 1710

Museumsstrasse 7
Access: Not open to public
Public transportation: U2 (Volkstheater)

Otto Wagner

7.-**4**

The Neustiftgasse 40 (1909) and Döblergasse 4 (1911) apartment houses were built on two adjoining plots. They exemplify Otto Wagner's position on urban housing, their simplicity being an expression of the socio-economic conditions (see explanatory notes by O. Wagner). The last city apartment that Otto Wagner occupied (1911–1918) is located in the Döblergasse building. It has contained the Otto Wagner Archive of the Academy of Fine Arts of Vienna since 1985.

Döblergasse-Neustiftgasse Apartment Buildings 1909

Neustiftgasse 40,
Döblergasse 4
Access: by appointment (Döblergasse 4)
Public transportation: Tram line 46 (Strozzigasse)

7.-**5** | *Paul Sprenger, Joh. Georg Müller, Franz Sitte*

Altlerchenfelder Church 1846, (1849–61)

Lerchenfelder Strasse 111
Access: Open to public
Public transportation: Tram line 46 (Schottenfeldgasse)

Built on the inner edge of the former suburban fortifications of the city, the church is the clearest reflection of the upheavals in architecture that followed the politically unsuccessful civil revolution of 1848. Construction on this large church was begun by Paul Sprenger, who was head of the Imperial Building Authority and ardently propagated Classicism as the official style. It was finally completed by Johann Georg Müller, Eduard van der Nüll and Franz Sitte and is considered a masterpiece of Early Historicism.

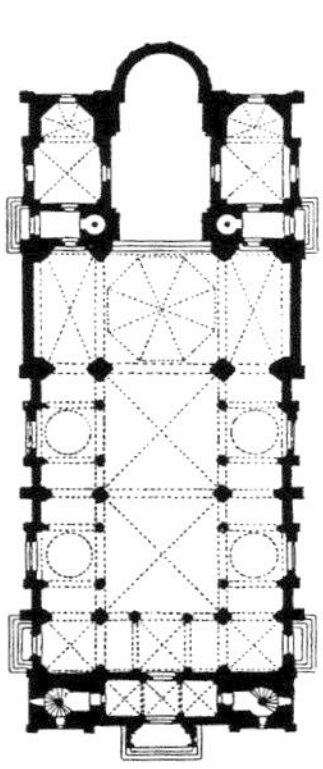

7.-**6** | *Georg Driendl and Gerhard Steixner*

Skala Bar and Restaurant 1987

Neubaugasse 8
Access: Open to public
Public transportation: U3 (Neubaugasse)

The bar cum restaurant is situated in the basement of a Gründerzeit building. The lighting and its transitory materialization serve to distract from the fact that it is located below street-level. A complex sequence of rooms is emphasized by heterogeneous surfaces such as sanded, dull and polished metal; bare, lacquered and pre-rusted iron; diverse kinds of glass and mirrors as well as variously treated stone and wooden surfaces.

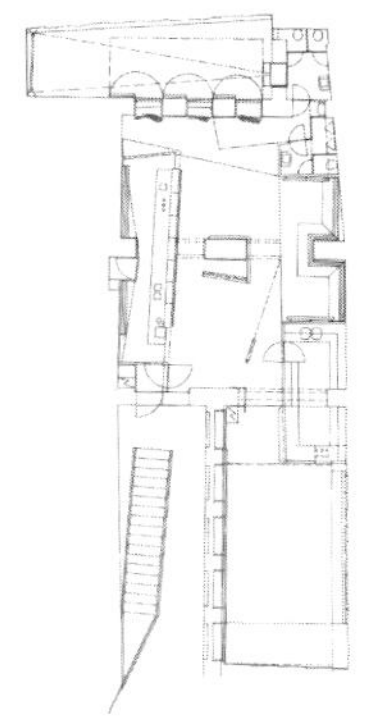

Zentralsparkasse (Central Savings Bank) Mariahilf-Neubau 1914

Mariahilfer Strasse 70
Access: During business hours
Public transportation: U3 (Neubaugasse)

The former headquarters of the "Anglo-Austrian Bank II" reveals Loos as an ingenious semantician. It is, at the same time, Loos' answer to Otto Wagner's Postsparkasse (Post Office Savings Bank), which he was not in complete agreement with. Not only the choice of material but also the monumental treatment of a very small space lend the impressive, black granite portal the appearance of a strong box. A dark entrance hall leads to rooms of different height all the way to a high and bright banking hall which is exclusively top-lit. The interior was renovated in 1973.

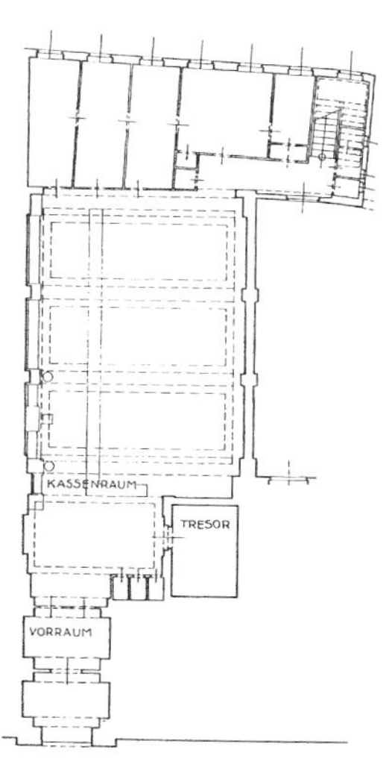

Spittelberg

Burggasse, Spittelberggasse, Siebensterngasse
Access: Open to public
Public transportation: U2, U3 (Volkstheater)

The section of the district behind the former court stables has undergone several "changes in image". It took its name from the "Wiener Bürgerspital" (Viennese Civic Hospital), which had owned the grounds since 1525. Spittelberg lies approximately 20 metres higher than the area immediately in front of it. This gave it strategic importance during the Turkish siege of Vienna; both Sultan Suleiman and Cara Mustapha had their encampment here. The development dates back to the 17th century and has largely retained its original form. This is due to the fact that the area was one of the most disreputable parts of Vienna until the First World War.

8.-**1**

Robert Oerley

Studentenheim (Students' Hostel) (Formerly Luithlen Sanatorium) 1907

Auerspergstrasse 9
Access: Not open to public
Public transportation: U2 (Rathaus)

Robert Oerley has left behind a legacy of a remarkable number of noteworthy buildings in Vienna. Now in use as a students' hostel, the interior of the Luithlen Sanatorium has been largely altered. However the street façade, with its horizontal divisioning and double and triple partitioned windows with embossed glass panes, retains its imposing presence. The glass canopy as well as the roof structures containing the former operating theatres no longer exist (reconstruction in the sixties).

8.-**2**

Joseph Allio, Josef Kornhäusel, et al.

Theater in der Josefstadt 1822

Josefstädterstrasse 76
Access: During performances
Public transportation: Tram line J (Lederergasse)

The original intent of this theatre complex is now lost due to its numerous reconstructions. Furthermore, while it was once a free-standing structure, it is now completely surrounded by residential buildings. Its construction history is correspondingly complex: an existing hall from the 18th century was extended by Kornhäusel in 1882. After Max Reinhardt took over as director, further reconstructions were undertaken in the 1920s by Carl Witzmann, who in the process also incorporated the historical substance of the building. The entire complex was again renovated by Otto Niedermoser in the 1950s.

Johann Lukas von Hildebrandt

8.-**3**

The curvilinear twin-towered façade of the church is the highlight of one of the loveliest, architecturally most "beautifully composed" squares in Vienna. The frontage, which sweeps out in the centre and swings back towards the towers, reflects a varied graduated hall with a nearly circular oval nucleus. The ceiling frescoes are an early work by the Austrian painter Franz Anton Maulbertsch. Work on the adjoining cloister wing began prior to the construction of the church itself and was completed in the mid-18th century.

Piaristenkirche
1716

Jodok Fink-Platz
Access: Open to public
Public transportation: Tram line J (Lederergasse)

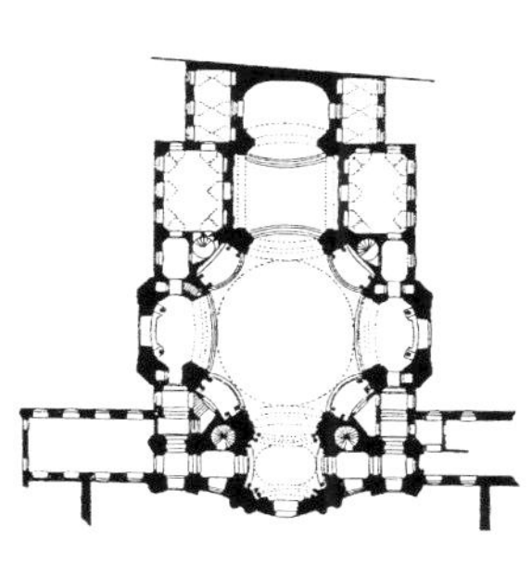

Julius and Wunibald Deininger

8.-**4**

An amazing school building with a clear typological concept, a centrally located auditorium and two side wings. The plan reflects the work of Julius Deininger and his son Wunibald. The latter had studied under Otto Wagner and was probably responsible for the design of the building. The exquisite majolica tilework was designed by Richard Luksch.

New Academy of Trade and Commerce
1906

Hamerlingplatz 5–6
Access: By appointment
Public transportation: Tram lines 5, 33 and J (Albertgasse)

8.-**5**

Boris Podrecca

Branch Office of the Österreichische Spar-Casse (Austrian Savings Bank) 1994

Josefstädterstrasse 75-77
Access: Business hours
Public transportation: Tram lines 5, 33, J (Albertgasse)

This bank branch was constructed in the former Albert-Kino (cinema) in the Josefstadt district and forms a dialogue with the students' hostel on a more or less optical level. In converting this movie hall into a bank, Podrecca tried to retain all the "memorabilia" in order to retain a historical context. The former projection room is now the director's office and the former theatre now serves as the banking hall. An urban transformation.

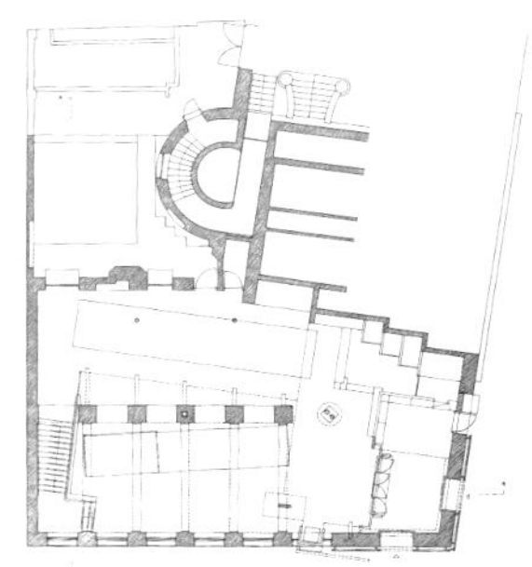

8.-**6**

Caesar Poppovits

Ludo-Hartmann-Hof 1924

Albertgasse 13–15
Access: Not open to public
Public transportation: Tram lines 5, 33 and J (Albertgasse)

This explicitly "inner city" housing estate is one of the very few of its kind in Vienna. It is particularly noteworthy for its unusual ground plan. The setback creates a small square which again differentiates it from the other historical buildings around it. The dense development of the area gave rise to rather small inner courtyards, evoking a resemblance to residential barracks. The details, on the other hand, are kept very unpretentious and "homely".

Boris Podrecca

8.-**7**

The six storey high students' hostel rises above a two storeyed glazed base zone. The fact that it is a refurbished house is not immediately noticeable because Podrecca cleverly altered the proportions of the building. The ground floor allows a view into the function halls making it "communicative". A convincing low-cost adaptation.

Korotan Hotel and Students' Hostel 1991

Albertgasse 48
Access: Not open to public
Public transportation: Tram line J (Albertgasse)

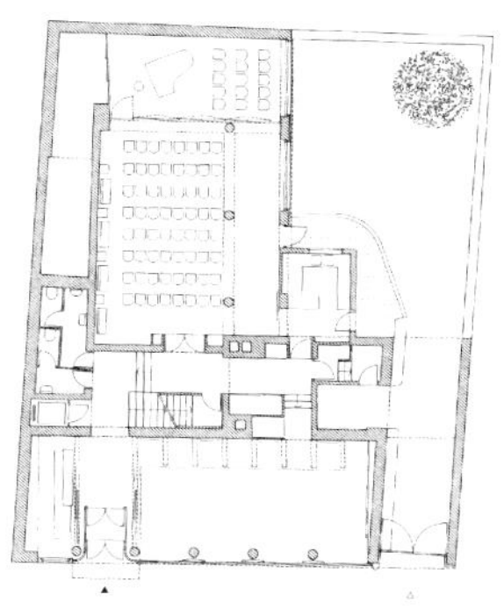

Elsa Prochazka

8.-**8**

A museum is a museum is a museum. A Folk Museum is a special kind of museum, allowing a glimpse of the history of different cultures. The renovation and adaptation of the interior was executed with great sensitivity: the new arrangement of the exhibits and the design of the showcases have been done with an awareness of the historical substance of the building and the new lighting is effective without being dramatic. The variety of the showcases is a pleasure in itself and contributes to the harmony of the presentation.

Folk Museum 1994

Laudongasse
Access: Opening hours
Public transportation: Tram lines 5, 33 (Laudongasse)

9.-**1** | *Heinrich von Ferstel*

Votivkirche
1856

Rooseveltplatz
Access: Open to public
Public transportation: U2 (Schottentor)

Originally located outside the defensive wall, the Votivkirche is one of Heinrich von Ferstel's early works and was erected to commemorate a failed assassination attempt on Emperor Franz Josef. Ferstel adopted the classical schema of French cathedrals as his prototype, discarding the mixture of diverse architectural styles in the sense of strict Historicism. By avoiding the use of elements from other epochs he built a derivative that is "more Gothic" than most of its famed prototypes were.

9.-**2** | *Gregor Eichinger, Christian Knechtl*

Stein Café-Restaurant
1985

Währinger Strasse 6
Access: Open to public
Public transportation: U2, tram lines 1and 2 (Schottentor)

Stein Café can be seen as having been implanted into an already existing spatial structure. Limited interventions – integration of the lighting, the bar and old objects such as the suspended clock into the concept – determine the design of the space. As a result it has grown somewhat organically, with each phase of its development visible in "layers", as it were. In 1987 the café was expanded by the addition of Stein Restaurant's Diner. Its adjoining rooms are under continuous reconstruction and reorganization.

Leopold Bauer 9.-3

Actually the result of disastrous planning, the headquarters of the Austrian National Bank later underwent extensive alterations. Of Leopold Bauer's ambitious project, only the plans involving the printing-office building were implemented before the First World War. After the war it was transformed into the main building by Ferdinand Glaser and Rudolf Eisler, who also changed the banking hall in the process of reconstruction. The fifth floor housing the general administration offices was destroyed by fire.

Nationalbank
1913

Otto-Wagner-Platz 3
Access: Not open to public
Public transportation: Tram lines 43, 44 (Landesgerichtstrasse)

Otto Wagner 9.-4

One of Otto Wagner's large and stately apartment buildings, the house affords a splendid view of the Landesgerichtsstrasse. Originally built by Wagner for his own use, it was granted its building permit on 29th December 1887. It gains prominence in the context of town-planning due to its special location along three streets (Universitätsstrasse, Garnisongasse and Garelligasse). Each storey contains two upper middle-class apartments of approximately 300 m^2 living space.

Universitätsstrasse Apartment Building
1887

Universitätsstrasse 12
Access: Not open to public
Public transportation: U2 (Schottentor)

9.-**5**

Heinrich von Ferstel

Institute of Chemistry, University of Vienna 1868

Währinger Strasse 10
Access: Open to public
Public transportation: U2 (Schottentor)

Even before Heinrich von Ferstel began the construction of the nearby University building, he was able to make a head-start in planning the scientific institutions by building the Institute for Pharmaceutical Chemistry. He was given necessary support by the chemicist Josef Redtenbacher. Built on a square ground-plan, the brickwork structure is almost free-standing. The main façade facing Währingerstrasse is marked by a broad but shallow central bay – one may assume a connection to the eminent Classicist buildings in its close proximity.

9.-**6**

Wolfgang Tschapeller (Library)

Sigmund Freud's Apartment 1991

Berggasse 19
Access: Opening hours
Public transportation: Tram line D (Schlickgasse)

Berggasse 19 is a Viennese address of international renown. Sigmund Freud lived and worked here for decades until he was forced to emigrate to London. From this one place the whole of 20th century thought was revolutionized. Seen from this perspective, the memorial is more a genius loci than a museum. The traditional middle-class world of a joint-family was the cradle of a global revolution in thought. In the process of expanding the lecture room, Wolfgang Tschapeller also built a library and an emergency staircase. The consistent use of contemporary materials such as steel, wire cables and fibreglass, creates a deliberate contrast to the surroundings.

Altes Allgemeines Krankenhaus (Old General Hospital) – Narrenturm 1783

Allgemeines Krankenhaus, Spitalgasse
Access: Open to public
Public transportation: Tram lines 5, 33 (Lazarettgasse)

This extensive complex was opened in 1784 after Joseph II's reform of the entire health and public relief system. Located outside the city wall, it served to isolate the sick from the rest of the populace. It consists of low-rises grouped around numerous large courtyards, with the Narrenturm (Fools' Tower) situated on the main axis (Alserstrasse). Canevale refers to the Classicism of the French Revolution and the extant prison architecture. This "Panopticon" – consisting of a central building with a surveillance wing – facilitated the observation of inmates. The tower now houses the Museum of Pathology. In the future, departments of the University of Vienna will be relocated to the old hospital building.

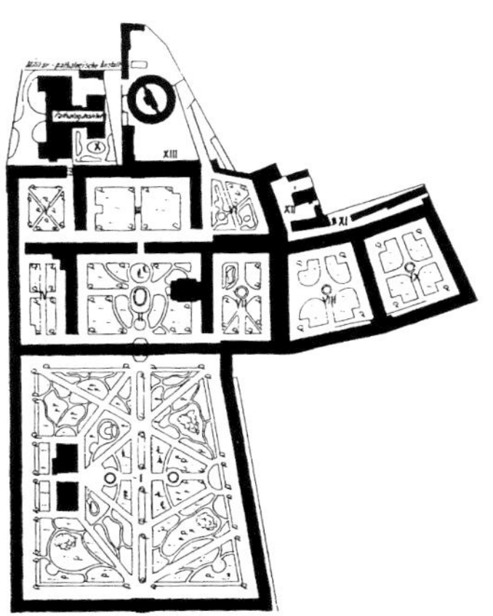

9.-**8** | *Hans Puchhammer*

Wasagasse Apartment Building 1984

Wasagasse 28,
Dietrichsteingasse
Access: Not open to public
Public transportation: Bus 40A (Bauernfeldplatz)

Built in 1847 and designed by Ölzelt, this building underwent extensive renovation under the supervision of Hans Puchhammer. The wing facing the courtyard of this typically Viennese Bassenahaus (translator's note: a house with decorative enameled basins, built in the corridors for communal use – implying a lack of running water in the individual apartments) was demolished and rebuilt, whereby two new staircases and a lift were added providing access to each double loaded wing. The unequal elevations of the wings facing the street and the courtyard result in an interesting floor plan and staggered landings.

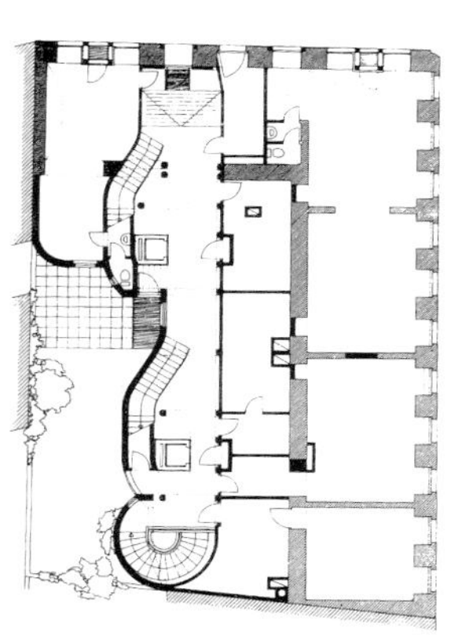

9.-**9** | *Isidor Canevale*

Josephinum (Surgical-Medical Academy) 1783

Währinger Strasse 25
Access: Open to public
Public transportation: U2, tram lines 37and 38 (Sensengasse)

The academy was built in the vicinity of the new Allgemeines Krankenhaus (General Hospital) during the health reforms undertaken by Joseph II. The French design of the cour d'honneur is rare in traditional Viennese architecture. The understated façade is also organized in French Classicist tradition. The Museum of Medical History, with its exceptional collection of wax figures used for educational purposes, is one of the institutions also located here.

Otto Wagner

9.-**10**

A chapel to St. John had to be demolished to make way for the Stadtbahn (Gürtel line). However, the Traffic Commission engaged Otto Wagner to construct a new chapel on Klammgasse, next to the viaduct over the Währingerstrasse. This small symmetrical structure with its central cupola was probably built after 1897 (ref. Otto Graf). The projecting structure attached on the side of the apsis is not by Wagner, but was added later.

Joanniskapelle
1895

Währinger Gürtel, Klammergasse
Access: By appointment
Public transportation: Tram lines 40 and 41 (Volksoper)

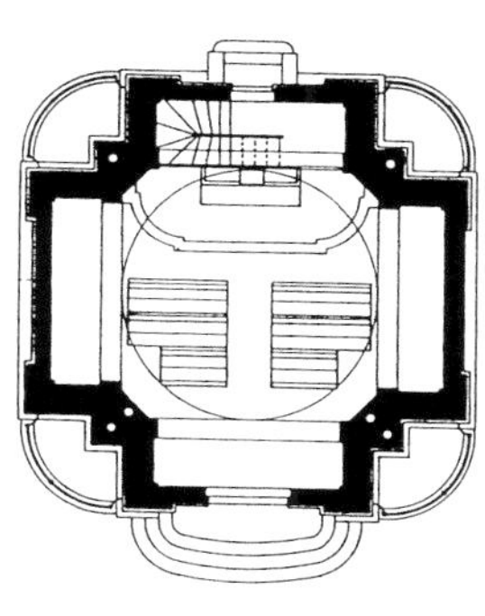

Theophil von Hansen

9.-**11**

The first residential block built for civil servants in Vienna, the Rudolfshof marks a historical step in the direction of residential buildings that were to dominate the city between the Ring and the Gürtel. An unusual aspect of Hansen's construction were the "Pavlatch" courtyards (wooden, glazed circulation galleries along the walls of the inner courtyard), which belonged to a specific Viennese architectural tradition. However, these were later sacrificed in favour of the patio in large residential buildings.

Rudolfshof
1871

Hörlgasse 15, Türkenstrasse 14, Schlickplatz 5
Access: Not open to public
Public transportation: U2 (Schottentor)

9.-**12**

Colonel Karl Pilhal, Major Karl Markl

Rossauerkaserne (Rossauer Barracks) 1865

This gigantic complex was not built by architects but by army officers as a reaction to the civil revolution of 1848. Similar to the civic armoury in the 3rd district, this too is a brickwork building. The closed structure, however, has a far more martial appearance due to its towers and battlements. It was intended to be the counterpart to the Franz-Josefs-Kaserne on Stubenring (demolished in 1898); it now serves as police barracks.

Schlickplatz
Access: Not open to public
Public transportation: Tram line D (Schottenring)

9.-**13**

C. M. Carlone, F. and C. Canevale, F. S. Rosenstingl

Servitenkirche 1651, (1667–77, 1754–56)

This church was the earliest oval centralised building in Vienna. Three stages of planning are recognisable: following the initial phase of construction by Carlo Martino Carlone in 1651–61, the church was largely completed by Franz and Carlo Canevale in 1667–77. The east towers were erected anew in the 18th century according to the plans by F.S. Rosenstingl. The longitudinal orientation of the main hall is emphasized by the elongated choir and antechamber.

Servitengasse, Grünentorgasse
Access: Open to public
Public transportation: Tram line D (Schlickgasse)

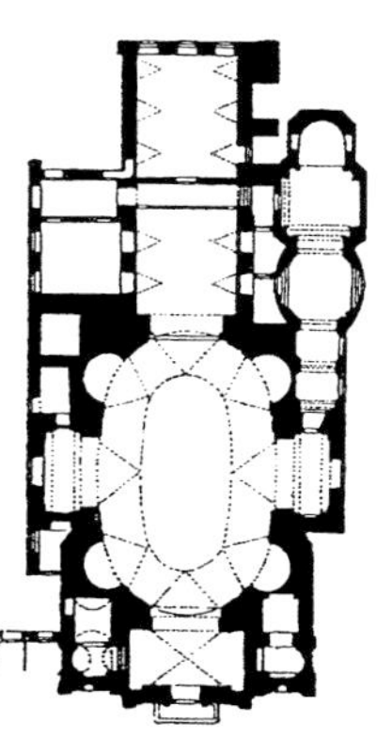

Domenico Egidio Rossi, Domenico Martinelli 9.-**14**

This garden palace was originally planned as the starting point of a baroque remodelling of the district "Lichtental" founded by Prince Johann Adam Lichtenstein. Its closed cubical organisation, however, is remarkably severe for a garden palace. The frescos are by Johann Michael Rottmayr and Andrea Pozzo and others. The main building has housed the Museum of Modern Art – Ludwig Foundation since 1979.

Garden Palais Liechtenstein (currently Museum of Modern Art) 1691, (1705–06)

Fürstengasse 2
Access: Open to public
Public transportation: Tram line D (Fürstengasse)

Theodor Jäger 9.-**15**

Friedrich Achleitner has proven beyond doubt that the flight of steps does not figure as prominently in Heimito von Doderer's novel of the same name as one tended to believe. The steps, nevertheless, are an important landmark of Vienna and make the hilliness of the area apparent. Similar to its baroque predecessors, the double flight of steps with its fountain and various platforms can make climbing stairs a conscious act.

Strudlhofstiege 1910

Strudlhofstiege
Access: Open to public
Public transportation: Tram lines 37, 38 and 40 (Sensengasse)

PVA, Old-Age Insurance Company for Workers 1955

Rossauerlände 3
Access: Not open to public
Public transportation: U4 (Rossauerlände)

Office architecture during the post war period though predominantly functionalist had an unsure look about it in the context of city planning. By orienting the y-shaped plan of the multi-storeyed part of the building toward the Danube Canal, Schuster succeeded in creating a dominant position next to the Ring Tower. The roof garden designed like a running sun-screen is a conscious reference to the architecture of the 30s.

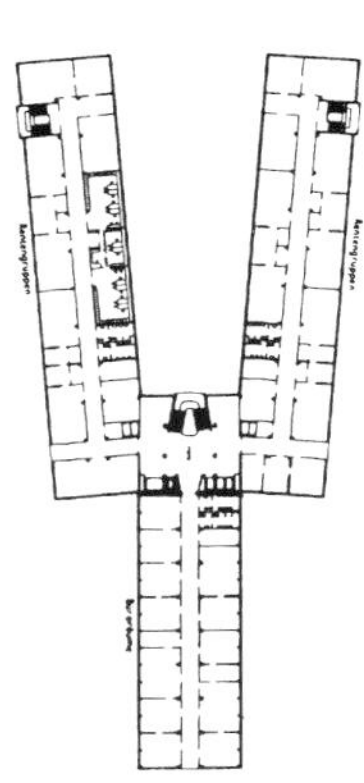

Supplementary Recommendations

4.-**8s**	Starhemberg-Schönburg Garden Palace Johann Lukas von Hildebrandt	1700 Rainergasse 11
5.-**9s**	Central Savings Bank Reinprechtsdorfer Strasse Friedrich Kurrent and Johannes Spalt	1969 Reinprechtsdorfer Strasse 8
5.-**10s**	Rüdiger Hof Oskar Marmorek	1902 Hamburgerstrasse 20
6.-**6s**	Mariahilfer Strasse Office Building Heinz Neumann	1994 Mariahilfer Strasse 123
6.-**7s**	Gumpendorfer Strasse Apartment Building Timo Penttilä	1984 Gumpendorfer Strasse, Stiegengasse
6.-**8s**	Casa Piccola Shoe Shop Boris Podrecca	1984 Mariahilfer Strasse 1b
7.-**8s**	Film House Helmut Heistinger	1994 Spittelberggasse 3
7.-**9s**	Apartment Building Günther Holnsteiner	1995 Lindengasse 16
9.-**17s**	Management Book Service Eichinger oder Knechtl	1993 Augasse 5–7
9.-**18s**	Covered Market Nussdorfer Strasse Friedrich Paul	1879 Nussdorfer Strasse 22, Kapellengasse 2–4, Alserbachstrasse 1–3
9.-**19s**	Stadtbahnstation Rossauer Lände Otto Wagner	1900 Rossauer Lände
9.-**20s**	Fernwärme (District Heating) Wien Friedensreich Hundertwasser	1990 Spittelauer Lände 43
9.-**21s**	Stadtbahnstation Alserstrasse Otto Wagner	1896 Hernalser Hauptstrasse, Hernalser Gürtel

MAP No. 4

10th District
Favoriten

10th District, Favoriten index numbers 10.-**1** … 10.-**24s**

Buildings worth visiting – Suggestions by Viennese architects:

10th District:

Maria Auböck:
Umspannwerk (Transformer Plant), Index no. 10.-**1**

Coop Himmelblau:
Bank Branch, Index no. 10.-**2**

Heidulf Gerngross:
Angeligasse Housing Complex, Index no. 10.-**7**

Eugen Kastner, Fritz Waage

Umspannwerk – Transformer Plant 1928

Humboldtgasse 1–5, Sonnwendgasse
Not open to public
Public transportation: U1 (Südtiroler Platz)

The architects consciously separated the transformer plant from the rest of the dense residential neighbourhood. Various areas for technology and administration were to be built on a triangular site. The architects confronted the block development, closed on one side, with a spatially differentiated and open structure on the opposite side. Both façades are held together by a continuous base zone and overlapping sculptural elements on the "prow" of the building. Despite this complexity the spatial division is astonishingly clear – a hall each was conceived for the three-phase, two-phase and continuous current areas.

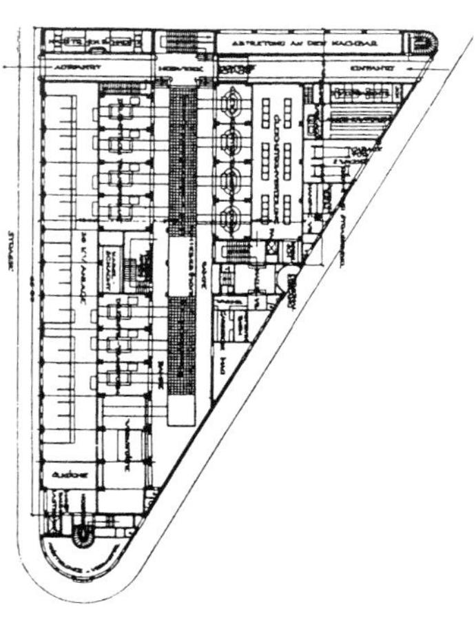

Günther Domenig ranks amongst the foremost architects of the "Graz School". This building not only brought renown and publicity to his client (Bank Austria, formerly the Zentralsparkasse – Central Savings Bank of the City of Vienna), but also provided the entire pedestrian zone with an architectural symbol of its own. This building is anti-contextual and negates any reference to history or to place. Domenig's individualistic attempt is toward the redefinition of the location. A bio-technical metaphor emerges in the interior composed of ventilation pipes, cable ducts and lighting fixtures.

Bank Branch Favoriten 1975

Favoritenstrasse 118
Access: Open to public
Public transportation: U1 (Reumannplatz)

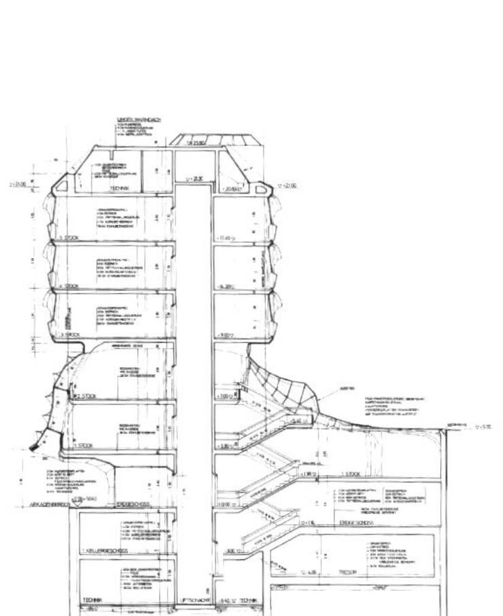

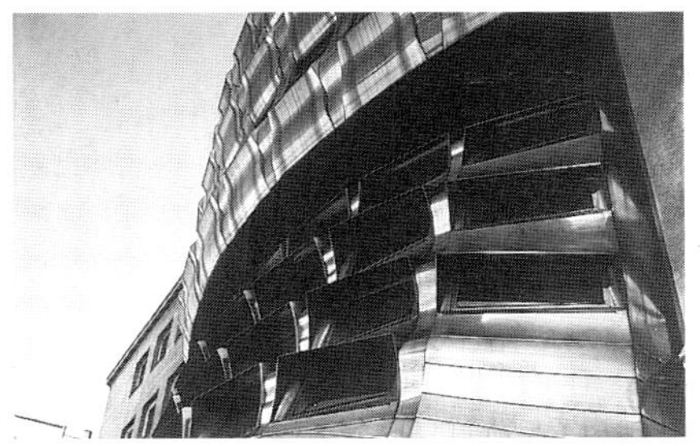

10.-**3** | *Clemens Holzmeister*

Pfarrkirche zur Heiligen Familie (The Holy Family Parish Church) 1964

Puchsbaumplatz 9
Access: Open to public
Public transportation: Tram line 6 (Absberggasse)

Clemens Holzmeister counts as one of the master church builders in the Austria of the 20th century. His buildings are characterised by a reduced Modernism and a strong element of pathos. Through the positioning of the 10 storey high church tower on the street-corner, the construction signals its dominance in the context of city planning in an otherwise unremarkable environment.

10.-**4** | *Rob Krier*

Schrankenberggasse Apartment Block 1983

Schrankenberggasse 18–20
Access: Not open to public
Public transportation: U1, tram line 6 (Absberggasse)

Built between 1983–86, this construction consists of two structures – a corner building and a central building. The metropolitan typology of the façade is in contradiction to the small divisioning of the apartments within. Krier attempts to divert attention from the reality of social housing by the classical façade and baroque forms in the floor plan. The desire for high-quality architecture is evident though the design itself has suffered from financial restrictions.

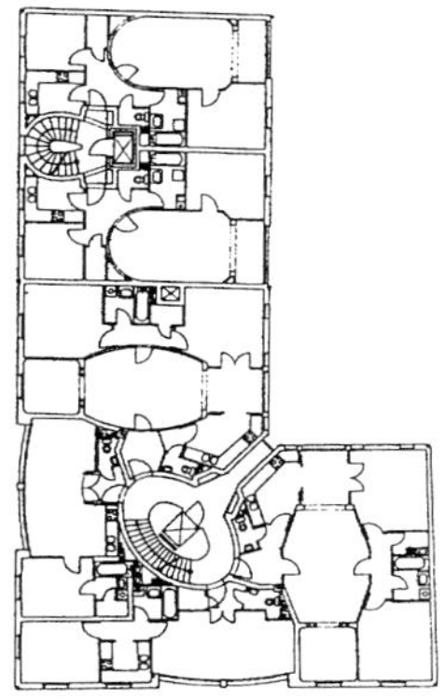

Absberggasse Secondary School 1994

Absberggasse 50
Access: By appointment
Public transportation: U1, tram line 6 (Absberggasse)

The city of Vienna's Programme 2000 for School Buildings has led to the construction of approximately 80 school buildings so far. Through the construction of the Absberggasse Secondary School, Rüdiger Lainer brought about a change of paradigms in the field of Viennese school architecture. He has interpreted the rigid regulations set by the school authorities intelligently in this project by not attempting to embellish the commonplace with expensive materials but by achieving spatial excellence through available means. The school includes 12 regular classrooms, a day care area and two gymnasiums as prescribed by the authorities.

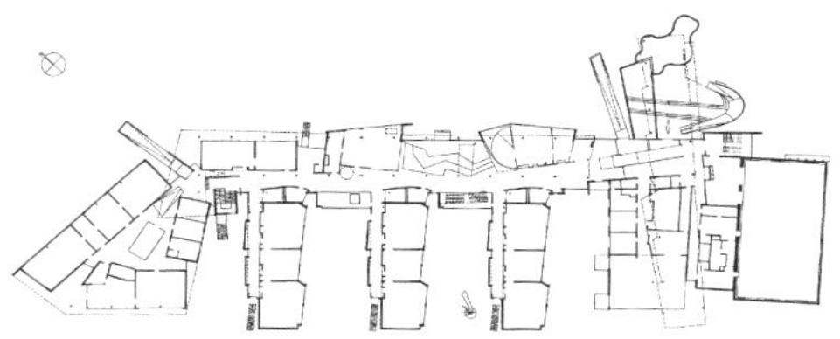

10.-6

Robert Kramreiter

Friedenskirche
1935

Quellenstrasse 197
Access: Open to public
Public transportation: U1, tram line 6 (Gellertplatz)

The uncompromising symmetry of the exterior is partially broken in the interior and is emphasized by the monumentality of the structure. Vaulted arches of various sizes are a recurrent motif in the arrangement. The relation between walls and openings is evocative of a Romanesque church. A striking feature is the echeloned structure of the façade. Depending on the position of the viewer, it lends the corner bays the appearance of towers although they do not actually exceed the height of the eaves of the nave.

10.-7

Harry Glück and Partner (W. Höfer, R. Neyer, T. Spychala)

Inzersdorfer Strasse – Angeligasse Housing Complex
1971

Hardtmuthgasse,
Zur Spinnerin, Inzersdorfer Strasse 113, Gussriegelstrasse
Access: Not open to public
Public transportation: Tram line 65 (Davidgasse)

The housing association "Junge Generation" (Young Generation) attempted in the 70s to revise the old pattern of social housing. The terraced apartments were allotted generous open spaces and the "urban luxury" of a swimming pool on the roof. This luxury was made possible through a particularly economical floor-plan (central corridor circulation) and pre-fabricated construction. The 222 apartment complex follows a block pattern, but breaks with the typology of the perimeter block.
The largest terraced apartment buildings of this kind are: the Alt Erlaa residential towers, 23rd district, Anton Baumgartnerstrasse, Vienna.

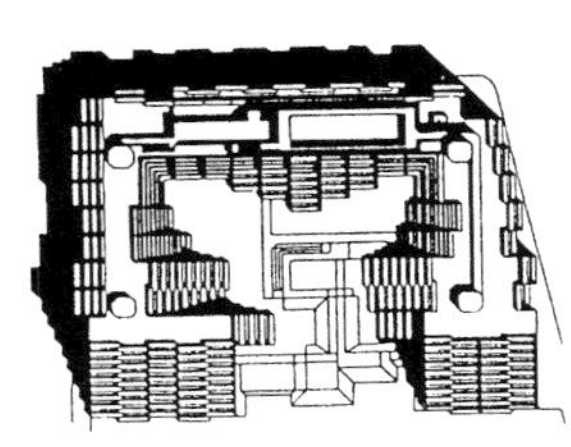

Amalienbad (Amalien Baths) 1923

The Amalienbad was an attempt to supplement the municipal development projects in Vienna and was intended to promote the health and well-being of the working classes. In addition to the "Tröpferlbad" (public sitz baths), there were steam baths and a swimming pool with natural lighting. It is one of the most beautiful indoor swimming-pools in Vienna and is remarkable for its partially original fittings and interior decor. Extensive renovations have brought the Amalienbad back to its full grandeur.

Reumannplatz 9
Access: Open to public
Public transportation: U1 (Reumannplatz)

10.-**9** | ***Siegfried Theiss, Hans Jaksch***

Quarin-Hof
1923

Appearing like a closed structure on the outside, the detailed decor of this inward facing complex is concentrated around the inner courtyard. The southern side of the five-storeyed complex is interrupted by a gateway.

Quaringasse 10–12,
Braunspergengasse,
Zur Spinnerin
Access: Not open to public
Public transportation: Tram line 65 (Windtenstrasse)

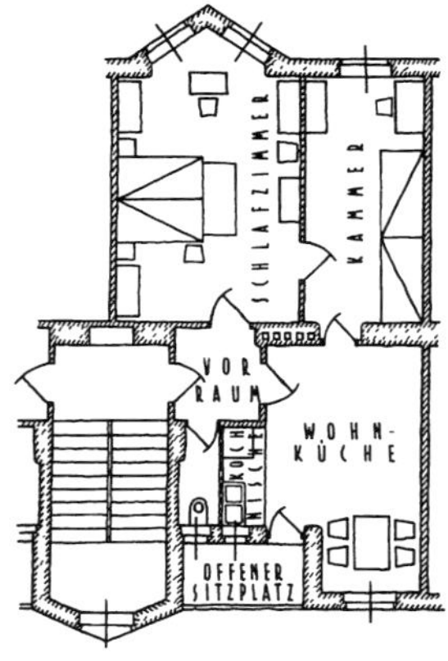

10.-**10** | ***Atelier 4 – K. P. Erblich, Z. Vesselinov, M. Hirschler et al.***

Business Park Vienna
1990

The Business Park Vienna, constructed by the Wienerberger Real-Estate Corporation, is a new office centre that has meanwhile changed hands. Office centres are symbols of financial and economic prosperity. The flexible and technically well-equipped offices are available in the lower building as well as in the 22 storeyed high-rise with a restaurant on the top floor. The shopping area on the ground floor corresponds to the usual standards expected of such service areas, and offered in all larger cities.

Wienerbergstrasse 11
Access: Shops open to public, viewing of offices by appointment
Public transportation: Tram line 65 (Windtenstrasse)

George Washington Estate 1927

This estate is one of the largest of its kind in Vienna and typologically can be said to belong to the typically solemn super blocks. The characteristic bathos is mellowed by the provincial details in the form of gateways, turrets and oriels. The enclosed courtyards were designed by Robert Oerley, while the more open structure facing Triesterstrasse is the work of Karl Krist. Different species of trees were planted in each of the courtyards.

Wienerbergstrasse, Untere Meidlinger Strasse, Kastanienallee
Access: Only open areas
Public transportation: Tram line 65 (Windtenstrasse)

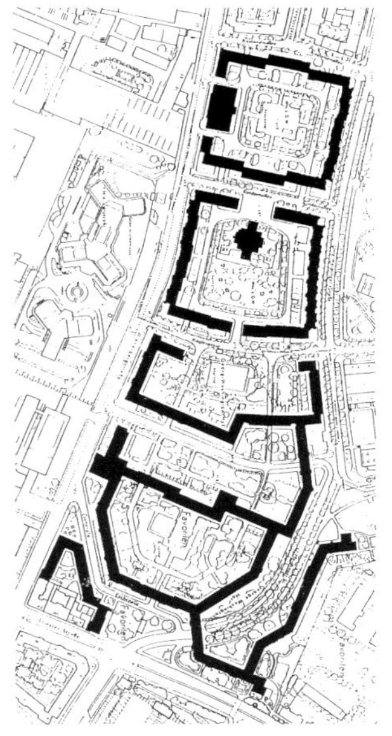

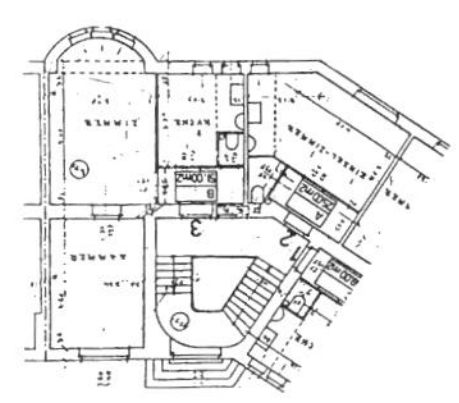

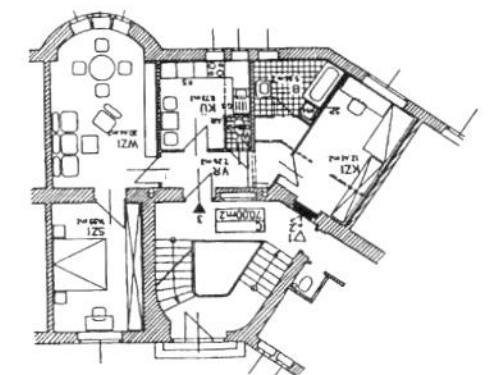

10.-**12** | *Karl Schwanzer*

Philips-Haus
1962

Triester Strasse 64–66
Access: Not open to public
Public transportation: Tram line 65 (Windtenstrasse)

An inofficial landmark of Vienna since 1963, the Philips building stands on the heights of the Wienerberg, at one of the most sensitive corners of the city – on the southbound main road (Trieste Federal Highway). Its reinforced concrete structure, protruding on either side (Robert Krapfenbauer, Dykerhoff and Widtmann were responsible for the statics), greets all visitors approaching Vienna from the South. The neighbouring high rise Business Park (1994) has undermined its original significance considerably.

10.-**13** | *Hans Prutscher*

Karmeliterkirche
1928

Stefan-Fadinger-Platz 1
Access: Open to public
Public transportation: Tram line 65 (Stefan-Fadinger-Platz)

Hans Prutscher questions traditional church architecture very minutely here. The building fulfills all the requirements of sacred architecture: a twin-tower façade, a rhythmic succession of yokes and an apse in the interior. The details, however, are still original though the building was badly damaged during the Second World War. The reconstruction of the church is a reflection of the "Zeitgeist" of the 50s.

Franz Schuster, Franz Schacherl

10.-**14**

Schuster and Schacherl placed the development on the outer edge of the irregular site, while the gardens were laid out casually along the external accesses in the enclosed area thus created. The houses of the estate bear witness to Franz Schuster's cooperation with Heinrich Tessenow through the controlled approach to form and material. Only a handful of the row-houses are preserved in their original state today.

Am Wasserturm Housing Estate 1924

Raxstrasse, Windtenstrasse, Weitmosergasse, Altdorferstrasse
Access: Not open to public
Public transportation: Tram line 65 (Windtenstrasse)

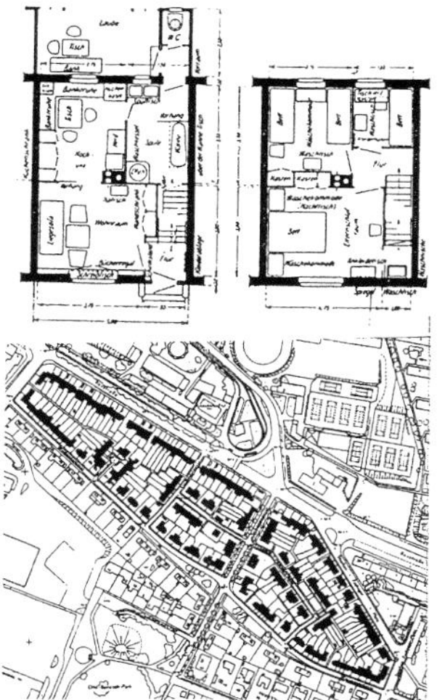

F. Schuster, F. Pangratz, S. Simony, E. Wörle

10.-**15**

Named after the Prime Minister of Sweden Per Albin Hanson, who made the building possible through her "Swedish Aid" programme, this residential complex is a reflection of the true conditions following the war. With a small variety of windows and identical sloping roofs it mirrors the council housing approach of the early 20s. The primary school is by Hermann Stiegholzer (1949), the "Volkshaus" by Franz Schuster (1954–55) and the kindergarten by Maria Tölzer.

Per-Albin-Hanson Housing Estate West 1947

Favoritenstrasse, Selma-Lagerlöf-Gasse, Pichelmayergasse
Access: Only open areas
Public transportation: Tram line 67 (Alaudagasse)

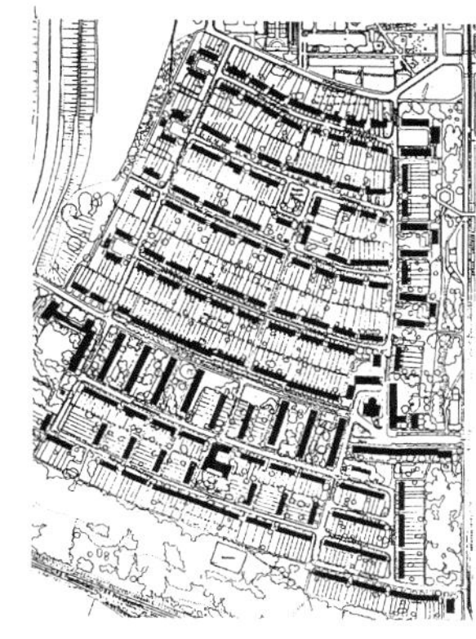

The Wienerberg Residential Complex 1978

Otto-Probst-Platz, Otto-Probst-Strasse, Hugo-Meisl-Weg, Tesarekplatz
Access: Not open to public
Public transportation: Tram line 67 (Otto-Probst-Strasse)

The Wienerberg residential complex situated in southern Vienna was built by Otto Häuselmayer, who won a two-stage architectural competition in 1978. His prize-winning project and plans were executed in three stages. Over 2000 apartments, a church, a primary school, a kindergarten as well as a shopping centre were constructed by several builders and architects. Residential blocks, row houses and villas are grouped along a Z-shaped main access street. These form an urban weave like a carpet and are within walking distance of each other.

The complex was realised within a span of over 17 years. The first stage of construction was commenced in 1981 involving over twenty architects. The houses, constituted of a maximum of four storeys, are incorporated in the partially protected landscape. The buildings by Otto Häuselmayer, Rudolf Lamprecht, Günther Oberhofer, Gustav Peichl, Otto Steidle, Helmut Wimmer and Heinz Tesar are particularly noteworthy (see legend).

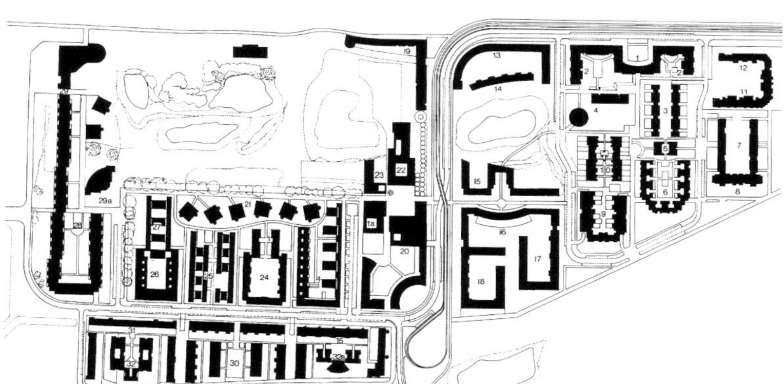

1/1a	Otto Häuselmayer (Housing, Church)
2	Sepp Frank Heinz Neumann
3	Manfred Nehrer
4	Norbert Gantar Friedrich Waclawek (Children's Day Care Centre)
5	Erich Bramhas
6	Karlheinz Gruber Stefan Bukovac
7	Kurt Hlaweniczka Thomas Reinthaller Franz Requat Erich Traxler
8	Elise Sundt
9	Heinz Lemberger
10	Gerhard Kroj
11	Hugo Potyka
12	Rainer Mayerhofer
13	Josef Hinterhölzl
14	Rudolf Lamprecht Pauline Muchar
15	Herbert Prehsler
16	Richard Hübschmann
17	Georg Lisner
18	Günter Krisch
19	Karl Leber Heinrich Matha
20	Helmut Wimmer
21/22	Gustav Peichl (Housing, School)
23	Heinz Tesar (Children's Day Care Centre)
24	Werner Obermann
25	Günther Oberhofer
26	Otto Steidle
27	Harry Glück
28	Edgar Göth
28a	Edgar Göth (Children's Day Care Centre)
29	Engelbert Eder Rudolf Weber
30	Walter Lagler
31/31a	Project Building

Tesarekplatz Church, School and Crèche 1992

Tesarekplatz
Access: Open to public during church services, by appointment
Public transportation: U1, tram line 67 (Tesarekplatz)

Tesarekplatz is the cultural centre of the Wienerberg Estate. Häuselmayer's church is typologically a basilica. A transom band runs between the steel framework and the screen, accentuating the difference between the non-supporting wall and the constructive pillars. The primary school by Peichl forms the north end of the complex; a white structure with a vaulted centre and an arched roof cover the classrooms in the outer wings. The crèche, built by Tesar, was consciously planned as the smallest structure in proportion to the houses around it.

Salvatorkirche am Wienerfeld 1976

Surrounded as it is by otherwise monotonous architecture, the Salvator Church succeeds in creating an atmosphere of calm and contemplation. Under the roof, a varied wooden framework unfolds itself along a longitudinal axis, lending the building a stringent modular character while at the same time leaving it pleasantly subdued. The lighting is extremely subtle. The interior contains a tryptich by Herbert Boeckl. Spalt fully incorporated the surroundings in the planning of the structure.

Neilreichgasse, Hetzkaplatz
Access: Open to public
Public transportation: Tram line 67 (Frödenplatz)

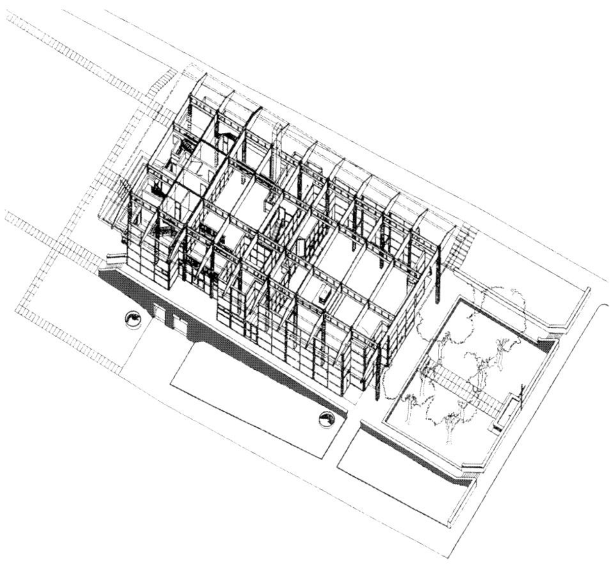

Students' Hostel 1992

Erlachplatz,
Van der Nüll Gasse 26–28
Access: Not open to public
Public transportation: U1
then Bus 14A (Erlachplatz)

One of the major differences between a students' hostel and a hotel lies in the communication between the inhabitants. Unfortunately, most hostels are treated today like hotels. Schweighofer, however, emphasizes the necessity of communication. He keeps the students' "cells" consciously small in order to focus on the qualities of communication in the common areas. These again are so small that communication between the residents becomes unavoidable. The hostel remains a well conceived model – with all the advantages and disadvantages.

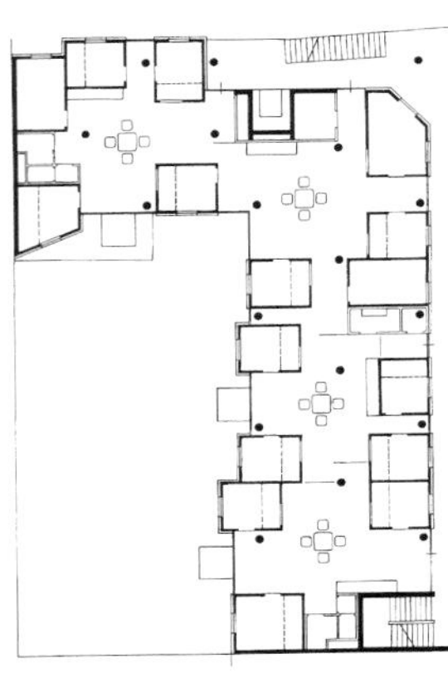

Supplementary Recommendations

10.-**20s**	Städtisches Ökohaus Günther Lautner, Peter Scheifinger, Rudolf Szedenik, Cornelia Schindler	1995 Puchsbaumplatz 15
10.-**21s**	Evangelical Cemetery Church Theophil von Hansen	1857 Triesterstrasse, Gudrunstrasse
10.-**22s**	Kundratstrasse Montagekirche Ottokar Uhl	1963 Kundratstrasse next to 17
10.-**23s**	Twin-Primary School Jagdgasse Manfred Nehrer, Reinhard Medek	1992 Jagdgasse 22
10.-**24s**	Spinnerin am Kreuz Hans Puchspaum	1451 Triester Strasse next to 52

Buildings worth visiting – Suggestions by Viennese architects

11th District:

Hermann Czech:
Simmeringer Haide Estate, index no. 11.-**11**

Dietmar Steiner:
Alberner Hafen (silos)

Manfred Wehdorn:
Lueger Church, Main Cemetery (as a parallel to Steinhof), index no. 11.-**6**

11.-**1** | *Franz Kapaun*

Simmering Gasometers 1896

No other building dominates the south-east entry to Vienna giving it an urban character like the gasometers in Simmering. Only four of the original complex remain today. These cylindrical brickwork structures are grouped in pairs and form an echelon toward the city giving them a town planning relevance. The outer wall of the buildings, while concealing the technological world within, is also capable of revealing it on the exterior. The gasometers will be adapted to contain apartments, students' hostels and shops in the near future.

Simmeringer Haide, Guglgasse, Döblerhofstrasse
Access: Not open to public
Public transportation: U3, bus 80A (Modecenterstrasse)

11.-**2** | *Hermann Czech with Wolfgang Reder*

Rosa Jochmann School 1991

The diversity of this school is mainly on the levels of semantics, design and interpretation. It is a building on second glance as Hermann Czech himself says: "This building is the most conventional school of Vienna. I have accepted the constrictions - painlessly. Only an open school would be fit for children — a school in which the acquisition of knowledge was more focused – like work on a farm".

Fuchröhrenstrasse 21-25
Access: by appointment
Public transportation: Tram lines 71 and 72 (Geysstrasse)

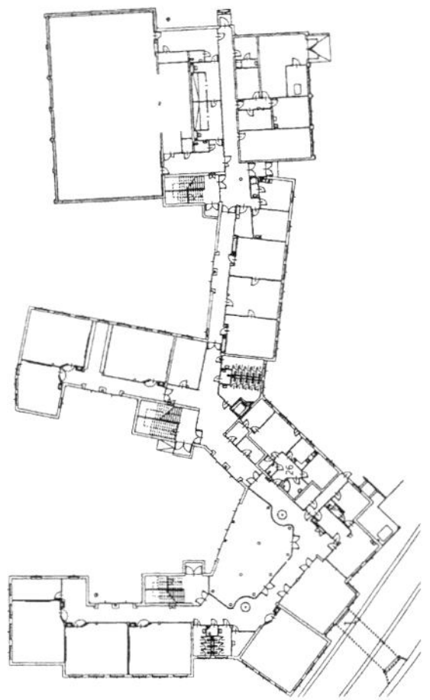

Evangelical Church 1962

The site is in a commercial and industrial area of Simmering and for this reason the approach to the church is via a semi-public atrium, which is also the access for the community centre. The lighting and the use of an abstracted symbol of the cross contribute to the contemplative aura of the high interior. The white washed lattice of the reinforced concrete framework forms the cross along the sides of the interior. A lighted cross spans the entire wall above the glazed area behind the altar.

Braunhubergasse 20
Access: Open to public
Public transportation: Tram lines 71 and 72 (Weissenböckstrasse)

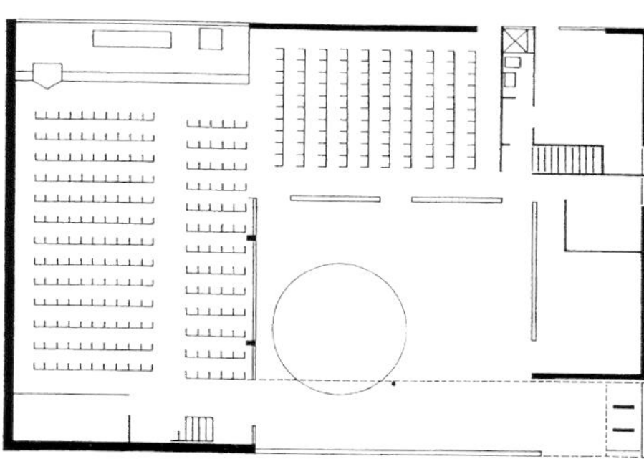

Franz Kaym, Alfons Hetmanek 11.-4

Weissenböck Estate 1922

The estate was built in two phases and also presents two different approaches. The earlier part consists of narrow row-houses with attached large gardens for self-sufficiency. The green areas were later reduced in size and a denser development resulted. The buildings of the next phase are detatched and consist of four apartments each, which are grouped around a central square with trees.

Simmeringer Hauptstrasse, Weissenböckstrasse, Wilhelm-Kress Platz
Access: Only open areas accessible
Public transportation: Tram lines 71 and 72 (Weissenböckstrasse)

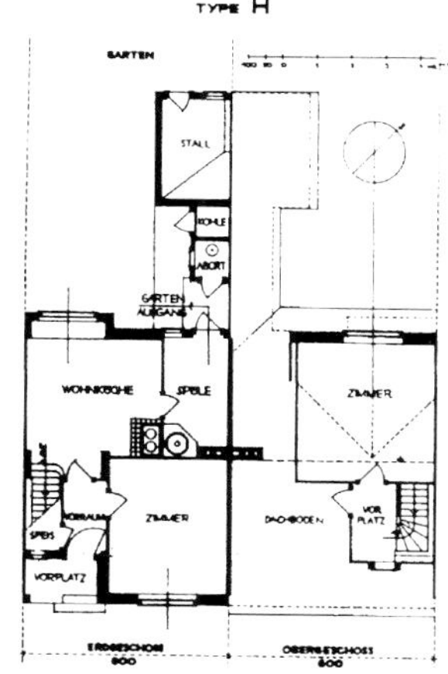

11.-5

Colin, Spranger, Jacopo da Strada, Pietro Ferrabosco

Neugebäude
1569

Simmeringer Hauptstrasse 337, Neugebäudestrasse
Access: Not open to public
Public transportation: Tram lines 71 and 72 (Zentralfriedhof – 2nd gate)

The hunting lodge for Maximillian II was built 1569 onwards close to the game stock in the woods along the Danube. Not much remains of the splendid terraced gardens today. During the reign of Maria Theresia the grounds were used as a depot for gun powder. Parts of the Renaissance palace were used to build the Schönbrunn palace, in particular the Gloriette. The palace was integrated into the Zentralfriedhof (Main Cemetery) grounds in the 19th century.

11.-6

Karl J. Mylius and Alfred F. Bluntschli, Max Hegele

Zentralfriedhof, Lueger Gedächtnis Kirche (Main Cemetery, Lueger Memorial Church)
1870,1908

Simmeringer Hauptstrasse 337
Access: Not open to public
Public transportation: Tram lines 71 and 72 (Zentralfriedhof)

The Central Cemetery was opened in 1874 and expanded for the first time at the turn of the century. The Hasenauer student Max Hegele won the competition in 1900 and was commissioned to build the 2nd gate and the mortuary as well as the Dr. Karl Lueger Memorial Church. Apart from the heavy application of Jugendstil elements, Hegele was also inspired by Historicism. Extraordinary from the typological point of view is the placing of the twin towers of the central building on to the rear façade. The gateway, on the other hand, is coordinated more organically. On the whole the structure manages to convey the required hallowed atmosphere.

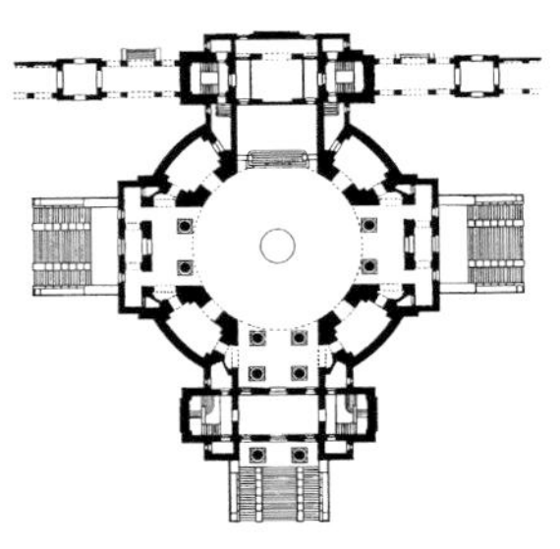

The crematorium lies within a walled-in region that originally belonged to the grounds of the Neugebäude. Although Holzmeister's project was only placed third in the competition, it was nevertheless accepted because it was by consensus considered to best maintain the historical substance of the Neugebäude. Holzmeister incorporated the crematorium and the adjoining arcades while retaining the original axis of the grounds. Holzmeister fulfilled the requirements of the construction (consecrated space, cremation facility) by using an expressionistic vocabulary of forms. The building was expanded by the architect in 1965–69.

Krematorium
1921

Simmeringer Hauptstrasse 337
Access: Open to public
Public transportation: Tram lines 71 and 72 (Zentralfriedhof)

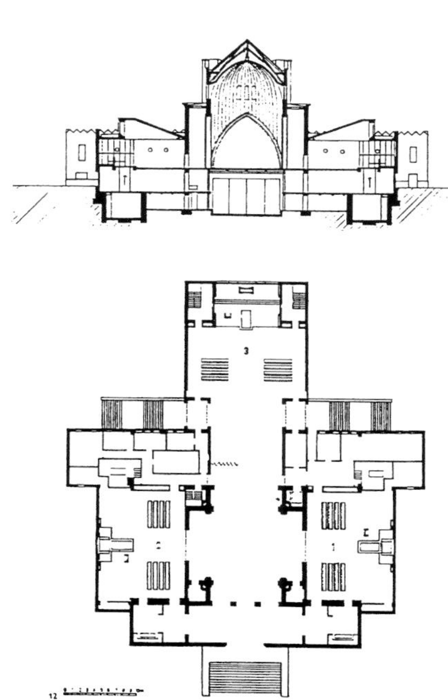

11.-**8** | *M. Cufer, O. Hasler, W. Stelzhammer, et al.*

Leberberg Housing Estate (North) 1994

Rosa Jochmann Ring
Access: Not open to public
Public transportation: Tram line 71 (Leberberg)

The pressure of the new housing offensive in Vienna gave rise to this suburban estate at the beginning of the 90s. It was based upon an already existing development concept from the 70s and consisted of approximately 4,000 apartments. Especially noteworthy is the residential building by Walter Stelzhammer, as well as the one by Margarethe Cufer and Othmar Hasler with its integrated child-care centre. Located close by is the new spiritual welfare centre with the St. Benedikt church (Wolfgang Zehetner, Hans Walter Michl, Walter Zschokke).

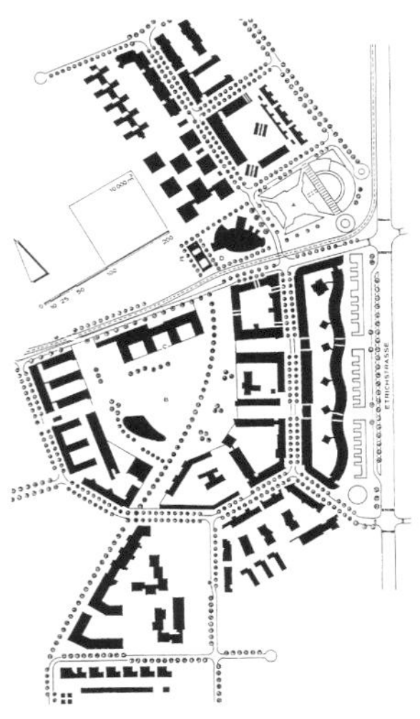

11.-**9** | *Spiegelfeld/Holnsteiner, Janowetz/Wagner, Sarnitz et al.*

Leberberg Housing Estate (South) 1994

Reimmichelgasse
Access: Not open to public
Public transportation: Tram line 71 (Leberberg)

The estate was built along Rosa Jochmann Ring, south of the large park, with residential buildings by Spiegelfeld/Holnsteiner, Janowetz/Wagner, Heidecker/Neuhauser/Zwingl, August Sarnitz and Blazica/ Spinadel and a kindergarten by Othmar Hasler. The original development plans were altered and the building of the varied structures was coordinated by the Werkstatt Wien. The complex consists of public passageways and individual free-standing structures. The residential complex by Schwalm-Theiss, who optically differentiates the linear, one to three storey buildings through vivid colorations, is located further south.

The largest school built as a part of Vienna's "School Building Programme 2000" is situated in the heart of the "Leberberg" housing development. Designed to accommodate 750 students, it consists of 13 classrooms for primary school, 12 classrooms for secondary and day school each, three adjoining gymnasiums and a dining hall. The architects chose reinforced concrete construction with a glass enclosure, the structure of which suggests great precision. At the same time, however, it contrasts the playful vivacity of children with a pragmatic Cartesian grid.

Svetelskystrasse Primary and Secondary School 1994

Svetelskystrasse 4–6
Access: By appointment
Public transportation: Tram line 71 (Leberberg)

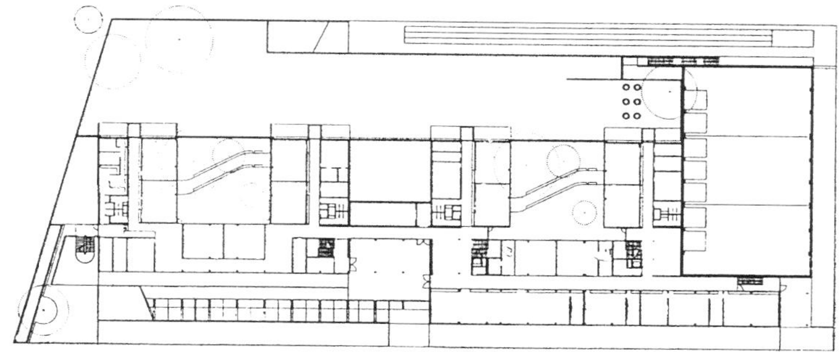

Schmidgunstgasse 1991

Schmidgunstgasse 61
Access: Not open to public
Public transportation: Tram line 71 (Zinnergasse)

Dense low-rise and row house developments have only a modest tradition in Vienna. A type of courtyard building was developed in the vicinity of the Leberberg housing estate, offering the inhabitants both a semi-urban density as well as a garden. The curved frontage of the buildings opens a surprising array of perspectives of the exterior. The individual buildings themselves have a U-form and a central access, thus creating a small private courtyard and an open garden.

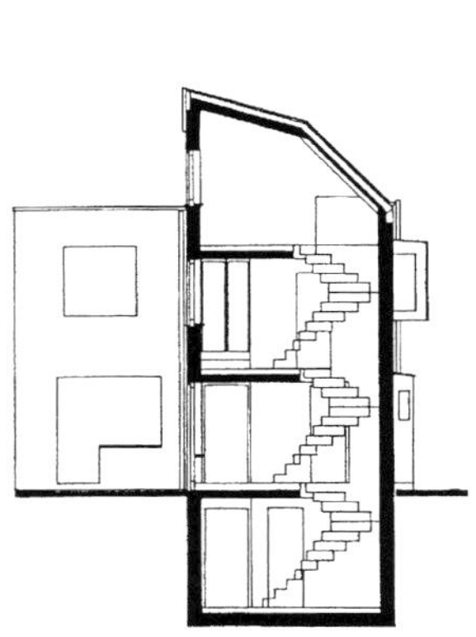

Supplementary Recommendations

11.-**12s** Kindergarten
Margarete Schütte-Lihotzky
1968
Rinnböckstrasse 47

11.-**13s** The Mautner-Markhof factory
1850
Simmeringer Hauptstrasse 101

Buildings worth visiting – Suggestions by Viennese architects

12th District:

August Sarnitz:

Walks: Hoffingergasse Estates, Index no. 12.-**6**
Walks: Rosenhügel Kleingartensiedlung (garden estate) Index no. 12.-**10**

12.-**1** | *Josef Frank*

Leopoldine-Glöckel-Hof 1931

Josef Frank brought life into the closed corner block by giving the façade a subtle colour scheme. This led to the municipal housing complex being called "Aquarell-Hof". The individual character of this otherwise simply structured building was lost when its colouring was ignored during renovation.

Steinbauergasse, Gaudenzdorfer Gürtel, Herthergasse, Siebertgasse
Access: Only open areas
Public transportation: Tram lines 6 and 18 (Margareten-gürtel/Arbeitergasse)

12.-**2** | *Karl Ehn*

Bebel-Hof 1925

This superblock cannot be said to be as clear a form of socialist "self-representation" by the architect, as for example his Karl-Marx-Hof. Ehn rejects the inclusion of "literary" allusions in favour of the dynamism conveyed by balconies and windows that enclose the corners. The residential towers, set deep into the block emphasize the corners of the building, while the rounded tower stresses the central axis. A row of shops along the ground floor of the main façade also serves as a terrace.

Steinbauergasse, Aßmayergasse, Klährgasse, Längenfeldgasse
Access: Not open to public
Public transportation: U4, U6 (Längenfeldgasse)

Walter Stelzhammer

12.-**3**

Building on a gap-site requires considerable innovation, restrictions of site present a challenge, particularly when high-quality apartments are to be planned. Stelzhammer, however, succeeded in designing 19 excellent apartments despite the narrow courtyard. A succession of arches unifies the street front, while the courtyard is organised through trellises, balustrades and by foot bridges connecting the living areas. "A varied light and spatial concept led to high quality apartments even on this narrow site. This is made possible by means of split level apartments, a pergola along the courtyard façade and spatial expansion through the trellis along the fire wall" (Dietmar Steiner).

Mandlgasse Apartment Building 1990

Mandlgasse 25–27
Access: Not open to public
Public transportation: U6 (Niederhofstrasse)

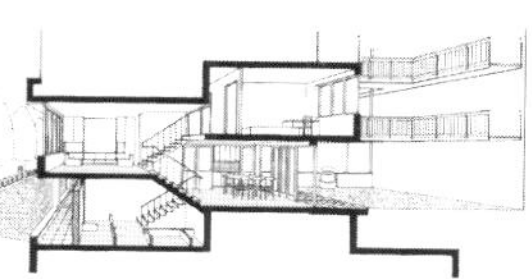

Wilhelm Flattich

12.-**4**

The residential buildings in Eichenstrasse are unique examples of workers' housing in Vienna. The brickwork, in particular, is evocative of English housing of this kind. In spite of its relatively small structure, this functional housing along the southern railway is reminiscent of monumental industrial architecture.

Workers' Housing of the Southern Railway Company 1870

Eichenstrasse 5–21
Access: Not open to public
Public transportation: U6 (Philadelphiabrücke)

12.-**5** | *Gustav Peichl*

Meidling Rehabilitation Centre 1966

Untermeidlinger Strasse 26-28, Kundratstrasse
Access: Not open to public
Public transportation: U4, bus 10A (UKH-Meidling)

The rehabilitation centre for brain-damaged patients was built in Meidling according to the plans of Dr. Mifka, who is a specialist for nervous disorders. The entire star-shaped building is a prefabricated structure made of reinforced concrete. It contains a unit with 52 beds and associated research, rehabilitation and occupational therapy facilities. There is a large terrace on each floor for patients and visitors.

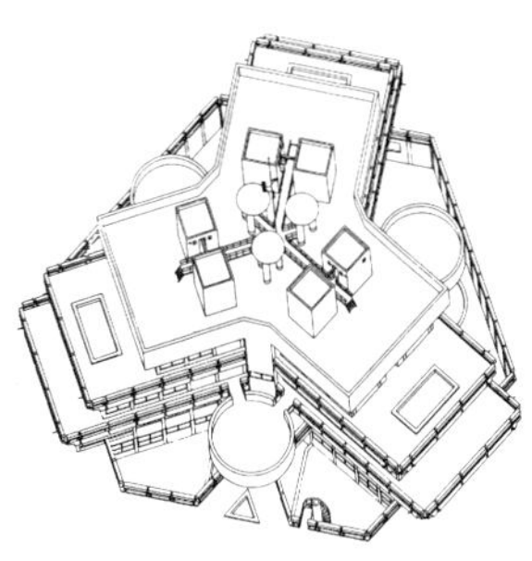

12.-**6** | *Josef Frank with Erich Faber*

Hoffingergasse Housing Estate 1921

Hoffingergasse, Stegmayergasse, Elsniggasse, Sonnergasse, Schneiderhangasse
Access: Only open areas
Public transportation: Tram line 62 (Altmannsdorfer Strasse)

This building is a reflection of Frank's refusal to accept any exterior constrictions imposed on him. All the houses are equipped with a small garden and are essentially built along an east-west axis. The architect reacts to deviations in the layout of the roads by changing the axis of the houses. An additional opening up of the development is achieved through the layout of the Oswaldgasse avenue. Most plots have a small garden house in addition to the residential unit. The inhabitants of the estate were required to contribute 2000 hours of work on the construction site.

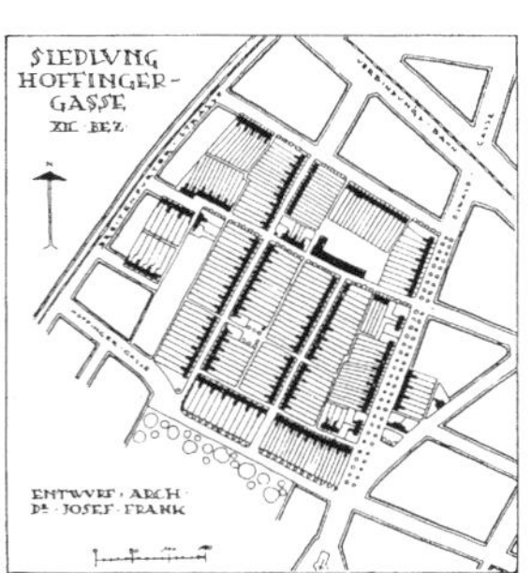

Rüdiger Lainer, Gertraud Auer

12.-**7**

A new corner block at the intersection of Hetzendorfer Strasse and Rothenburgstrasse was built jointly by the Werkstatt Wien (Günther Holnsteiner, Markus Spiegelfeld) and Rüdiger Lainer for a common building corporation. Lainer and Auer divided the 22 apartments into 2 blocks, which are connected by a bridge and are accessed through a common staircase. Layering and modelling of the outer wall led to a sculptural interplay between flat surfaces and cubical forms. The well-defined colouring of both the houses lend them a high degree of individuality.

Apartment Building
1993

Rothenburgstrasse 2
Access: Not open to public
Public transportation: Tram line 62 (Altmannsdorfer Strasse)

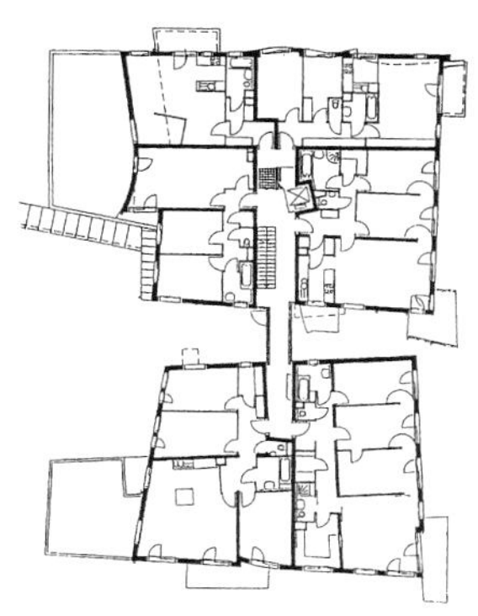

V. Hufnagl, T. and W. Windbrechtinger et al.

12.-**8**

Built at the end of the 60s, the 2,151 apartment housing estate "Am Schöpfwerk" was an attempt to react to the mistakes of the 50s. On the basis of a critical exhibition put together for the Austrian Society of Architecture by Hufnagl and Windbrechtinger, the architects sought to reformulate the subject of Viennese housing complexes of the inter-war period. A variety of apartments (terraced, maisonette, split-level) and a combination of public services were planned to create a new urban form. Architects: V. Hufnagl, E. Bauer, L. Parenzan, J. Peters, M. Pribitzer, F. Waclawek, T. and W. Windbrechtinger.

Am Schöpfwerk
Housing Estate
1967

Am Schöpfwerk,
Lichtensterngasse,
Zanschkagasse
Access: Not open to public
Public transportation: U6 (Am Schöpfwerk)

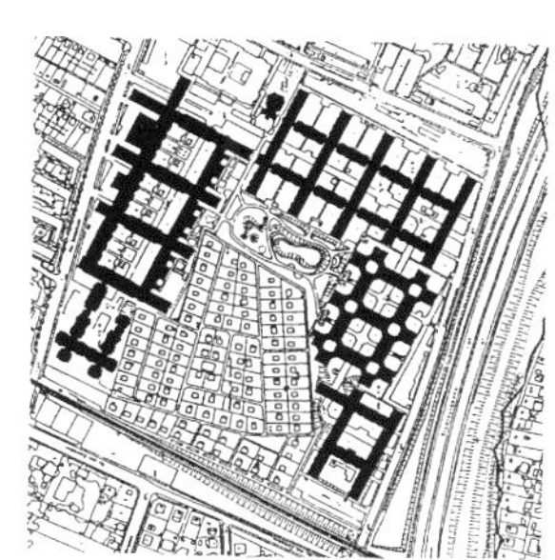

12.-**9** | ***Manfred Nehrer and Reinhard Medek***

Rohrwassergasse School 1993

Rohrwassergasse 2/
Margarete Seemann Weg 1
Access: By appointment
Public transportation: Tram line 62 (Schloss Hetzendorf)

The Rohrwassergasse School belongs to the category of hall schools. The original concept, however, was not to build a school that would be open all day. The core of the school is a well-lit, two-storeyed hall with a visible, trapezium sheet metal and steel roof: a homey and well-proportioned space, it allows the students to identify with "their" school.

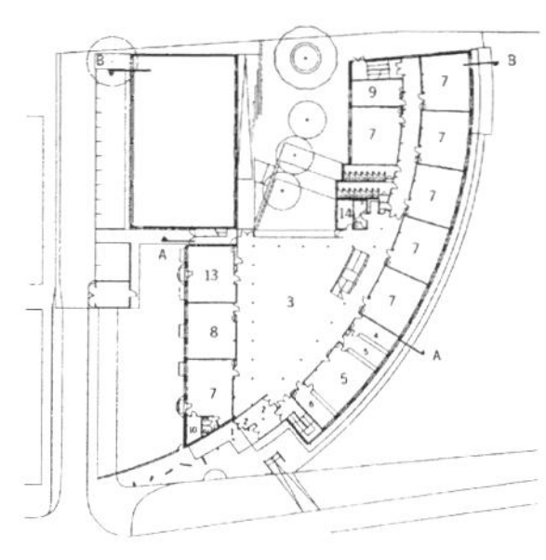

12.-**10** | ***Hugo Mayer, Emil Krause***

Rosenhügel Garden Estate 1921

Atzgersdorfer Strasse, Defreggerstrasse, Endergasse, Rosenhügelstrasse
Access: Only open areas
Public transportation: Tram line 62 (Atzgersdorfer Strasse)

The 543 house estate was built by the society "Pioneers of Rosenhügel" and was one of the largest self-sufficient estates of its kind in Vienna. Its varied construction consists of 5 types of ground plans with 16 variations, with a constant garden size of 350 m^2. The estate is modelled after the English garden cities, though the immediate reference is Hannes Meyer's Friedhofssiedlung in Basle. The adjoining society building was destroyed by fire in 1968.

Boris Podrecca

12.-**11**

Public Square Design in Meidling
1989; 1995

Pedestrian zones attempt to win back space for pedestrians and shoppers in traffic-congested city centres. They are an economic and political necessity in the face of the increasing pressure exerted by the many shopping centres on city peripheries. The redesign of the Meidlinger Hauptstrasse pedestrian zone is exemplary for the way it has again lent the district an urban flair, and is not merely an attempt to beautify or atone for the loss of urban space.

Meidlinger Hauptstrasse pedestrian zone
Access: Open to public
Public transportation: U4 (Meidling Hauptstrasse)

Josef Paul Kleihues, N. Hensel, W. Höfer, K. Becker

12.-**12**

Rollingergasse
1985

In this 180 unit housing complex, Kleihues refers to one of the main contributions of social utopia – the Familistère (1859 onwards) by Jean Baptist Godin (1817–88) – where the access is through a glass-roofed atrium. Such atrium courtyards were to symbolize community, family and solidarity and have thus become the basic semantic creed of fundamental socialism. The individual apartments are in keeping with social housing standards, where atria mutate to oversized circulation halls. Characteristic elements of design had to be sacrificed due to economic restraints.

Rollingergasse 16–20
Access: Not open to public
Public transportation: U4, bus 15A (Ruckergasse)

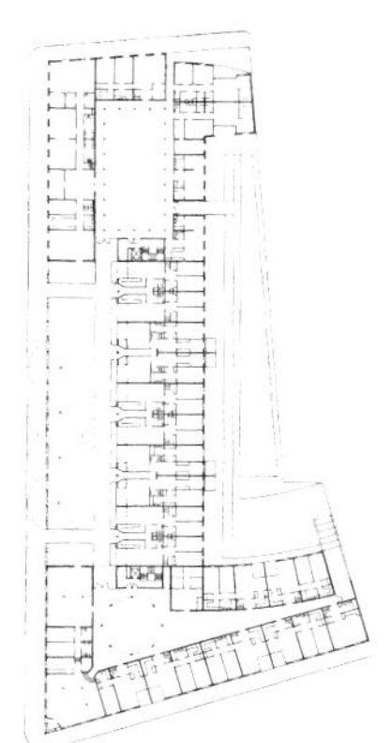

Michael Schluder and Hanns Kastner

Altmannsdorf Garden Hotel 1994

Hoffingergasse 26–28
Access: Open to public
Public transportation: Tram line 62 (Altmannsdorfer Strasse)

New hotels in Vienna attempt to uphold the expectations of the guests, whereby the traditional image of Vienna has priority over other considerations. Seen in this context, the refurbishment of the Altmannsdorf Garden Hotel appears to be a pleasant exception. The design of the hotel rooms, their fittings and the accesses have been given individual attention, forming an agreeable contrast to the monotonous uniformity of international hotel chains. The numerous views and lines of sight react to the layout of the gardens. Colour scheme by Oskar Putz, statics by Oskar Graf. The site has had a varied past: an Augustinian cloister stood here in the 14th century, the Frankl residence since 1819, the Karl-Renner-Institute since 1976 and a hotel since 1981.

Supplementary Recommendations

12.-**14s**	Rosenkranzkirche Hetzendorf (Rosary Church), Interior decoration Friedrich Achleitner, Georg Gsteu	1956 Marschallplatz
12.-**15s**	Hetzendorf Kindergarten Johann Georg Gsteu	1968 Marschallplatz 6
12.-**16s**	Stadtbahn bridge over the Zeile (Wienzeile bridge) Otto Wagner	1895 Gumpendorfer Gürtel, Linke Wienzeile

MAP No. 7

13th District Hietzing

13th District, Hietzing index numbers 13.-**1** … 13.-**36**s

Buildings worth visiting – Suggestions by Viennese architects:

13. Bezirk:

Adolf Krischanitz:
Beer House, index no. 13.-**12**

Gustav Peichl:
Beer House, index no. 13.-**12**

Carl Pruscha:
Beer House, index no. 13.-**12**

Roland Rainer:
Werkbund Housing Estate, index no. 13.-**23**

August Sarnitz:
Residential building in Wattmanngasse, index no. 13.-**8**
Scheu House, index no. 13.-**15**

13.-**1**

Otto Wagner

Stadtbahn – Imperial Pavilion 1898

Schönbrunner Schloss-Strasse
Access: During opening hours
Public transportation: U4 (Hietzing)

The Imperial Pavilion dates from 1898 and is part of the underground line that follows the course of the River Wien. Its significance was more symbolic than practical, as it was only used once – namely, when the Wiental Line was inaugurated by Emperor Franz Josef. The octagonal, domed central hall has a second internal dome. A large fresco depicts the city of Vienna. Today the Imperial Pavilion is utilised by the Museum of the City of Vienna as a museum. It was renovated by Adolf Krischanitz in the 'eighties.

13.-**2**

Franz von Segenschmid

Schönbrunn Palmery 1881

Schönbrunn Palace Park
Access: Opening hours
Public transportation: U4 (Hietzing)

At the time it was erected (1879–82) within the precincts of the Botanical Garden, it was one the largest buildings of its kind in the world, measuring 114 m long, 25 m high and 29 m wide. The architect based his plans on mid-19th century English and French greenhouses he had studied in the course of a business trip. By dividing the translucent masses into a central pavilion and flanking wings, the design is indebted to the prototype of palace buildings and thus conforms to traditional ideas of representative architecture while utilising innovative materials like glass and steel. The greenhouse was heavily damaged during World War II, rebuilt in the 1950's and, after long neglect and decay, renovated by Herbert Prehsler and the successors to the construction firm Wagner-Biró.

Schönbrunn Palace 1696
Schönbrunn Park 1705

Schönbrunner Schloss-Strasse
Access: Open to the public
Public transportation: U4 (Schönbrunn)

The palace was conceived by J.B.Fischer von Erlach and Emperor Leopold I. as an Austrian answer to Versailles. Originally, the plan was to build the palace at the top of the hill where the "Gloriette" now stands. A more modest design by J.B.Fischer von Erlach was later adopted for financial reasons, which was carried on by his son J.B.Fischer von Erlach after the father's death, and completed by Nicolaus Pacassi during the reign of Maria Theresia. Schönbrunn Palace Park is the most important and best preserved Baroque garden in Austria and was laid out by Jean Trehet in 1705. The main vistas also feature garden architecture, including the Gloriette (J.F.Hetzendorf von Hohenberg, 1772–75, converted into a café by F.Ullmann, 1996) and the Menangerie (Jean Nicolas Jadot, 1751). The zoo (Menagerie) is currently being renovated and adopted by H.Lechner.

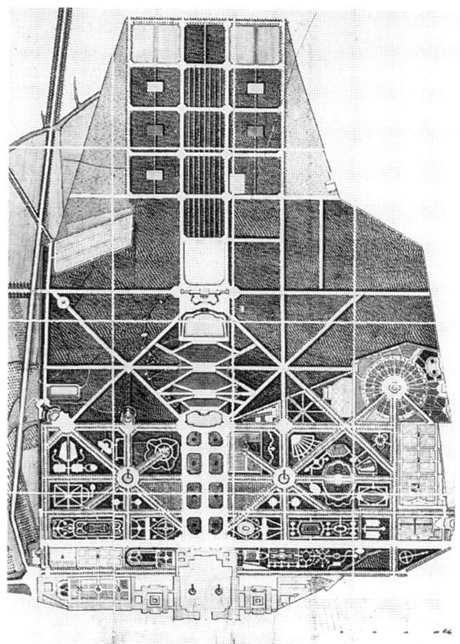

13.-**4** *Josef Plečnik and Josef Czastka*

Adaptation of the Weidmann House 1901

Hietzinger Hauptstrasse 6
Access: Not open to the public
Public transportation: U4 (Hietzing)

Josef Plečnik's alterations to an existing building were changed once more in the early 1920's by Rudolf Goebel, especially by the addition of top storeys to the side wings. This early work, whose "Baroque" concept already hints at the sensitivity with which Plečnik would later adopt and exploit local building traditions, stamps the young Slovene architect as one of Wagner's most original disciples.

13.-**5** *Robert Oerley*

Villa Wustl 1912

Auhofstrasse 15
Access: Not open to the public
Public transportation: Tram line 58 (Wenzgasse)

Oerley integrated a conservatory which had belonged to the previous building (a palace belonging to the Duke of Brunswick) into his new villa for the industrialist Richard Wustl.
The architect's most significant achievement is to strike a balance between the highly differentiated spatial forms of the interior – which are also apparent on the exterior, i.e. in the garden front – and a clearly articulated and symmetrical façade. The architect included the vases he designed for the Secession in the ramp. The interior of the building has been altered extensively since.

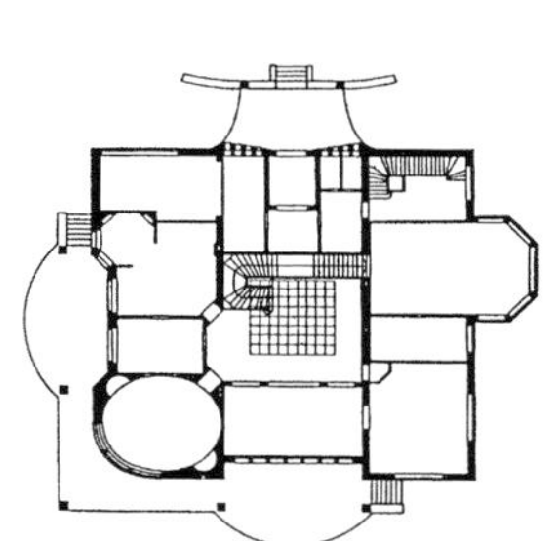

Adolf Loos

13.-**6**

Like the Horner House, this residential building is a highly sophisticated minimalist version of a family residence. With only an area of 10 square metres and one central load-bearing column at his disposal, Loos developed a highly differentiated spatial concept that is also legible on the exterior. Loos deployed copies of fragments of the Parthenon Frieze to harmonise the structure of the northern façade on the one hand, and, on the other, to give the concept of architectural sculpture a novel twist.

Rufer House
1922

Schliessmanngasse 11
Access: Not open to the public
Public transportation: U4 (Braunschweiggasse)

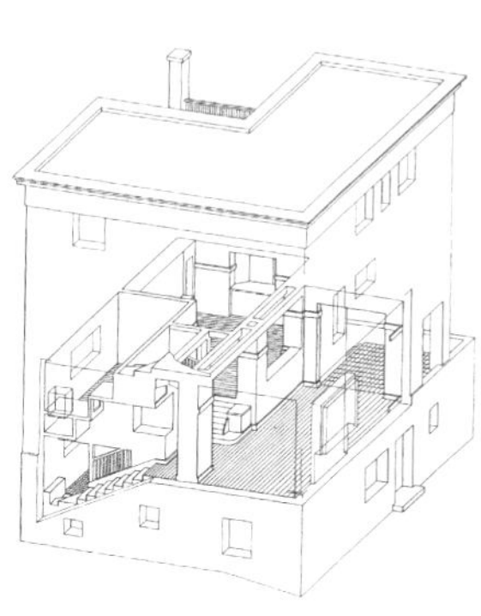

Gunther Wawrik, Hans Puchhammer

13.-**7**

Office buildings in the 'seventies were dominated by the demand for flexibility and adaptability. Both elements have been very successfully integrated in this small office building: a widely spanning concrete frame allows free utilisation of the available space. The transparent glass membrane also reveals an expressionist construction underneath.

Grothusen I
1970

Aufhofstrasse 41a
Access: Not open to the public
Public transportation: U4 (Unter St.Veit)

13.-**8**

Ernst Lichtblau

Residential building, Wattmanngasse 1914

This early work by the Wagner disciple Ernst Lichtblau is dominated by dark, sculptural relief bands. The prominence given to the horizontal, however, also reflects the open-minded and dynamic traits that characterised the later work of the architect, especially his pavilion for the Austrian Werkbund Exhibition in 1930.

Wattmanngasse 29
Access: Not open to the public
Public transportation: U4, bus 56B, 58B (Tirolergasse)

13.-**9**

Siegfried C. Drach

Malfatti Housing Estate 1930

This small housing estate (1930–32) by Drach was developed parallel to Josef Frank's Viennese Werkbund Housing Estate. The houses are built in the form of a terrace and treated individually. The roof terraces are accessible and add to the comfort offered by the houses, in spite of their restricted size. The guiding principle of the estate is not unlike Frank's: i.e. instead of building monotonous blocks, that would unfailingly reveal their identical contents (e.g. domestic spaces) but would neglect the psychical needs of their residents, the architect chose formal variety while at the same time avoiding any excessive display.

Franz-Schalk-Platz 1–15
Access: Not open to the public
Public transportation: Tram line 60 (Gloriettegasse)

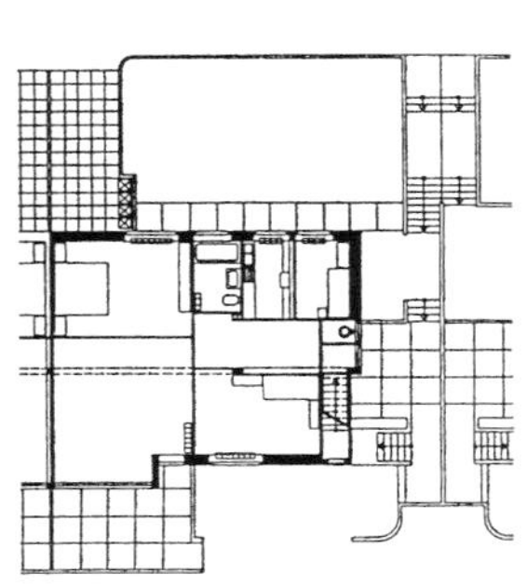

Villa Skywa-Primavesi 1913

Gloriettegasse 18
Access: Not open to the public
Public transportation: U4, tram line 60 (Gloriettegasse)

Two corresponding factors played a role in the design of this magnificent villa: uninterrupted expanses of masonry were avoided in favour of receding layers and disparate elements combined with one another to form one unified overall design. This villa represents the zenith of a sophisticated form of Viennese domestic culture that catered to a bourgeois clientele and ended with the advent of World War I. However, the self-assurance with which Hoffmann proclaims the function of this building in its façade was already being diluted in earlier residential buildings by the architect (and those of his rival Loos) and substituted by the stress laid on their internal appointment.

Bösch House
Roland Rainer's House
1968

Weidlichgasse 17,
Weidlichgasse 17a
Access: Not open to the public
Public transportation: U4, bus 56B (Tiroler Gasse)

The two houses at Weidlichgasse 17, comprising the residence of the architect Roland Rainer (1964–66) and Weidlichgasse 17a, the residence of the Bösch family (1968–70), were originally erected on the same plot. The architect's residence was conceived as an atrium building in keeping with his philosophy of domestic living. It is sealed off from the street and opens up onto the garden. It also represents the architect's homage to the atrium houses in China and is adopted to conform to its topographical situation on the slope of a hill.

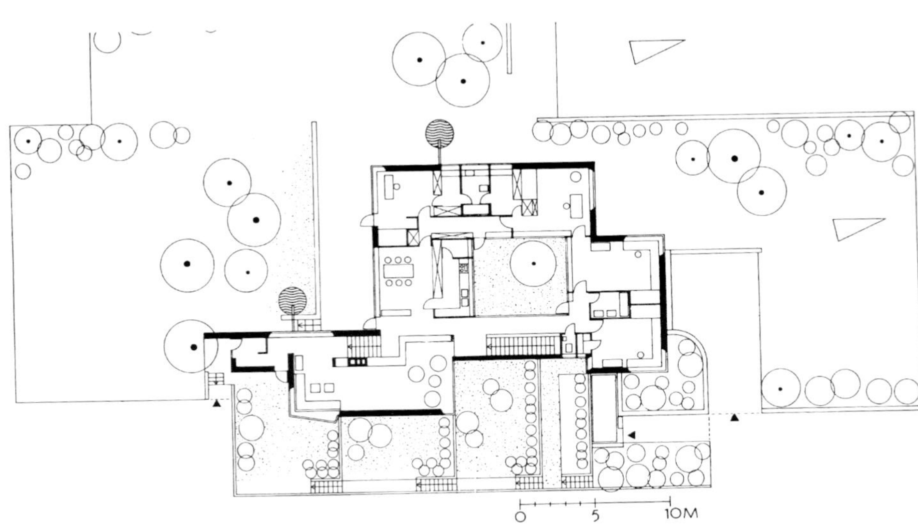

Beer House
1929

Wenzgasse 12
Access: Not open to the public
Public transportation: U3, tram line 60 (Gloriettegasse)

It was no accident that Frank propounded valid criteria for innovative thinking and setting standards and, above all, pleaded for the abandonment of what he saw as pointless and dogmatic regularity in an article devoted to this villa in the publication "Das Haus als Weg und Platz". The evolution of the floor plan owes something to Loos' spatial programme and reveals a very free succession of rooms that is also legible on the exterior in the form of "spatial pockets" (J. Frank). Unfortunately the sophisticated internal spatial concept has been seriously compromised by recent structural alterations. The building has a compact street façade, while the garden front comprises a wide variety of balconies and terraces.

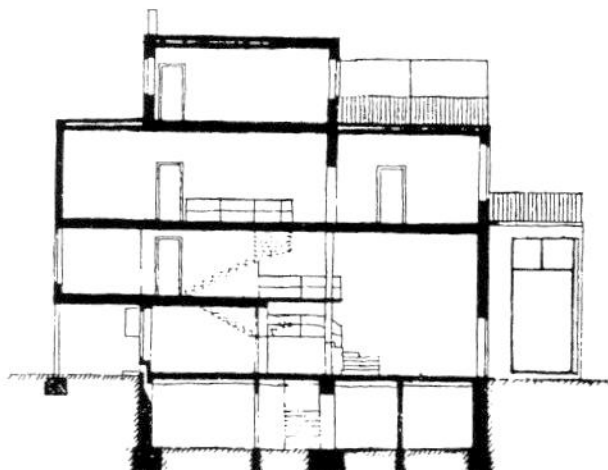

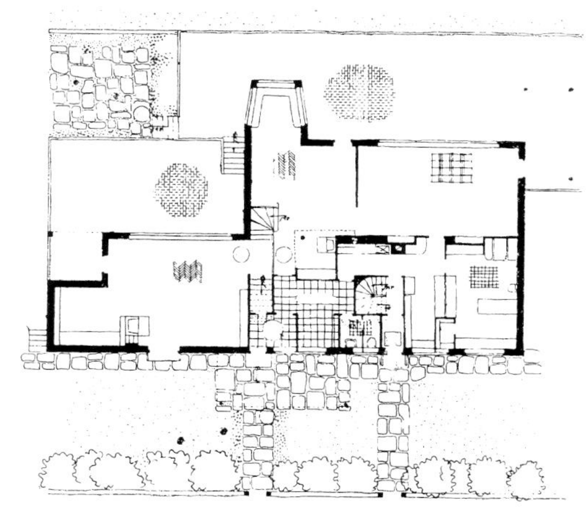

13.-**13** | *Theiss, Jaksch, Melicher, Schwalm-Theiss, Gressenbauer*

Secondary School Wenzgasse 1930 (1990)

Wenzgasse 7
Access: By prior appointment
Public transportation: Tram line 60 (Gloriettegasse)

The school was actually built in three stages: the original building housing the girls' Lyceum was built in the years 1906–09 and then extended by the architectural duo Jaksch and Theiss between 1930 and '31. The young Bernard Rudofsky was also employed as a junior associate on this building, which was extraordinarily modern by Austrian standards. A generous use of glass and glass tiling ensured that the interior was well lit and the restrained design gave rise to an appropriate sobriety, although the choice of materials prevents this from becoming merely lifeless. In 1990–95, the school was extended yet again by the architectural studio of Melicher, Schwalm-Theiss & Gressenbauer, who also renovated the older fabric.

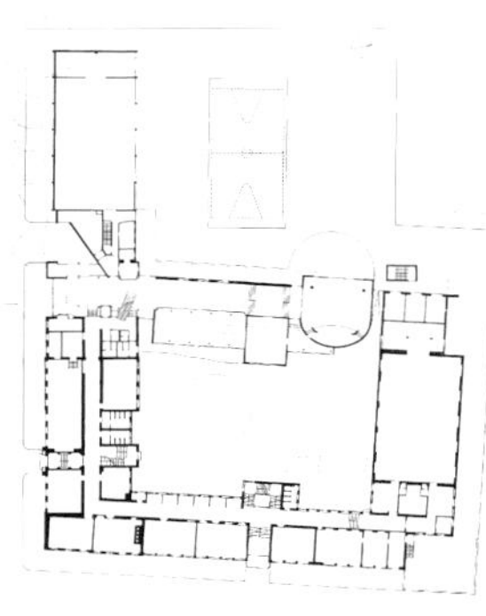

13.-**14** | *Adolf Loos*

Strasser House 1918

Kuppelwiesergasse 28
Access: Not open to the public
Public transportation: Tram line 58 (Fleschgasse)

Loos integrated an existing 19th century building so subtly into his design that it is now very difficult to locate. The building represents a preliminary stage of the architect's subsequent "spatial designs". The complexity of the interior corresponds to Loos' treatment of the façade – and the latter is completely legitimised only by the former. The "protuberances" are typical of this early stage in the evolution of Loos' concept of space: they later lost their significance in favour of the "blocking" of buildings and a more systematic treatment of their façades.

Scheu House
1912

Larochegasse 3
Access: Not open to the public
Public transportation: Tram line 58 (Fleschgasse)

This family home, which also contains an additional apartment on the top floor with its own entrance, boasts of a generous balcony in front of each of the east facing bedrooms. The uncompromising arrangement of the block (both of the terraces recede 4 metres in a building that measures a total of 16 metres) is mirrored by the treatment of the windows, whose different sizes are based on combinations of one module. The house met with resistance from the building authorities at the planning stage, who demanded that the owner cover the building with vegetation and that the architect submit plans for the neighbouring plot. The latter, however, were never realised.

13.-**16**

Josef Plečnik

Residential Building, Beckgasse 1900

Beckgasse 30
Access: Not open to the public
Public transportation: Tram line 60 (Gloriettegasse)

Plečnik's contribution was made at a very late stage in the planning of this building. Apart from a few corrections to the interior, he was only really able to influence the design of the façade – and this is accordingly unorthodox. The plaster was uniformly covered with prefabricated ornamentation: it is hardly possible to formulate the dichotomy between underlying structure and decoration more clearly than here.

13.-**17**

Adolf Loos

Horner House 1912

Nothartgasse 7
Access: Not open to the public
Public transportation: U4, bus 55B (Tolstoigasse)

Whatever pretensions Loos might indulge in when carrying out some of his larger assignments and in the furnishings of his buildings, he always strove to produce cheap housing. The Horner House is a good example of the latter kind of pragmatism: here Loos managed to erect a family home on a minimal plot measuring 10 x 11m that only contains load-bearing outer walls - in complete conformity with the architect's concept of the wall as a protective and structural element that should be made subservient to the requirements of the interior arrangement.

Steiner House
1910

This is a house with some surprising elements: building regulations only allowed for a street front with one storey and a dormer window, while the garden front is three-storied and highly articulated. The transition between the two scales is achieved with the aid of a semi-circular roof structure. The interior features – in spite of the uninterrupted storey levels – a differentiated "spatial" concept because of the differing heights of the rooms. The atelier of the builder, the painter Lilly Steiner, is situated behind the large window in the street front.

St. Veit-Gasse 10
Access: Not open to the public
Public transportation: Tram line 58 (Hummelgasse)

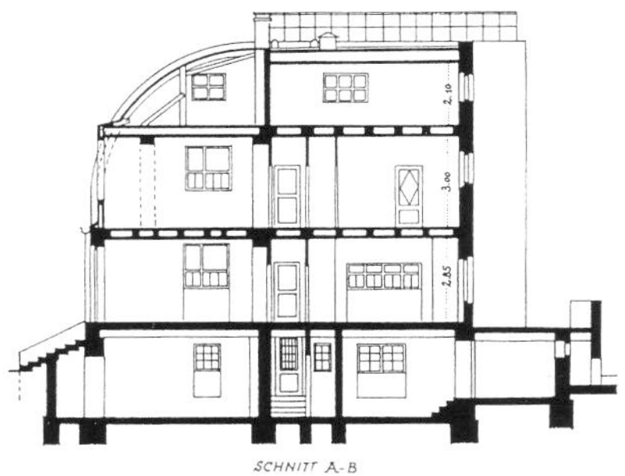

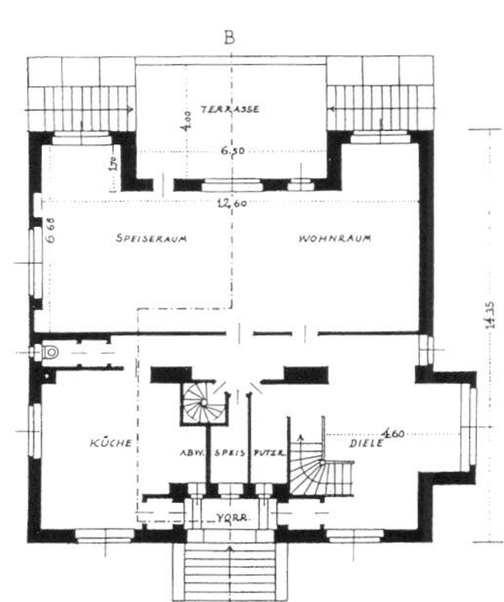

Luigi Blau

T. House
1983

Gogolgasse 58
Access: Not open to the public
Public transportation: U4, bus 54B (Gogolgasse)

The floor plan of this family home acquiesces both to the topography of the site and the traditions of Viennese Modernism. A north-eastern slope with little sun and a terrace on the street front were amongst the obstacles facing the architect. The interior of the building reveals a highly differentiated series of rooms that are stacked behind one another and reveal surprising perspectives and vistas. The built-in furnishings were designed by the architect.

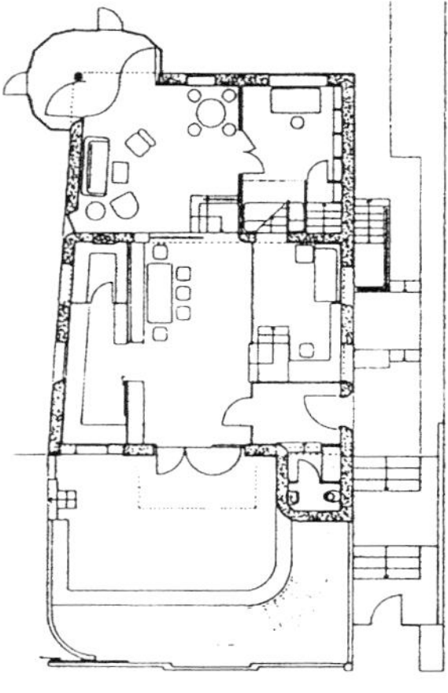

13.-**20**

Josef Lackner

Konzils-Gedächtniskirche (Vatican Council Memorial Church) 1965

Lainzerstrasse 138
Access: Open to the public
Public transportation: Tram lines 60 and 62 (Jagdschlossgasse)

Church building was characterised by the spirit of change and renewal within the Catholic Church in the Sixties. The process of "opening" and "democratisation" within the church itself made new concepts of church architecture possible.
Lackner developed a very diversified church interior over a square ground plan that features heavy external walls and an internal gallery (cloisters) at first floor level. A peripheral band of skylights allows enough light to penetrate the interior and gives the ceiling the impression of "hovering" visually.

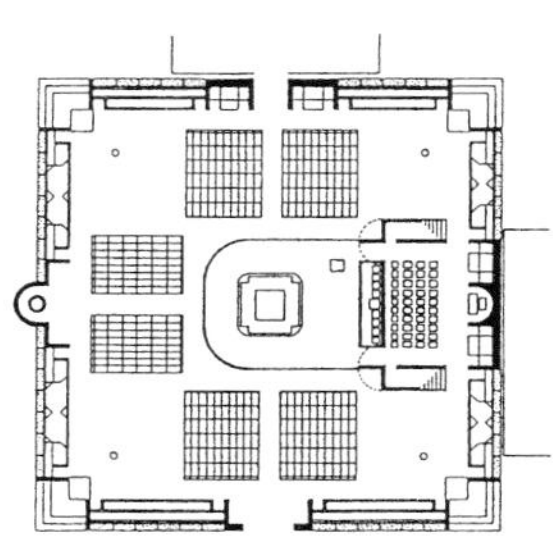

Roland Rainer

13.-**21**

When the Austrian broadcasting agency ORF was restructured in the late 'sixties, it was furnished with a new architectural image, which was reflected by the subsequent erection of provincial ORF studios by Gustav Peichl on a federal level and the ORF Centre on the Küniglberg by Roland Rainer. In compliance with the ORF's role as a medial broadcasting agency, the building features a very specific architectural language: prefabricated reinforced concrete structures, functional arrangement, integrated solar shades, etc. Rainer succeeded in relieving and structuring the large-scale building with the help of smaller individual functional structures. It was constructed between 1968 and 1976 and has been subject to constant modifications ever since.

ORF Centre
1968

Würzburggasse, Küniglberg
Access: By appointment
Public transportation: U4, bus 58B (ORF Zentrum)

Karl Schartelmüller

13.-**22**

This development represents a rather belated attempt by a civil architect to revive the settlement model. The Lockerwiese estate is not of the self-supporting type favoured in earlier complexes, but a purely residential complex. The terrace houses with their small gardens are sometimes grouped together to become large blocks and form curving streets and small squares that also include public spaces.

Lockerwiese Settlement
1928

Wolkersbergenstrasse,
Engelhartgasse,
Versorgungsheimstrasse
Access: Not open to the public
Public transportation: Tram lines 60 and 62 (Wolkersbergenstrasse)

Werkbund Housing Estate 1930

Jagdschlossgasse, Veitingergasse, Woinovichgasse, Jagicgasse
Access: Only public areas
Public transportation: U4, bus 54B (Gobergasse)

Josef Frank, the initiator of the Werkbund Housing Estate (1930–32), was the only Austrian to be involved in the celebrated Weissenhof project in Stuttgart. Five years after its completion, his competing plan for Vienna was inaugurated as the Werkbund Housing Estate in 1932. Alongside the élite of domestic architects, Frank also invited internationally renowned figures whom he felt had been ignored at the planning stage in Stuttgart. The layout of the estate, with its curved streets that seem to inevitably open out onto small squares, reflect Frank's theoretical maxim of "planned contingency" and were intended to evoke the living quality of an ensemble that had gradually evolved. The houses themselves represent a wide variety of types – the spectrum ranges from detached family homes to semi-detached and terrace houses –

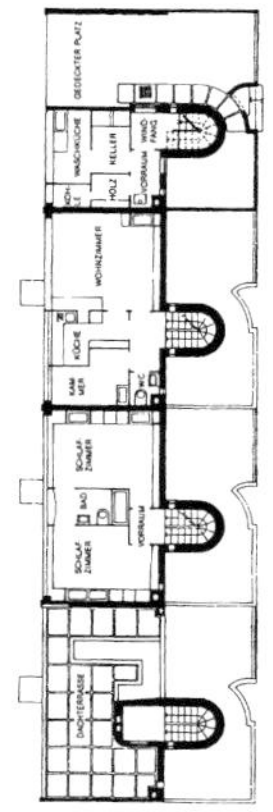

Lurcat

Frank

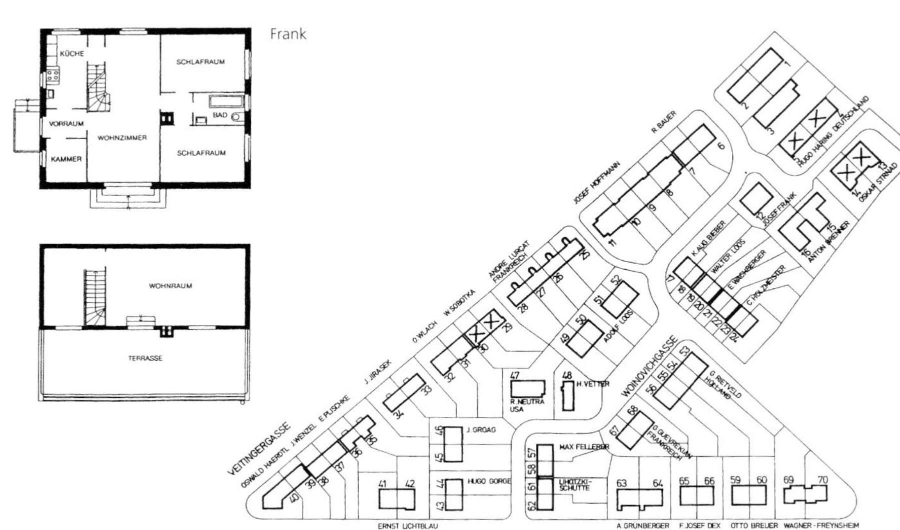

whose ground plans were intended to impart to the contemporary visitor an impression of possible domestic arrangements on very restricted ground plans. Lazlo Gabor, a Hungarian artist, was responsible for the colouring of the façades. This housing estate is the "most concentrated package" of high quality architecture in the international style in Austria, whereby the two houses designed by Adolf Loos represent a high point in compactness and spatial complexity. The whole complex was renovated by Adolf Krischanitz and Otto Kapfinger in the years 1983–85, who left untouched sensible adaptations that had been introduced by later residents.

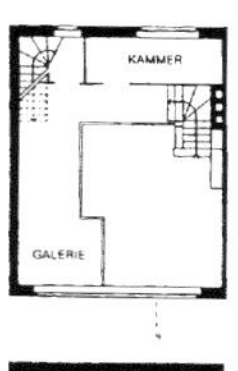

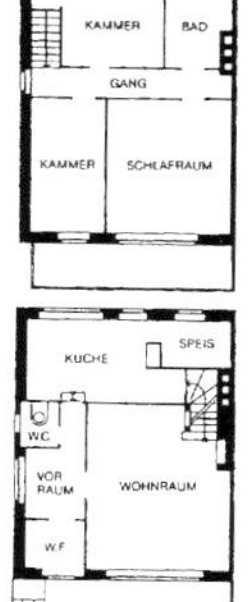

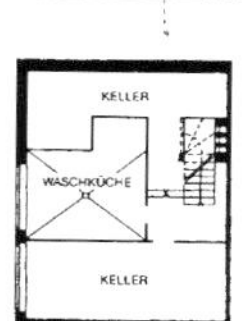

A. Loos

13.-**24**

Gustav Peichl

Dominican Convent
1963

This convent building for 100 girls attempts to integrate a more family-oriented structure into a boarding school situation. Five identical wings housing 20 girls each adjoin one another in alternating fashion and are connected to the main wing containing the refectory and gymnasium by "cloisters". This precise geometry is carried out in reinforced concrete with wooden fenestration, while the surrounding vegetation lends the building some of the mellowness of age.

Schlossberggasse 17,
Seuttergasse 1
Access: Not open to the public
Public transportation: U4, bus 54B (Seuttergasse)

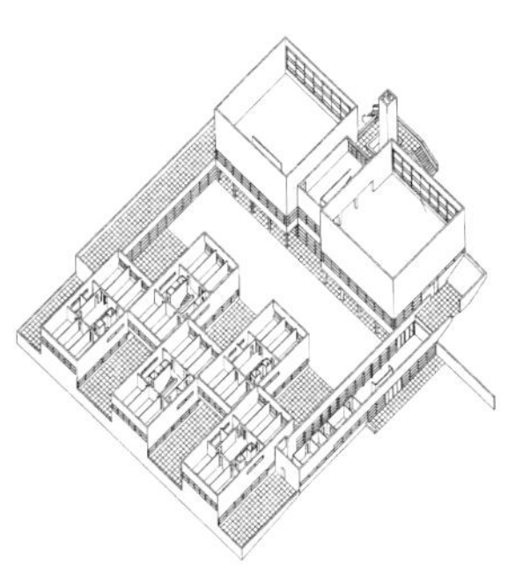

13.-**25**

Carl von Hasenauer

Hermes Villa
1882

Although the main structure of the building, which was erected as a hunting lodge for Empress Elisabeth, seems somewhat studied in its picturesqueness, the whole complex has been integrated very effectively into the surrounding landscape.

Lainzer Tiergarten
Access: Open during public events
Public transportation: Bus 60B (Lainzer Tor)

Fritz Judtmann, Egon Riss

13.-**26**

T.B.C. Pavilion of the Lainz Hospital 1929

The hospital complex was erected by Josef Klingsbigl and Johann Nepomuk Scheiringer between 1908 and 1913, only to be later extended by a block for the treatment of tuberculosis patients by Fritz Judtmann and Egon Riss in 1929–30. The sober but not unpleasant execution of this building, which is architecturally the most interesting in the hospital complex, expresses an overriding confidence in the success of modern science in its generous fenestration and manifold use of stepped and receding masses.

Wolkersbergenstrasse 1
Lainzer Krankenhaus, Pav. VIII
Access: Not open to the public
Public transportation: Tram lines 60 and 62 (Krankenhaus Lainz)

Elsa Prochazka

13.-**27**

School in Hietzinger Hauptstrasse 1992

This extension to an existing secondary school that dates back to the Monarchy was carried out with great sensitivity. While the building proved highly controversial during the construction phase, the result is a well proportioned cube with a perforated façade and yellow majolica tiles. This allows a sense of critical detachment to the older stucco façade to evolve, without shirking the responsibility of creating an architectural link between the older building and new annex. The spatial concept allows for four classrooms, two dividing rooms, a library and ancillary rooms. The classrooms face east and are enlivened by small bay windows that protrude outwards, affording each of these otherwise conventional classrooms their own private niches.

Hietzinger Hauptstrasse 166
Access: By prior appointment
Public transportation: Bus 53B (Wolfrathplatz)

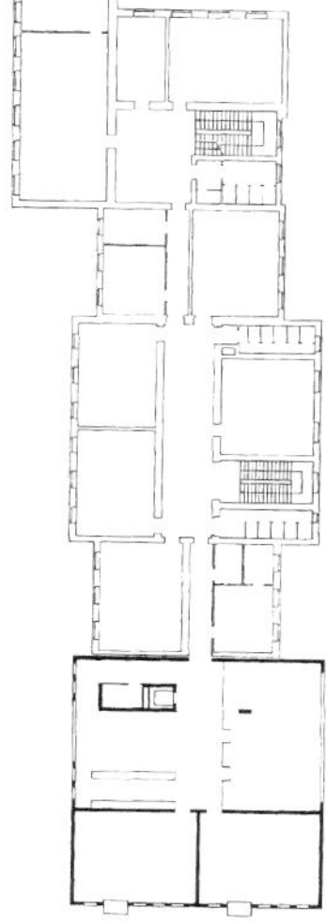

Supplementary recommendations

13.-**28s**	Office building BKK-2, Christoph Lammerhuber, Axel Linemayr, Franz Sumnitsch, Florian Wallnöfer, Johann Winter, Evelyn Wurster	1991 St. Veitgasse 50
13.-**29s**	Pavilion for Handicapped Children of the Neurological Hospital Rupert Falkner, Anton Schweighofer	1969 Riedelgasse 5, Rosenhügelstrasse
13.-**30s**	Porpaczy Residence Roland Hagmüller	1984 Wittgensteinstrasse 50
13.-**31s**	Knobling Residence Heinz Tesar	1985 Grobeckergasse 4
13.-**32s**	Ekazent Hietzing Wolfgang and Traude Windbrechtinger	1962 Hietzinger Hauptstrasse 22
13.-**33s**	Stoessl House Adolf Loos	1911 Matrasgasse 20
13.-**34s**	Bettelheim House Wilhelm Holzbauer	1966 Joseph-Lister-Gasse 22
13.-**35s**	Residential building Gert M. Mayr-Keber	1989 Schweizertalstrasse 44
13.-**36s**	Residential building Ernst Lichtblau	1922 Meytensgasse

MAP No. 8

14th District
Penzing

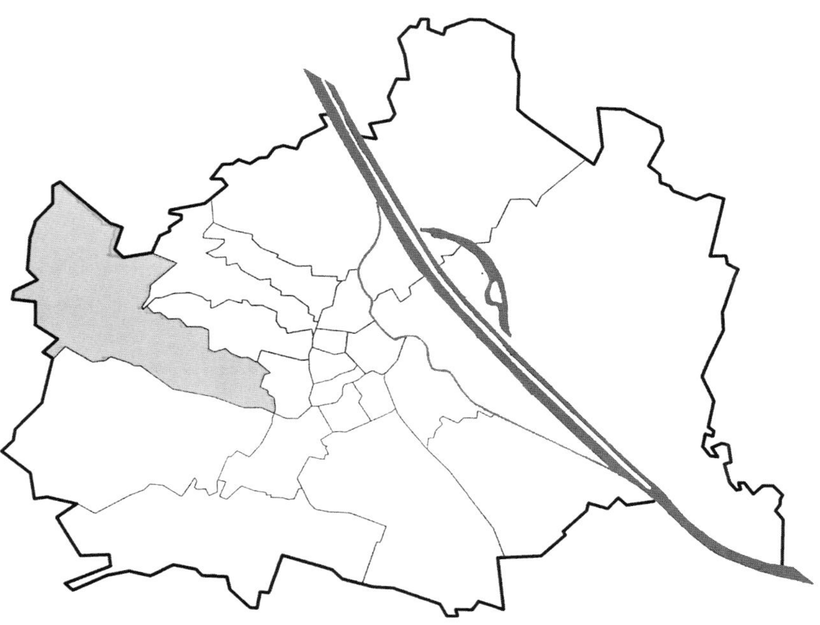

14th District, Penzing index numbers 14.-**1** ... 14.-**19s**

Buildings worth visiting – Suggestions by Viennese architects

14th District

Otto Graf (art historian):
Church of St. Leopold, index no. 14.-**9**

Rüdiger Lainer – walking route:
Garden allotments at Am Flötzersteig, between Blümelhubergasse and Steinbruchstrasse (en route to Otto Wagner's Church of St. Leopold)

Gustav Peichl:
Church of St. Leopold, index no. 14.-**9**

Marta Schreieck:
Kinkplatz School, index no. 14.-**6**

Heinz Tesar:
Pastoral Care Centre Baumgarten, index no. 14.-**4**

Franziska Ullmann:
Church of St. Leopold and hospital complex, index no. 14.-**9**

14.-**1** | *Anton Schweighofer*

Muthsamgasse 1986

Anton Schweighofer significantly enriched public housing by introducing the topos of "centralised spaces" into his ground plans. Most of the rooms in this particular project open out onto generously proportioned balconies, which dominate the external design as a "loggia curtain" and introduce a Mediterranean flair into this Viennese building. The cylindrical asbestos cement cladding stretches through five stories and lends this residential building an unusually monumental appearance (colossal order).

Muthsamgasse 3
Access: Not open to the public
Public transportation: Tram lines 10 and 49 (Laurentiusplatz)

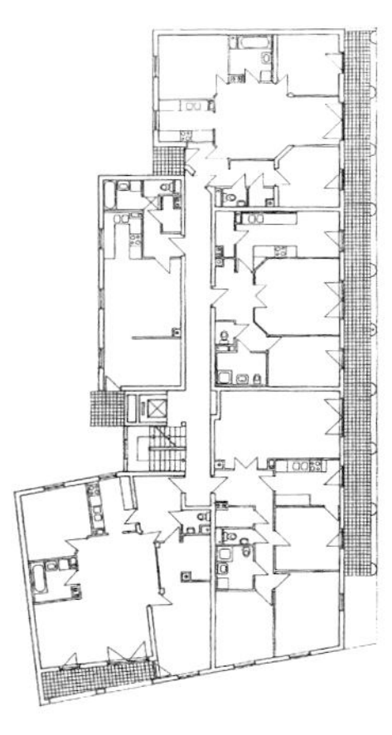

14.-**2** | *Robert Oerley*

Zeiss Works 1915

The Zeiss Works production facility was originally situated on an exposed urban site and perfectly reflects the different forms of expression that early industrial architecture could still harmonise with one another: on the one hand, it clearly proclaims its profane purpose by emphasising constructive elements, but on the other, the building (which once stood on its own) could intimate the commercial hegemony of this well-known manufacturer of optical precision instruments through its exposed situation and the deployment of architectural masses. The latter are rather reminiscent of sacred architecture. The building now serves a different purpose.

Abbegasse 1
Access: Not open to the public
Public transportation: Tram line 46, bus 48A (Waidäckergasse)

Residential building Matznergasse 1993

Matznergasse 8/
Goldschlagstrasse 169
Access: Only in part
Public transportation: U3, tram line 52 (Diesterweggasse)

The "residential community" now occupying the former premises of a coffin factory set new standards in urban living from a social, conceptual, legal (residents' association) and architectural point of view. Awarded with the Adolf Loos Prize in 1996, this building displays a hybrid structure of apartments, a restaurant, lecture rooms, an assembly hall. And swimming pool with approx. 2,000 m² communal space and approx. 6,000 m² living space. BKK-2 members: C Lammerhuber, A.Linemayr, F.Sumnitsch, F.Wallnöfer, J.Winter and E.Wurster

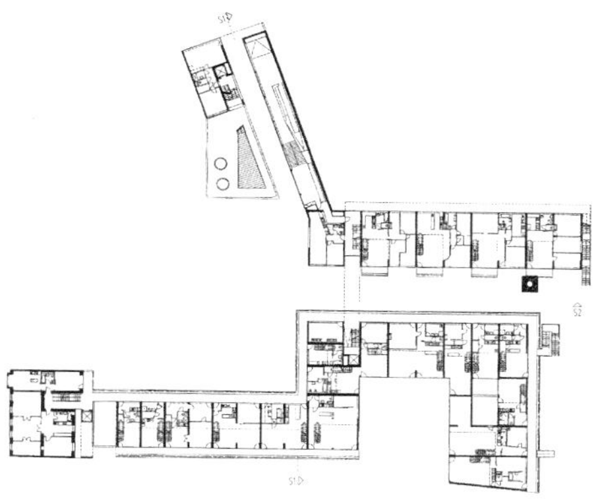

14.-**4** | ***Johann Georg Gsteu***

Pastoral Care Centre Baumgarten 1960

Hütteldorferstrasse 280
Linzer Strasse
Access: By prior appointment
Public transportation: Tram line 49 (Baumgarten)

The spatial qualities of the church only unfold in the interior, where a cruciform band of light reaches from the roof to the floor. The projecting reinforced concrete structure rises over a square ground plan and has the appearance of a split cube as a result of its central band of lighting. The exterior of the complex is also arranged symmetrically with the four square corner wings housing the parsonage, sacristy, parish hall and belfry, respectively.

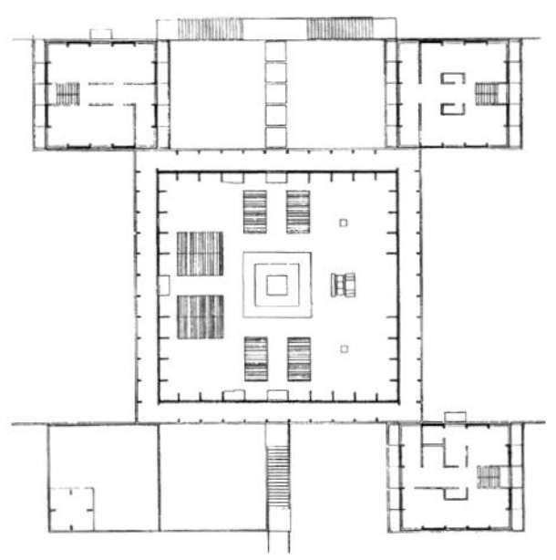

14.-**5** | ***Otto Schönthal, Boris Podrecca***

Villa Vojcsik 1901 GGK Atelier Building 1984

Linzer Strasse 375
Access: Not open to the public
Public transportation: Tram line 49 (Bahnhofstrasse)

Otto Wagner conferred the assignment of erecting this villa in typical suburban surroundings on his pupil Otto Schönthal. Although it stands in the middle of a terrace, the title "villa" is not without certain justification. The central corpus of the building remains autonomous in the manner of Otto Wagner and is only connected to the neighbouring houses by low wings. The upper windows of the latter reach up to the roof-line and are reminiscent of Josef Hoffmann's contemporary Palais Stocklet project in Brussels. The villa was later renovated by Boris Podrecca (1975–82) who also erected a wooden structure as a GGK atelier in the garden (1984–86).

School Waidhauenstrasse/ Kinkplatz 1994

"I wanted to create a school building where the unpleasantness characteristic of schools in general was not so apparent" (Helmut Richter). The result of this aesthetic resolution is a translucent wedge-shaped cube of glass that houses the school hall and the tripartite gymnasium. Three parallel wings with conventional classrooms jut out from the back of this and consist of concrete skeleton structures with prefabricated ceiling elements. Richter catered to the extensive spatial needs of a specialist secondary school with 20 classes with the aid of vigorous plasticity of his forms. The spatial openness of the school building also intimates a new openness in the pedagogical approach to education.

Kinkplatz 21
Access: By prior appointment
Public transportation: Tram line 49, bus 47A (Baumgartner Friedhof)

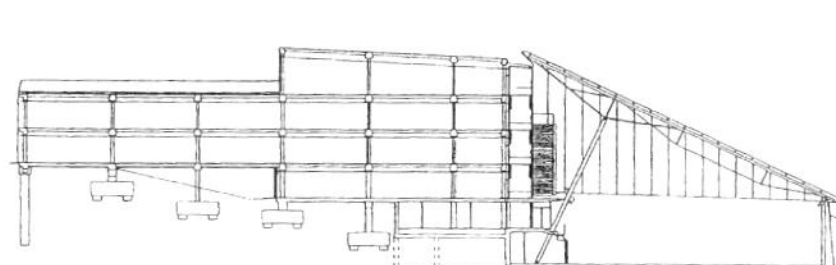

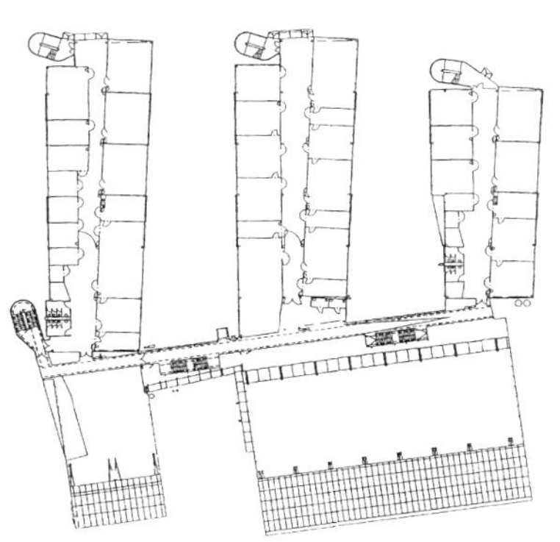

14.-**7** | ***Otto Wagner***

1st Wagner Villa 1886

This sumptuous suburban villa in an eclectic "Neo-Renaissance" style at the edge of the Vienna Woods in Hütteldorf was originally erected as Wagner's own home in 1886. The pergola to the right of the building was glazed over in 1895 and that on the left converted into a studio in 1899. Two inscriptions emblazoned on the main façade help clarify Wagner's architectural thinking: "Sine arte sine amore non est vitae" and "Sola domina necessitas". The building has since been altered and the interior no longer has its original appearance.

Hüttelbergstrasse 26
Access: Not open to the public
Public transportation: Tram line 49, bus 148 (Wien West I Camping Site)

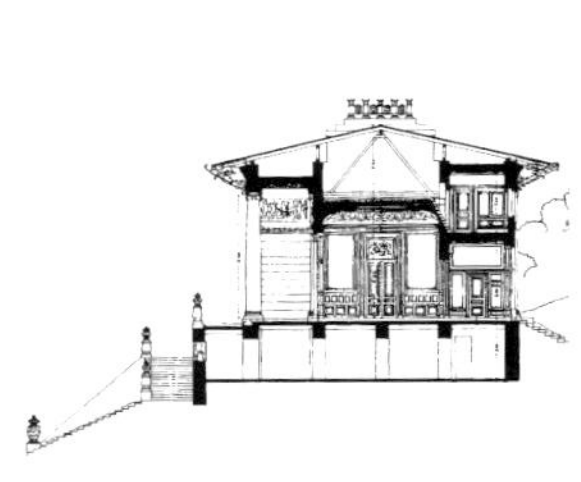

14.-**8** | ***Otto Wagner***

2nd Villa Wagner 1912

A quarter of a century after he built his first villa (which he later sold to the variety impresario Ben Tiber) Wagner built a house alongside it that can be interpreted as a protest against the "picturesque" patriotic style that was popular in the years leading up to World War I. The building permit was granted on 8th August, 1912. Wagner sold the house on 25th September, 1916, because he no longer wanted to live in the house where his wife had died. (Otto Graf)

Hüttelbergstrasse 28
access: none
Public transportation: Tram line 49, bus 148 (Wien West I Camping Site)

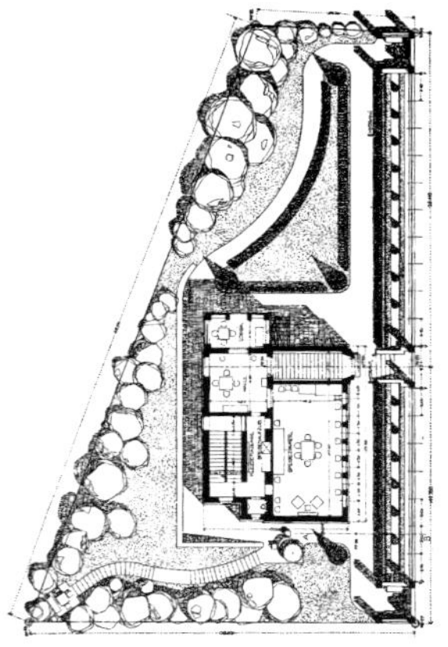

Church of St. Leopold 1905

Baumgartner Höhe 1
Access: During opening hours
Public transportation: Tram line 46, bus 48A (Psychiatrisches Krankenhaus)

The design adopted for the new psychiatric hospital was the outcome of a competition (1902–04) and stuck closely to Wagner's own layout. However, Wagner only actually built the Church of St. Leopold whose plan can be dated between November 1903 and March 1904 (Otto Graf). It is perched on the western slopes of the Vienna Woods like a splendid tiara and establishes an almost mytho-poetic relationship with the city of Vienna lying below. The building is an architectural masterpiece and an "absolute must" on the itinerary of every visitor to Vienna.

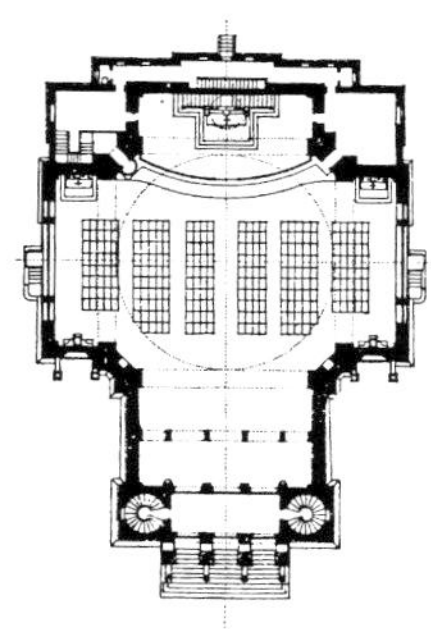

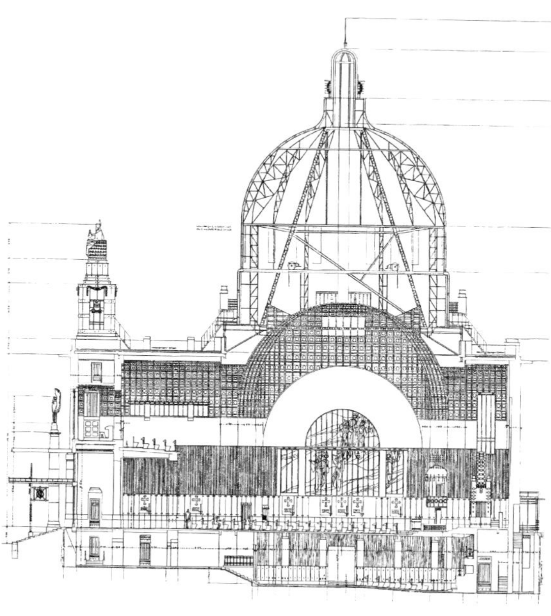

City of the Child
1969

The "City of the Child" is, conceptually speaking, an open youth hostel run by the Municipality of Vienna, where children are put into family homes with autonomous care. Alongside the five family homes, a library, gymnasium, swimming pool, refectory and a theatre are all deployed along a linear structure. A symbolic gesture, where the spatial shell reflects sociological demands.

Weidlingau, Mühlbergstrasse, Hofjägerstrasse
Access: By prior appointment
Public transportation: U4, bus 151 (Weidlingau)

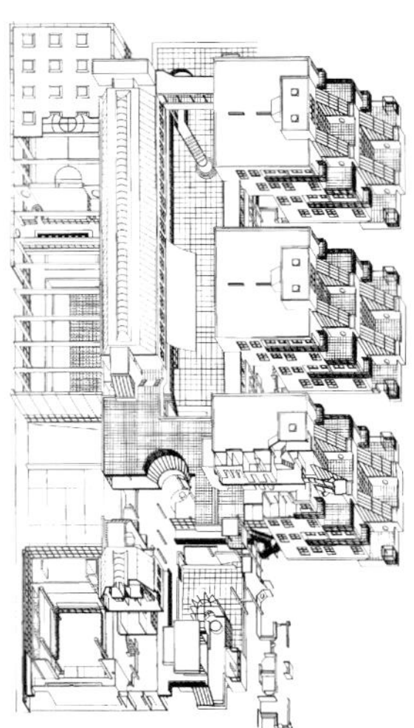

Supplementary Recommendations

14.-**11s**	Diesterweggasse Primary School Gustav Peichl	1976 Diesterweggasse 30
14.-**12s**	Waidhausenstrasse Rüdiger Lainer, Gertraud Auer	1987 Waidhausenstrasse 24
14.-**13s**	Residential building, Penzinger Strasse Karl Fischl	1901 Penzinger Strasse 40
14.-**14s**	Baumgartner Höhe Franz Berger	1902 Baumgartner Höhe 1, Steinhof Psychiatric Hospital
14.-**15s**	Hackinger Steg D. Henke, M. Schreieck, W. Ziesel	1995 Hackinger Kai
14.-**16s**	Bacher House Wilhelm Holzbauer, Friedrich Kurrent, Johannes Spalt (Arbeitsgruppe 4)	1963 Günselgasse 20
14.-**17s**	Annex to the Technical Museum (entrance hall) Atelier in der Schönbrunner Straße	1993 Mariahilferstrasse 212
14.-**18s**	Grothusen II Warehouse and Office Building Gunther Wawrik	1979 Albert-Schweitzer-Gasse 5
14.-**19s**	Sebastian Kelch Gasse Josef Frank	1928 Sebastian Kelch Gasse 1–3

MAP No. 9

15th District Rudolfsheim-Fünfhaus 16th District Ottakring 17th District Hernals 18th District Währing

15th District, Rudolfsheim-Fünfhaus Index numbers	15.-**1** ... 15.-**14s**
16th District, Ottakring Index numbers	16.-**1** ... 16.-**10s**
17th District, Hernals Index numbers	17.-**1** ... 17.-**7s**
18th District, Währing Index numbers	18.-**1** ... 18.-**11s**

Buildings worth visiting – Suggestions by Viennese architects

15th District:

Marta Schreieck:
Stadthalle, Stadthallenbad, Index no. 15.-**2**

16th District:

Maria Auböck:
Kongressbad 16th District, Index no. 16.-**4**
Margarethe Cufer:
Heilig-Geist Kirche, Index no. 16.-**3**
Adolf Krischanitz:
Heilig-Geist Kirche, Index no. 16.-**3**
Rüdiger Lainer – walking route:
Wurlitzergasse in Ottakring, between Wilhelminenstrasse and Effingerstrasse
Dietmar Steiner:
Church of the Holy Ghost, Index no.-**3**

17th District:

Carl Pruscha:
Heuberg Housing Estate with gardens, Index no. 17.-**5**

Seipel-Dollfuss Church (Kanzlerkirche) 1933

Vogelweidplatz 7–8
Access: Open to the public
Public transportation: U6 (Burgasse)

The church was built in 1932 to commemorate the death of the Austrian chancellor, Ignaz Seipel. The body of his successor Engelbert Dollfuss was also interred here after he was assassinated during a putsch staged by the illegal Nazis. The church soon became a shrine of the Austrian Fascist Movement, which led to the caskets of both chancellors being removed immediately after the "Anschluss" between Austria and Germany. Holzmeister based the design of his building on Austrian monastery architecture and adopted it to conform the topography of the extensive site and the requirements of a pastoral care centre with adjoining accommodation for a parish priest and pastor.

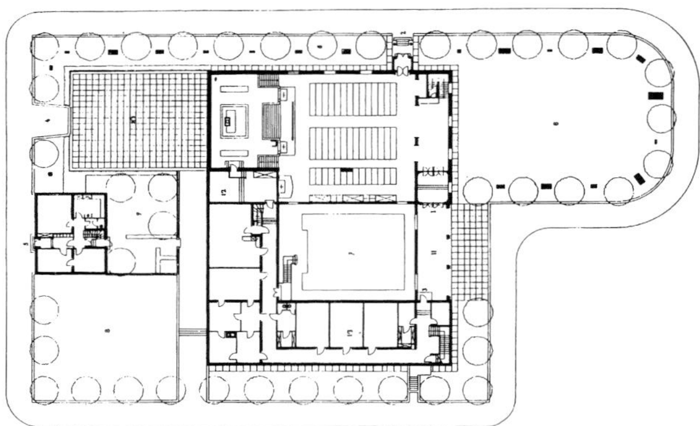

In the immediate vicinity of the Westbahnhof, the Stadthalle in Vienna was built as a result of an international competition. Capable of holding an audience of between 15,000 and 20,000 people, the Stadthalle is the largest hall of its kind in Austria. The reinforced concrete structure slants in towards the centre (Prof. Baravalle) and rises outwards with the increasing height of the tribunes. A large indoor swimming pool was added in 1971–1974; the foyer renovated and a small hall (Hall E) added in 1994.

Stadthalle, Halle E, Stadthalle Swimming Pool 1994

Vogelweidplatz, Märzstrasse, Gablenzgasse
Access: Open to the public
Public transportation: U6 (Burggasse/Stadthalle)

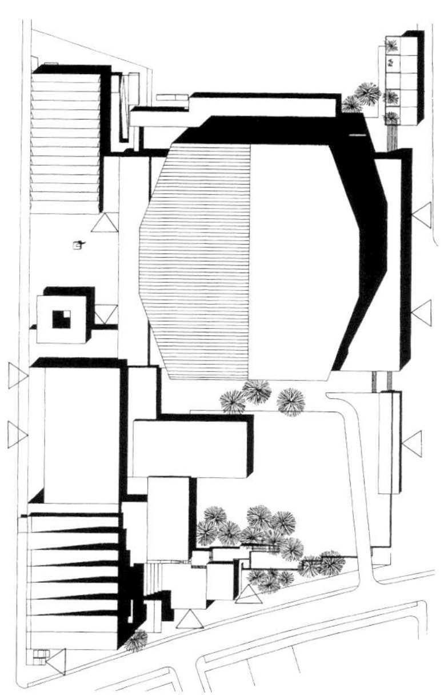

15.-**3**

Leopold Bauer

Vogelweid-Hof 1926

Hütteldorferstrasse 2A, Wurzbachgasse, Sorbaitgasse
Access: Not open to the public
Public transportation: U6 (Burgasse)

Leopold Bauer was a Wagner disciple, who soon turned away from his mentor's "rationalism" and embraced a much more picturesque approach that he favoured for residential buildings and which also reflected significant social and emotional qualities. He attempted to increase these qualities by, amongst other things, integrating painting in the arcades of the "Vogelweid Hof", which gave rise to the nickname "fairy tale castle".

15.-**4**

Georg Driendl, Gerhard Steixner

Special School for Children with Visual Disabilities 1992

Zinckgasse 12–14
Access: By prior appointment
Public transportation: Tram lines 9 and 49 (Beingasse)

To build a special school for children with visual disabilities on an empty lot in a block of houses is a twofold challenge to an architect: alongside the prerequisite and complex practical requirements, the problem of daylight and haptic quality becomes paramount. The highly compact school building contains eight classes and utilises a wide range of materials (softwood and hardwood, fair-faced concrete, clinker, terrazzo, ceramics, glass and stucco) and highly sophisticated lighting to stimulate the sensual perceptions of the pupils.

Otto Polak-Hellwig

The "Heimhof" was built as a so-called single kitchen house, in which catering for the residents from a central kitchen was served in a dining hall or with the aid of food elevators. After it was extended in 1926, the building contained a total of 246 apartments. A kindergarten, sun terraces and a central laundry were put at the residents' disposal alongside the central kitchen. The socialist Auguste Fickert initiated the project with the objective of improving the living standard of working couples.

Heimhof
1921

Pilgerimgasse 22–24,
Oeverseestrasse 25-29,
Wurmsergasse 45-47,
Johnstrasse
Access: Public spaces only
Public transportation: U3 (Johnstrasse)

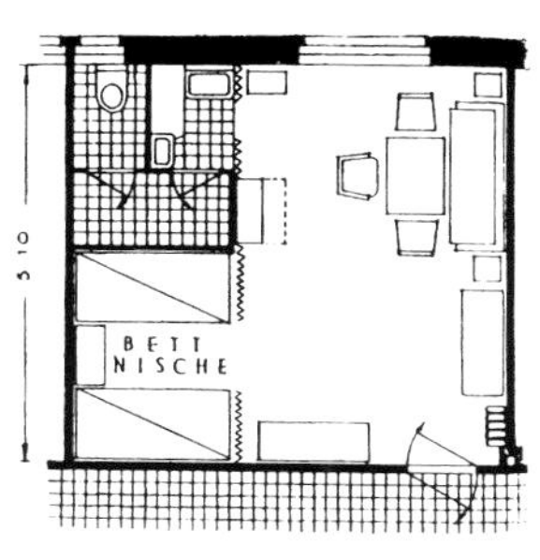

Oskar Strnad

The oeuvre that Oscar Strnad actually built is relatively modest compared to his influence as teacher and writer. Alongside a handful of family homes, including a villa in Cottagegasse and the Wassermann Villa, parts of the Winarsky Hof and this residential complex in Holochergasse are among the largest buildings he was able to realise. Strnad, who, in his early buildings and particularly in his interiors, oscillated between a rococo-like delicacy and Biedermeier-like transparency, modelled this work on the simplicity that his long-standing partner Josef Frank cultivated in residential projects for the Municipality of Vienna.

Residential Complex Holochergasse
1931

Holochergasse 40,
Loeschenkohlgasse 30–32,
Oeverseestrasse,
Preysingerstrasse
Access: Not open to the public
Public transportation: U3 (Johnstrasse)

15.-**7** | *Hugo Mayer*

Residential Complex Schmelz 1919

Possingergasse, Gablenzgasse, Minciostrasse, Oeverseestrasse, Mareschplatz
Access: Public areas only
Public transportation: U3, bus 10A (Akkonplatz)

Hugo Mayer was a leading representative of the Viennese garden city movement and collaborated with Adolf Loos on the Heuberg Estate project. Here on the Schmelz, Mayer combined a built-up periphery (which, incidentally, was the first part of the project to be erected) with free-standing inside blocks. The complex had a laundry, a meeting hall, shops and baths. In the final design, vernacular traditions and streamlined elements vie against one another.

15.-**8** | *Friedrich Kurrent*

Residential Building Nobilegasse 1985

Nobilegasse 51–53
Access: Not open to the public
Public transportation: U3 (Johnstrasse)

It is often difficult to find a good example of "new architecture in old surroundings". In the case of this 30 m wide building in a predominantly 19th century district, Kurrent adroitly places the stairwell next to the façade, which results in a split-level organisation and arrangement of the building. Thus, the uniform façade contrasts with the tower containing the stairs (Friedrich Achleitner points out that this is a citation of the building of the Stadtwerke Graz, Steinbüchel-Rheinwall, 1928–32).

Friedrich von Schmidt

15.-**9**

The church, which was built in close proximity to the Linienwall (outer rampart, now marked by the route of the Stadtbahn), is an attempt by Friedrich Schmidt to synthesise the fundamentally opposed topoi of oblong and centralised ground plans. The building can best be seen from a passing vehicle when its different silhouettes can unfold to optimal effect.

Fünfhaus Parish Church (Maria vom Siege) 1864

Mariahilfer Gürtel
Access: Open to the public
Public transportation: U6, tram line 6 (Mariahilfer Gürtel)

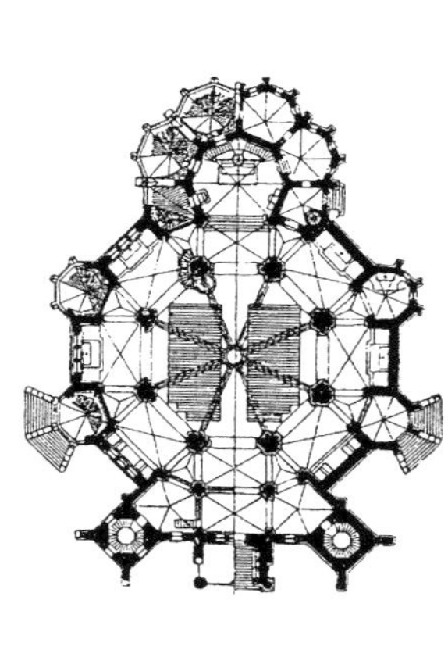

Johann Georg Gsteu

15.-**10**

The adaptation of this late 19th century building to serve as the subsidiary branch of a retail bank was carried out in two stages and is interesting for a number of architectural and practical reasons. The circular form of the windows sprang functionally from the "pressure pipe solution" and formally from arched windows and the clock motif of the original façade. The interior has been given variety with the aid of a gallery floor. The large steel and glass entrance was added in 1989.

Savings bank 1970

Sparkassenplatz 4/
Ullmannstrasse
Access: Open to the public
Public transportation: Bus 9A (Sparkassenplatz)

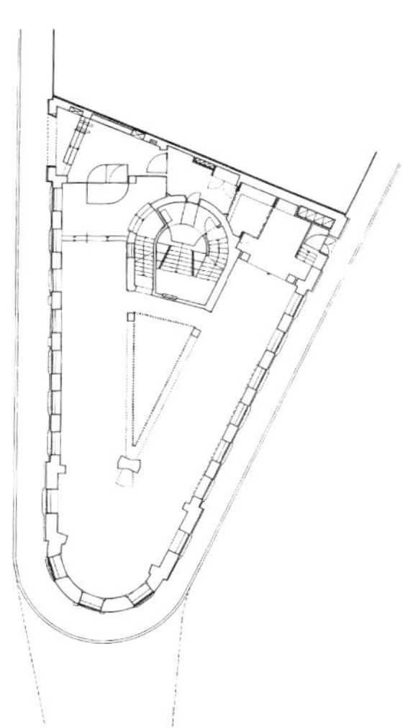

Residential Complex "Wohnen Morgen" 1974

Anschützgasse, Jheringgasse, Siebeneichengasse, Weiglgasse
Access: Public areas only
Public transportation: U3, tram lines 52 and 58 (Anschützgasse)

An architectural competition entitled "Wohnen Morgen" ("Living Tomorrow") was mounted in all Austrian federal provinces in the Sixties. The winning project by Wilhelm Holzbauer reveals a mixed utilisation concept (street front and garden court) that deftly mingles public and private areas. The public front features commercial premises and is enlivened by arcades; the garden courts achieve a maximum of privacy through their terrace-like arrangement. This complex represents a highly successful prototype for redevelopment in urban areas.

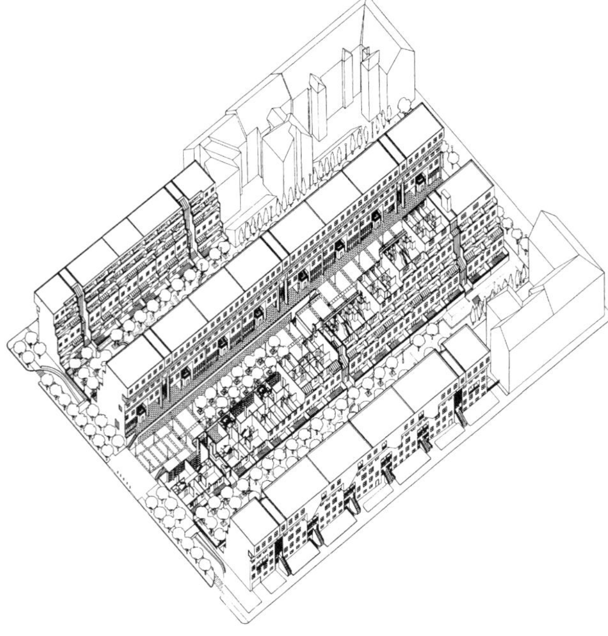

Special Kindergarten Schweizerspende 1948

During the period of reconstruction following World War II, Franz Schuster was able to create an example of humane and cheerful architectural language in this building. The slightly curvilinear site with it cog-like layout of radiating refectories and playgrounds is an impressive example of spatial differentiation between exterior and interior. Each play group has its own separate access independent of the main entrance. The building was later enlarged by Dimitris Manikas.

Auer-Welsbach-Park
Access: By prior appointment
Public transportation: Tram lines 52 and 58 (Penzingerstrasse)

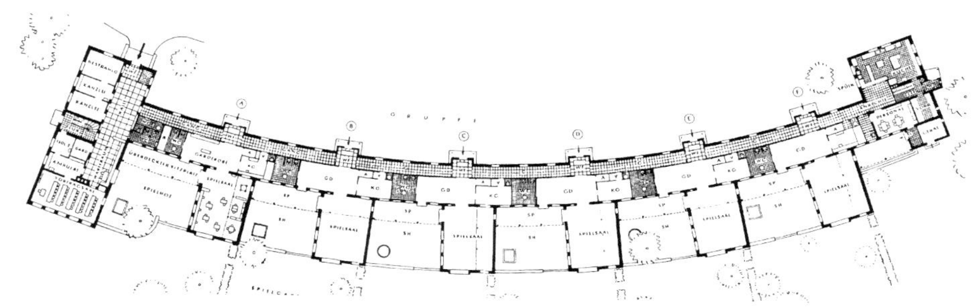

16.-**1**

Theodor Bach, Leopold Simony

Jubilee Buildings 1898

Maderspergerstrasse, Wernhardtstrasse, Gutraterplatz Roseggerstrasse
Access: Not open to the public
Public transportation: U4, tram line 10 (Gutraterplatz)

These apartment buildings were erected by the "Franz Joseph Jubilee Endowment" fund and represent an early alternative to the widespread tenement housing of the period. An attempt was made to compensate for the numerous defects and shortages that made life intolerable in the latter in these new buildings: only 45% of the total area was actually built up so as to achieve better ventilation and lighting conditions and many of the apartments were equipped with toilets, in order to improve sanitation. This type of development is an early predecessor of the council housing erected by the Municipality of Vienna: one may surmise that its conservative and representative façade and innovative spatial organisation exercised a great deal of influence on municipal architects.

16.-**2**

Manfred Nehrer and Reinhard Medek

Laboratory building 1993

Hasnerstrasse 127/ Koppstrasse 116
Access: Not open to the public
Public transportation: Tram line 46 (Possingergasse)

The functional consistency of this approx. 15,000 m² large laboratory and office building is impressive. One third of the area is used by Austria Tabak for laboratories, the other two thirds consist of flexible rental space for offices with the appropriate fittings. Everywhere the necessary flexibility has been carried over into the visual design: in the bands of windows, the framework of supporting columns and the aluminium cladding on the façade. Access to interior is through three atria (lifts and stairs) and two corridors. The objective was to create attractive working places in all parts of the building with the aid of natural lighting.

"Inspired by new building technologies, Plečnik succeeded [...] in further developing an age-old spatial topos that has always been associated with the Church into a lively, new and promising form that can be understood and appreciated by all" (F. Achleitner). Plečnik's building reveals innovative elements at all levels: even the erection of a pastoral care centre in a working class area was a revolutionary act. The use of reinforced concrete allows the architect to develop a new type of spatial concept; one that not only reinterprets the classic prototype of the basilica, but also investigates the sensuous possibilities of this new material. The "unfinished" air (façade) was not intended by the architect, but undoubtedly represents an added attraction for present-day sensibilities.

Heilig-Geist Kirche (Church of the Holy Ghost) (Schmelz Parish Church) 1910

Herbststrasse 82
Access: Open to the public
Public transportation: U6, tram line 9 (Koppstrasse)

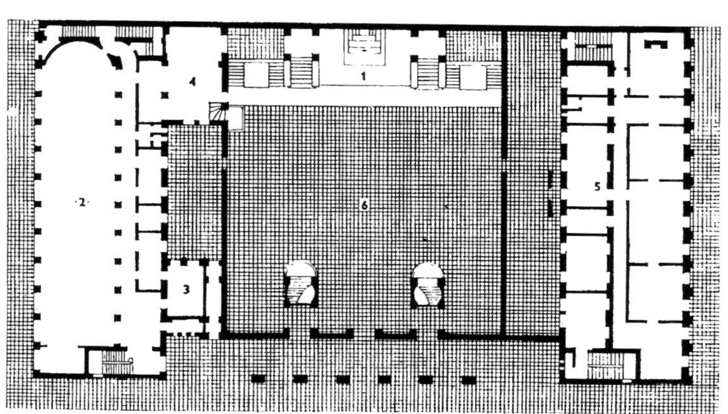

16.-**4**

Erich Leischner

Kongress Bad
1928

During the inter-war period, the erection of recreational facilities was a supplementary measure to the housing projects of the Municipality of Vienna. The atmosphere of this sport complex as a centre of working class culture is still quite palpable even today. This is undoubtedly helped by the mixture of sobriety (i.e. the simple coloured wooden cladding) and the playfulness of the details. Even though this large complex does not exude the luxury of the more cosmopolitan seaside resorts of the period, it nevertheless convincingly reflects the openness, physical culture and above all self-confidence that the Socialist Party strove to cultivate, especially in its early history.

Kongressplatz
Access: During opening hours
Public transportation: Tram line 43 (Hernals)

16.-**5**

Otto Wagner

Sanatorium for Lupus Patients
1909

The "Lupusheilstätte" is situated in the present day Wilhelminen Hospital complex . In principle, the H-shaped building is functionally arranged as all patients' quarters face south. Wagner's innovation was to create smaller rooms "to cater to the individuality of the patients" (Otto Wagner, Explanatory Report). The façade was carried out in terra nova and embedded with two centimetre thick blue glass plates as decoration.

Montléarstrasse 37,
Wilhelminenspital Pavillon 24,
Access: Not open to the public
Public transportation: Tram line 46 (Rankgasse)

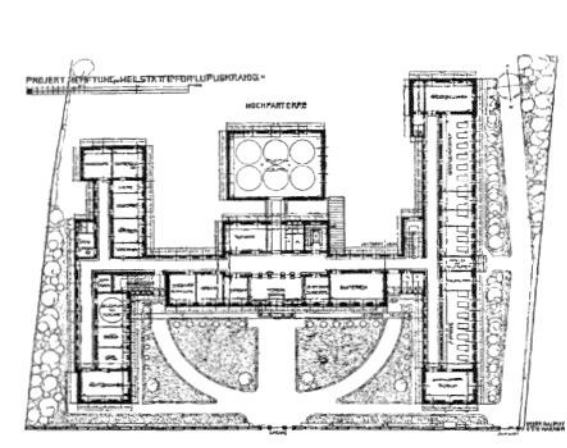

Sandleiten Hof
1924

This major residential development (1576 apartments) was realised by a large number of architects. Two different types of buildings were used: so as to avoid monotony, the blocks have curvilinear ground plans and are grouped around courts and squares, with their lines adapted to meet the topographical situation. The built up blocks are replaced by free-standing houses in the transition area between the development and the adjacent suburban villas. The complex became a showpiece project for the Municipality of Vienna because of its autonomous infrastructure, which could boast of its own library and post office. The team of architects included E.Hoppe, O.Schönthal, F.Matuschek, S.Theiss, H Jaksch, F.Krauss and J.Tölk.

Sandleitengasse, Steinmüllergasse, Metschlgasse, Baumeistergasse
Access: Public areas only
Public transportation: Tram line 44 (Sandleitengasse)

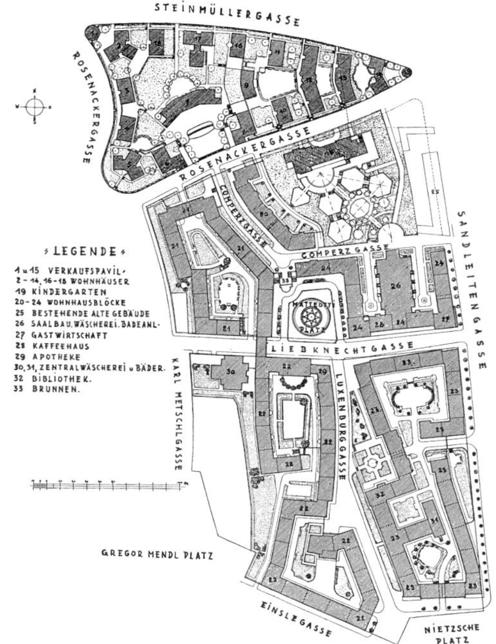

16.-**7**

Ottokar Uhl

Residential Building, Festgasse 1977

Festgasse 12–14,
J.-N.-Berger-Platz 7–9
Access: Not open to the public
Public transportation: Tram line J (Berger Platz)

Uhl was able to realise this first resident-participation scheme for the Municipality of Vienna. The basic framework is a reinforced concrete transverse wall system with a net span of 7.6 m and a depth of 15 m (11.4 to 16.8 m, depending on the inclusion of loggias or balconies). The location of kitchen wells was predetermined, together with those of the baths and toilets. The tenants were allowed to influence the ground plan of each apartment and, from the fourth floor upwards, the façade as well. The roof garden was designed by Gunnar Martinsson.

16.-**8**

Adolf Krischanitz

Housing estate Engilgasse 1992

Engilgasse
Access: Not open to the public
Public transportation: 45B bus (Funkengerngasse)

This residential project has three wings and was built on a corner site in an area that is characterised by loosely scattered detached and semidetached houses. Access is from the north, from the slightly elevated Pschorngasse, over two gangways that lead to the 1st floor of each stairwell, both of which are wedged between the residential wings. The three residential wings all have the same oblong arrangement, the outer ones being two and the middle wing three stories high. They contain clearly articulated three-room floor plans whose sitting rooms face south. As far as possible the flights of stairs have been designed to stop in front of the apartment doors so that these threshold areas can also act as a filter. Colour scheme by Oskar Putz.

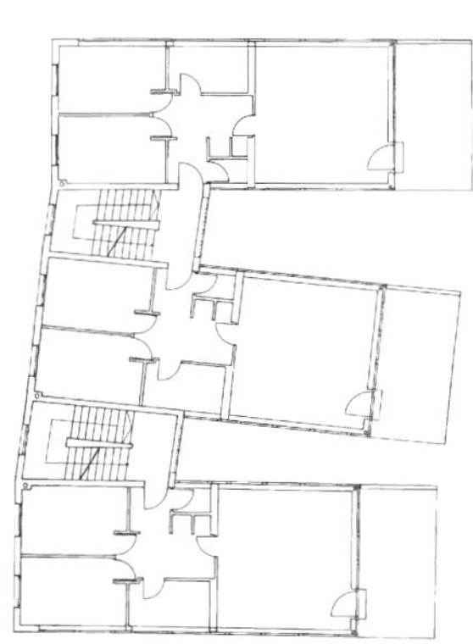

Konrad Lorenz Institute for Behavioural Research 1992

Savoyenstrasse
Access: By prior appointment
Public transportation: Tram line 44, 146B bus (Schloss Wilhelminenberg)

The Konrad Lorenz Institute for Comparative Behavioural Research of the Austrian Academy of Sciences came into being with the adaptation, extension and rebuilding of Otto König's now legendary Biological Station. Anton Schweighofer transformed a scattered medley of buildings into a new unified complex: the institute comprises laboratories, aquaria, free flight aviaries, a library and communal facilities. The main construction materials used were wood and glass.

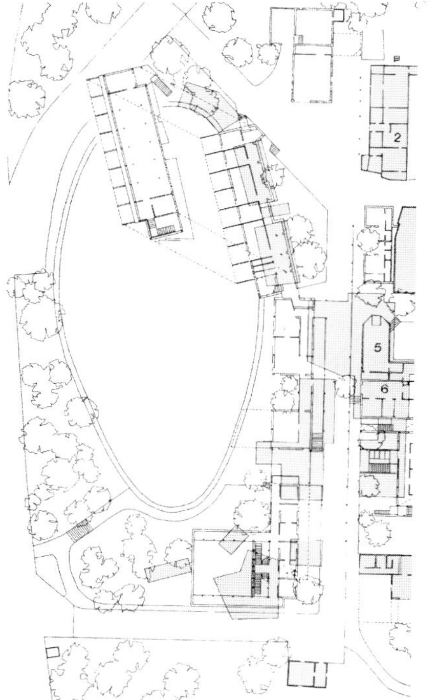

Wiedenhofer Hof
1924

Zeillergasse, Beringgasse, Liebknechtgasse, Pretschgogasse
Access: Not open to the public
Public transportation: U2, tram line 43 (Hernals)

For Josef Frank, who was actually an adherent of the settlement movement and a critic of large-scale "palaces for the people", the Wiedenhofer Hof must have really meant overstepping the boundaries of acceptable density in residential developments (another floor was added in the 'fifties). In spite of this, the main front building facing the Kongresspark gives a good idea of Frank's feeling for scale, formal richness and clarity of organisation. Because of its red colouring, the building was facetiously called the "paprika basket" and, with rather more animosity, the "red fort".

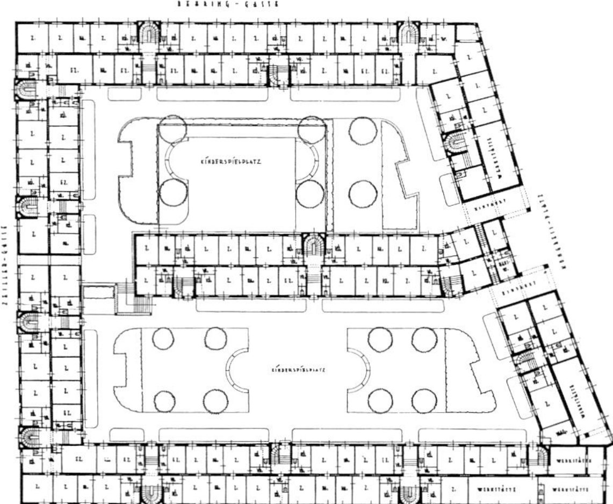

Residential Building Frauenfelderstrasse 1991

This building is a prime example of a new reappraisal of the modern architecture in Viennese residential development. The team of architects were able to realise this concept (together with a residential building cooperative as committed principal), which combines the greatest possible spatial quality with a neutral ground plan. Access to the building is through an open stairwell portal and arcades: the apartments available are either on one level, split level or of the penthouse variety. The loggias of the split level maisonettes are equipped with sliding horizontal blinds that reach over two stories. These serve to optically reduce the scale of the six storey residential building.

Frauenfelderstrasse 14
Access: Not open to the public
Public transportation: U2, tram line 43 (Hernals)

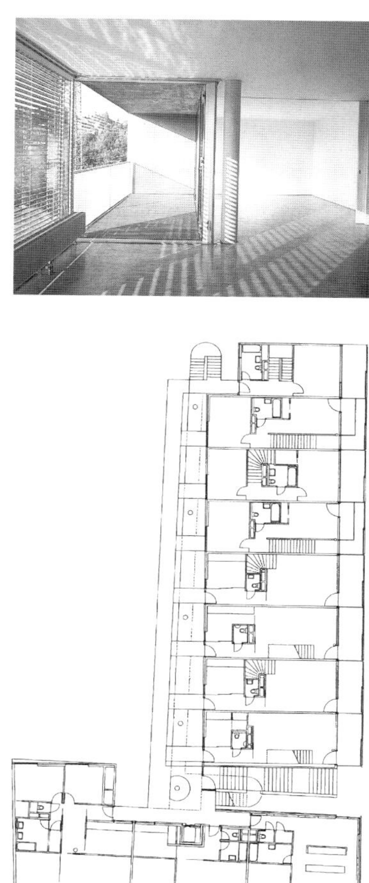

17.-**3** | ***Hermann Czech***

Schmidt House
1980

Seemüllergasse 29
Access: Not open to the public
Public transportation: Tram line 43 (Neuwaldegg)

This private house was planned to combine a family dwelling with a psychotherapeutic practice and to "fit in" on a topographical (slope, existing groups of trees and a swimming pool), functional (residence and practice) and cultural level (Viennese residential traditions, exemplified by Josef Frank and Adolf Loos). In terms of layout, the building consists of a cylinder (the library) between two cubes. The building, whose architectural vocabulary exploits conventions, both actively and passively exploits solar energy. "The building as a whole is a Viennese response to 'Post Modernism' and was early to reveal the limits of the same and to point to another intricacy of historical heritage" (Achleitner).

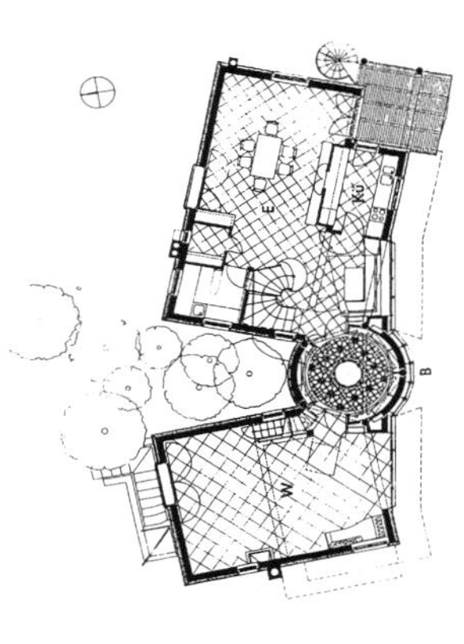

17.-**4** | ***Max Rieder, Wolfgang Tschapeller, Hans Peter Wörndl***

Residential Building Wittgensteingründe
1986

Neuwaldegger Strasse 38A
Access: Not open to the public
Public transportation: Tram line 43, 43B bus (Geroldgasse)

Neuwaldegger Strasse is situated in a valley between the Heuberg and the Schafberg hills and leads out of town directly into the Vienna Woods. The development, which was the first major assignment for a team of young architects, is at the end of this road. Its contemporary architectural vocabulary quite consciously sets itself apart from the bourgeois traditions of the surrounding suburban villas. The building is also characterised by an unusual diversity of materials and spatial differentiation.

Heuberg Housing Estate 1921

Kretschekgasse, Röntgengasse, Schrammelgasse, Plachygasse, Trenkwaldgasse
Access: Public areas only
Public transportation: Tram line 43, 44B bus (Siedlung Heuberg)

At the planning stage, Loos was chief architect of the Viennese Siedlungsamt (Settlement Office) and as such a committed exponent of the small-scale structures in "self-supporting" settlements at the edge of the city. He was convinced that these would contribute to an improvement of the living conditions and self-image of the working classes. It is by no means certain whether Loos was responsible for the layout as a whole, but he undoubtedly designed the houses in Plachygasse 1–13. They represent refinements of his prototype of "the house with one wall" that were designed in 1921 and built in 1923–24.

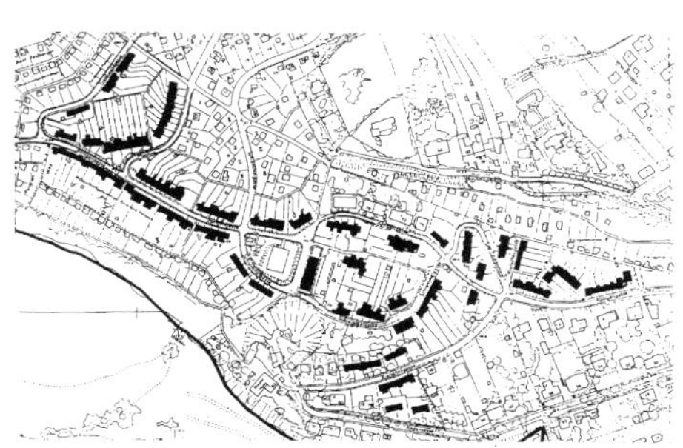

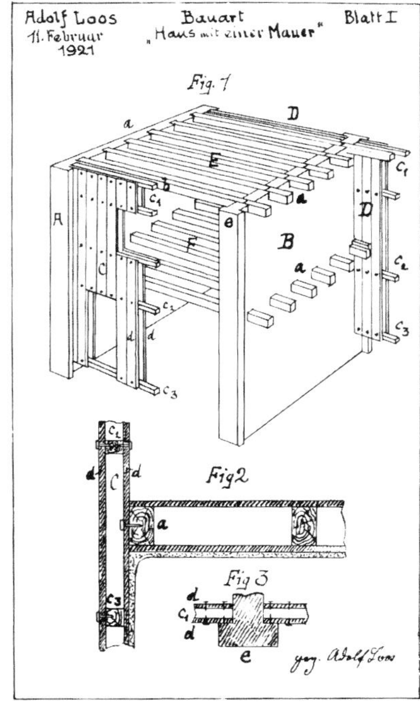

18.-**1**

Hubert and Franz Gessner

Gessner House
1907

Gessner's approach to volume is typical for the Otto Wagner School: a four-square building with broad eaves. The simple plaster facade and addition of English-style bay-windows is not very typical, and demonstrates the increasing influence of the Arts & Crafts Movement on buildings in Vienna, while the columns are more reminiscent of the Wiener Secession.

Sternwartestrasse 70
Access: Not open to the public
Public transportation: Tram lines 40 and 41 (Gersthof)

18.-**2**

Lois Welzenbacher

Arnold House
1923

Even in this early work Welzenbacher's sensitivity in merging his buildings with either the surrounding architecture or the landscape is visible. The concave plan is a response to the boundaries of the site, the classical-columned portal to the genteel suburban location. Any Biedermeier impression is eradicated by the use of "dropped" capitals.

Sternwartestrasse 83
Access: Not open to the public
Public transportation: Tram line 41 (Gersthof)

Designed during 1977–78, this school building was finished only in 1990. The long planning and realisation phase can be blamed on the complexities of school building in Vienna. Hollein has realized an impressive variety of spatial quality, diverse materials and light effects in a very limited space. A small city for small people, with space to explore, and safe spaces. This is the art of building as a didactic element.

Primary School Köhlergasse 1977

Gentzgasse/Köhlergasse
Access: Viewing by arrangement
Public transportation: Tram lines 40 and 41 (Weinhausergasse)

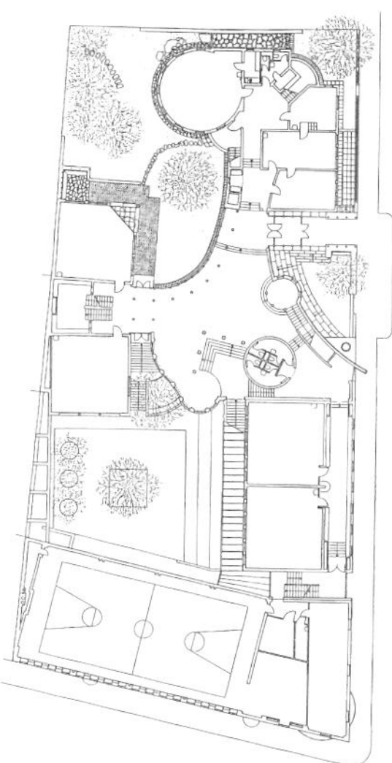

18.-**4** *H. von Ferstel, G. Sennholz, H. Goldemund, W. Hybler*

Türkenschanzpark
1885

This park was laid out on the initiative of Heinrich von Ferstel on defences from the time of the "Turkish Sieges" of Vienna. The landscaping was carried out by Gustav Sennholz. It is modelled on the flair of a refreshing alpine summer, and rendered picturesque by the use of artificial waterfalls, rockfaces and a chasm. The park was expanded by popular demand at the beginning of the 20th century.

Gregor Mendel Strasse,
Hasenauerstrasse,
Max Emanuel Strasse
Access: Open to the public
Public transportation: Buses 37A and 40A (Gregor Mendel Strasse)

18.-**5** *Adolf Krischanitz*

House
1989

The entrance and the southern part of the garden are connected to a public path, while the private part of the garden is a gently sloping north face. Krischanitz responded to this with a parabola-shaped plan ending with a "shield", and to the north in the vertex of the parabola, a glazed conservatory. The roof and walls are made of timber, the "shield" is masonry with an interesting facade.

Franz Barwigweg
Access: Not open to the public
Public transportation: Tram line 41 (Pötzleinsdorf)

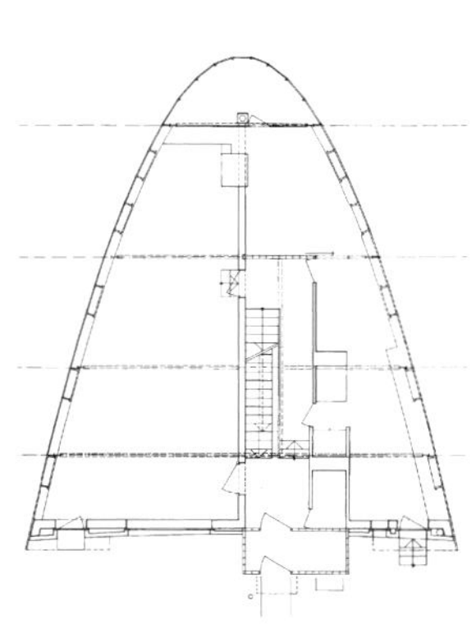

Moller House
1927

Loos was living in Paris when he designed this house, a family house that fits in neatly with the series of buildings he designed during his emigré period. As with the Tristan Tzara House in Paris, the austere symmetry of the street-facing facade melts into clearly human lines in the layout of the rooms in the interior. The private garden side contrasts with the public street-facing facade. Only the outer walls are load-bearing, with facilitates the visual connection of the rooms inside.

Starkfriedgasse 19
Access: Not open to the public
Public transportation: Tram line 41 (Scheibenbergstrasse)

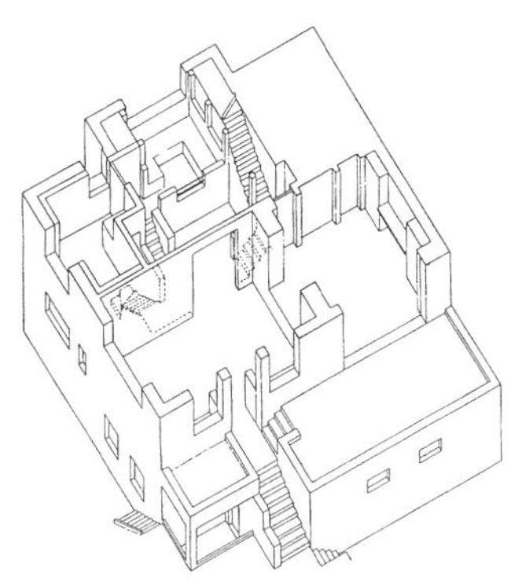

Private House
1988

Cultural values are concentrated in this house, a made-to-measure family home. The building articulates the dualism of private bedrooms on the lower two floors and reception rooms with transparent glass on the top, third storey: this also makes optimal use of the slope for the view.

Pötzleinsdorfer Höhe 25a
Access: Not open to the public
Public transportation: Tram line 41, Bus 41A (Pötzleinsdorfer Höhe)

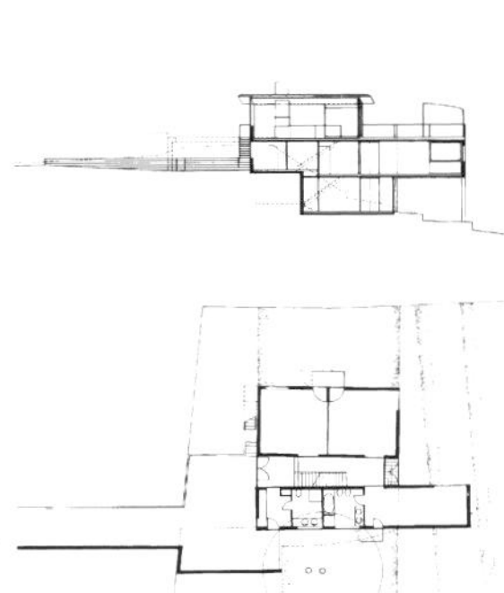

Supplementary Recommendations

15.-**13s**	Apartment House Franco Fonatti	1988 Gebrüder Langgasse 16
15.-**14s**	Bezirksgericht Fünfhaus (Courts) Günther Oberhofer	1995 Gasgasse 1–7
16.-**10s**	Secondary School Atelier 18: Eder, Pal, Weber, Wieden	1994 Koppstrasse 110
17.-**6s**	Richthausen Bridge over the Suburban line Otto Wagner	1896 Richthausenstrasse, Hernalser Friedhof
17.-**7s**	Holy Hof Rudolf Perco	1928 Heigerleinstrasse 104
18.-**8s**	Terraced housing Roland Rainer	1984 Pötzleinsdorfer Strasse 178–180
18.-**9s**	Suburban line station, Gersthof Otto Wagner	1896 Gersthofer Strasse, Währinger Strasse, Gentzgasse
18.-**10s**	Hans Radl School Viktor Adler	1958 Währingerstrasse 173–181
18.-**11s**	House Hans Glas	1932 Wilbrandtgasse 23

MAP No. 10

19th District
Döbling

19th District, Döbling Index numbers 19.-**1** … 19.-**32s**

Buildings worth visiting – Suggestions by Viennese architects

19th District:

Heidulf Gerngroß:
Karl Marx Hof, Index number 19.-**25**

Hans Hollein:
Karl-Marx-Hof, Index number 19.-**25**

19.-**1** | *Josef Hoffmann*

Klose-Hof
1924

This council housing scheme designed for the City of Vienna by Josef Hoffmann consists of 140 flats and is located in a traditionally upper middle class residential district. In inserting a single residental tower Hoffmann disrupted the standard courtyard layout of such residential building. He reduced his beloved classical architecture details to a level appropriate to the project. The building is one of the finest erected as part of Vienna's council housing programme at that time, as are the sculptures by Anton Hanak.

Philippovichgasse 1,
Werkmanngasse,
Fickertgasse, Peezgasse
Access: Limited to exterior viewing
Public transportation: Tram line 38 (Glatzgasse)

19.-**2** | *Adolf Loos*

Duschnitz House
1915

A felt manufacturer who profited from World War I and, still during its course, commissioned Loos to develop his house and make space for an art collection and add a music room. Loos altered little of the original building, expanding it mainly by the addition of cubes, which also created the terraces. A 16th century ceiling was installed in the study. The organ salon is one of the architect's most grandiose interior designs.

Weimarer Strasse 87
Access: Not open to the public
Public transportation: U4 and bus 10A (Blaasstrasse)

Adolf Loos

19.-**3**

A further example of Loos' spatial planning showing that his pragmatism can satisfy the demands of restructuring a building, even though the architect was often regarded as dogmatic. In this case the large house was extended to the south and east, with additions clearly visible from the outside but no break with the original building being visible inside.

Mandl House
1916

Blaasstraße 8
Access: Not open to the public
Public transportation: U4, Bus 10A (Blaasstraße)

Josef Frank, Oskar Wlach

19.-**4**

Once Josef Frank had freed himself from the 'constraints' (as he saw it) of symmetry he began to dissolve closed building volumes and develop space horizontally. The next step was to reject the straight line. In this house in the Chimanistraße the two architects grouped the variously sized building volumes according to their function around an open terrace that was oriented towards the garden.

Bunzl House
1936

Chimanistrasse 18
Access: Not open to the public
Public transportation: Tram line 38 (Gatterburggasse)

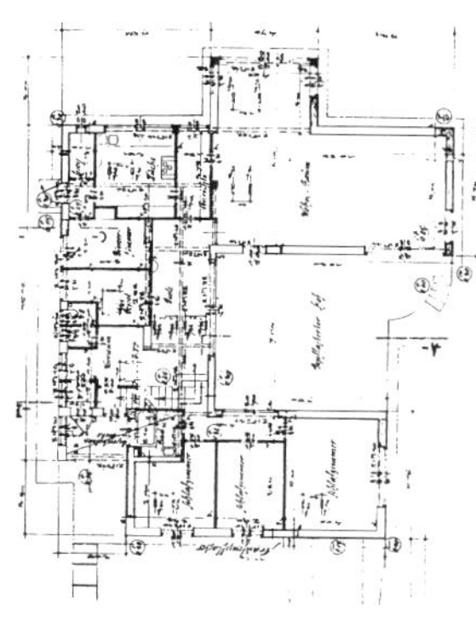

19.-**5**

Anton Schweighofer

Housing Gatterburggasse 1989

This residential apartment house built in Grinzing for the city of Vienna has as its main theme the central space plan. In the middle of the flat there is an undefined square room that can be used differently: as a dining room, living room or play room. The adjoining rooms, all of the same size, are functionally neutral and offer a maximum of flexibility. The two buildings are recognisable externally as simple Modernist buildings with their white plaster facades and curved roof.

Gatterburggasse 2c
Access: Not open for viewing
Public transportation: Tram line 38 (Gatterburggasse)

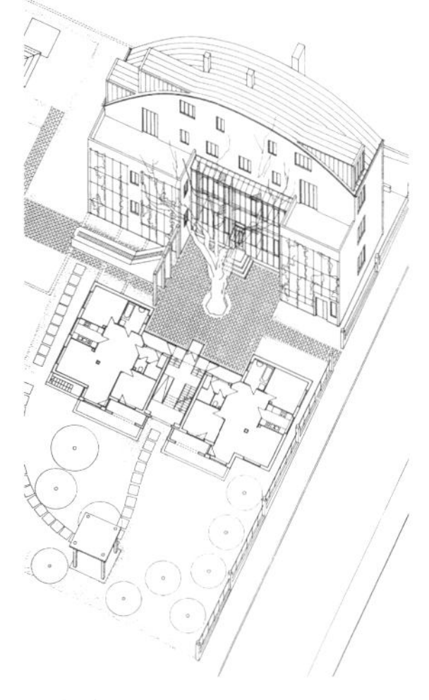

19.-**6**

Anton Schweighofer

Institute Building for the University of Agriculture 1967

University buildings are on the one hand functional buildings but on the other representative of a public building culture. This institute building was one of the first really modern university buildings built after the Second World War, and is comparable to Ernst Hiesmayer's Law Faculty (1969–83). In both cases the belief in scientific progress is symbolised by technical aesthetics. Schweighofer's dynamic organism has a facade of pre-rustcoated steel, a technical innovation of the 1970s. Spacious halls and a clearly organised plan are evident in this building.

Peter-Jordan-Strasse 82
Access: Viewing by arrangement
Public transportation: U4, Bus 37A (Dänenstrasse)

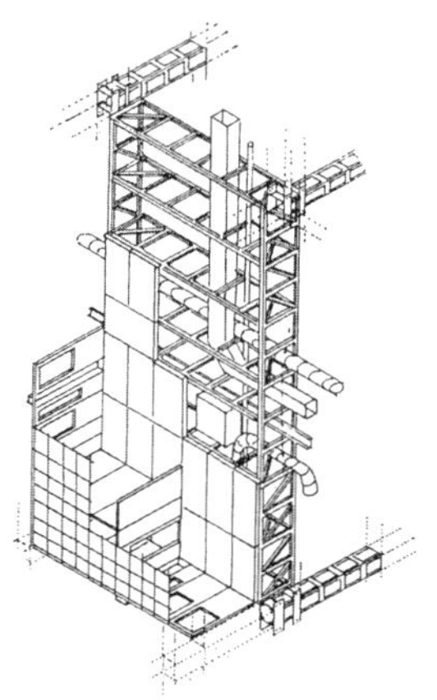

Houses in the Wilbrandtgasse 1913

Josef Frank was in charge of the project for an ensemble of which only two buildings were realised. House number 3 is a remarkable object to which Frank applies his, later published, ideas about an architectural design that looks as if it was unplanned. The street facade is axial in principle but contains surprising deviations that give the building the impression of having grown over a long period of time. The relationship of this front facade to the articulated and terraced garden front is full of tension as in the Moller House by Adolf Loos, built a decade later.

Wilbrandtgasse 3 and 11
Access: Not open to the public
Public transportation: Tram line 41 (Scheibenbergstrasse)

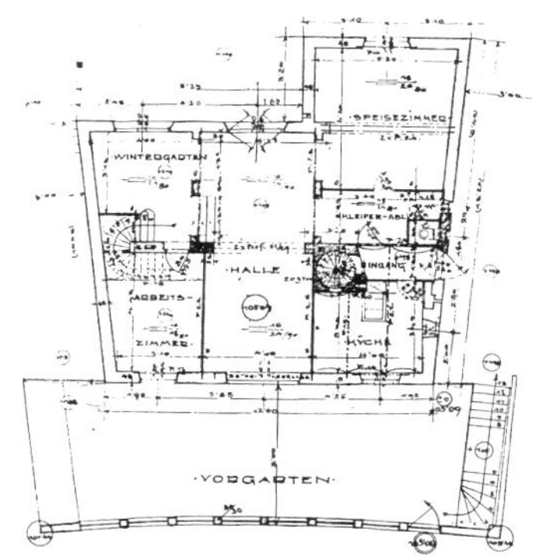

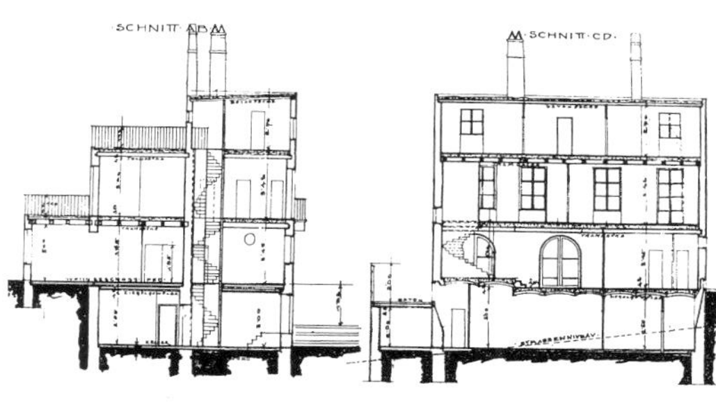

19.-**8** | *Richter/Gerngroß, Schweighofer, Mang, Mang-Frimmel, et al.*

Housing on the Gräf & Stift estate 1981

The City of Vienna held an architectural competition in autumn 1981 for a housing estate on the former Gräf & Stift industrial estate. The final cooperation between the winners resulted in a variety of diverse forms. Western building: (1) Helmut Richter, Heidulf Gerngross, (2) Anton Schweighofer (3) Johann Brennig, Helmut Christen, Michael Stepanek, Christoph Thetter, Helmut Wimmer; Eastern building: Günther Lautner, Peter Scheifinger, Rudolf Szedenik, Walter Hoffellner, Bernd Stanzel, Ernst Hoffman.

Weinberggasse 70–74
Access: Outside open to viewing
Public transportation: Bus 35A (Kratzlgasse)

19.-**9** | *Clemens Holzmeister*

Church of St. Judas Thaddäus in der Krim 1924

Holzmeister was able to complete only the part of the church facing the street (1924–32). Although he related the building to the eaves of the adjoining buildings he provides the church with a prominent feature by placing an extended tower on the front. The church was damaged during World War II and was completed in 1957 with the building of the nave.

Budinskygasse 19
Access: Open to public viewing
Public transportation: Suburban train (Schnellbahn) 45, Bus 35A (Rodlergasse)

Primary School in der Krim 1961

This primary school with eight classes is grouped around a central courtyard. Each classroom has an open space attached to it so that classes can be held in the open. So doing, the architect has broken with the traditional type of school building and offered a novel solution. The clarity of plan and the economy of construction (exposed concrete, plaster and timber) contribute to the convincing composition.

Flotowgasse 25
Access: Viewing by arrangement
Public transportation: U4, Suburban train (Schnellbahn) 45 (Krottenbachstrasse)

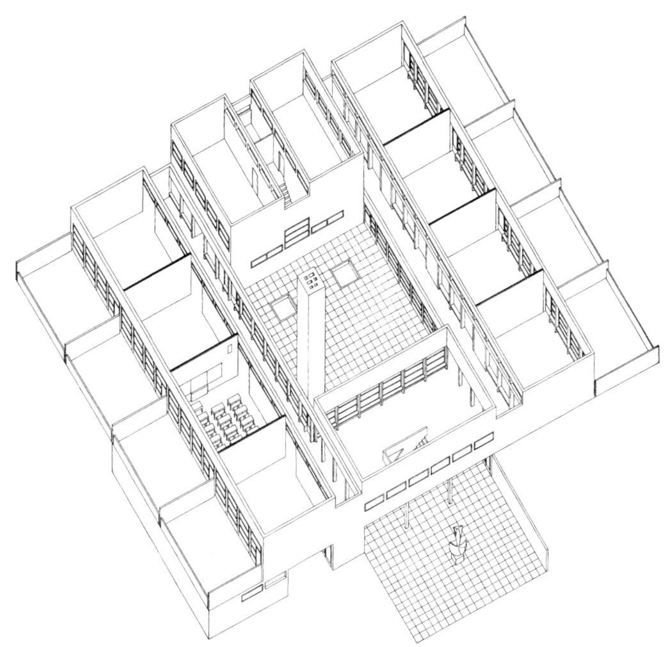

19.-**11** | ***Josef Hoffmann, Josef Kalbac***

Housing Silbergasse 1951

This modest housing scheme of 70 flats was built around a tower-like apartment block which acts as the centre of the complex. Identical windows were used everywhere including the stairwell. The simplicity of the design by the then 81 year old Josef Hoffmann corresponds to similar council housing of the immediate post-war period. The planned pergola to the street no longer exists.

Silbergasse 2–4
Access: Not open to the public
Public transportation: Tram line 38 (Silbergasse)

19.-**12** | ***Karl Mayreder***

Zacherl factory 1888

This building, for a pesticide factory, integrated an earlier complex of buildings from 1873. The use of Persian forms was legitimised by the fact that one of the ingredients for the pesticide was imported from Persia. This factory is a unique example of imaginative building in Vienna's urban landscape.

Nusswaldgasse 14
Access: Not open to the public
Public transportation: Tram line 38 (Silbergasse)

Josef Hoffmann

19.-**13**

The Sonja Knips House gives the impression of being a simple building. On closer inspection one sees that Hoffmann's tendency to decorate has yielded a schematic, restrained arrangement, and the complicated layering of walls with smooth surfaces broken by applied decorative elements. The garden facade has a more pronounced articulation than the street facade. The building develops lengthwise along the road, and even at its broadest is only two rooms deep.

Knips House
1924

Nusswaldgasse 22
Access: Not open to the public
Public transportation: Tram line 37 (Barawitzkagasse)

Jan Kotera

19.-**14**

The only known work by the Otto Wagner student Jan Kotera from Czechoslovakia is this house of impressive dimension. Kotera divided the volume into two almost independent buildings grouping a residential tract around a courtyard and connecting a service tract on the side. The facade is brought to life not only through the use of expressionist decorative forms, an imaginative diversion from the classical, but also by the use of plaster and brick masonry. Tne terracotta surface of the upper storey gives that level the character of an attic.

Lemberger House
1914

Access: Not open to the public
Public transportation: Tram line 38 (An den langen Lüssen)

19.-**15**

Siegfried C. Drach

House in the Leopold Steiner Gasse 1935

This house has elements typical of the Viennese variations on the "Neue Sachlichkeit", on occasion ironically referred to as "charming" by contemporaries. Closed walls, an almost picturesque solution to the actual building and the stress on line by reducing the cornices, the architect takes a dynamic approach, but not at the expense of individual comfort, and (let's say it just once) and gives the house a certain "Gemütlichkeit".

Leopold-Steiner-Gasse 45
Access: Not open to the public
Public transportation: Tram line 38 (Paradisgasse)

19.-**16**

Josef Hoffmann

Housing estate Kaasgraben 1912

Building several houses together to form an ensemble with the character of a housing estate is an interesting way to try and create a certain unity in the suburbs. Hoffmann approaches the task with skill. He arranges the buildings on the edge of the site, to keep the spaciousness a house needs. The architecture is simple and radiates "upright" middle-class style without being unduly stolid. The building data make a mockery of the whole project, because it was precisely the middle-class for whom it was built that suffered financial ruin after World War I.

Kaasgrabengasse 30/32, 36/38, Suttingergasse 12/14, 16/18
Access: Not open to the public
Public transportation: Tram line 38 (Paradisgasse)

Wilhelm Holzbauer

19.-**17**

House for an art collector
1978

This Post-Modern house for an art collector was built in the tradition of the upper-class houses of the turn of the century with an extensive system of rooms. Both semantically and formally the architect separates the reception area (entrance pavilion, living room, dining room) with a marble facade from the private sleeping areas with a plaster facade. Differentiated rooms and exclusive furnishing materials characterize the atmosphere of cultivated living.

Kaasgrabengasse 110
Access: Not open to the public
Public transportation: Tram line 38 (Paradisgasse)

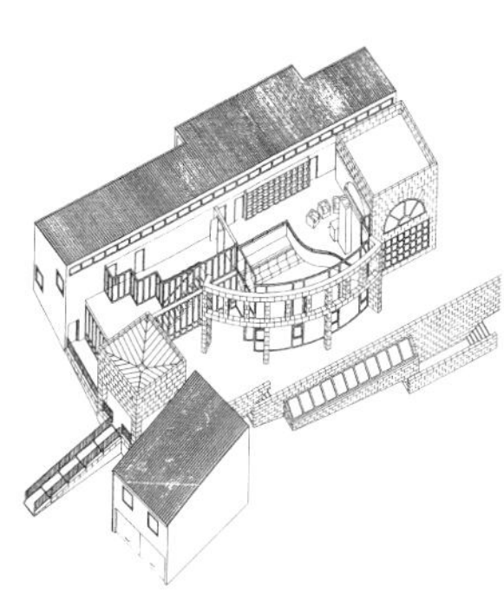

Gustav Peichl

19.-**18**

Peichl House
1960

The outer dimensions of this house are the result of the rules for building on a narrow sloping plot in this area. The street facade of the white cuboid building looks austere, broken only by a horizontal strip of window. The south-facing garden side is completely gazed and faces the vineyards. An example of the Viennese style of living, oriented to the principles of the Movement Classical Modern.

Himmelstrasse 47
Access: Not open to the public
Public transportation: Tram line 38 (Grinzing)

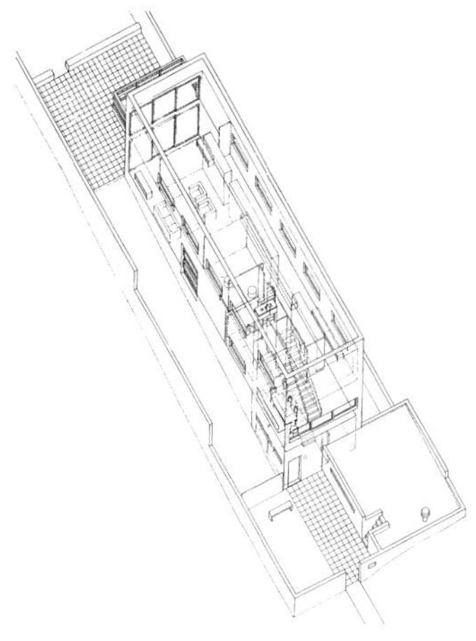

19.-**19**

Adolf Krischanitz

House in Salmannsdorf 1986

Salmannsdorfer Strasse 66
Access: Not open to the public
Public transportation: U6, Bus 35A (Salmannsdorf)

Reconstructing existing buildings has always been an important part of the Viennese way of life. Since Adolf Loos, the Modernists have been using transformation, adaptation, regulation and even partial renewal in an attempt at a semantic dialogue with history. The house in Salmannsdorf is a case in point: the interior structures were almost entirely renewed, and the outer face extended, adapted and renewed (the colour concept way by Oskar Putz). Colour contrasts and a mixture of materials are characteristic of Krischanitz' latest projects.

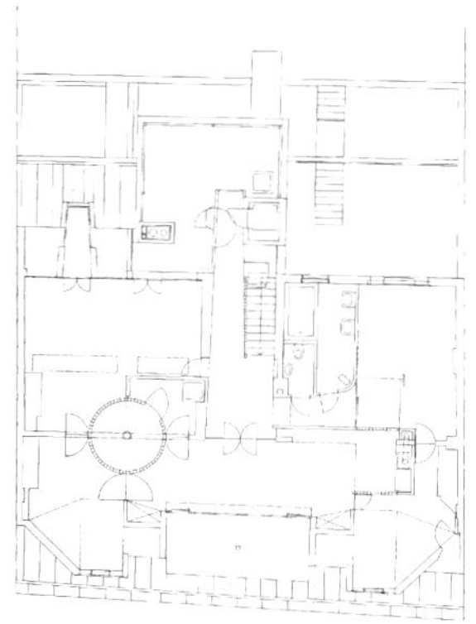

19.-**20**

Oskar Strnad, Oskar Wlach (Josef Frank)

House in the Cobenzlgasse 1910

Cobenzlgasse 71
Access: Not open to the public
Public transportation: Bus 38A (Oberer Reisenbergweg)

A building from the period when Oskar Strnad, Oskar Wlach and Josef Frank worked closely together. The building is classical "once again", not "still" classical. That this classicism is applied in a deliberately reflective and fragmentary manner can be seen by the extraordinary position of the portal, which is not facing the street. The difference in levels of the sloping plot is dealt with by various flights of steps. The building was designed by a group who were critical authorities on building activities in Vienna in the inter-war period.

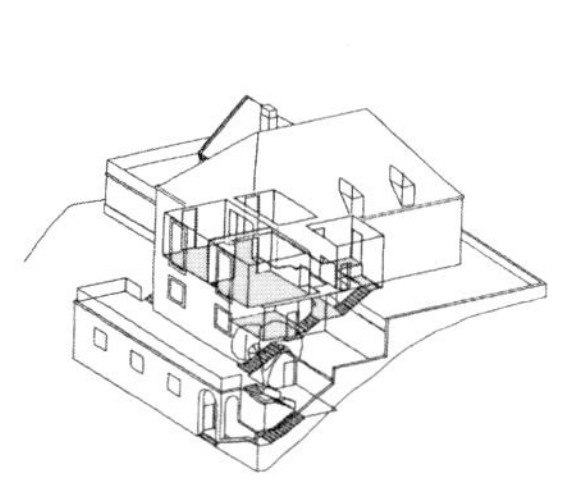

Moll House II
1906

Painter Carl Moll's second residence (see Moser-Moll: 18th District, Starkfriedgasse19) is near Hoffmann's Brauner and Henneberg houses. Hoffmann built a tower-like addition to a nearly square living area, with the kitchen on the ground floor and the upper storey being the painter's studio. This division is made clear through the use of plaster on the addition while the main building is clad in asbestos shingle. The additions made in 1928 changed the building considerably, and it was then renovated in 1971/72 by Erich Boltenstein.

Wollergasse 10
Access: Not open to the public
Public transportation: Tram line 37 (Geweygasse)

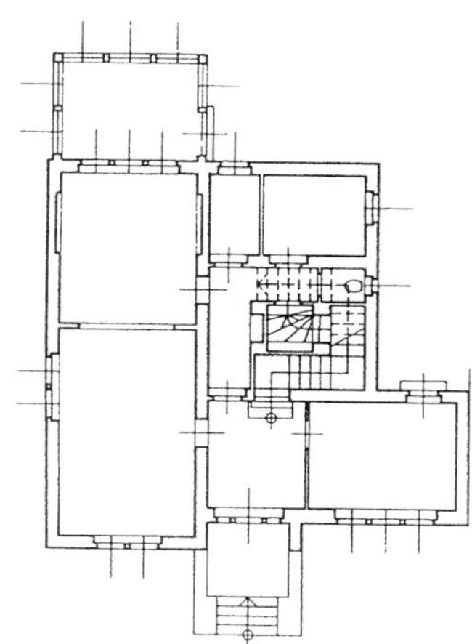

Ast House
1909

Steinfeldgasse 2,
Wollergasse 12
Access: Not open to the public
Public transportation: Tram line 37 (Hohe Warte)

The Eduard Ast House was built as the final contribution to the Hoffmann conglomerate on the Hohe Warte, and is located on a corner plot between the Spitzer and Moll houses. Hoffmann made use of this position by constructing a raised walled terrace, which he connected to the lower storey of the building. The building is square in plan, with only the stairwell breaking out of the form. An ingenuous rhetorician, Hoffmann applies his classical architectural vocabulary in an unorthodox manner, for example by fluting the entire outer wall.

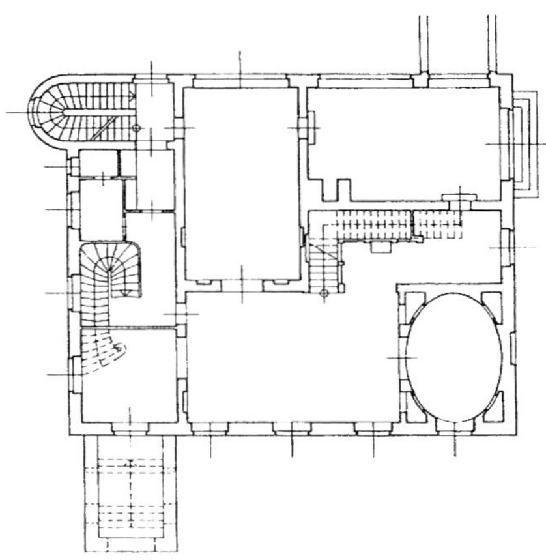

Spitzer House
1901

Hoffmann considered this building and the Moll Moser and Heneberg houses part of a group. Here too, elements of the English Arts & Crafts Movement dominate the different sections of the building. The projecting entrance hall, the upper part of which can be used as a terrace, also breaks up the facade. The glazed alcove on the street facade is part of the house owner´s photography studio. The interior has been slightly altered, but the exterior is in a good state of repair.

Steinfeldgasse 4
Access: Not open to the public
Public transportation: Tram line 37 (Hohe Warte)

Josef Hoffmann

19.-**24**

Moser-Moll House I
1900

The tension in this semi-detached house built for the Viennese painters Carl Moll and Kolo Moser results from a calculated balance between homogeneity and pronounced differentiation. The semi-hipped roof and half-timbered gable end, and the strong relationship to the landscape (also evident in the interiors), contradict the urban typology of the semi-detached house. It typifies the inherent conflict of building a semi-rural housing estate like the "Vienna Cottage District" in the city. Hoffmann´s design was inspired by English country houses.

Steinfeldgasse 8,
Geweygasse 13
Access: Not open to the public
Public transportation: Tram line 37 (Geweygasse)

Karl Marx Hof and Svoboda Hof 1926

Heiligenstädter Strasse, Grinzinger Strasse, Boschstrasse
Access: The courtyards are open to viewing
Public transportation: U4 (Heiligenstadt)

The Karl Marx Hof is considered the flagship of the social housing apartment buildings erected by Vienna's City Council. And not by accident: it is not the biggest apartment block (it has 1325 dwellings, whereas the Sandleiten Hof has 200 more), but none of the other "superblocks" project such a demonstration of the power of the Social Democratic movement. Its monumental size, above all its closed lower storey and tower-like projections were promptly misunderstood by the Austrofascists, and the result was a bloody battle for the "Red Fortress" in 1934. The architectonic achievement of the Otto Wagner student Karl Ehn is in the articulation of the approximately 1 km long street-facing facades.

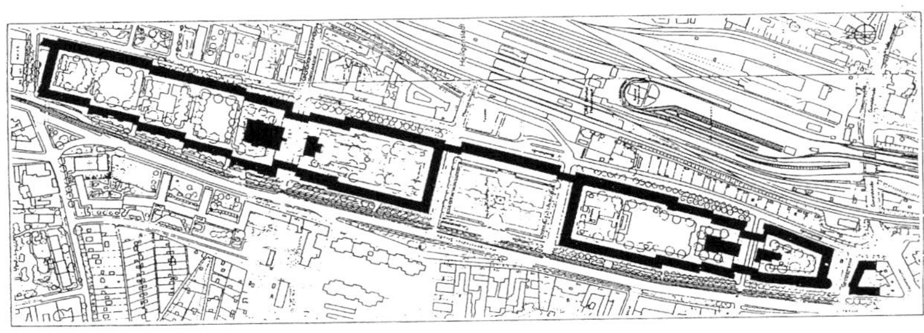

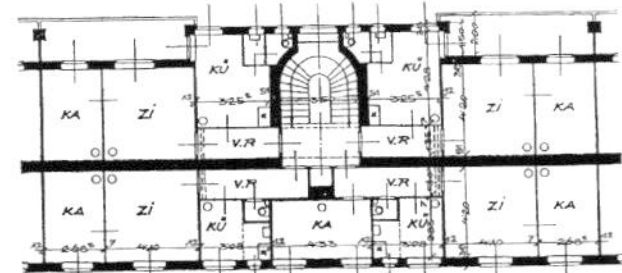

Office Building
1992

This building won the 1993 Adolf Loos Prize for Architecture. It is also one of the few cases in Vienna where the owner and the architect were one and the same person. The architect built a simple, linear office building next to a brick building dating from 1897, which he was using as his office. He was more interested in the realisation of the idea than the use of expensive-looking materials. Grey concrete breeze blocks, equal-sized windows and a protruding glazed stairwell are the characteristics of the architecture. A remarkable achievement when compared to other office blocks.

Muthgasse 107
Access: Not open to the public
Public transportation: Bus 11A, 39A (Mooslackengasse)

Supplementary Recommendations

19.-**27s**	House R. Boris Podrecca	1990 Kosselgasse 17
19.-**28s**	Offices, Grinzinger Allee Ulrike Janowetz	1991 Grinzinger Allee 18
19.-**29s**	Offices, Grinzinger Allee Heinz Neumann	1994 Grinzinger Allee 3
19.-**30s**	Hackenberggasse Günther Oberhofer	1990 Hackenberggasse 17–19/ Raimund Zoder Gasse 10–16
19.-**31s**	House S. F. Luigi Blau	1975 Hansi Niese Gasse 18
19.-**32s**	House Ernst Hoffmann	1994 Koschatgasse 2

MAP No. 11

20th District
Brigittenau

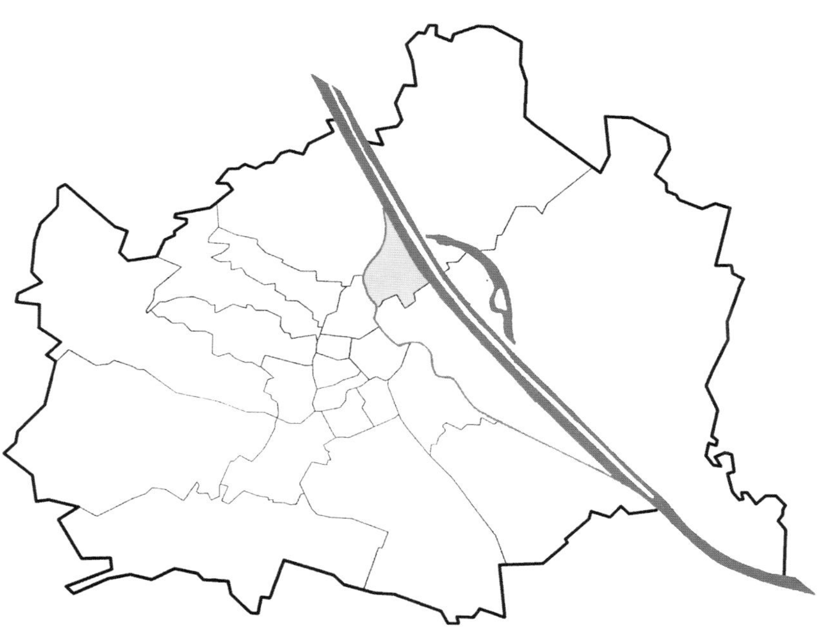

20th District, Brigittenau Index numbers 20.-**1** … 20.-**7s**

Buildings worth visiting – Suggestions by Viennese architects

20th District

August Sarnitz:

Nußdorfer-Wehr, Index number 20.-**1**
Winarsky Hof, Index number 20.-**3**
Basler Versicherung, Index number 20.-**6**

Nussdorf Weir and Locks 1894

At the beginning of the Danube Canal
Access: Open to the public
Public transportation: Suburban train (Schnellbahn) 40 (Nussdorf)

Otto Wagner planned this weir with its administrative building (1894–1898) to act as well as a gateway on the water to the city. Two larger-than-life lions on either side of the barrier "guard" the city. Otto Wagner himself claimed to have produced 1500 drawings for the structures. This weir was restructured from 1971–75 to fit in with flood protection plans for the whole city. Wagner's original "needle weir" was replaced by two segmented locks. The relocation of the highway beside it caused the gateway, with its lions, to lose its significance.

H. Glück, W. Holzbauer, H. Hilmer & C. Sattler 20.-**2**

Housing „Vollwertwohnen" Hartlgasse 1985

Hartlgasse, Dammstrasse, Pappenheimgasse
Access: Not open to the public
Public transportation: Tram line 33 (Jägerstrasse)

The "Vollwertwohnen" initiative was started by the city council to initiate architecture of high quality in its social housing programme. International architects were invited to work with local architects on the project, which also includes the housing scheme in Rollingergasse (Index No.12.-**5**).
Section by Holzbauer: Flats and maisonettes.
Section by Glück: Maisonettes with terraces and with a roof-top swimming pool.
Section by Hilmer/Sattler: Flats around a glass-roofed atrium.

P. Behrens, J. Hoffmann, J. Frank, O. Strnad, O. Wlach, et al. 20.-**3**

Housing Winarsky Hof and Otto Haas Hof 1924

Stromstrasse 36–38, Winarskystrasse, Durchlauf-strasse, Pasettistrasse
Access: Not open to the public
Public transportation: U6 (Dresdner Strasse)

Vienna's best architects were commissioned by the City of Vienna to erect this prestige housing scheme. As a consequence the formation of the blocks is varied. The individual buildings in the Winarskyhof develop into interlocking courtyards along a symmetrical axis, although the outer buildings are arranged in a somewhat looser fashion. Adolf Loos planned a stepped-back building for the Otto Haas Hof built at the same time, but it was not realized. Architects: P. Behrens, J. Hoffmann, J. Frank, O. Strnad, O. Wlach, K. Dirnhuber, F. Schuster, M. Lihotzky.

20.-**4**

Rudolf Perco

Housing Friedrich Engels Platz 1930

Friedrich Engels Platz, Wehlistrasse, Leystrasse, Forsthausgasse, Kapaunplatz
Access: Not open to the public
Public transportation: Tram line 31 (Friedrich-Engels-Platz)

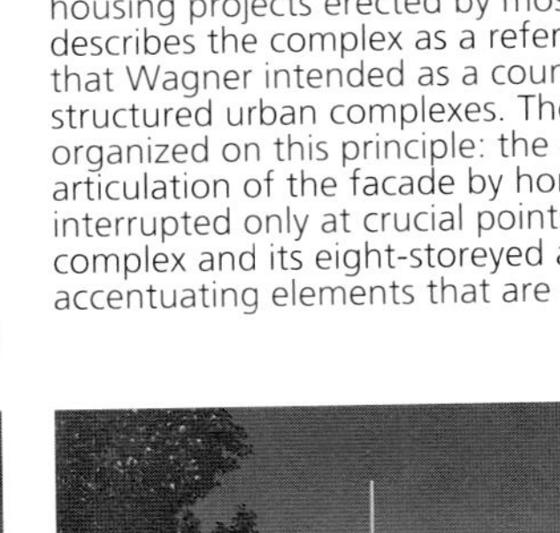

The particularly large-scale metropolitan character of the architecture of this superblock (1930–33) is a more direct consequence of Otto Wagner's teachings than the Viennese social housing projects erected by most of his students. Manfredo Tafuri describes the complex as a reference to the "happy interruption" that Wagner intended as a counterpoint to the usual evenly structured urban complexes. The building volume itself is also organized on this principle: the economical and constant articulation of the facade by horizontal bands and cornices is interrupted only at crucial points, such as the entrance to the complex and its eight-storeyed apartment towers, by additional accentuating elements that are overlaid on the structure.

20.-**5**

Heinz Neumann, Eric Steiner

Housing Handelskai 1994

Handelskai, Friedrich Engels Platz
Access: Viewing only from outside
Public transportation: Tram line 31 (Friedrich-Engels-Platz)

The building corresponds to the linearity of the river Danube, with a tower accentuating the corner at Friedrich Engels Platz. Facing the Handelskai is a two-storey base containing a supermarket and parking lots, above which is a circulation level with a view over the river. The architects describe the concept of flats on a supporting frame facing the Handelskai as "floating beams", whereas the Friedrich Engels Platz facade comprises two-storey maisonnette flats.

Basler Versicherungen Office building 1990

The Danube Canal is one of Vienna's most important spaces. Any building constructed there enters into a visible dialogue with the beginnings of the inner city itself. Podrecca has achieved in this administrative building a reflection on Viennese architecture in that he has treated each of the three facades of the corner building differently: a glazed curtain wall faces the Danube Canal, a horizontal strip facade and a stuccoed perforated facade face the two subsidiary streets.The semi-public function of the administrative building is given additional emphasis by an interior courtyard open to the public.

Brigittenauer Lände 50–54
Access: Courtyard and restaurant open to the public
Public transportation: U4 (Friedensbrücke)

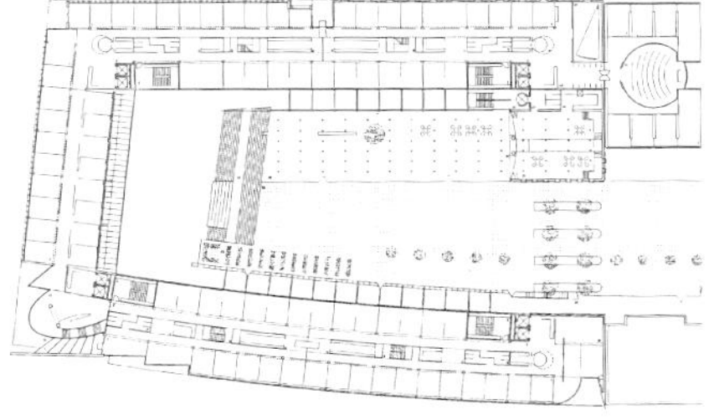

Housing Wexstrasse 1993

Jägerstrasse,Wexstrasse, Leipziger Platz
Access: Open areas only
Public transportation: U6 (Leipziger Platz)

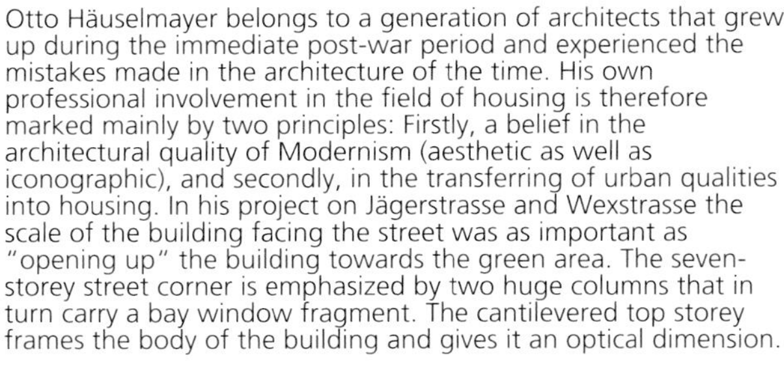

Otto Häuselmayer belongs to a generation of architects that grew up during the immediate post-war period and experienced the mistakes made in the architecture of the time. His own professional involvement in the field of housing is therefore marked mainly by two principles: Firstly, a belief in the architectural quality of Modernism (aesthetic as well as iconographic), and secondly, in the transferring of urban qualities into housing. In his project on Jägerstrasse and Wexstrasse the scale of the building facing the street was as important as "opening up" the building towards the green area. The seven-storey street corner is emphasized by two huge columns that in turn carry a bay window fragment. The cantilevered top storey frames the body of the building and gives it an optical dimension.

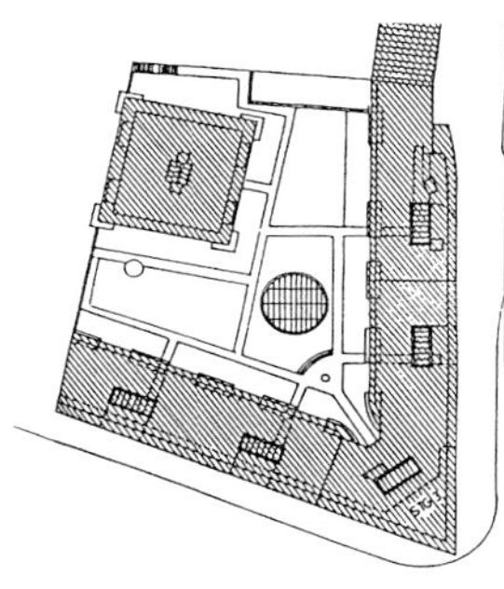

MAP No. 12

21st District
Floridsdorf

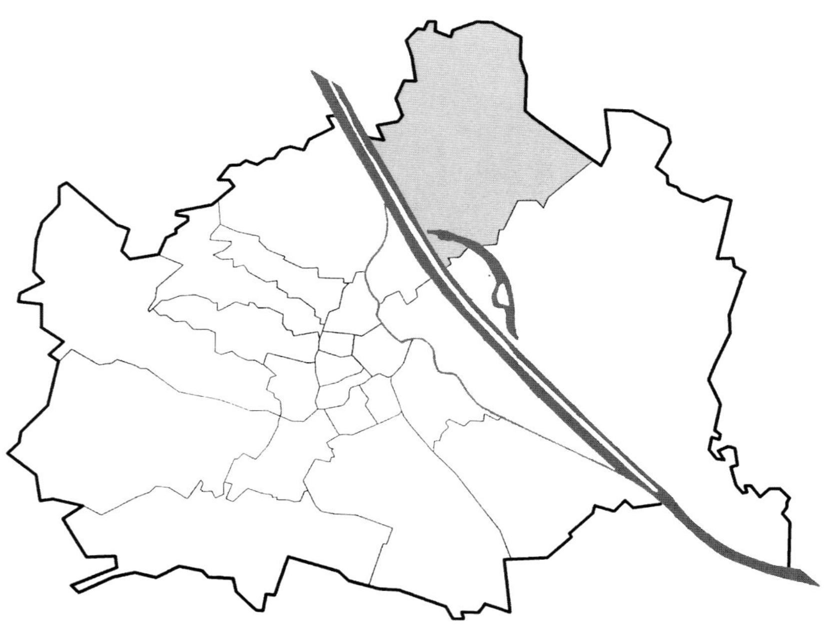

21st District, Floridsdorf Index numbers 21.-**1** … 21.-**22s**

Buildings worth visiting – Suggestions by Viennese architects

21st District:

August Sarnitz:
- Bank Austria Floridsdorf, Index No. 21.-**3**
- Housing, Index No. 21.-**16**
- Walk: Housing Siemensstrasse, Index No. 21.-**9**
- Walk: Paul Speiser Hof, Index No. 21.-**2**

21.-**1** | *Hubert Gessner*

Karl Seitz Hof
1926

The peripheral block formation defines, with an almost imperial gesture, an exedren shaped entrance square. The main entrance on the central axis is further emphasized by an extremely high gateway. The formality of the grand gesture is somewhat reduced by the use of decoration, though sparsely applied.

Jedleseer Strasse 66-94, Voltagasse, Bunsengasse, Dunantgasse, Edisongasse
Access: Open areas only
Public transportation: Tram line 26 (Koloniestrasse)

21.-**2** | *H. Glaser, K. Scheffel, E. Lichtblau, L. Bauer*

Paul Speiser Hof
1929

This spaciously dimensioned housing complex displays several innovative aspects in the context of the City of Vienna's social housing programme: the complex was conceived as a conventional, large court-centred housing scheme, but the details of the volumes and the facades differ from the norm, especially in the sections designed by Ernst Lichtblau. The corners are softened by stepped elements, and the symmetry of the facades deliberately disturbed by variations. One can presume that Josef Frank influenced the architect.

Franklinstrasse, Bodenstedtgasse, Grossmannplatz, Freytaggasse
Access: Open areas only
Public transportation: U6 (Floridsdorf)

Zentralsparkasse Floridsdorf (Bank Austria) 1971

Floridsdorf, Am Spitz 11
Access: During business hours
Public transportation: Tram lines 31, 33 (Am Spitz)

The transformation of the existing corner building by an extension is an example of an intelligent contemporary approach to a historical building substance. The three-storey, hall-like addition has a louvered facade to its south, which can be used to regulate natural light in the banking hall. Both parts of the building remain autonomous in their aesthetic and architectural language.

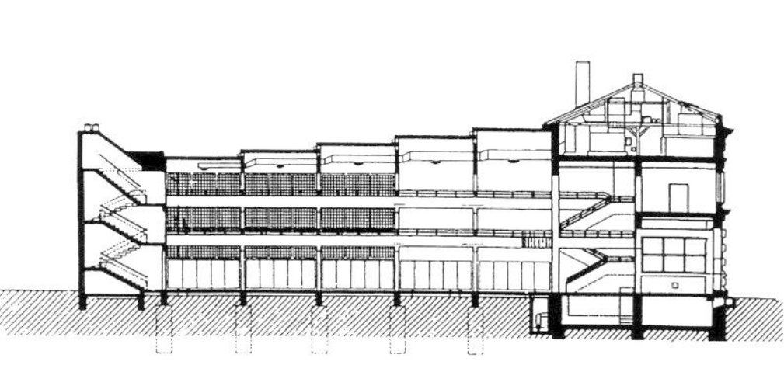

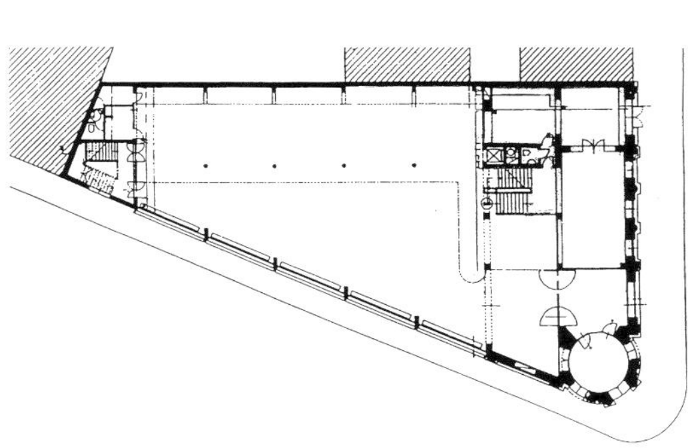

21.-**4**

Wilhelm Schütte, Margarete Schütte-Lihotzky

Special school Floridsdorf 1960

Franklinstrasse 27-33
Access: Open to the public by arrangement
Public transportation: U6 (Floridsdorf)

Wilhelm Schütte and Margarete Schütte-Lihotzky count as two of the most important Austrian architecture theorists of the 20th century. Their involvement in several fields, from the household (the Frankfurt kitchen) to education (kindergartens, schools) is well documented. The almost square class rooms in this school are lit from two sides; the free seating was an innovation at the time. A conceptual approach to school building was placed in opposition to formal aestheticism.

21.-**5**

Heidulf Gerngroß, Werkstatt Wien

Loftsiedlung Vienna Floridsdorf 1994

Ödenburgerstrasse 87
Access: Not open to the public
Public transportation: S3 (Jedlersdorf)

An exemplary housing area called the 'Viennese Loft' was built on Vienna's periphery (1994–1997) to realize the idea of a partly finished but inhabitable loft apartment. The fixed core of a loft apartment comprising the sanitary core with a kitchen and a gallery staircase form the fixed part of the loft. A second level for bedrooms, children's rooms or studies can be built in later as needed. Each two-level apartment has 95 m^2 initially inhabitable, and can be expanded to 127 m^2. This self-build model is an attempt to counter increasing costs in social housing construction; the result is a greater net area for the same cost. Seventeen loft apartments are grouped around an internal courtyard. They are built of brick and painted a bright yellow and a neutral white. In the immediate vicinity there is a council home for young people, run by the City and built on the same principle, at Mitterhofgasse 2, 21st District.

H. Wimmer, E. Reichl, P. Zauchenberger and K. Koller

21.-**6**

This 93-apartment housing scheme designed by Helmut Wimmer and Eva Reichl forms a typical Viennese peripheral block. Starting from Brünner Strasse a circulation system has established a continuous sequence of space from the urban realm to the individual apartment. This circulation system consisting of ramps, open stairways, staircases and galleries also establishes a complex spatial relationship between horizontal and vertical urban space. Different apartment types (flats, maisonettes, gallery-access flats) guarantee a variety of uses that illustrate urban heterogeneity. That the balconies and verandas are well-used proves that the inhabitants accept the variety provided by the scheme.

Housing Brünner Strasse 1993

Brünner Strasse 31/
Gerichtsgasse 12
Access: Not open to the publlic
Public transportation: Tram line 31 (Schlingermarkt)

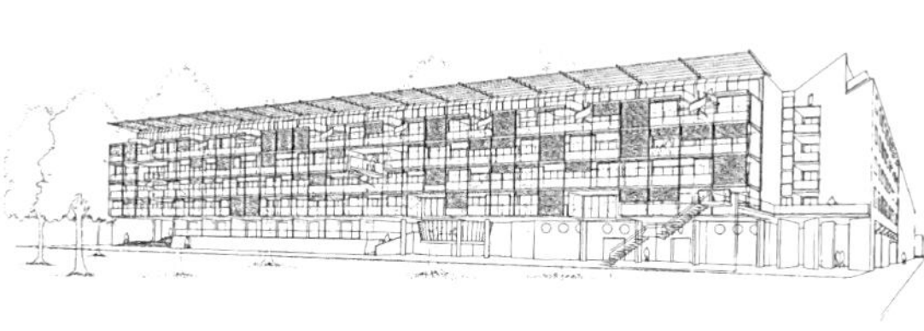

Ottokar Uhl et al.

21.-**7**

Ottokar Uhl, a pioneer of participatory building in Austria, realized this exemplary housing scheme together with sixteen families. The building is experimental and specially oriented to the needs of children, hence the name. Two separate buildings face a communal garden courtyard with shared facilities. The relatively large flats and maisonettes are constructed with load bearing party walls, leaving considerable freedom for the facades and interiors to be designed by the users. The project was realized within the financial constraints of the state's housing subsidy programme.

Housing 'Living with Children' 1980

Jeneweingasse 32,
Wienergasse 6
Access: Not open to the public
Public transportation: Tram line 26 (Hopfengasse)

21.-**8** **Heinz Neumann**

Office building
1991

This office building for a mass media company, is a metaphor for naval architecture, as it was commonly used at the beginning of the Modern Movement. The building is apparently at anchor. Service balconies run round the front of the glass facades, which are structurally separated from the production floors. The three office floors are cantilevered over the entrance like a ship's bridge. This is one of the few examples of newer office architecture in Vienna.

Ignaz Köck Strasse/
Lundenburgergasse
Access: Viewing by arrangement
Public transportation: Tram lines 31 and 33 (Shuttleworthstrasse)

21.-**9** **Franz Schuster**

Housing Siemensstrasse
1950

This scheme was built by Franz Schuster between 1950–53 according to the principles of a housing estate that incorporated the Garden City concept. Two-storey rows of houses were planned and fitted out so that the small flats could later be combined into larger ones. Built with the simplest of building materials and suitably landscaped, this complex is an example of socially relevant housing.

Siemensstrasse, Ruthnergasse, Scottgasse, Wanklackergasse
Access: Not open to the public
Public transportation: Bus 30A, 31A (Ruthnergasse)

Viktor Hufnagl

21.-**10**

In a manner similar to that in the housing scheme "Am Schöpfwerk", reference is made here to large areas of housing around courtyards, a specifically Viennese form of architecture. It took almost a decade (until 1982) to realize the competition results of the first phase of a competition held in 1973. The individual courts are connected to each other and relate to the dimensions and proportions of the structures of the surrounding settlements. The relatively low building density made the pleasant proportions possible.

Housing
Gerasdorfer Strasse
1980

Gerasdorfer Strasse 61
Access: Not open to the public
Public transportation: Bus 32A (Ratzenhofergasse)

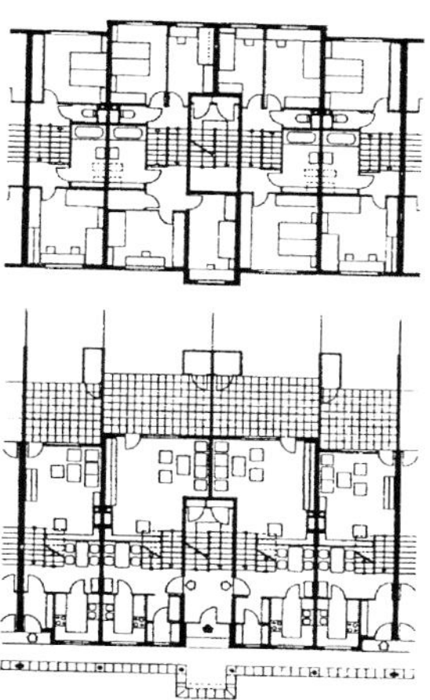

Atelier 18 – Eder, Pal, Weber, Wieden

21.-**11**

The backbone of this two and three-storey settlement is a village-green-like area. At crossroads and entrances four storeys have been used.
All communal facilities, such as schools and kindergartens, are accessible on foot. Flats for the disabled are on the ground floor. Gardens for the tenants reinforce the social ideals of the settlements of the 1920s.

Housing
Ernst Theumerhof
1977

Empergergasse,
Koschiergasse
Access: Not open to the public
Public transportation: Tram line 31 (Empergergasse)

21.-**12** | ***Martin Treberspurg, Georg W. Reinberg, Erich Raith***

Housing
1993

Brünnerstrasse-Empergergasse
Access: Not open to the public
Public transportation: Tram line 31 (Empergergasse)

This scheme of 215 social housing units is part of a larger urban extension area to the north of Vienna. It was conceived as a low energy scheme: solar windows, transition areas with conservatories, ventilation systems with heat recovery systems that allow energy consumption to stay below 40 kw/m²a. The 330 metre long block facing the street (Brünnerstrasse) is a many-layered shield for the court-oriented flats. To the east this block protects ten three-storey rows each with four terrace houses from wind and traffic noise. The whole is an attempt at energy-saving architecture. Energy planning: Office Schmied-Schwelch.

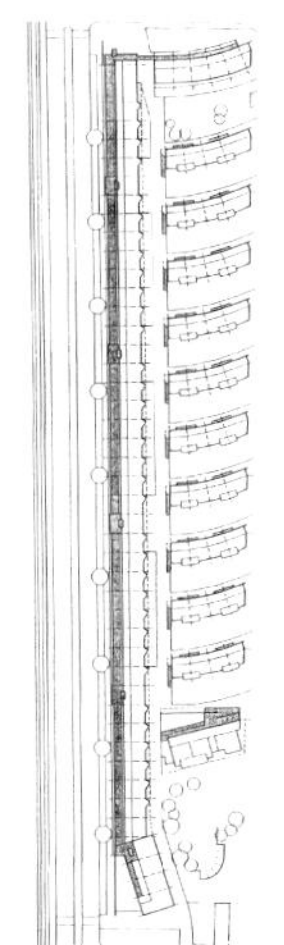

21.-**13** | ***Häuselmayer, Melicher, Schwalm-Theiss, Gressenbauer***

Housing Ocwirkgasse
1994

Ocwirkgasse 7
Access: Not open to the public
Public transportation: Tram lines 31 and 33 (Empergergasse)

This large housing area at the further end of Brünner Strasse is primarily a collection of a large number of flats and neither the planning concept nor the architectural design have evoked a positive resonance. However, some of the smaller buildings inside the scheme are remarkable. The small church with a small forecourt by Häuselmayer can be seen as an attempt to insert a functional centre into the project. Häuselmayer has developed on his earlier church concept on the Wienerberg, and uses a vaulted roof. Also in the immediate vicinity is a remarkable housing block by Melicher/Schwalm-Theiss and Gressenbauer which reacts sensitively to everyday living needs through its scale and differentiation.

Gustav Peichl, Rudolf F. Weber

21.-**14**

The large school centre at Hanreitergasse designed by Gustav Peichl and Rudolf F. Weber consists of five functionally differentiated building volumes around an attractive courtyard, thereby creating a small "school town": an elliptical, metal-clad entrance building; a landscaped, vaulted gymnasium; two school blocks with class rooms oriented towards the south-east; and a crèche oriented towards the north-east. Transparent glass bridges connect the oval entrance building with the school blocks. The clarity of order is emphasized by the sensitive use of materials.

Primary and secondary school Hanreitergasse 1994

Hanreitergasse 2,
Ocwirkgasse
Access: Viewing by appointment
Public transportation: Tram line 31 (Brünner Strasse/Gerasdorfer Strasse)

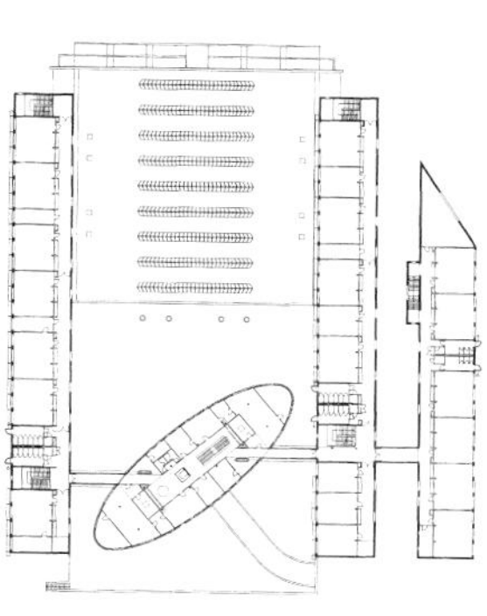

Stefan Hübner/Peter Leibetseder

21.-**15**

This primary school and music school together with the adjacent church by Otto Häuselmayer form the spiritual centre of the new housing area along Brünner Strasse. On the periphery of the city, schools take over the demands of public architecture. In this case a heterogeneous, differentiated and collaged architectural language lies somewhere between postmodern and fragmentary design approaches.

Primary School, Music School Schumpeterweg 1992

Schumpeterweg 3
Access: Viewing by appointment
Public transportation: Tram line 31 (Empergergasse)

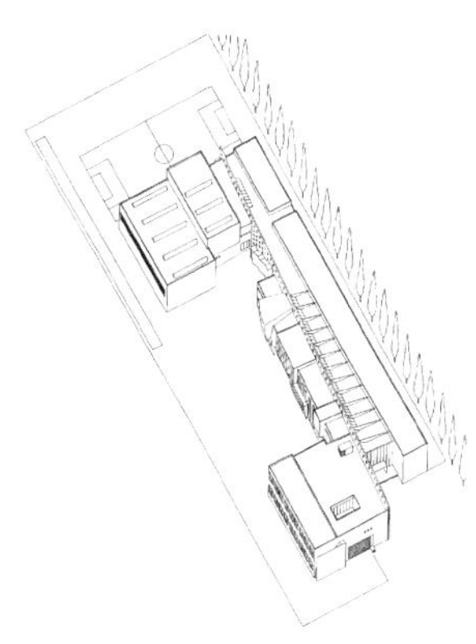

21.-**16**

Jean Nouvel

Housing
1994

Leopoldauerstrasse 168
Access: Not open to the public
Public transportation: Bus 29A (Eipeldauerstrasse)

Jean Nouvel was invited by a private building society to design this housing project. Within the limitations set by the regulations of Vienna's housing subsidy programme and building regulations, Nouvel came up with an interesting loft type construction with maisonette-like aspects. By using staircases that penetrate the building, maisonettes, and gallery corridors, Nouvel has developed a completely new housing pattern for Vienna. Vertical walls covered with creepers ensure individual privacy.

21.-**17**

Kurt Heidecker, Herbert Neuhauser

Housing
"Intercultural Living"
1994

Satzingerweg
Access: Open areas only
Public transportation: Bus 31A (Doeltergasse)

The aim of this project was to create a housing area that provided the best possible conditions for encouraging good neighbourly relations. The flats are connected by gallery corridors to the courtyard, the central space. The broad vestibules at the entrance to the flats create a spatial division and are open to additional uses. A large opening in the kitchen-cum-dining room connects the gallery corridor to the flats. The project "intercultural living" was devised by the research team Leitner, Reppé and Appelt.

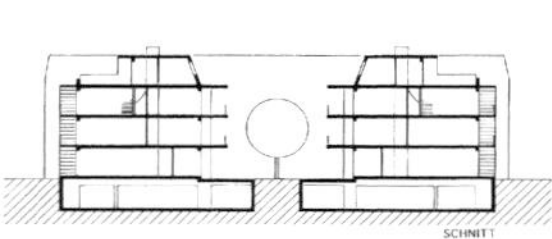

Frauen-Werk-Stadt 1994

Eight female architects were invited by the Women´s Office of the City of Vienna to a workshop to develop structural, functional and building proposals to reinforce female-friendly urban planning.The overall plan is by Franziska Ullmann. The concept for 350 apartments and a children's day-care centre (Elsa Prochazka) was carried out by various housing societies. The project, initially called the "Frauen-Werk-Stadt" was renamed "Margarethe Schütte-Lihotzky Hof" to celebrate the architect´s 100th birthday.

Donaufelderstrasse
Access: Open areas only
Public transportation: U6, Tram line 26 (Alfred Nobel Strasse)

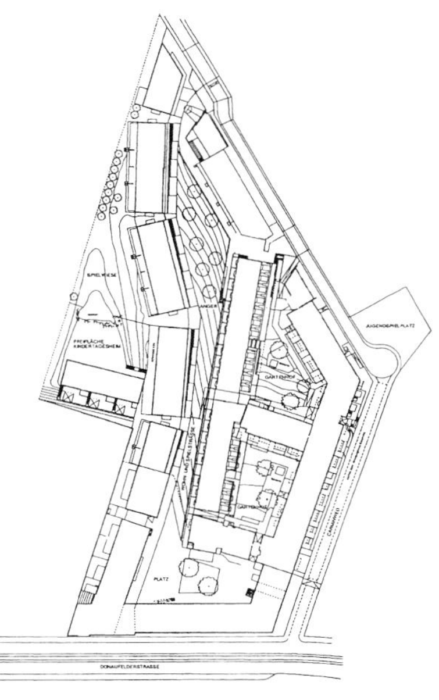

Primary School Zehdengasse 1993

This comb-shaped two and three-storey all-day primary school emphasizes its individual functions with strong volumetric forms, and occupies the entire trapezoidal site. Free spaces and built forms complement each other in a dense complex. The zinc facade forms a contra-punctual rhythm with the perforated window facade. The corridors are by contrast completely glazed.

Zehdengasse
Access: Viewing by appointment
Public transportation: Bus 31A (Doeltergasse)

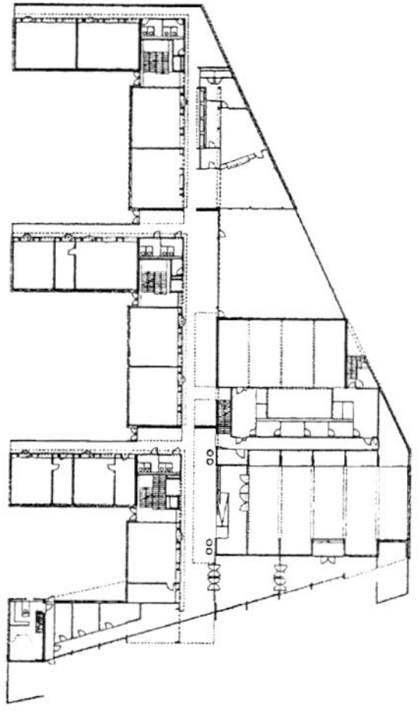

Supplementary Recommendations

21.-**20s**	Housing Anton Böck Gasse Eva Ceska, Friedrich Priesner	1993 Anton Böck Gasse 4
21.-**21s**	Dorotheum Floridsdorf Egon Kastner, Fritz Waage	1931 Pitkagasse 4
21.-**22s**	Children's Day Care Center of the City of Vienna Markus Geiswinkler	1993 Gschweidlgasse 1

MAP No. 13

22nd District Donaustadt

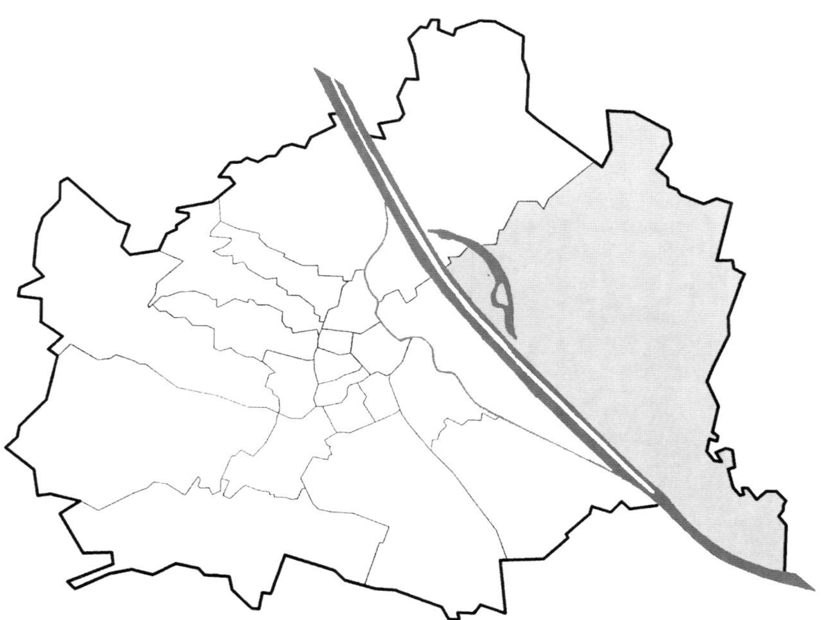

22nd District, Donaustadt Index numbers 22.-**1** … 22.-**37s**

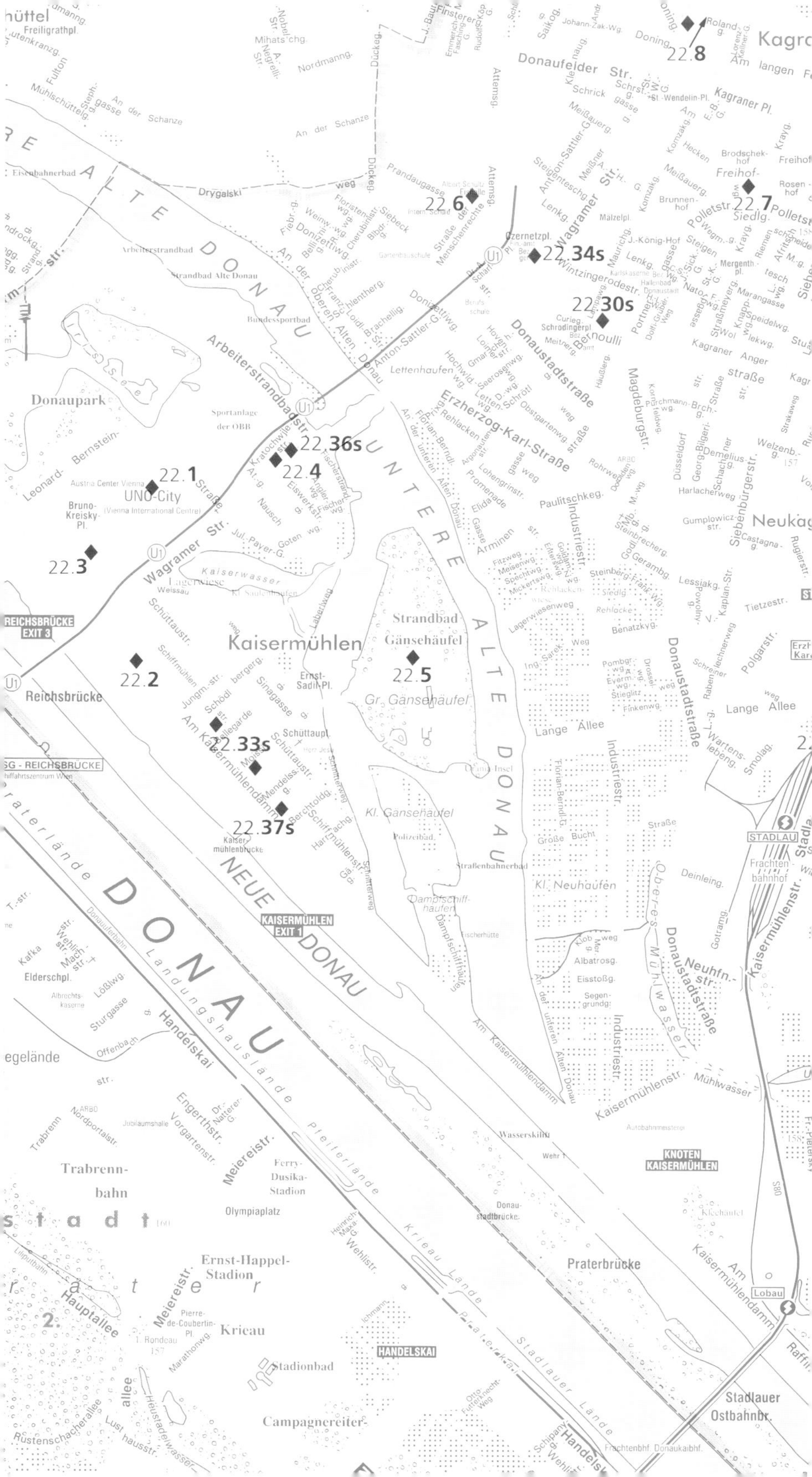

22.1
22.2
22.3
22.4
22.5
22.6
22.7
22.8
22.30s
22.33s
22.34s
22.36s
22.37s
ALTE DONAU
UNTERE ALTE DONAU
NEUE DONAU
DONAU
Donaupark
UNO-City
(Vienna International Centre)
Austria Center Vienna
Bruno-Kreisky-Pl.
Kaisermühlen
Strandbad Gänsehäufel
Gr. Gänsehäufel
Kl. Gänsehäufel
Kl. Neuhaufen
Reichsbrücke
REICHSBRÜCKE EXIT 3
KAISERMÜHLEN EXIT 1
KNOTEN KAISERMÜHLEN
HANDELSKAI
Wagramer Str.
Donaustadtstraße
Erzherzog-Karl-Straße
Industriestr.
Kaisermühlenstr.
Am Kaisermühlendamm
Arbeiterstrandbadstr.
Leonard-Bernstein-Str.
Schüttaustr.
Donaufelder Str.
Kagraner Pl.
Magdeburgstr.
Siebenbürgerstr.
Lange Allee
Handelskai
Meiereistr.
Trabrennbahn
Ernst-Happel-Stadion
Krieau
Stadionbad
Praterbrücke
Stadlauer Ostbahnbr.
Prater
Hauptallee
Stadlau
Lobau
Neukagran
Kagran

Buildings worth visiting – Suggestions by Viennese architects

22nd District:

Rüdiger Lainer – Walks:
Wagramer Strasse, from the Erzherzog Karl-Strasse to Donaustadtstrasse, Index No. 22.-**3**, 22.-**4**, 22.-**17**, 22.-**18**, 22.-**19**, 22.-**20**

Eichinger oder Knechtl:
Guggenheim Museum Vienna (Hans Hollein) – as yet unbuilt.

August Sarnitz:
Donauturm

Margherita Spiluttini (architecture photographer):
Donauturm

22.-**1** | *Johann Staber*

UNO-City (Vienna International Centre) 1973

Wagramer Strasse, Donaupark
Access: Viewing by arrangement
Public transportation: U1 (Kaisermühlen)

The efforts of the former Austrian Chancellor, Bruno Kreisky, to establish Vienna as a third United Nations location after New York and Geneva, led to an international competition for the new UNO Centre in 1970. Although the jury awarded a first prize, it was the project which won the 4th prize, by Johann Staber, that was realized. The Y-form, significant in plan, has no spatial relevance and its urban dimension is controversial. A large conference centre (1983–87) was added to the complex, now known as the Vienna International Centre.

22.-**2** | *Cufer, Czech, Delugan, Delugan-Meissl, Loudon (Master Pla*

Danube City 1992

Wagramer Strasse
Access: Open areas only
Public transportation: U1 (Kaisermühlen)

After the fall of the Iron Curtain in 1989 a new "Founders' Era", similar to the era of urban expansion of the 19th century, was declared in Vienna. An increase in the population, the economic upturn and an increased role for Vienna as a mediator between Eastern and Western Europe were expected to take place. The 'Danube City' was to be a bipolar second centre for the city and a new impulse to the city. The World Exhibition Vienna-Budapest to take place on this site was cancelled after the negative results of a referendum, so that the site was freed earlier than expected for future use. The land-use concept was undertaken by Hans Hollein and Coop Himmelblau, the master plan prepared by Adolf Krischanitz/Heinz Neumann, the buildings were designed by Holzbauer (office tower), Hollein (primary school) and Cufer, Delugan, Loudon etc. (housing).

Andromeda Tower 1993

This office and residential building (1993–97) occupies a special urban position as a gateway to the entire Danube City complex. The elliptical form of the tower reacts formally to the concave building volumes of the UNO City. The external skin is interrupted twice by a three-storey, slanting glass element that houses multi-level lobbies. The top four floors house flats, with balconies cut into the elliptical building volume.

Wagramer Strasse
Access: Not open to the public
Public transportation: U1 (Kaisermühlen)

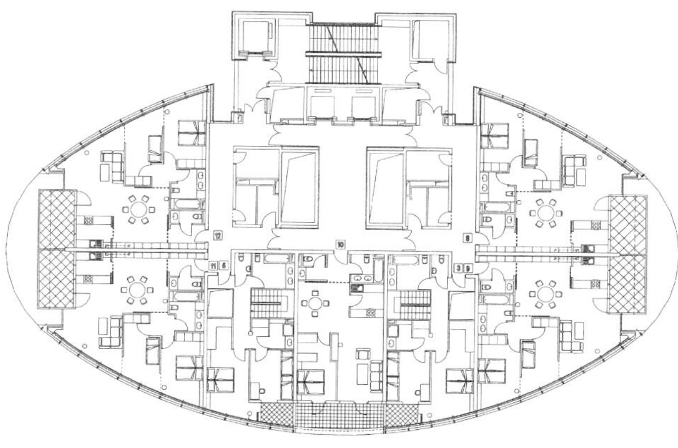

Residential Towers Wagramerstrasse 1994

Wagramerstrasse/
Kratochwjlestrasse
Access: Not open to the public
Public transportation: U1 (Kaisermühlen)

Three remarkable 25-storey residential towers are being built between Wagramerstrasse and Kratochwjlestrasse, along the axis of the Underground. The site plan has been designed to afford a minimum of mutual shadow and the maximum view. The technology and construction are the most complicated in Coop Himmelblau's residential tower, with a 'climatic facade', a sky lobby for residents, heat storage and conservatories. The flats are based on an open-plan loft concept. Gustav Peichl's residential tower is cylindrical and emphasises the tower form, whereas NFOG (Nigst, Fonatti, Ostertag, Gaisrucker) have designed their tower with differentiated solar shading façade elements.

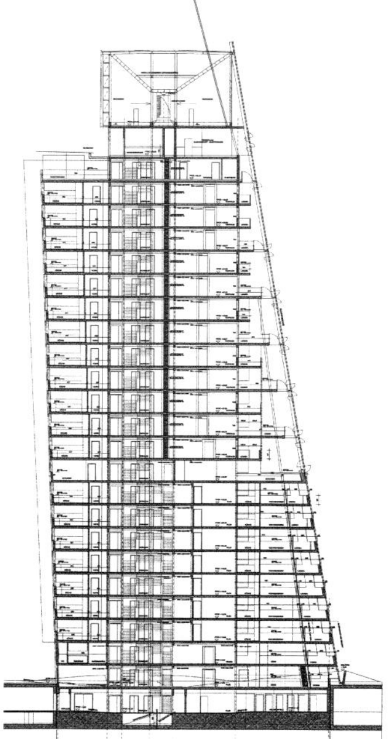

Coop-Himmelblau

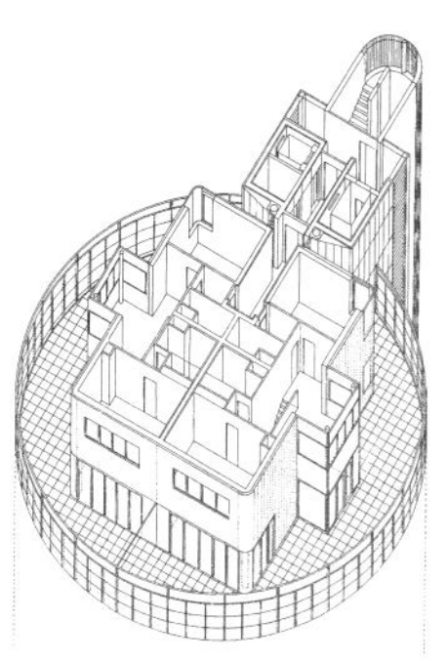

Peichl

Max Fellerer, Eugen Wörle

Gänsehäufel, Open Air Public Baths 1948

This is the first open-air baths complex to be built after the Second World War and can accommodate 30,000 visitors. An orthogonal circulation system overlays the biomorphic form of the island. The pavilions are built between and partly around the existing trees. The changing rooms are constructed of a reinforced concrete skeleton system.

Moissigasse 21
Access: Open to the public
Public transportation: Bus 90A (Gänsehäufel)

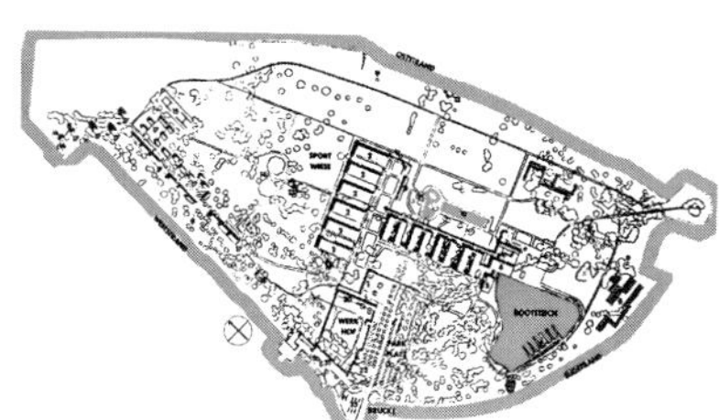

22.-6 | ***Sepp Müller, with Alfred Berger and Werner Krismer***

Ice Sports Hall
1990

Dr. Adolf Schärf Platz
Access: Open to the public
Public transportation: U1
(Donauzentrum)

The planning of this ice sports hall started in 1990, when a new sports hall was needed for the planned Expo '95 Vienna Budapest.The winner of a national architectural competition with invited international participation was Müller/Berger/Krismer's project, which, after slight modifications, was built in a record twenty months. A grandiose glass palace has been created. Its technical perfection and formal clarity is pleasing to both sport participants and visitors. The building programme called for two equally large ice rinks, one a training rink without a spectator gallery, and the second, a performers' rink, with a seating capacity for 4,350 spectators.

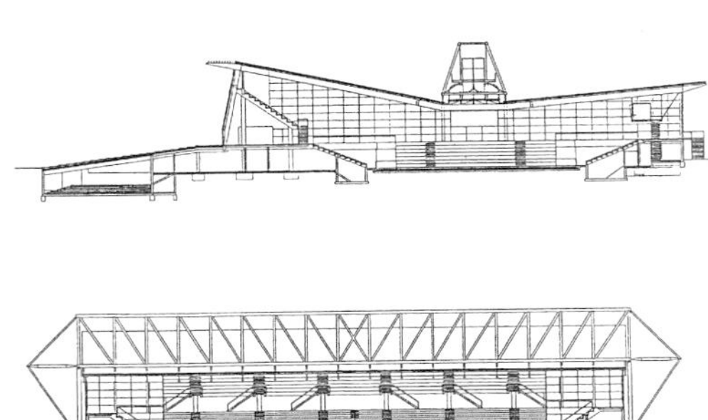

A garden estate that displays a great deal of heterogenity, with a curved street running through the site and complemented by a small square. The small buildings with attached gardens are mainly laid out in rows or form courts. Following the housing strategy, several house types were used, containing altogether 1,042 flats.

Housing estate Am Freihof 1923

Kagraner Platz, Siebenbürgenstrasse, Steigenteschstrasse, Polletstrasse
Access: Not open to the public
Public transportation: Tram lines 25 and 26
Steigenteschgasse)

22.-**8** | *E. Frauendorfer, J. Gsteu, E. Mang, K. Mang, et al.*

Housing Josef-Bohmann-Hof 1973

Ehrlichweg, Ohnsorgweg, Absolonweg, Urteilweg, Boeklweg, Kubinplatz
Access: Open areas only
Public transportation: Bus 31A (Doeltergasse)

On the basis of a common concept, each architect here has expressed an individual style in his section. The section by Johann Osten is remarkable for the communal use of the central access corridor by the addition of a common room, as well as for the layout of the flats, which offer quality above the average usual for social housing. The central organization of the kitchen, the living room and the balcony within the flat results in minimal circulation space. The roof is partially used as a communal space. Architects: E. Frauendorfer, J. Gsteu, E. Mang, K. Mang, A.Obermann, A.Pal, U.Schrittwieser, G.Schuster, M.Stein.

22.-**9** | *Johannes Spalt*

Housing Varnhagengasse 1984

Varnhagengasse 9
Access: Not open to the public
Public transportation: Tram line 25 (Konstanziagasse)

The building relates to the scale of the two neighbouring buildings and achieves a distinctive character due to the projecting bay windows constructed in timber. The different heights within the flats (2.5 m for the bedrooms, 2.75 m for the living rooms) and the ensuing split-levels result in interesting sections and spaces.

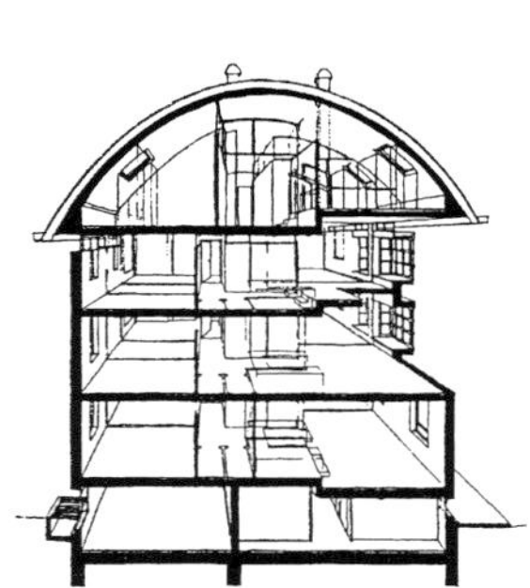

The plans of this apartment building were intended to provide functionally neutral spaces. The great degree of flexibility and variety of use made possible within the house contrasts with the ordered and restrained facade, which presents itself in the language of appropriate contemporary building. Only he who can remain silent is also open to dialogue.

Housing Heinrich Lefler Gasse 1994

Heinrich Lefler Gasse 24
Access: Not open to the public
Public transportation: U1, Tram line 25 (Langobardengasse)

22.-**11**

Stelzhammer, Katzberger, Bily, Melicher, Schwalm-Theiss e

Housing Mühlgrundweg 1993

Hardeggasse 69
Access: Not open to the public
Public transportation: U1, Tram line 25, Bus 92A (Strandbad Stadlau)

The housing group consists of 180 flats and 28 terrace houses. The urban design concept by Melicher, Schwalm-Theiss and Gressenbauer envisaged the stepping down of the building volumes towards the south. The two buildings by Paul Katzberger and Karin Bily have flexible plans, whereas the terrace houses by Walter Stelzhammer take advantage of the sloped site to create split levels with an interior staircase, as the master plan envisaged.

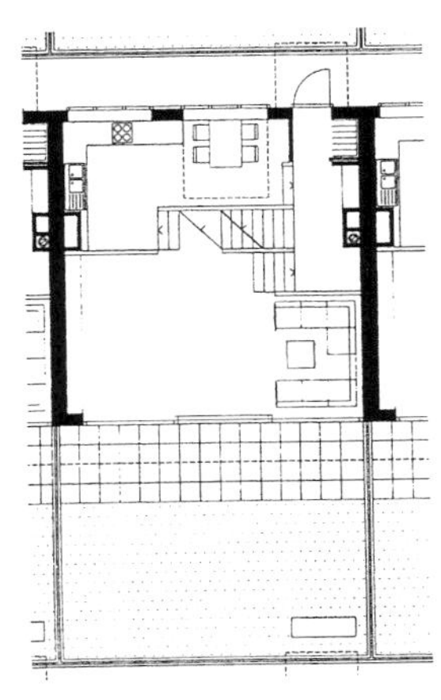

22.-**12**

G. Reinberg, M. Treberspurg, E. Raith, Kislinger and Trudak

Housing Kamillenweg 1989

Kamillenweg/Pappelweg/Haselnussweg
Access: Not open to the public
Public transportation: U1, Tram line 25, Bus 96B (Kanalstrasse)

Ever since the oil crisis of 1973, architects have been trying to examine the energy consumption balance of their buildings. Solar houses with active and passive solar energy use make an important contribution to ecological living. The ten houses in this group have been the subject of extensive writing in specialist and popular magazines and are considered important contributions to a new style of housing. The verandah house type consists of light skeletal timber constructions, conservatories towards the south and a massive façade towards the north.

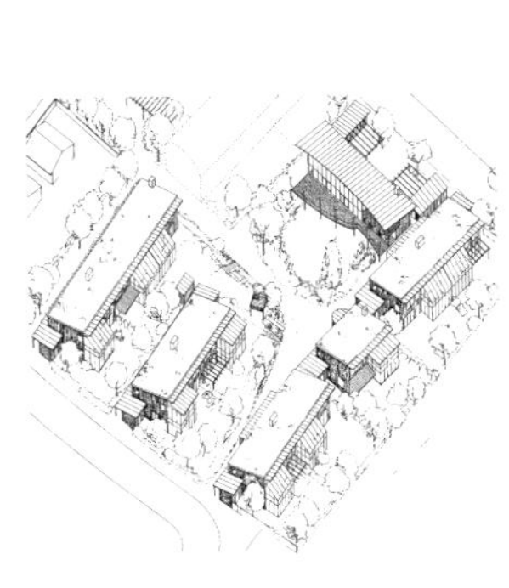

Roland Hagmüller

22.-**13**

This housing scheme by Roland Hagmüller in Stadlau (1990–92) was awarded the Adolf Loos Prize. There is a mix of terrace houses and flats on this residential site. The extra space in the roof-top ateliers and the wooden wall construction within a prefabricated reinforced concrete skeleton system are remarkable.

Housing Pappelweg 1990

Pappelweg 1–34
Access: Not open to the public
Public transportation: U1, Tram line 25, Bus 96B (Kanalstrasse)

Boris Podrecca/Gotthard Eiböck

22.-**14**

On the periphery of the city north of the Danube, this housing block by Boris Podrecca makes an urban statement comparable to the major housing blocks of the inter-war years. A 200 metre long residential block acts as the starting point for new buildings along the Wulzendorfstrasse in Aspern. The five-storey building contains a mixture of flats, duplexes and triplexes.

Housing Kapellenweg 1986

Kapellenweg 36–38
Access: Not open to the public
Public transportation: Tram line 25 (Langobardenstrasse/ Kapellenweg)

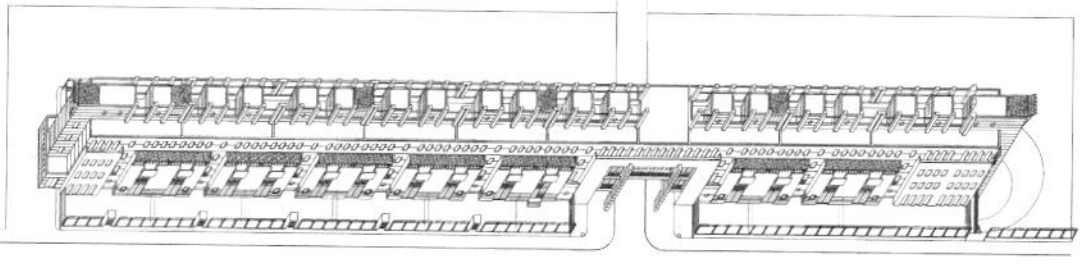

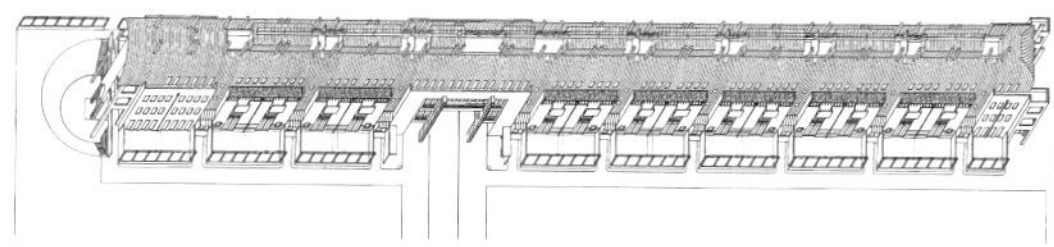

22.-**15** | ***Viktor Hufnagl***

Housing Zschokkegasse 1992

Zschokkegasse 91
Access: Not open to the public
Public transportation: U1, Tram 25 (SMZ Ost)

The four-storey housing block by Hufnagl is in the immediate vicinity of Roland Rainer's housing scheme in the Tamariskengasse. In contrast to many housing schemes on the urban periphery, this design is based on an inner access road with glass-roofed atria. The balconies and terraces facing this area help to create a variety of divisions. This and the variety of detail make it a controlled, semi-public area. There are signs here of the social utopian ideals of Jean Baptiste Godin (1817–88), especially his Familistère (from 1859).

22.-**16** | ***Roland Rainer***

Housing Tamariskengasse 1993

Tamariskengasse 102
Access: Not open to the public
Public transportation: U1, Tram line 25 (SMZ Ost)

Roland Rainer's convincing solution for building on the urban periphery is low-rise high-density housing. It also satisfies the demand for having a house of one's own without wasting land. Ground level courtyard houses and two-storey terrace houses with a garden for families, flats and maisonettes above for childless families. The entire housing scheme is accessible on foot. There is a kindergarten and pensioners´ flats in the centre of the site.

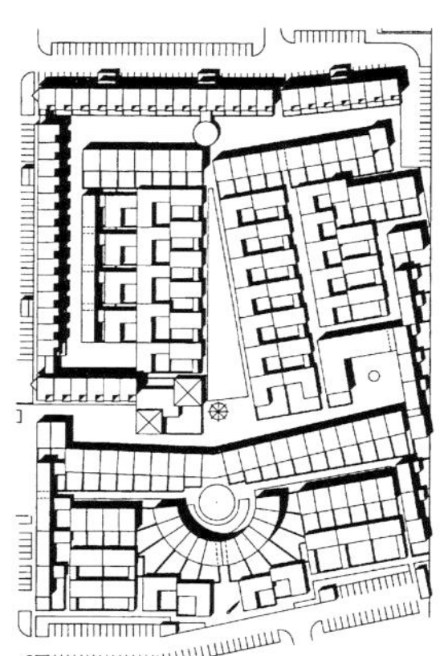

Ablinger/Vedral, W. Stelzhammer, M. Cufer

Housing Wulzendorf (West) 1993

The urban design concept for the housing scheme "Ostarichi" was developed by Walter Stelzhammer in 1991. The concept attempts the maximum possible integration of the western green spaces in courtyard form, while Bergengasse is rhythmically traversed by 'bridges' containing flats. The buildings follow an orthogonal layout: a three-storey north-south oriented building by Walter Stelzhammer is intersected by four 4-storey east-west oriented buildings by Ablinger and Vedral. Margarethe Cufer has built terrace houses in the courtyards as well as housing and a kindergarten at the northernmost end of the site. Between the two stands Walter Stelzhammer's pastoral care centre. A total of 204 flats and 24 terrace houses.

Bergengasse
Access: Not open to the public
Public transportation: Tram line 25 (Oberdorfstrasse)

Sarnitz, Haselwanter, Linsberger, Wimmer, Spiegelfeld, Holnsteiner

Housing Wulzendorf (Ost) 1993

The development on the eastern side of the Bergengasse is also based on Walter Stelzhammer's urban design concept, although in this case three residential courts and one row of terrace houses were planned. The large residential court to the north with flats and roof-top maisonettes were planned by August Sarnitz. The housing with flexible sliding walls in the flats, situated at where the roads cross, was planned by Helmut Wimmer, and the adjacent housing court by Günther Holnsteiner and Markus Spiegelfeld. The terrace houses with louvered solar protection on the facade was planned by the architects Haselwanter and Linsberger. The white stucco façades on all the buildings unite the different buildings, a total of 180 flats.

Bergengasse 4
Access: Not open to the public
Public transportation: Tram line 25 (Oberdorfstrasse)

22.-**19** | ***G. Peichl, M. Kohlbauer, P. Katzberger, NFOG et al.***

Housing Erzherzog Karl Stadt 1994

Several building phases were foreseen in the overall concept for this settlement of 2,000 flats by Peichl and Kohlbauer. The varied external spaces hold the promise of a pleasant living atmosphere. Housing blocks with two wings, flats, terrace houses and a round tower building offer different types of accommodation. Architects: Gustav Peichl, Rudolf F.Weber, Martin Kohlbauer, Peter Nigst, Paul Katzberger, Karin Bily, Micheal Loudon, NFOG (Nigst, Fouatti, Ostertag, Gaisrucker), Gruppe ARCA.

Access: Open areas only
Public transportation: Tram line 25 (Oberdorfstrasse)

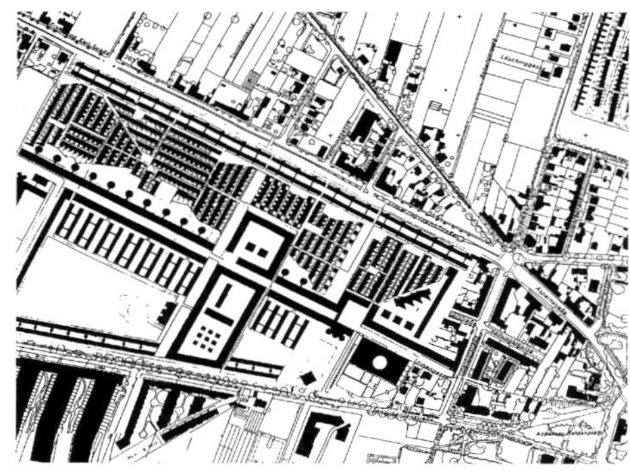

22.-**20** | ***Martin Kohlbauer***

Secondary School Eibengasse 1992

This secondary school was the winning entry in one of the few nation-wide architectural competitions. The compact, white stucco building combines all the diverse functions of a school in a cubical volume, and a circular central courtyard introduces formal tension into the complex. However, the internal organisation of the building manages to break up the optical symmetry caused by the circular court, and deliniates the functions in a differentiated manner.

Eibengasse 56–58
Access: Viewing by appointment
Public transportation: Tram line 25 (Oberdorfstrasse)

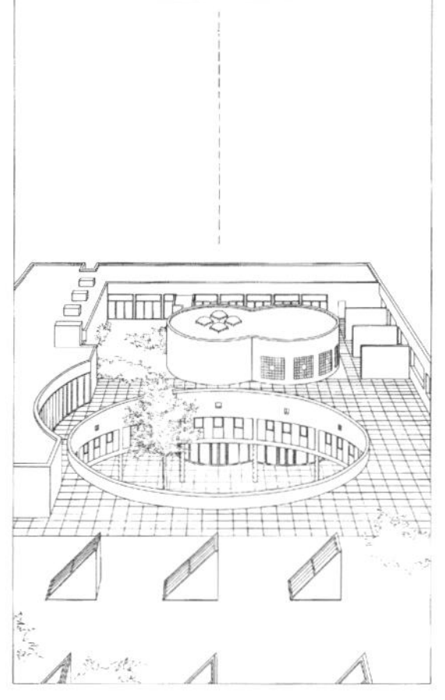

Housing estate Biberhaufenweg 1981

"The housing in Biberhaufenweg was the beginning of new expectations and standards in Vienna's social housing programme. Historically it belonged to the 'Little Architecture' period, during which fundamental questions of architecture were dealt with in exemplary fashion in small projects"(Dietmar Steiner). The three typologically basic forms of urban development – the square, the street and the green – have been handled by three architects. Häuselmayer, Pruscha and Tesar have put their personal signatures on the differentiated needs raised in this project, while a unified choice of colours and materials give the buildings additional coherence.

Biberhaufenweg
Access: Open areas only
Public transportation: Bus 85A, Bus 93A (Benjowskygasse)

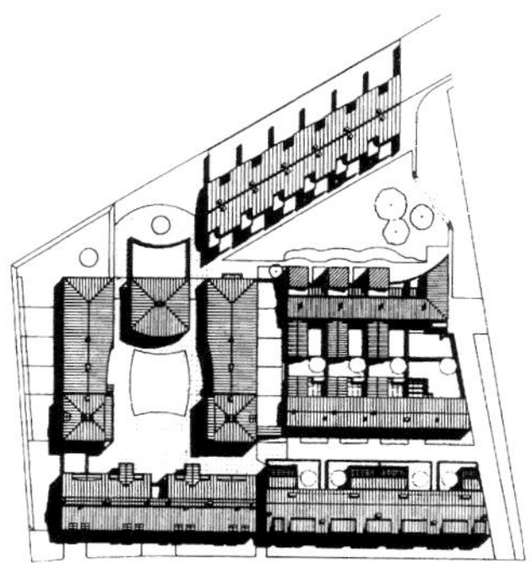

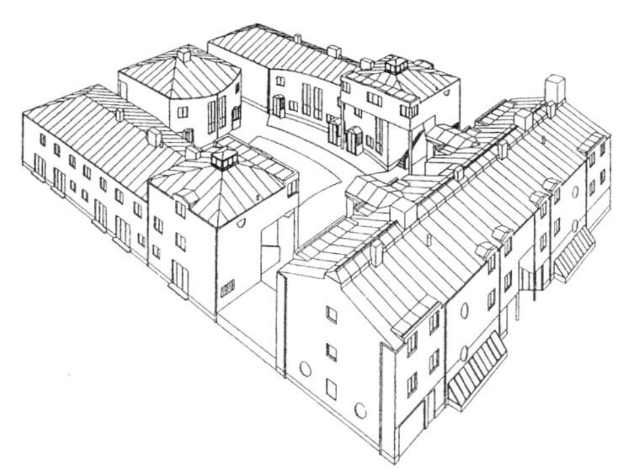

22.-**22** | *Rüdiger Lainer and Gertraud Auer*

Housing Siegesplatz/ Benjowskygasse 1991

The site on the south front of Siegesplatz square lies in the old centre of Aspern. The long, narrow plot (20 x 130 m) with varied building regulations led to a typologically differentiated solution. Different types of buildings (a low building on Siegesplatz, gateway houses, terrace houses, flats and an apartment block) paradigmatically represent the "pars pro toto" for a possible comprehensive urban situation.

Siegesplatz 21/
Benjowskygasse 11
Access: Not open to the public
Public transportation: U1, Bus 26A (Aspern Siegesplatz)

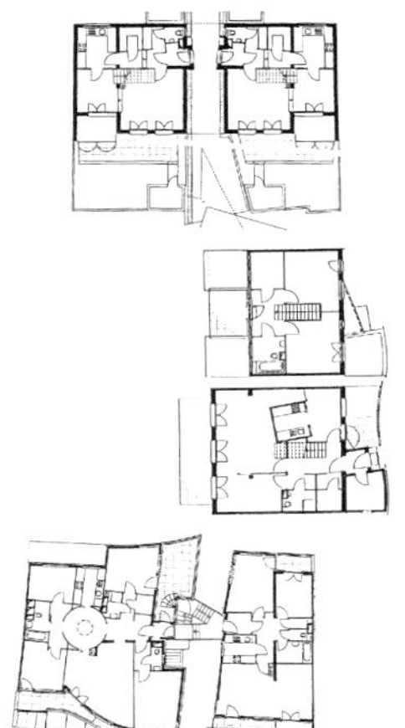

22.-**23** | *Günther Domenig*

Secondary School Simonsgasse 1993

Günther Domenig, the main proponent of the Graz School of architecture, has, with this building, brought a touch of inimitable style to Vienna. Domenig has restricted himself to economical methods. "Even the curved part of the building is limited to a relatively brief section of the entire block length. The rationalism of the right angle dominates even though the first impression of the building is that of organically formed volumes" (W. M. Chramosta).

Simonsgasse
Access: Viewing by appointment
Public transportation: Bus 26A (Eßling Schule)

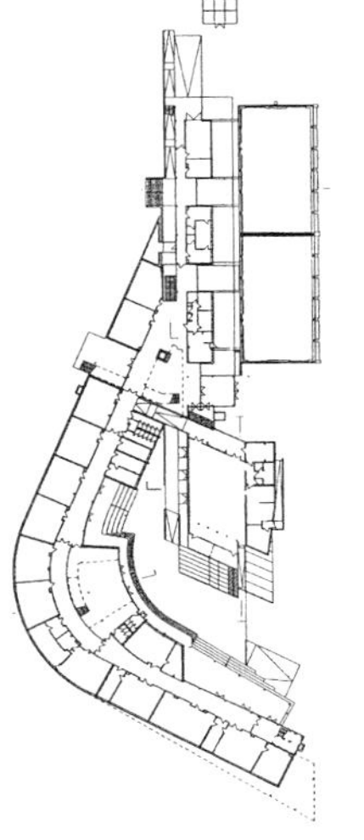

Housing Pilotengasse 1989

This medium-sized housing estate with 200 units has, in contrast to the nearby housing in Biberhaufenweg, a stringent system of linear building volumes. These are not organized, as those in Biberhaufenweg are, on the basis of a typological order, but glean their cohesion from a systematic series arranged around a fictive centre. The three teams of architects, Herzog and de Meuron, Krischanitz and Steidle & Partners have developed a subtle interpretation of the terrace house. Krischanitz has, in cooperation with Oskar Putz, used a strongly differentiated colour concept for the individual terrace houses.

Pilotengasse/Hausfeldstrasse
Access: Open areas only
Public transportation: U1, Tram line 25, Bus 97A (Goldregengasse)

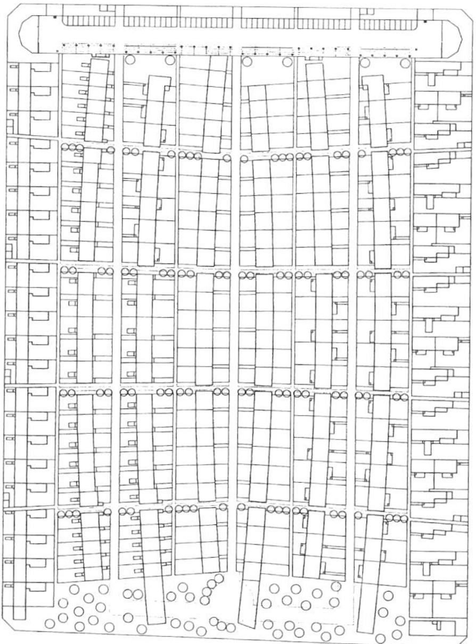

22.-**25** | ***Hempel, Fonatti, Baldass, Weiser, Gerngroß***

Housing Wiethestrasse 84 1991

The housing on Wiethestrasse, based on the urban design concept by Helmut Hempel, has taken up the challenge of establishing a new identity on the periphery: three teams of architects under Markus Spiegelfeld's project management team from the Werkstatt Wien developed a new typology of terrace houses and have erected a settlement with synthetic coherence rather than one of continuous invariance. Both the plans and the spatial division of the terrace houses offer a spatial experience uncommon in council housing: split-level flats and some double-height spaces.

Wiethestrasse
Access: Not open to the public
Public transportation: Bus 99B (Wiethestrasse)

22.-**26** | ***Helmut Hempel, Franco Fonatti***

Housing Gladiolenweg 1983

This row of eight terrace houses lies in the vicinity of a 1920s housing estate. The terrace houses were reinterpreted in an innovative way, using passive solar energy and environmentally acceptable building materials. The spatially differentiated interior organisation includes a glass-roofed interior court with plants, an atelier-type attic space and living space with higher ceilings.

Gladiolenweg 21
Access: Not open to the public
Public transportation: Buses 95B and 96B (Gladiolenweg)

Multipurpose Hall and Parish Building
1984

Quadenstrasse 53
Access: Open to the public
Public transportation: Buses 95 and 96B (Am Heidjöchl)

Life on the periphery also sets new challenges to church building. The architects have managed here to create a spatial collage consisting of traditional elements such as semi-circular arches and contemporary building technology such as prefabricated concrete elements, without entirely giving up the traditional spatial sequence of a centrally organized church with its vestibule, narthex and nave. They have attempted to create a church centre acceptable to the inhabitants as a community house. On the lower floor there is a meeting room and a kitchen.

(Quadenstrasse)

(Rennbahnweg)

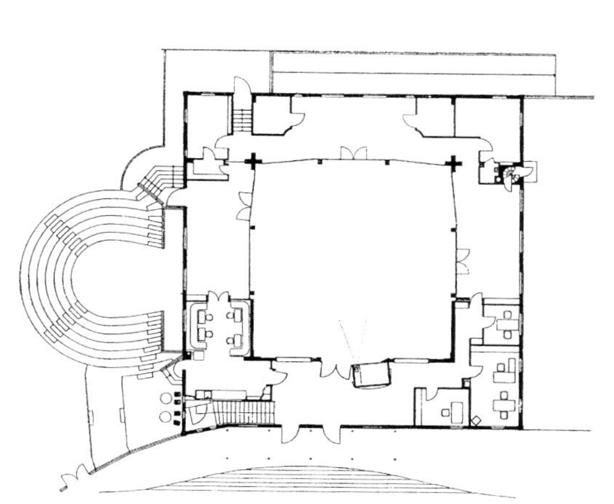

Atelier 4

Primary School Pastinakweg 1991

Pastinakweg 10
Access: Viewing by appointment
Public transportation: Bus 86A (Korianderweg)

This two-storey all-day primary school for twelve classes has a two-storey entrance hall organized as in a U-form around a central court. "Atelier 4 has achieved a respectable school on the Pastinakweg, one that aims primarily at gaining the acceptance of the children and not that of architectural critics or other architects" (W. M. Chramosta). The architects in Atelier 4: K. P. Erblich, Z. Vesselinov, M. Hirschler, P. Scheufler, G. Schweighofer.

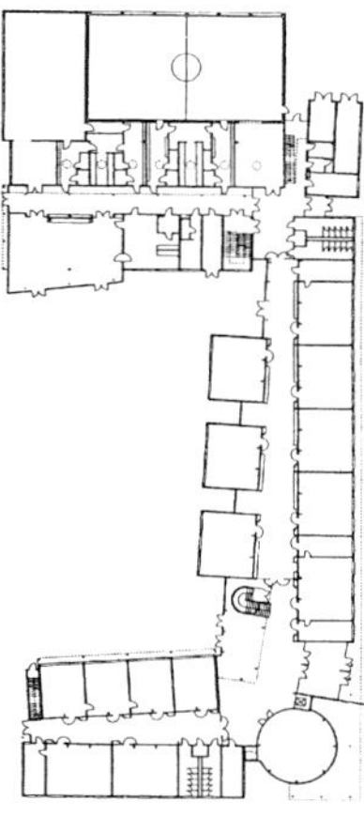

Supplementary Recommendations

22.-**29s** Housing Estate Süssenbrunn
Otto Häuselmayer
1995

22.-**30s** School Kagran
Roland Rainer
1967
Bernoullistrasse 3

22-.**31s** Primary school Viktor Wittner Gasse
Sepp Frank
1993
Viktor Wittner Gasse 50

22.-**32s** House Hinterberger
Andreas and Gerda Gerner
1993
Plankenmaisstrasse 43

22.-**33s** Housing
BKK-2, Christoph Lammerhuber, Axel Linemayr, Franz Sumnitsch, Florian Wallnöfer, Johann Winter, Evelyn Wurster
1991
Schiffmühlenstrasse 48

22.-**34s** Employment exchange
Bernhard Denkinger
1996
Prandaugasse 58

22.-**35s** Zentralsparkasse (now Bank Austria) Stadlau
Johann Georg Gsteu
1978
Stadlauer Strasse, Langobardenstrasse

22.-**36s** Primary school
NFOG (Nigst, Fonatti, Ostertag, Gaisrucker)
1994
Wagramerstrasse 45

22.-**37s** Housing and Shopping Centre
Ernst Hoffmann
1993
Am Kaisermühlendamm 87–92

MAP No. 14

23rd District
Liesing

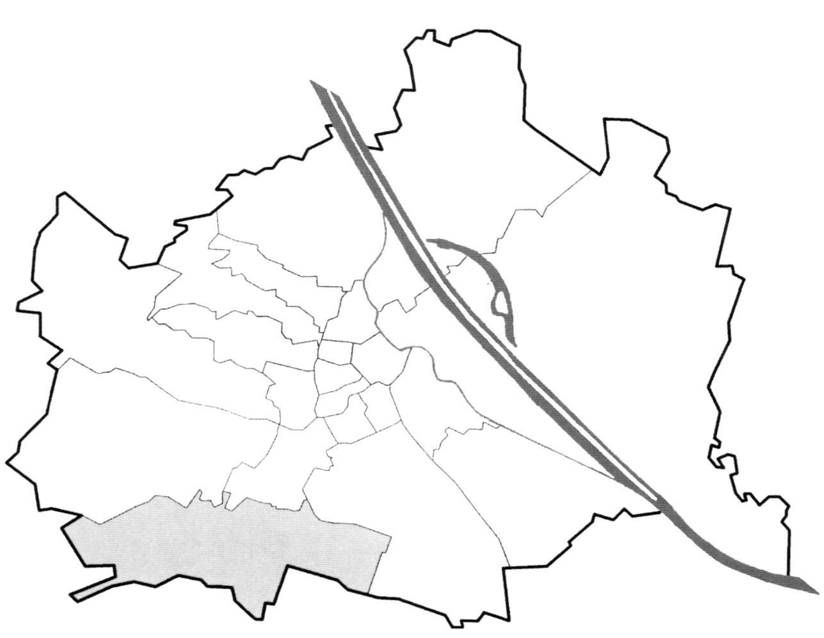

23rd District, Liesing Index numbers 23.-**1** … 23.-**13s**

Friedensstadt
am Wienerwald
Krankenhaus Lainz
Penzinger Wiese
Teichwiese
Hohenauer Wiese
Hermesstraße
Lainzer-Bach-Str.
Friedenszeile
Dr.-Schober-Str.
Wittgensteinstr.
Speisinger Str.
Rosenhügelstraße
Franz-Asenbauer-G.
Mauer
Maurer Hauptpl.
Endresstraße
Maurer Lange G.
Kroissbg.
Kadoltsbg.
St.-Georgen-Bg.
Maurer Bg.
Haymogasse
Anton-Krieger-G.
Rudolf-Waisenhorn-G.
Rodauner Str.
Breitenfurter Straße
Promenadewg.
Reiche Liesing
Ketzergasse
Rodaun
Kaltenleutgebner Straße
Hochstraße
Perchtoldsdorfer Heide
Perchtoldsdorf
Liesinger Pl.
Wiener Gasse
Donauwörther Str.
Ob. Sossen
Zugberg
Neuberg
23.7
23.13s
23.6
23.12s
23.5
23.3

Buildings worth visiting – Suggestions by Viennese architects

23rd District:

Luigi Blau:
Employment office (Arbeitsamt) Liesing, Index No. 23.-**2**

Underground Stations
U6 Line
1990

Perfektastrasse
Access: Open to the public
Public transportation: U6 (Perfektastrasse)

The opening of the south line of the U6 in 1995 lengthened Vienna's Underground system by 5.2 km, providing it with five additional station buildings of outstanding quality and two technical halls. Johann Georg Gsteu began in 1990 with the architectural design of the U6 South after the technical planning had already been finalized. In spite of this he did not restrict his work to superficial cosmetics. The forms are based on the technical production methods of profiled aluminium sheets manufactured by pull pressing, which was used in the building along with bluish streaked concrete and glass. Gsteu's attempt at justifying the design by basing it on the technical production methods of the materials was similar to the approach used first by Otto Wagner a hundred years previously.

This is one of the most emphatic tributes to the Bauhaus tradition in Viennese inter-war architecture. The largely transparent street front with the well-lit staircase extension faces a more opaque garden facade. This one-sided opening derives from the function of the building. Plischke concentrated public circulation on the ground floor, grouping the waiting rooms around a central hall. The building has received more international than national recognition. This official indifference continued up to the 1990s, but meanwhile the building has been beautifully restored by Hermann Czech (1998) to its original condition.

Employment Office Liesing 1932

Dr. Neumann Gasse 7
Access: Not open to the public
Public transportation: Bus 60A (Dr. Neumann Gasse)

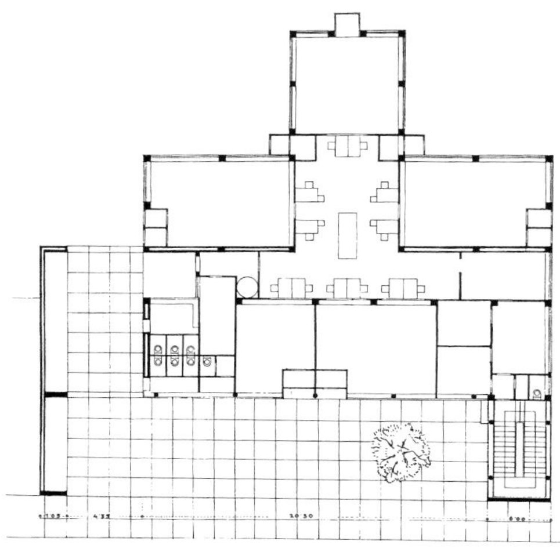

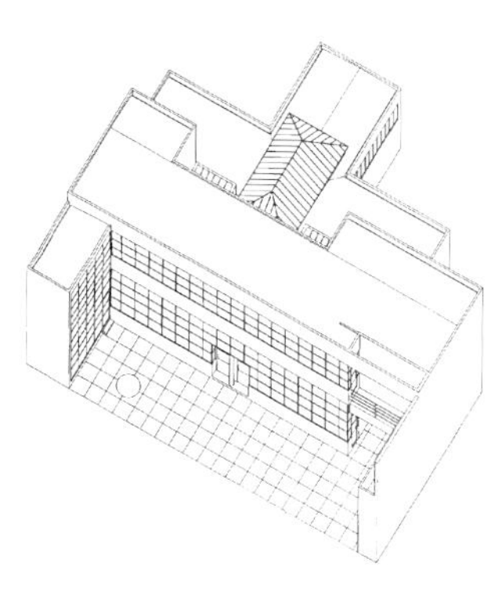

Boris Podrecca

School Dirmhirngasse 1990

Boris Podrecca's school in Dirmhirngasse acts as an extension to the small school building across the street. The two buildings are connected optically and functionally by a glass bridge. The new building consists of two parts separated by the main stairway and glazed hallway . The gym is situated under the court to gain space and to provide additional open space for pupils on its roof.

Dirmhirngasse 138
Access: Viewing by appointment
Public transportation: Suburban train (Schnellbahn)1 and 2 (Liesing)

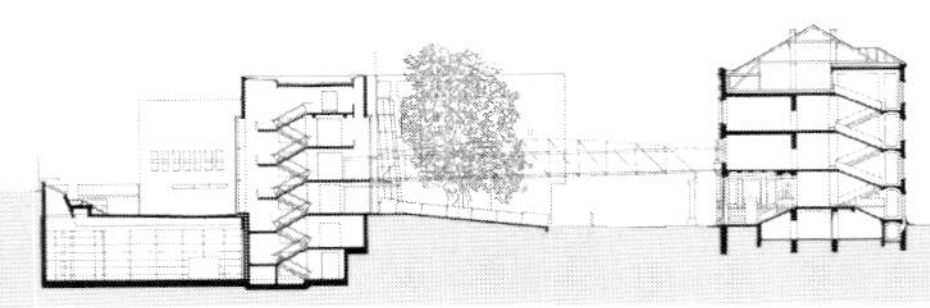

Brunner Strasse
1986

Brunner Strasse in Liesing is one of the most heavily frequented roads in the south of Vienna. A social housing cooperative society was offered a plot adjoining this road. Helmut Richter proposed to set back the actual housing block, in order to create a glazed buffer zone against the noise of the traffic. The flats themselves have a small quiet interior court and are oriented exclusively towards the garden. In terms of materials and functions this is a consistent work in the spirit of Modernism.

Brunner Strasse 26-32,
Autofabrikgasse 7
Access: Not open to the public
Public transportation: Bus 66A (Carlbergergasse)

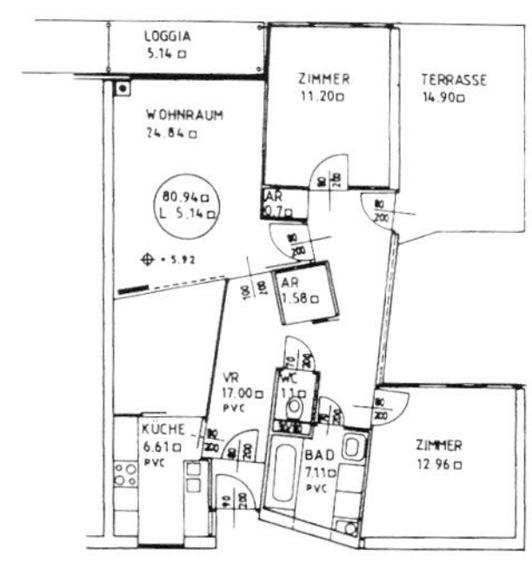

23.-5 | *Rob Krier, Hedwig Wachberger and Peter Gebhart*

Housing Breitenfurter Strasse 1981

Rob Krier drew up the master plan for this housing following his urban planning principle. The central round building and the two edge buildings are by Krier himself. In the sphere of social housing, Krier uses the postmodern architectural vocabulary with which he defines his concept of urban space: streets, squares and blocks. The result is a small, synthetic town in itself on Vienna's periphery.

Breitenfurter Strasse 380–413
Access: Open areas only
Public transportation: Buses 253, 254 and 354 (Hoferstiege)

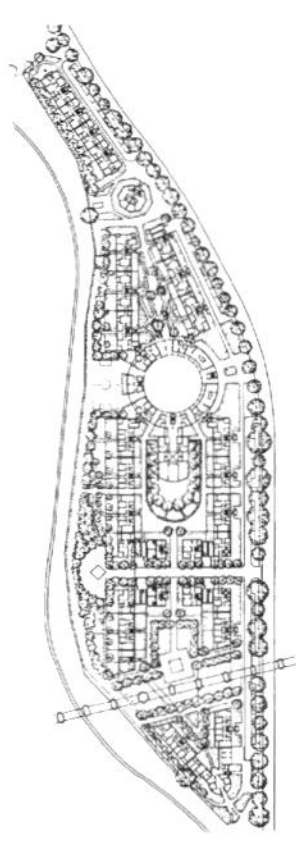

23.-6 | *Roland Rainer*

Housing Mauerberg 1956

Roland Rainer's philosophy of high-density low-rise has been applied to this sloping site in an exemplary manner. It was considered impossible to build on this south sloping site: Rainer has realized a housing scheme based on ecological principles which are still valid today.

Rodauner Strasse, Mauerbergstrasse, R. Waisenhorngasse, Lerchthalergasse
Access: Open areas only
Public transportation: Bus 60A (Maurer Berg)

Fritz Wotruba, Fritz G. Mayr

23.-**7**

The sculptor Fritz Wotruba has succeeded in additionally enhancing the mythical atmosphere of a small hill through the archaic nature of the concrete cubes of the church. The sculptural exterior of the building reveals the plastic imagination of the sculptor, a flat concrete roof slab largely robs the interior of its spatial qualities. The technical realization was handled by the architect Fritz G. Mayr.

Church of the Holiest Trinity ("Zur Heiligsten Dreifaltigkeit") 1965

Georgenberg, Maurer Lange Gasse 137, Rysergasse
Access: Open to the public
Public transportation: Bus 60A (Kaserngasse)

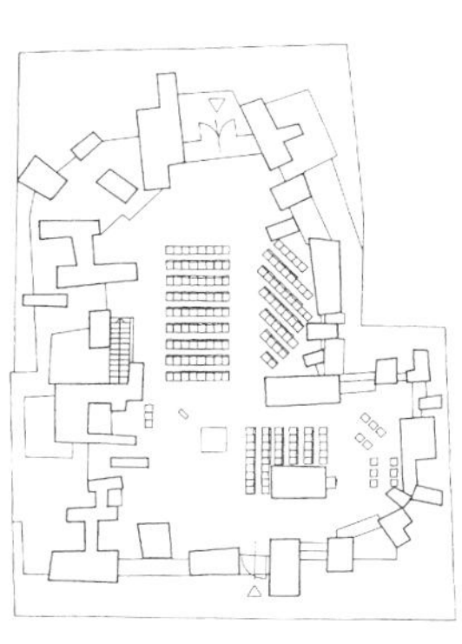

Martin Kohlbauer

23.-**8**

Situating a heating plant in the southern part of the Vienna basin demands a strong urban form and a contemporary interpretation of a lost industrial building culture. The huge vaulted roof and setting part of the building ten metres underground allowed the housing of two gigantic incinerators, the pump hall and the entire service station, including the administrative functions.

Thermal Power Station 1993

Heizwerkstrasse
Access: Not open to the public
Public transportation: Bus 67A (Heizwerkstrasse)

Housing Othellogasse 1986

Othellogasse,
Jochen Rindt Strasse
Access: Open areas only
Public transportation: Bus 67A (Birostrasse, J. Rindt Strasse)

The master plan conceived by Melicher, Schwalm-Theiss und Gressenbauer developed an open comb-like structure, closed towards the north and open towards the south. "The level, trapezoidal site has two large urban elements: the square over the underground parking garage which spans the distance between the border blocks and the curved row, and the group of individual houses. It thus deals elegantly with the general problem of any residential situation, namely the transition from the automobile world to the pedestrian world" (W. M. Chramosta). The team of architects: Melicher, Schwalm-Theiss and Gressenbauer, Cufer, Gruss and Gruss and Schandl.

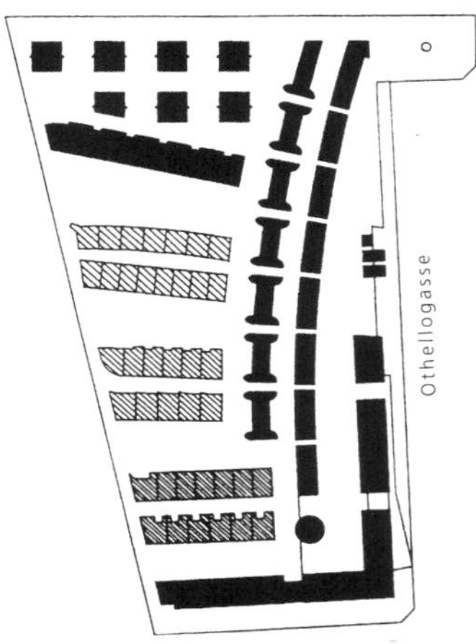

Housing Traviatagasse 1991

Abraham's masterplan for the four groups of architects (Abraham, Buck/Giencke, Lautner/Scheifinger/Szedenik/Schindler and Pruscha, was the result of a restricted competition.. Abraham gives a new identity to the formless periphery of the city by the means of a rigid geometry. The architects answer the challenge with typological and partly traditional residential forms: Abraham's answer is vertical living in terrace houses, Pruscha organises an introverted, multi-storeyed detached courtyard house, Buck/Giencke rework the stepped housing type and Lautner/Scheifinger/ Szedenik/Schindler react with a mixed residential form. The geometry and the strongly introverted living pattern are atypical for Vienna.

Traviatagasse, Pfarrgasse, Kolpingstrasse
Access: Not open to the public
Public transportation: Bus 16A (Pfarrgasse/ Traviatagasse)

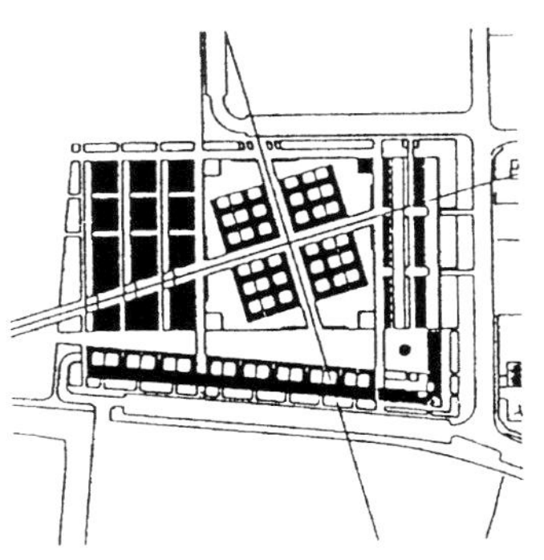

Supplementary Recommendations

23.-**11s**	Johann Gottek Estate Helmar Zwick	1979 Johann Gottek Gasse
23.-**12s**	Widtmann House Hans Puchhammer, Gunther Wawrik	1966 Lechthalergasse 21
23.-**13s**	Private Residence in Mauer Dieter Henke, Marta Schreieck	1983 Rudolf Waisenhorn Gasse 148

Vienna Surrounding Districts

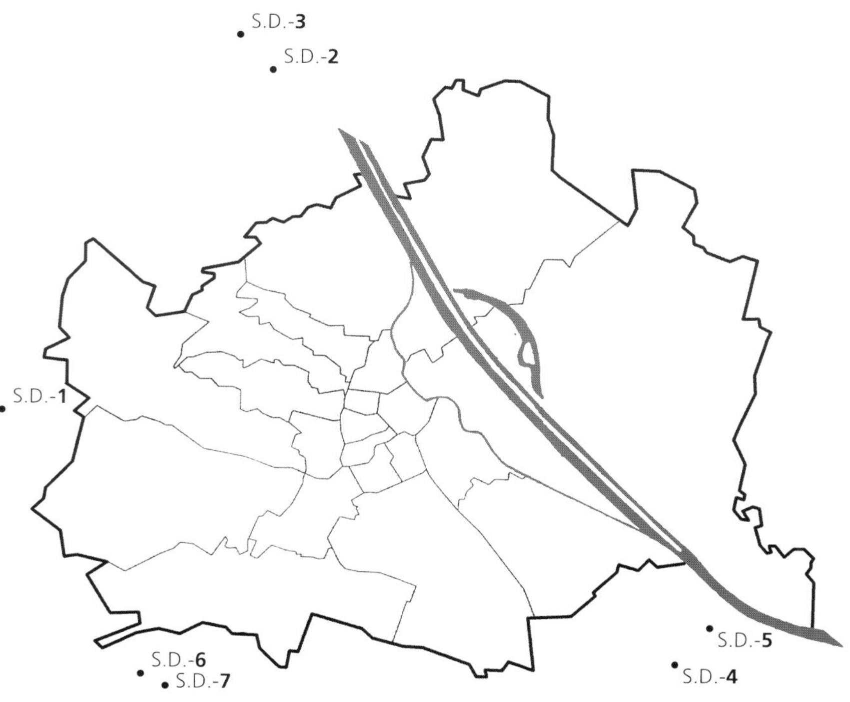

Vienna Surrounding Districts Index numbers S.D..-**1** … S.D.-**9s**

S.D.-**1** | ***Josef Hoffmann***

Sanatorium Purkersdorf 1904

Purkersdorf, Wiener Strasse 74
Access: Not open to the public

Josef Hoffmann's major work in Vienna is known for "the clarity of its disposition, a consequence of its formal finish, and above all the extreme simplicity of its cube form, which is, for 1904, as avant-garde as Frank Lloyd Wright's Larkin Building in Buffalo, Mackintosh's Scotland Street School in Glasgow or Otto Wagner's Postal Savings Bank" (Eduard Sekler). It was planned for the director, Viktor Zuckerhandl, as a sanatorium with baths and physiotherapy facilities. Built in reinforced concrete, it has partially visible constructions, such as the stairwell and the dining area. The interior is the work of the Wiener Werkstätte, and the furniture designs are considered some of the most significant of the period. Thoroughly renovated in 1995, it can now be viewed again in its original splendour.

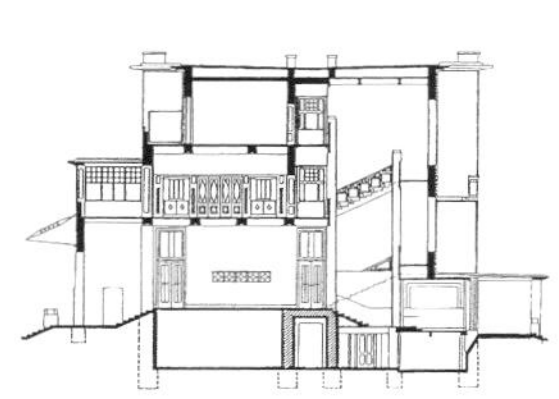

S.D.-**2** | ***Heinz Tesar***

Schömer Central Office 1985

Klosterneuburg, Aufeldstrasse 17–23
Access: Viewing by arrangement

The Schömer Company's administration building was built between 1985 and 1987 by Heinz Tesar, winner of an invited competition. All the offices are accessible from a central space formed by a generously dimensioned atrium extending to the full height of this four storey building. The core of the hall is double staircase with a functional and a sculptural element. The walls of the central hall house an extensive collection of contemporary Austrian art, the Essel Collection.

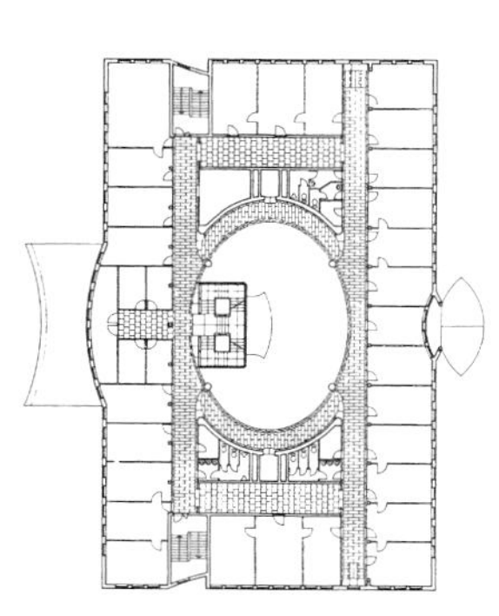

Heinz Tesar

S.D.-**3**

The idea behind this project was to create a community centre for the Protestant community in Klosterneuburg. It fulfils this function along with the existing parish building from 1907. A small elliptical building for circa 150 people, and an almost Baroque treatment of light. Square windows on the south façade and circular roof lights in exposed concrete result in an intense play of light and shadow; immaterial light being a metaphor for divinity. Adjacent to the church is a semi-detached house built between 1991 and 1994 by Heinz Tesar, Am Ölberg 26–30.

Protestant Church Klosterneuburg 1992

Klosterneuburg
Franz Rumpler Strasse 14
Access: Please contact the church office for opening hours

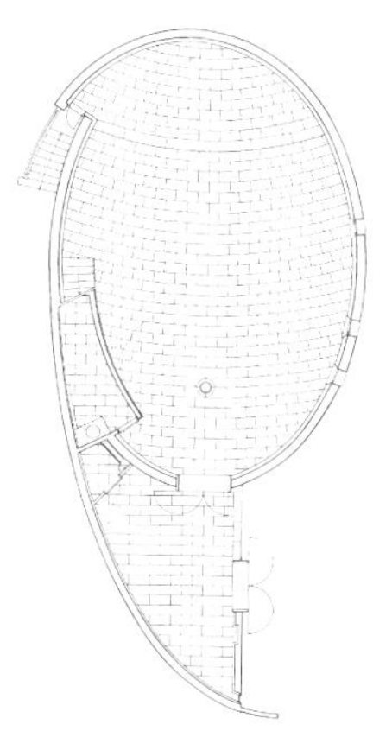

Hermann Czech

S.D.-**4**

Hermann Czech's theoretical work on Adolf Loos and Viennese Modernism forms the basis of the realisation of this building. Loos' concept of the 'space plan' was combined in a manneristic fashion with Gottfried Semper's thoughts on clothing in architecture. This apparently spontaneous surburban house is in reality an architectonic combination of the architectural theories of Semper, Loos and Frank.

House M. 1977

Schwechat, Kranichgasse 7
Access: Not open to the public

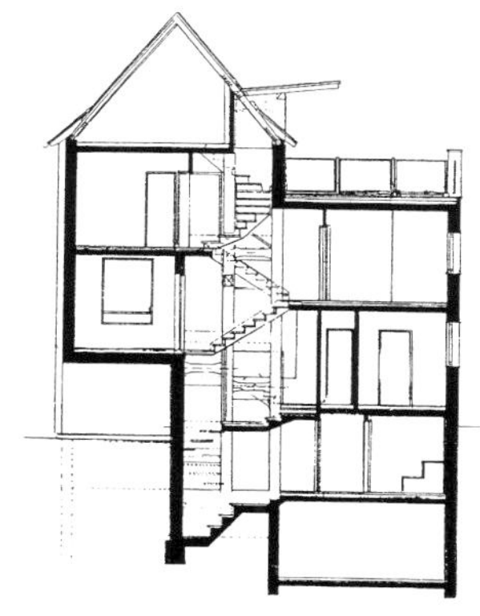

S.D.-**5**

Waagner-Biró

Pipeline Bridge for the ÖMV 1958

Access: Open to the public

The refinery at Schwechat, part of the Austrian Mineral Oil Administration (OMV), an oil company, is in itself a unique play of industrial architecture and light, especially at night. The pipelines also have a special architectural character. The suspension bridge, with its Y-shaped pylons, is a remarkable demonstration of the anonymous engineering skills of the post war period. It connects the refinery with the docks and oil storage tanks in the Lobau at Schwechat-Mannswörth, at the river mark 1,914.3 km of the Danube River.

S.D.-**6**

Hans Hollein

Council Rooms Perchtoldsdorf 1975

Perchtoldsdorf, Marktplatz, Council Building
Access: Viewing by arrangement

This early work by Hans Hollein, built 1975–1976, is remarkable for its spacious solution and precise detail. The new urban structure demanded an adaptation of the space in Perchtoldsdorf's Town Hall, an old listed building. The renovation was based on the principle that new design elements be integrated into the existing building. All the furniture was designed by the architect specifically for this project.

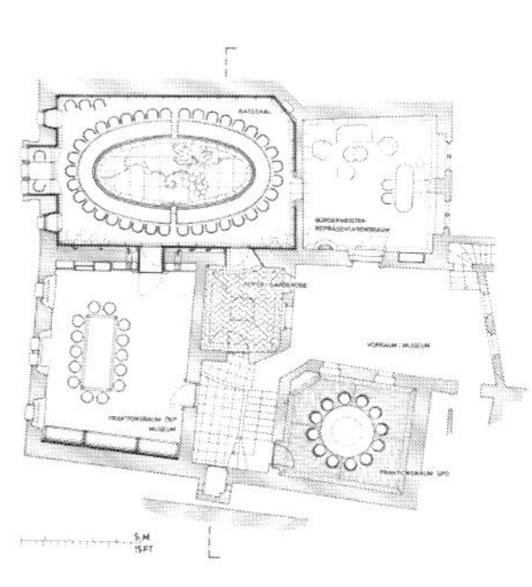

Fire Station 1981

The small-scale structures in the little town of Perchtoldsdorf suggested breaking up the fire station into three parts: the rescue services in one independent building on Donauwörther Strasse, next to it the covered festivities´ area, and the fire station itself. The roof over the festivities´ area acts as a joint between the rescue services and the fire brigade. For functional and safety reasons the access roads are separate from each other. Built between 1981 and 1983. "The basic idea was to erect a building that kept to the scale of the local structures and could be experienced as part of a whole" (Heinz Tesar).

Perchtoldsdorf,
Donauwörther Strasse 29
Access: Viewing by arrangement

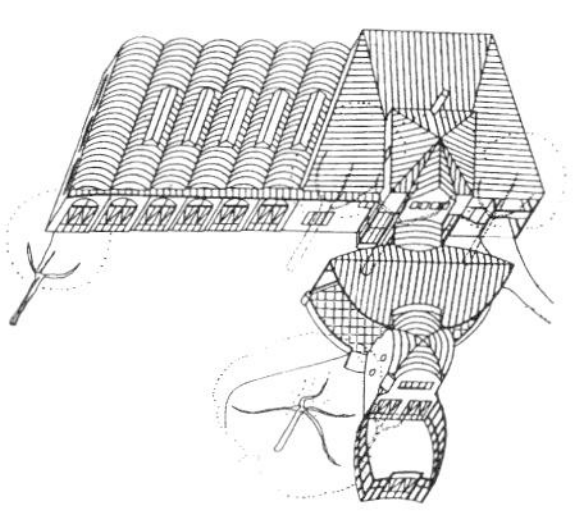

Supplementary Recommendations

S.D.-**8s**	Government Officers´ Housing, Rannersdorf Heinrich Tessenow, Mayer, Mang	1921 Schwechat-Rannersdorf, Stankagasse 8–18
S.D.-**9s**	Government Offices, Perchtoldsdorf IGIRIEN, Werner Appelt, Franz Eberhard Kneissl, Elsa Prochazka	1984 Perchtoldsdorf, Marktplatz 11

Notes on Vienna's Contemporary History

The impression Vienna conveys still today is primarily that of a typical 19th century capital. Functioning as it did as centre of the Habsburg Empire, the city combined both economic functions and financial services with the cultural representational requirements of the bourgeoisie and the large-scale demand for industrial and cultural goods. This capital city and imperial residence, this "infinitely expandable metropolis" for which Otto Wagner had developed his visions for the modern city was, in 1918, deprived of essential functions. With the collapse of the Habsburg monarchy, Vienna, which had always regarded itself on a par with the dynamic capitals of Berlin and Paris, forfeited much of its significance as a metropolis. In the divided Europe of 1945, it was transformed into a kind of border city, in danger of becoming old and antiquated. Vienna began to live off its past. With the fall of the Iron Curtain in 1989, the city reverted to its former position in Europe's centre, a position that has, up to now, remained a purely geographical phenomenon, even though, with the opening-up of the East European states, political hopes were raised of Vienna taking on its former role, and serving as metropolis for the countries once part of the Habsburg monarchy. However, Berlin, and also Prague and Budapest have proved themselves to be superior, or at least serious, rivals. The Austrian capital lacks the dynamism and open-mindedness to gain the trust of large development corporations, international companies or transnational institutions. When, in 1995, a site analysis comparing Vienna with German cities was presented, the headline in a Vienna daily ran, "Still beautiful, but old." The German cities were credited with better-qualified labour markets, superior technology, cheaper housing and office facilities and a better transport network. Vienna's culture, traditionally pushed by the marketing specialists in their tourist brochures, was, it went on, not modern enough, and the prevailing high environmental standards not a decisive enough factor on their own. Those with their political slogans proclaiming a "New Gründerzeit", a "Vienna without borders", were thus brought back down to earth, but the search for a new identity has not yet begun. There can be no denying that proceeding along a course that would transform Vienna into a metropolis cannot be a political end in itself, involving the risk of social conflict and political insecurity. Yet the possible decision against such an orientation is again hardly compatible with Vienna's (and its citizens') sense of its own importance as former imperial city, and its inherent desire both to have its place alongside the other famous cities of the world and be of international significance.

The skepticism shown towards the idea of Vienna becoming a European metropolis has many causes, which only partly lie within the sphere of urban politics. In those fields, however, which do come under the jurisdiction of local politicians, the uncertainty as to which course the city should now take is clearly to be seen. Influenced by spectacular urban projects such as the "grands travaux" in Paris under Mitterand, the Docklands in London or the Reichstagsgelände in Berlin, the former self-confidence asserts itself again and again - namely that Vienna should become a metropolis with a role to play in the world. Symbolic of this confidence are plans for large-scale urban projects such as the development of a new highly technicized district on the north bank of the Danube. Over 50 years ago, on the other hand, the art historian and publicist Hans Tietze made the point in his history of Vienna that throughout those periods when the city had made strides towards becoming a metropolis, the mentality and political horizon of its population had remained provincial. This has time and time again been fundamental to the objections raised against any incisive intrusion into the cityscape; the last occasion being for instance opposition to the representational power displayed by architectural elements of the newly planned museum quarter in the former Messepalast, which were conceived as a demonstration of a progressive and democratic cultural policy. This and the history of numerous other unsuccessful attempts to modernize Vienna form the basis for the following notes on Vienna's contemporary history.

Whereas many of the earlier urban projects such as that of Otto Wagner for the reorganization of Karlsplatz failed for financial or bureaucratic reasons, later projects have come up against opposition of a more diffuse nature; diffuse because it is seldom a question of the population manifestly demonstrating against a given project, or of an open debate taking place between those in favour and those against. What manifests itself here is possibly a result of a confinement syndrome: the architect Karl Mayreder already complained a century ago that the monotony resulting from the enforced historicism of the facades gave the city the look of a military barracks. Those confined seem in the meantime to have grown so accustomed to these aesthetics that the pure mention of the world "modern" in connection with architecture is enough to make the hackles rise. If an explanation needs to be found for the Viennese inclination to fight over the city's profile, it ought to be mentioned that these conflicts have taken place during times of extreme political stability. The approximately 20 years of ongoing Christian-Social rule between 1897 and 1918 were followed by the 70 year-period of absolute majority for the Social Democratic Party, the latter interrupted solely by two successive dictatorships from 1934 –1945, and the division as a result of the war into 4 zones of occupation between 1945 and 1955. Considering such political permanence within the city's administration, the emotional rebellion blocking many a contemporary architectural project can be interpreted as a syndrome, as a means of expressing discontent with change in general, with the incursions of modernity and with the pace of modernization, without running the risk of political instability.

The antagonistic manner in which local government was conducted can be traced back to Karl Lueger (1844 –1910), that legendary populist, and the revolutionary urban policies of his Christian-Social Party carried through at the end of the previous century. As in other large cities of the time, Mayor Lueger's period of office saw a rapid expansion within the administration itself, and a more professional approach to public services. In comparison to other European cities, the number of council employees increased at an extraordinary rate; the 2000 civil servants and several hundred workers of the pre-Lueger era were increased to 30.000, the current count being approximately 70.000. As a result, the city council in Vienna became, after the state, the largest employer and important conferrer of commissions. The reasons for this were, in addition to the general increase in services, the extensive local political reforms, for example the municipalization of energy supplies and public transport. The Christian-Social Party treated the civil service as a political source of power – a factor that began to shape the way local government was to function. Appointments and promotions, as well as the award of contracts for official projects to private firms were used to reward long-serving party members, and win over new ones. From district level to that of the city administration, the interests of public administration and ruling party began to overlap. It was at this time that the city first began to function as developer, and also had considerable social aid to distribute. For this reason the administration became vulnerable for a finely meshed lobbyism, going beyond pure economic power groups such as exist in American cities, and affecting the entire enfranchised population. Two aspects of Vienna's public life are still today influenced by this phenomenon: then, as now, people have a close affinity with districts or older parts of districts, whose almost village-like sense of community appears to relate back to the heyday of the lower middle-class Christian-Social clubs and their sense of tradition. A Viennese is therefore torn between two conflicting loyalities - to the city and to, for example, Josefstadt, Währing or Ottakring, the latter sentiment with its inherent touch of folklore. Secondly Vienna has become since the Lueger era a political city in the way that urban theorists paradoxically describe premodern cities. Lueger's politics first led to the idea that an administration which provided for, and saw to, the welfare of its citizens, could greatly influence the living conditions and conduct of the same. The Viennese still today have a strong belief in the absolute power of the mayor to regulate life in general and, as a less welcome consequence, to believe that he is responsible for all urban phenomena, from immigration and the traffic jam to urban aesthetics.

In 1919, the Social Democrats took over from the Christian-Social administration, and, until very recently, could always rule with an absolute majority. City administration, bureaucracy, party and economic institutions were forced to cooperate even more closely as, with the collapse of the Habsburg monarchy, the wealthy classes were ruined, and, as a result, many aspects of the economy that were of communal relevance ceased to function. Urban policy of the inter-war years led to Vienna being given the epithet "red", achieving fame above all on account of its ambitious and social municipal housing policy, which, within a few years, was to lead to the building of 60.000 apartments, and its efficient system of welfare.

The influence of the city, which in 1920, had become a federal state in its own right, and that of its administration, ranged from municipal banking institutions (Zentralsparkasse) to a cinema chain (KIBA), from restaurants and canteens (WÖK) to council-owned swimming baths and sportsgrounds, from kindergartens to the board of the state radio, and to the city's largest advertising agency (Gewista). From a democratic point of view, such concentration of power is questionable, but in the case of "Red Vienna", it was not only legitimated by comfortable majorities in practically every single election, but also backed by the active participation of large sections of the population - every second (!) Viennese was a member of the Social Democratic Party. Thousands of functionaries involved themselves in an honorary capacity in cultural, sporting, educational and charitable organizations supporting the work of the city administration, thus lending Social-Democratic municipal policy an almost unchallengeable authority. In politically critical times such as the 1927 election year, even public figures such as Sigmund Freud and Robert Musil who normally steered clear of political parties, openly supported the Viennese Social-Democratic Party. In the Seventies and Eighties, however, there was increasing scepticism shown towards this intermingling of political administration, businesses closely linked to the council, and Party. An analysis was made of the district of Favoriten, which ascertained that 50 % of the Social Democratic Party functionaries were also employed by either state or city council. Those in important positions in banks, insurance companies and other institutions owned by the council were also very often leading party officials.[1] A conflict of interests was unavoidable: a Social-Democratic district chairman could, for example, not only be the "mayor" (Bezirksvorsteher) of a single district, and deputy mayor of the city itself, but also chairman of a public development corporation that harboured interests in the district of which he was mayor, thus bringing him into conflict with his electorate. The Social Democratic Party was, according to the critics, in danger of forgoing its function as mediator between large sections of the population and the city authorities, and of tending to serve the interests of the civil servants.

Alongside the image projected by "Red Vienna", there was, after 1945, another, just as compelling. The "Third Man", with Orson Welles as cynical gangster profiting from the tension between the occupying powers signified a city without a future. The decaying city was also used by John Irving, who had studied in Vienna in 1964, as theme in his novel "Hotel Newhampshire": obscure bars, grimy lodging houses on the once so renowned Kärntnerstrasse are the pad of long-serving prostitutes. As to be expected, in "Newhampshire" a group of otherwise easy-going anarchists is planning an attack on the Opera House and the antiquated ceremonial that lends the city a last vestige of aesthetic charm. Vienna, or more particularly its centre, had indeed lost its metropolitan flair, but did not possess the strength to turn the tables. Here too the specific political characteristics of the city provide many an explanation: although 90 % of the districts

1 See Herbert Stammer: Party organization based on the Austrian Socialist Party's political organization in Favoriten, PhD thesis, Vienna 1979.

were in the hands of the Social Democrats, the First District, the "Inner City" remained Conservative. Until recently, this distribution of political power determined the general trend in urban planning. The Social Democratic majority on the City Council regarded the First District as enemy territory - this was at least how the latter's Conservative "Bezirksvorsteher" saw it. Political decisions such as the discontinuance of inner-city bus routes, special taxes levied on catering businesses, the introduction of petty night-time noise reguations and generally neglecting to invest, made life in the "City" increasingly provincial. These were at any rate the complaints of the Conservative politicians, the hotel owners, the businessmen and the real estate agents. A large number of restaurants and cafés closed down in the Sixties, and, compared to the former population of 100.000, there were now only 25.000 people living in the First District. Criticism was also voiced in progressive-liberal circles. To quote from the newly-founded weekly magazine "Profil", which, at the onset of the Seventies, began to play an influential role in Viennese politics by disclosing numerous cases of corruption and abuses of power, "In contrast to the bombed-out cities of Germany, urban planning did not, in less badly damaged Vienna, begin at the centre (which would have conceivably made harmonious development from the centre outwards possible) but, as though one was looking for areas in which to experiment, on the periphery." When a Social Democratic City Councillor seriously proposed using old gravestones to pave St. Stephen's square, the caustic likening of the city to a graveyard came as no surprise.

However, this decline of the "City" and its loss of charm, albeit temporary, cannot be solely be attributed to the political power struggle. It also reflects the image the Viennese themselves have of their city. The maps, the tourist brochures, the books and the films have, for over 100 years, all contributed together with the architecture towards producing a conical-shaped conception of the city, with concentric circles representing politics, culture, urban living, recreation and industry arranged round its religious centre - the city not as mechanism, but as a biomorphic organism. Any interference in the hierarchical structure of this organism necessarily leads to a feeling of insecurity and loss of bearings. This is why the converting of the city centre into a kind of museum could count on the tacit approval of the citizenry. Vienna has been built, it can only be added to in ways that are in keeping with the times. The builders of the Ringstrasse, their work often mistakenly compared with Baron Haussman's "deconstruction" of the old Paris, already adhered to this principle, solicitously filling in the still empty Glacis, with its military but not as yet politically representative character, with the cultural buildings of the liberal-democratic era. It only took a few street regulations for Karl Kraus in 1900 to issue an impassioned warning that Viennese literature, at home in the coffee-houses in danger of being demolished, could fall victim to modernity and the new streams of traffic. To the Viennese way of thinking, if one had to have urban modernity, then the "Sirk-Ecke" opposite the Opera quite sufficed, the Social Democrats thus being left with the task of solving the housing problem in the zones betwee the suburbs and the open country.

Up to the end of the Sixties, the administration of Vienna was a comparatively easy task, but then, as in other larger cities, new forms of political life began to assert themselves. It was, in fact, exactly at this point that the urban model associated with "Red Vienna", which had replaced uncontrolled urbanity and its inherent dangers by social security and cultural stability, began to erode. In May 1973, the Viennese Social Democrats lost a referendum, the first ever to be held in Vienna, on whether 40 trees in a park should be felled to provide land required for the building of a university institute. The exemplary effect could not have been greater, for here for the first time a relatively unimportant ecological issue had caused the question to be asked whether prominent public building projects were always socially acceptable. The fact that the referendum on the "Sternwartepark" was greatly influenced by Vienna's most popular daily added to the political disconcertion. Compared with the city's written constitution, the question of political representation was suddenly to be seen from a different angle: how far, in a society thirsting for adventure and so easily influenced by the media, could a party risk planning 2-3 decades in advance and not have public support ? And was the citizenry still homogenous enough to accept schematic urban planning in such vital fields as population growth, traffic volume and housing supply ? The Social Democratic Party had been warned: with the 1964 Landtag election looming up, an opinion poll was held for the first time aimed at ascertaining the electorate's attitude towards both the redevelopment of old city districts, and council housing policy. In a show of traditionalism, the majority voted against the demolition of Gründerzeit districts and the erection of new housing in these areas, thus opposing the priorities set by the City Council. There were also new demands: traffic noise and air pollution were quoted as pressing problems. The building of old people's homes and hospitals, the maintenance of water standards, and the protection of the green belt were considered by the electorate to be just as important as the erection of houses.[2] In contrast, interest in a municipal social and welfare policy, with which the image of "Red Vienna" had been so closely linked, rapidly declined. The results of this opinion poll put Vienna's governing party in an embarrassing situation, for it had based its image essentially on municipal housing. The Seventies brought about the re-emergence of older conceptions of what "city" implied. Projects aimed at reviving some sort of local identity were now considered by the politicians as worthy of support. During the following years, the opposition Conservative Party was not without success in its drive to set cultural initiatives reviving traditional forms of urban life. It was here that the local restaurants and bars played a major part, and, as organizers of poetry readings, discussions and cabaret performances, were to give people a general feeling of security and familiarity as they went about enjoying these different forms of urban entertainment. Consciously or unconsciously, one fell back on a tenacious element of Vienna's urban structure, for the city is characterized by the small functional mix, ranging from small grocers' shops, cafés, restaurants, and tobacconists to the highly specialized "Trafik" selling newspapers and magazines and offering a wide range of services in cramped ground-floor premises. The originators of this "local district culture", one would, in the Viennese dialect, more precisely talk about "Grätzel neighbourhood culture" in order to describe the almost familiar atmosphere prevailing in particular corners of individual districts, were probably themselves surprised at the fact that it was they who had provided the decisive impulse for a re-urbanisation of the city. In the Eighties it was precisely this small reanimated functional mix of shops and forms of entertainment that gave Vienna highly effective publicity, in addition to the fact that the numerous cafés, restaurants and bars provided avantgarde architects, with too little to do, with a field in which to experiment.

It was this swing in opinion, away from the magic "big number" in housing to the quality of life in the city and the questions it posed, that formed the background to the ecological reorientation in the municipal policy of the Seventies. Architecture as a sign was allotted an important role in the sense of "speaking architecture", but it is an architecture that is forever in danger of becoming trite. A completely novel idea was the commissioning in 1977 of the painter, ecologist and fantastic realist Friedensreich Hundertwasser with the building of a council apartment block, allowing him to put into practice his conception of "anti-architecture". The building has since become a magnet for tourists doing their rounds. Hundertwasser became famous as author of the "Verschimmelungsmanifest", an esoteric manifesto protesting against rationalism in architecture, countering it by the colourful framing of windows, uneven floors, non-angular walls, and the fertilization of the building's garden with the house's own sewage. Ever since this turnabout, the city council has regularly commissioned artists

2 Sozialwissenschaftliche Studiengesellschaft. 32. report, August 1964; a report on opinion polls relating to problems in Vienna, p. 5

close in style to the "Vienna School of Fantastic Realism" to design houses or facades under the supervision of civil engineers. The eco-social alternative to this debatable aesthetic radicalism, and certainly of greater significance for the urban theoretical debate, was provided by the architect Harry Glück, whose residential parks - the best-known being in Alt-Erlaa with its 3.031 apartments - were officially presented at the Europalia '87 in Antwerp as an advancement in Viennese social housing. The multi-storey terraced residential buildings, each with a roof-top swimming pool, communal recreational facilities and integrated areas of green saw their justification along ethological lines. What they attempted was the quadrature of the circle, the bringing of town and country into harmony with each other.[3]

The rapidly increasing diversity of life-styles and vested interests of post-industrial societies has made urban planning more difficult. In the search for new points of reference, marketing strategies and site management are coming increasingly to the fore. Commercialization, of which tourism represents only one of the many elements, is forcing new aesthetic and emotional concepts of the commodity "city" to be found. In Vienna too, municipal policy oscillates between structural planning and architectural modes. Urban projects and basic concepts alternate at a fast rate. The eco-social movement of the Seventies was followed in the Eighties by the twin option, paradoxical as it was, for urban expansion north of the Danube and urban renovation in the inner-city areas. The debates of the Nineties were again dominated by individual image-building projects such as Hans Hollein's shopping mall on St. Stephen's Square, a late post-modernist reaction to competition from cities abroad, and projects in various districts that were similarly upheld by the reputation of the architects planning them. Now that large-scale linear social planning had come to an end, these were to correspond to the increasing social fragmentation of the city according to age, sex, culture as well as other criteria: "Sun City", "Intercultural Living", "Frauen-Werk-Statt" ...

Vienna is being forced to mediate between the isolationist leanings of its citizens and the demands of a metropolis. The last few years have seen the introduction of forms of entertainment that at least in scale conform to the image a metropolis projects. These new forms of urban entertainment include the open-air operatic film festival in front of the city hall in summer, the artificial ice-rink there in winter, the Danube Island festival, the ski-jumping and snowboard competitions on Heldenplatz and Karlsplatz, the Christmas markets extending well beyond the actual season etc., all accompanied by an indirectly subsidized catering industry. Urban policy is being staged rather than conceived; but that was already the secret of Karl Lueger's success.

3 Cf. Wohnen in Wien. Wohnbau mit Gesinnung, Vienna 1987 (Contribution at the Europalia 1987, Antwerp)

Chronology

Index	Building	Planned/Start of Construction	Architect
		1161–1918	
1.**77**	St. Ruprecht's Church (Ruprechtskirche)	1161	
1.**14**	St. Michael's Church (Michaelerkirche)	1220	Antonio Beduzzi, Ernest Koch
1.**1**	St. Stephen's Cathedral (Stephansdom)	1230	Hans von Prachatitz, Hans Puchspaum, et al.
1.**16**	Hofburg		
	Hofburg-Schweizerhof, Imperial Chapel	1279	Jean-Nicolas Jadot de Ville-Issey, et al.
	Hofburg-Leopoldine Wing	1547	Philiberto Luchese, Burnacini, et al.
	Hofburg-Stallburg	1558	
	Hofburg-Amalienburg	1575	Ferrabosco, Nicolaus Pacassi, et al.
	Hofburg-National Library	1719	Johann Bernhard Fischer von Erlach, et al.
	Hofburg-Imperial Chancellery	1723	Johann Lucas von Hildebrandt, Josef Emanuel Fischer von Erlach, et al.
	Hofburg-Michaelertrakt	1723	Josef Emanuel Fischer von Erlach, et al.
	Hofburg Winter Riding School	1729	Josef Emanuel Fischer von Erlach
	Hofburg-Outer Castle Gateway	1821	Luigi Cagnola, Peter von Nobile
	New Hofburg	1869	Gottfried Semper, Carl Hasenauer, et al.
1.**18**	St. Augustine's Church (Augustinerkirche)	1330	Dietrich Ladtner von Pirn, Johann Ferdinand Hetzendorf von Hohenberg
1.**58**	Minorite Church (Minoritenkirche)	1339	
1.**67**	Maria am Gestade	1343	Michael Knab, Friedrich von Klinkowström
1.**44**	Old Jesuit Church (Alte Jesuitenkirche)	1386	Carlo Antonio Carlone
2.**11**	Prater	1403	
10.**24s**	Spinnerin am Kreuz	1451	Hans Puchspaum
1.**56**	Ensembles	1535	
11.**5**	Neugebäude	1569	Colin, Spranger, Jacopo da Strada, Pietro Ferrabosco
1.**41**	Franciscan Church (Franziskanerkirche)	1603	Bonaventura Daum
4.**7**	Theresian Academy	1615	Giovanni Battista Carlone
1.**86**	Jesuit Church (Universitätskirche)	1626	Andrea Pozzo
1.**109s**	Dominican Church (Dominikanerkirche)	1626	Antonio Canevale, et al.
9.**13**	Servitenkirche	1651, (1667–77, 1754–56)	Carlo Martino Carlone, Franz und Carlo Canevale, Franz Sebastian Rosenstingl
1.**9**	Plague Column (Pestsäule)	1682	Johann Bernhard Fischer von Erlach, Ludovico Burnacini, Paul Strudel
1.**22**	Palais Lobkowitz	1685	Giovanni Pietro Tencala, Johann Bernhard Fischer von Erlach
1.**47**	Palais Harrach	1690	Domenico Martinelli
9.**14**	Garden Palais Liechtenstein (currently Museum of Modern Art)	1691, (1705–06)	Domenico Martinelli, Domenico Egidio Rossi
1.**65**	Palais Liechtenstein	1694	Domenico Martinelli, Gabriel de Gabriele
1.**38**	Town Palace of Prince Eugene (now the Ministry of Finance)	1695	Johann Bernhard Fischer von Erlach
13.**3**	Schönbrunn Palace	1696	Johann Bernhard Fischer von Erlach, Josef Emaunel Fischer von Erlach, Nicolaus Pacassi
3.**6**	Palais Schwarzenberg	1697, (1716–18), 1722, 1751, 1928	Johann Lukas von Hildebrandt, Johann Bernhard Fischer von Erlach, Josef Emanuel Fischer von Erlach, Andrea Altomonte, C. Schmidt
1.**51**	Palais Batthyány-Schönborn	1698	Johann Bernhard Fischer von Erlach
3.**7**	Belvedere	1700	Johann Lukas von Hildebrandt
4.**8s**	Garden Palace Starhemberg-Schönburg	1700	Johann Lukas von Hildebrandt
1.**8**	St. Peter's Church (Peterskirche)	1702	Gabriele Montani, Johann Lukas von Hildebrandt
13.**3**	Schönbrunn Park	1705	Jean Trehet Ferdinand v. Hohenberg
1.**104s**	Bohemian Court Chancellery (Böhmische Hofkanzlei) -now Verfassungs- und Verwaltungsgerichtshof	1708	Johann Bernhard Fischer von Erlach
7.**3**	Palais Trautson	1710	Johann Bernhard Fischer von Erlach

Index	Building	Planned/Start of Construction	Architect
1.**48**	Palais Kinsky (formerly Palais Daun)	1713	Johann Lukas von Hildebrandt
4.**3**	Karlskirche	1715, (1722–39)	Johann Bernhard Fischer von Erlach, Josef E. Fischer von Erlach
8.**3**	Piaristenkirche	1716	Johann Lukas von Hildebrandt
1.**57**	Chancellery	1717	Johann Lukas von Hildebrandt
7.**1**	Museum Quarter (Messepalast) -formerly Imperial Stables	1719, (1721–23)	Johann Bernhard Fischer von Erlach, Josef Emanuel Fischer von Erlach
1.**105s**	Vermählungsbrunnen (Josefs-Brunnen)	1729	Josef Emanuel Fischer von Erlach
1.**45**	Civic Arsenal (Bürgerliches Zeughaus) now Fire Brigade Headquarters	1731	Anton Ospel
1.**23**	The Donner Fountain (Donnerbrunnen)	1737	Georg Raphael Donner
1.**21**	Albertina	1745	Louis von Montoyer, Josef Kornhäusel
1.**87**	Academy of Sciences (formerly the aula of the University)	1753	Jean-Nicolas Jadot de Ville-Issey
9.**7**	General Hospital– Narrenturm	1783	Isidor Canevale, Josef Gerl
9.**9**	Josephinum (Surgical Medical Academy)	1783	Isidor Canevale
1.**20**	Palais Pallavicini	1783	Johann Ferdinand Hetzendorf von Hohenberg
6.**3**	Theater an der Wien	1797	Josef Reymund d. Ä., Franz Jäger
3.**11**	Palais Rasumovsky (now the Federal Geographical Institute)	1803, 1814	Louis Montoyer, Joseph Meißl jun.
4.**1**	Technical University Vienna	1816	Hofbaudirektion, Josef S. von Leytenbach, Peter von Nobile
1.**60**	Volksgarten, Theseustempel, Monument to Empress Elisabeth	1819 (1904)	Ludwig Remy, Peter Nobile, Friedrich Ohmann
8.**2**	Theater in der Josefstadt	1822	Joseph Allio, Josef Kornhäusel, et al.
3.**10**	Sünnhof	1823	Peter Gerl
1.**82**	Synagogue	1824	Josef Kornhäusel
1.**82**	Seitenstettenhof	1825	Josef Kornhäusel
1.**50**	Schottenhof	1826	Josef Kornhäusel
4.**4**	The Dittmann Apartment Building	1831	Josef Kornhäusel
1.**52**	Parliament Building of Lower Austria	1832	Alois Pichl
3.**20s**	Hoffmann Apartment Building	1833	Josef Kornhäusel, Anton Hoppe
3.**2**	Central Mint	1835	Paul Sprenger
2.**13s**	Johann-Nepomuk Church	1841	Carl Rösner
6.**4**	Evangelical Church (Gustav-Adolf Church)	1846	Ludwig Förster, Theophil von Hansen
7.**5**	Altlerchenfelder Church	1846, (1849–61)	Paul Sprenger, Johann Georg Müller, Franz Sitte
3.**8**	Arsenal, (Museum of Military History)	1849, (1852)	Sicardsburg, Nüll, Roesner, Rigel, Förster, Hansen, Mayr
11.**13s**	Mautner-Markhof Factory	1850	
1.**46**	Palais Ferstel (formerly the Austro-Hungarian National Bank)	1856	Heinrich von Ferstel
9.**1**	Votivkirche	1856	Heinrich von Ferstel
10.**21s**	Evangelical Cemetery Church	1857	Theophil von Hansen
1.**83**	Greek Orthodox Church	1858	Theophil von Hansen
1.**28**	Palais Todesco	1861	Ludwig Förster und Theophil von Hansen
1.**29**	State Opera	1861	Eduard van der Nüll und August Sicard van Sicardsburg
1.**93**	Palace of the Grand and German Master of the Teutonic Order, Archduke Wilhelm	1864	Theophil von Hansen
15.**9**	Fünfhaus Parish Church (Maria vom Siege)	1864	Friedrich von Schmidt
9.**12**	Rossauer Barracks	1865	Oberst Karl Pilhal, Major Karl Markl
1.**37**	Music Association Building (Musikverein)	1866	Theophil von Hansen
1.**91**	University and Museum of Applied Arts	1867	Heinrich von Ferstel, Ludwig Baumann

Index	Building	Planned/Start of Construction	Architect
9.**5**	Institute of Chemistry, University of Vienna	1868	Heinrich von Ferstel
1.**66**	Palais Epstein (now Municipal Education Authority Building)	1868	Theophil von Hansen
12.**4**	Workers' Housing of the Southern Railway Company	1870	Wilhelm Flattich
11.**6**	Main Cemetery (Lueger Memorial Church)	1870, 1908	Karl Jonas Mylius und Alfred Friedrich Bluntschli, Max Hegele
9.**11**	Rudolfshof	1871	Theophil von Hansen
1.**19**	Art History and Natural History Museums	1871	Gottfried Semper, Carl von Hasenauer
1.**31**	Academy of Fine Arts	1871	Theophil von Hansen
1.**71**	Stock Exchange (Börse)	1871	Theophil von Hansen
1.**63**	Parliament	1871	Theophil von Hansen
1.**62**	City Hall	1872	Friedrich von Schmidt
1.**54**	University	1873	Heinrich von Ferstel
1.**106s**	Residential Building Alois Hauser	1874	Alois Hauser
1.**64**	Burgtheater	1874	Gottfried Semper, Carl von Hasenauer
6.**1**	Depot for Backdrop and Decorations of the Court Theatres (currently studios of the Academy of Fine Arts)	1875,1993	Gottfried Semper, Carl von Hasenauer, Carl Pruscha
1.**74**	Schottenring Apartment Building	1877	Otto Wagner
9.**18s**	Covered Market Nussdorferstrasse	1879	Friedrich Paul
13.**2**	Palmery Schönbrunn	1881	Franz von Segenschmid
1.**61**	Stadiongasse Apartment Building	1882	Otto Wagner
1.**73**	Länderbank (former)	1882	Otto Wagner
13.**25**	Hermes Villa	1882	Carl von Hasenauer
2.**9**	Freudenau Racecourse	1885	Carl von Hasenauer, Adolf Feszty, Anton u. Josef Drexler
18.**4**	Türkenschanz Park	1885	Heinrich von Ferstel, Gustav Sennholz, Heinrich Goldemund, Wenzel Hybler
14.**7**	Wagner Villa I.	1886	Otto Wagner
9.**4**	Residential Building Universitätsstrasse	1887	Otto Wagner
1.**2**	Palais Equitable	1887	Andreas Streit
7.**2**	Volkstheater	1887	Ferdinand Fellner, Hermann Helmer
1.**40**	Ronacher	1887, (1991)	Ferdinand Fellner, Hermann Helmer, Luigi Blau
19.**12**	Zacherl Factory	1888	Karl Mayreder
3.**5**	Rennweg Apartment Buildings	1890	Otto Wagner
1.**4**	Anker House	1894	Otto Wagner
20.**1**	Nussdorf Weir and Locks	1894	Otto Wagner
12.**16s**	Stadtbahn (City Railway) Bridge over the Zeile (Wienzeile-Brücke)	1895	Otto Wagner
9.**10**	Joannis Chapel	1895	Otto Wagner
2.**4**	Giant Ferris Wheel	1896	Walter B. Basset, Hitchins (eng.)
11.**1**	Simmering Gasometers	1896	Dr. Franz Kapaun
18.**9s**	Suburban Line Station, Gersthof	1896	Otto Wagner
17.**6s**	Richthausen Bridge on the Suburban Line	1896	Otto Wagner
9.**21s**	Stadtbahn Station Alser Strasse	1896	Otto Wagner
13.**1**	Stadtbahn- Imperial Pavilion	1896	Otto Wagner
1.**36**	Stadtbahn and Suburban Lines	1896	Otto Wagner
1.**35**	Secession	1897	Joseph Maria Olbrich
1.**36**	Stadtbahn Station Stadtpark	1897	Otto Wagner
16.**1**	Jubilee Buildings	1898	Theodor Bach, Leopold Simony
1.**36**	Stadtbahn Station Karlsplatz	1898	Otto Wagner
6.**2**	Wienzeile Houses	1898	Otto Wagner
3.**15**	Portois & Fix Residential and Commercial Buildings	1899	Max Fabiani
1.**13**	Artaria House	1900	Max Fabiani
13.**16**	Residential Building Beckgasse	1900	Josef Plečnik

Index	Building	Planned/Start of Construction	Architect
19.**24**	Moser-Moll House 1	1900	Josef Hoffmann
9.**19s**	Stadtbahn Station Rossauer Lände	1900	Otto Wagner
1.**43**	Engel Pharmacy	1901	Oskar Laske
14.**13s**	Residential Building Penzinger Strasse	1901	Karl Fischl
13.**4**	Weidmann House (adaptation of)	1901	Josef Plečnik und Josef Czastka
19.**23**	Spitzer House	1901	Josef Hoffmann
5.**1**	Steggasse Apartment Building	1901	Josef Plečnik
14.**5**	Villa Vojcsik; Atelier Building GGK	1901, 1984	Otto Schönthal, Boris Podrecca
14.**14s**	Baumgartner Höhe	1902	Franz Berger
5.**10s**	Rüdigerhof	1902	Oskar Marmorek
1.**94**	The Wien River Constructions	1903	Friedrich Ohmann, Josef Hackhofer
1.**68**	Hohe Brücke	1903	Josef Hackhofer
1.**70**	Zacherl House	1903	Josef Plečnik
1.**94**	Customs Office Footbridge	1903	Friedrich Ohmann, Josef Hackhofer
1.**88**	Postal Savings Bank	1903	Otto Wagner
S.D.**1**	Sanatorium Purkersdorf	1904	Josef Hoffmann
3.**13**	Karl Borromäus Fountain (Lueger Fountain)	1904	Josef Engelhart, Josef Plečnik
14.**9**	Church of St. Leopold	1905	Otto Wagner
8.**4**	New Academy of Trade and Commerce	1906	Wunibald Deininger
19.**21**	Moll House II	1906	Josef Hoffmann
2.**1**	Schützenhaus	1906	Otto Wagner
5.**2**	Vorwärts – Printers and Publishers	1907	Hubert und Franz Gessner
18.**1**	Gessner House	1907	Hubert und Franz Gessner
8.**1**	Auersperg Sanatorium	1907	Robert Oerley
11.**6**	Lueger Memorial Church	1908	Max Hegele
1.**26**	Kärntner-Bar (Loos-Bar)	1908	Adolf Loos, Renovation: Hermann Czech, Burkhardt Rukschcio
1.**90**	Urania	1909	Max Fabiani
1.**15**	Loos House (formerly Goldman and Salatsch tailoring company)	1909	Adolf Loos
19.**22**	Ast House	1909	Josef Hoffmann
7.**4**	Döblergasse-Neustiftgasse apartment buildings	1909	Otto Wagner
16.**5**	Sanatorium for Lupus patients	1909	Otto Wagner
2.**5**	Krieau Trotting Race Assoc.	1910	Emil Hoppe, Marcel Kammerer, Otto Schönthal
9.**15**	Strudlhofstiege	1910	Theodor Jäger
13.**18**	Steiner House	1910	Adolf Loos
19.**20**	House in the Cobenzlgasse	1910	Oskar Strnad, Oskar Wlach (Josef Frank)
1.**10**	Knize Gentlemen's Outfitters	1910	Adolf Loos
16.**3**	Heilig-Geist Church (Schmelz Parish Church)	1910	Josef Plečnik
1.**5**	Trattnerhof	1911	Rudolf Krauß
13.**33s**	Stoessl House	1911	Adolf Loos
13.**5**	Villa Wustl	1912	Robert Oerley
13.**17**	Horner House	1912	Adolf Loos
13.**15**	Scheu House	1912	Adolf Loos
19.**16**	Kaasgrabengasse Housing Estate	1912	Josef Hoffmann
14.**8**	Wagner Villa II	1912	Otto Wagner
1.**102s**	Tuchlaubenhof	1912	Ernst Spielmann, Alfred Teller
1.**103s**	Manz Booksellers	1912	Adolf Loos
19.**7**	Houses in the Wildbrandtgasse	1913	Josef Frank, Oskar Wlach, Oskar Strnad
13.**10**	Skywa-Primavesi Villa	1913	Josef Hoffmann
9.**3**	National Bank	1913	Leopold Bauer
7.**7**	Central Savings Bank Mariahilf-Neubau	1914	Adolf Loos
13.**8**	Wattmanngasse Residential Building	1914	Ernst Lichtblau

Index	Building	Planned/Start of Construction	Architect
19.**14**	Lemberger House	1914	Jan Kotera
14.**2**	Zeiss Works (now Philips)	1915	Robert Oerley
19.**2**	Duschnitz House	1915	Adolf Loos
19.**3**	Mandl House	1916	Adolf Loos
13.**14**	Strasser House	1918	Adolf Loos
		1918–1945	
15.**7**	Residential Complex Schmelz	1919	Hugo Mayer
S.D.**8s**	Government Officers' Housing Rannersdorf	1921	Heinrich Tessenow, Mayer, Mang
15.**5**	Heimhof	1921	Otto Polak-Hellwig
11.**7**	Crematorium	1921	Clemens Holzmeister
12.**6**	Hoffingergasse Housing Estate	1921	Josef Frank with Erich Faber
12.**10**	Rosenhügel Garden Estate	1921	Hugo Mayer, Emil Krause
17.**5**	Heuberg Housing Estate	1921	Adolf Loos, Hugo Mayer
11.**4**	Weissenböckstrasse Estate	1922	Franz Kaym, Alfons Hetmanek
13.**6**	Rufer House	1922	Adolf Loos
13.**36s**	Residential Building	1922	Ernst Lichtblau
10.**9**	Quarin Hof	1923	Siegfried Theiss, Hans Jaksch
18.**2**	Arnold House	1923	Lois Welzenbacher
10.**8**	Amalienbad	1923	Otto Nadel, Karl Schmalhofer
22.**7**	Housing Estate Am Freihof	1923	Karl Schartelmüller
8.**6**	Ludo Hartmann Hof	1924	Caesar Poppovits
10.**14**	Am Wasserturm Housing Estate	1924	Franz Schuster, Franz Schacherl
17.**1**	Wiedenhofer Hof	1924	Josef Frank
19.**13**	Knips House	1924	Josef Hoffmann
19.**1**	Klose Hof	1924	Josef Hoffmann
20.**3**	Winarsky Hof and Otto Haas Hof	1924	Peter Behrens, Josef Hoffmann, Josef Frank, Oskar Strnad, Oskar Wlach, Karl Dirnhuber, Franz Schuster, Margarete Lihotzky
5.**7**	Reumann Hof	1924	Hubert Gessner
16.**6**	Sandleiten Hof	1924	Emil Hoppe, Otto Schönthal, Franz Matuschek, Siegfried Theiss, Hans Jaksch, Franz Krauß, Josef Tölk
19.**9**	Church of St. Judas in der Krim	1924	Clemens Holzmeister
12.**2**	Bebel Hof	1925	Karl Ehn
3.**18**	Raben Hof	1925	Heinrich Schmid, Hermann Aichinger
15.**3**	Vogelweid Hof	1926	Leopold Bauer
21.**1**	Karl Seitz Hof	1926	Hubert Gessner
3.**12**	Stonborough Wittgenstein House (now Bulgarian Cultural Assoc.)	1926	Paul Engelmann, Ludwig Wittgenstein
19.**25**	Karl Marx Hof und Svoboda Hof	1926	Karl-Ehn
3.**16**	Klopsteinplatz Apartment Block	1927	Walter Sobotka
18.**6**	Moller House	1927	Adolf Loos
10.**11**	George Washington Hof	1927	Karl Krist, Robert Oerley
2.**2**	Augarten Bridge	1928	Hubert Gessner
5.**4**	Diehlgasse Apartment Building	1928	Fritz Judtmann, Egon Riss
10.**1**	Transformer Plant	1928	Eugen Kastner, Fritz Waage
10.**13**	Karmeliterkirche	1928	Hans Prutscher
13.**22**	Lockerwiese Settlement	1928	Karl Schartelmüller
16.**4**	Kongress Bad	1928	Erich Leischner
5.**5**	Labour Exchange for the Metal and Timber Industry	1928	Hermann Stiegholzer, Herbert Kastinger
14.**19s**	Sebastian Kelch Gasse	1928	Josef Frank
17.**7s**	Holy Hof	1928	Rudolf Perco
13.**12**	Beer House	1929	Josef Frank with Oskar Wlach

Index	Building	Planned/Start of Construction	Architect
13.**26**	T.B.C.-Pavilion of the Lainz Hospital	1929	Fritz Judtmann, Egon Riss
21.**2**	Paul Speiser Hof	1929	Hans Glaser, Karl Scheffel, Ernst Lichtblau, Leopold Bauer
2.**8**	Prater Stadium	1929, 1956, 1985	Otto Ernst Schweizer, Theodor Schöll, Erich Frantl
13.**9**	Malfatti Housing Estate	1930	Siegfried C. Drach
13.**23**	Werkbund Housing Estate (Werkbundsiedlung)	1930	Josef Frank, Gerrit Rietveld, Josef Hoffmann, Adolf Loos, Heinrich Kulka, André Lurcat, Ernst A. Plischke, Hugo Häring, Anton Brenner, Oswald Haerdtl, Oskar Strnad, Walter Sobotka
20.**4**	Friedrich Engels Platz Housing	1930	Rudolf Perco
13.**13**	Wenzgasse Secondary School	1930 (1990)	Siegfried Theiss, Hans Jaksch, (Renovation: Theophil Melicher, Georg Schwalm-Theiss, Horst Gressenbauer
1.**49**	Herrengasse High-rise	1931	Siegfried Theiss, Hans Jaksch
12.**1**	Leopoldine Glöckel Hof	1931	Josef Frank
15.**6**	Holochergasse Residential Complex	1931	Oskar Strnad
21.**21s**	Dorotheum Floridsdorf	1931	Egon Kastner, Fritz Waage
1.**96s**	Altmann & Kühne	1932	Josef Hoffmann and Oswald Haerdtl
23.**2**	Employment Office Liesing	1932	Ernst Plischke
18.**11s**	House Hans Glas	1932	Hans Glas
15.**1**	Seipel-Dollfuss Church (Kanzlerkirche)	1933	Clemens Holzmeister
1.**113s**	"Zum Römertor"	1934	Heinrich Schmid, Hermann Aichinger
3.**4**	Neulinggasse Apartment Building	1935	Siegfried C. Drach, Alexander Osterberger
10.**6**	Friedenskirche	1935	Robert Kramreiter
19.**15**	House in the Leopold-Steiner Gasse	1935	Siegfried C. Drach
4.**5**	Funkhaus; Broadcasting Studios for Vienna and Lower Austria	1935	Clemens Holzmeister, Heinrich Schmid, Hermann Aichinger; Gustav Peichl
19.**4**	Bunzl House	1936	Josef Frank, Oskar Wlach
2.**3**	Augarten Flak Tower	1942	Friedrich Tamms
		1945–1974	
10.**15**	Per-Albin-Hansson Housing Estate West	1947	Franz Schuster, Friedrich Pangratz, Stefan Simony, Eugen Wörle
22.**5**	Gänsehäufel Open Air Public Baths	1948	Max Fellerer, Eugen Wörle
15.**12**	Special Kindergarten Schweizer Spende	1948	Franz Schuster
21.**9**	Housing Siemensstrasse	1950	Franz Schuster
19.**11**	Housing Silbergasse	1951	Josef Hoffmann, Josef Kalbac
1.**108s**	Haus der Magnesitwerke	1951	Erich Boltenstern
1.**75**	Ring Tower	1953 (1990)	Erich Boltenstern, Boris Podrecca
1.**34**	Museum of Viennese History	1954	Oswald Haerdtl
1.**59**	Volksgarten	1954	Oswald Haerdtl
1.**107s**	Café Prückel	1955	Oswald Haerdtl
9.**16**	PVA, Old Age Insurance Company for Workers	1955	Franz Schuster
12.**14s**	Rosary Church (Rosenkranzkirche) - interior decoration	1956	Johann Georg Gsteu, Friedrich Achleitner
1.**32**	Böhler House	1956	Roland Rainer
23.**6**	Housing Mauerberg	1956	Roland Rainer
1.**110s**	Ebendorferstrasse Student Chapel	1956	Ottokar Uhl
18.**10s**	Hans Radl School	1958	Viktor Adler
S.D.**5**	ÖMV Pipeline Bridge	1958	Waagner-Biró
3.**9**	Museum of the 20th Century	1959	Karl Schwanzer
14.**4**	Pastoral Care Centre Baumgarten	1960	Johann Georg Gsteu
19.**18**	Peichl House	1960	Gustav Peichl

Index	Building	Planned/Start of Construction	Architect
21.**4**	Special School Floridsdorf	1960	Wilhelm Schütte, Margarete Schütte-Lihotzky
3.**26s**	Hoffmann-La Roche	1960	Georg Lippert
19.**10**	Primary School in der Krim	1961	Gustav Peichl
5.**6**	St. Florian Parish Church	1961	Rudolf Schwarz
11.**3**	Evangelical Church	1962	Roland Rainer
15.**2**	Stadthalle, Halle E, Stadthalle Baths	1962, 1994	Roland Rainer
10.**12**	Philips House	1962	Karl Schwanzer
13.**32s**	Ekazent Hietzing	1962	Wolfgang and Traude Windbrechtinger
13.**24**	Dominican Convent	1963	Gustav Peichl
10.**22s**	Montagekirche Kundratstrasse	1963	Ottokar Uhl
3.**22s**	German Embassy	1963	Rolf Gutbrod
14.**16s**	Bacher House	1963	Wilhelm Holzbauer, Friedrich Kurrent, Johannes Spalt (Arbeitsgruppe 4)
1.**11**	Retti Candle Shop	1964	Hans Hollein
10.**3**	The Holy Family Parish Church (Pfarrkirche zur Heiligen Familie)	1964	Clemens Holzmeister
13.**20**	Konzils-Gedächtniskirche	1965	Josef Lackner
23.**7**	Church of the Holiest Trinity ("Zur Heiligsten Dreifältigkeit")	1965	Fritz Wotruba, Fritz G. Mayr
12.**5**	Meidling Rehabilitation Centre	1966	Gustav Peichl
23.**12s**	Widtmann House	1966	Hans Puchhammer, Gunther Wawrik
1.**25**	CM Boutique	1966	Hans Hollein
13.**34s**	Bettelheim House	1966	Wilhhelm Holzbauer
12.**8**	Am Schöpfwerk Housing Complex	1967	Viktor Hufnagl, E. Bauer, L. Parenzan, J. Peters, M. Pribitzer, F. Waclawek, T. and W. Windbrechtinger
22.**30s**	Secondary School Kagran	1967	Roland Rainer
19.**6**	Institute Building for the University of Agriculture	1967	Anton Schweighofer
1.**76**	Faculty of Law, University of Vienna	1968	Ernst Hiesmayr
13.**11**	Bösch House, Roland Rainer House	1968	Roland Rainer
13.**21**	ORF Centre	1968	Roland Rainer
12.**15s**	Hetzendorf Kindergarten	1968	Johann Georg Gsteu
11.**12s**	Kindergarten	1968	Margarete Schütte-Lihotzky
13.**29s**	Pavilion for Handicapped Children of the Neurological Hospital	1969	Rupert Falkner, Anton Schweighofer
5.**9s**	Zentralsparkasse (now Bank Austria) Reinprechtsdorfer Strasse	1969	Friedrich Kurrent and Johannes Spalt
14.**10**	Stadt des Kindes (City of the Child)	1969	Anton Schweighofer
1.**42**	Kleines Café	1970	Hermann Czech
1.**98s**	Dorotheergasse Galery	1970	Luigi Blau
13.**7**	Grothusen I	1970	Gunter Wawrik, Hans Puchhammer
15.**10**	Savings Bank Sparkassaplatz	1970	Johann Georg Gsteu
10.**7**	Inzersdorfer Straße-Angeligasse Housing Complex	1971	Harry Glück and Partners (W. Höfer, R. Neyer, T. Spychala)
1.**79**	Schottenring – Underground Station	1971	Wilhelm Holzbauer, Heinz Marschalek, Georg Ladstätter, Norbert Gantar (Architektengruppe U-Bahn)
21.**3**	Zentralsparkasse Floridsdorf (now Bank Austria)	1971	Friedrich Kurrent, Johannes Spalt
1.**6**	Schullin Jewellers I (now Deutsch Jewellers)	1972	Hans Hollein
22.**8**	Josef Bohmann Hof	1973	Egon Frauendorfer, Johann Gsteu, Eva Mang, Karl Mang, Annemarie Obermann, Alfred Pal, Udo Schrittwieser, Günther Schuster, Manfred Stein
22.**1**	Uno-City (Vienna International Centre)	1973	Johann Staber
15.**11**	Residential Complex "Wohnen Morgen"	1974	Wilhelm Holzbauer

Index	Building	Planned/Start of Construction	Architect
		1975–1997	
1.**84**	Wunderbar	1975	Hermann Czech
10.**2**	Central Savings Bank (now Bank Austria)	1975	Günther Domenig
S.D.**6**	Council Rooms Perchtoldsdorf	1975	Hans Hollein
19.**31s**	House S.F.	1975	Luigi Blau
10.**18**	Salvatorkirche am Wienerfeld	1976	Johannes Spalt
14.**11s**	Diesterweggasse Primary School	1976	Gustav Peichl
21.**11**	Housing Ernst Theumerhof	1977	Atelier 18: Eder, Pal, Weber, Wieden
1.**24**	Reiss Bar	1977	Coop Himmelblau – Wolf Prix und Helmut Swiczinsky
S.D.**4**	House M.	1977	Hermann Czech
18.**3**	Primary School Köhlergasse	1977	Hans Hollein
1.**75**	Branch of the Austrian Tourist Agency	1977	Hans Hollein
16.**7**	Residential Building Festgasse	1977	Ottokar Uhl
10.**16**	Wienerberg Residential Complex	1978	Otto Häuslmayer, Rudolf Lamprecht, Günther Oberhofer, Werner Oberman, Gustav Peichl, Otto Steidle, Helmut Wimmer
19.**17**	House for an Art Collector	1978	Wilhelm Holzbauer
22.**35s**	Zentralsparkasse Stadlau (now Bank Austria)	1978	Johann Georg Gsteu
23.**11s**	Johann-Gottek Estate	1979	Helmar Zwick
14.**18s**	Grothusen II Warehouse and Office Building	1979	Gunther Wawrik
17.**3**	Schmidt House	1980	Hermann Czech
21.**10**	Housing Gerasdorferstrasse	1980	Viktor Hufnagl
21.**7**	Housing "Living with Children"	1980	Ottokar Uhl u.a.
1.**53**	Demmer's Tea Shop	1981	Luigi Blau
1.**78**	Salzamt Bar and Restaurant	1981	Hermann Czech
1.**12**	Schullin Jewellers II	1981	Hans Hollein
23.**5**	Housing Breitenfurter Strasse	1981	Rob Krier, Hedwig Wachberger and Peter Gebhart
S.D.**7**	Fire Station	1981	Heinz Tesar
22.**21**	Biberhaufenweg Estate	1981	Heinz Tesar, Otto Häuselmayer, Carl Pruscha, Franz and Wilfried Wafler
5.**8**	Einsiedlergasse Apartment Building	1981	Heinz Tesar
19.**8**	Housing on the Gräf and Stift Estate	1981	Helmut Richter/, Heidulf Gerngroß, Anton Schweighofer, Karl Mang, Eva Mang-Frimmel, Johann Brennig, et al.
3.**19**	Hundertwasserhaus	1982	Friedensreich Hundertwasser
13.**19**	House T.	1983	Luigi Blau
22.**26**	Housing Gladiolenweg	1983	Helmut Hempel, Franco Fonatti
23.**13s**	Housing in Wien-Mauer	1983	Dieter Henke, Marta Schreieck
10.**4**	Schrankenberggasse Apartment Block	1983	Rob Krier
1.**97s**	Tromayer Gallery	1983	Anna-Lülja Praun
3.**21s**	Radetzkyplatz Bank Branch (Bank Austria)	1984	Luigi Blau
13.**30s**	Porpaczy Residence	1984	Roland Hagmüller
22.**27**	Multi-functional Hall and Parsonage	1984	IGIRIEN: Werner Appelt, Eberhard Kneissl, Elsa Prochazka
S.D.**9s**	Government Offices Perchtoldsdorf	1984	IGIRIEN: Werner Appelt, Franz Eberhard Kneissl, Elsa Prochazka
6.**7s**	Gumpendorfer Strasse Apartment Building	1984	Timo Penttilä
6.**8s**	Casa Piccola Shoe Shop	1984	Boris Podrecca
9.**8**	Wasagasse Apartment Building	1984	Hans Puchhammer
18.**8s**	Terraced Housing	1984	Roland Rainer
1.**81**	Kiang Restaurant	1984	Helmut Richter, Heidulf Gerngroß
22.**9**	Housing Varnhagengasse	1984	Johannes Spalt

Index	Building	Planned/Start of Construction	Architect
1.**72**	Baumann Studio	1985	Coop Himmelblau – Wolf Prix and Helmut Swiczinsky
1.**99s**	Wahliss Arcade	1985	Coop Himmelblau – Wolf Prix and Helmut Swiczinsky
1.**94**	Stadtpark Footbridge	1985	Hermann Czech, Alfred Pauser
9.**2**	Stein Café and Restaurant	1985	Gregor Eichinger, Christian Knechtl
20.**2**	Housing "Vollwertwohnen" Hartlgasse	1985	Harry Glück, Wilhelm Holzbauer, Heinz Hilmer & Christoph Sattler
1.**3**	The new Haas House	1985	Hans Hollein
S.D.**2**	Schömer Central Office	1985	Heinz Tesar
13.**31s**	Knobling Residence	1985	Heinz Tesar
15.**8**	Residential Building Nobilegasse	1985	Friedrich Kurrent
3.**14**	Petrusgasse Residential Building	1985	Hermann Czech
12.**12**	Rollingergasse	1985	Josef Paul Kleihues, N. Hensel, W. Höfer, K. Becker
19.**19**	House in Salmannsdorf	1986	Adolf Krischanitz
23.**9**	Housing Othellogasse	1986	Theophil Melicher, Georg Schwalm-Theiss, Horst Gressenbauer, Margarethe Cufer, Walter Gruss, Isabella Gruss, Johann Schandl
22.**14**	Housing Kapellenweg	1986	Boris Podrecca/Gotthard Eiböck
23.**4**	Brunner Strasse	1986	Helmut Richter
17.**4**	Residential Building Wittgensteingründe	1986	Max Rieder, Wolfgang Tschapeller, Hans Peter Wörndl
14.**1**	Muthsamgasse	1986	Anton Schweighofer
1.**92**	Falkestrasse Loft Adaptation	1987	Coop Himmelblau – Wolf Prix and Helmut Swiczinsky
7.**6**	Skala Bar and Restaurant	1987	Georg Driendl and Gerhard Steixner
14.**12s**	Waidhausenstrasse	1987	Rüdiger Lainer, Gertraud Auer
15.**13s**	House	1988	Franco Fonatti
7.**1**	Museum Quarter	1988	Laurids and Manfred Ortner
18.**7**	Prohazka House	1988	Rudolf Prohazka
2.**10**	Freudenau Hydro-Electric Plant	1988	Albert Wimmer, Herwig Schwarz, Gottfried Hansjakob, Toni Hansjakob
1.**114s**	Kix Bar	1988	Oskar Putz
1.**112s**	Kunstforum Bank Austria	1988	Gustav Peichl
1.**69**	Wrenkh Café and Restaurant	1989	Eichinger oder Knechtl
2.**6**	Lassallstrasse Office Complex; Bank Austria I and II, ÖMV, IBM	1989	Wilhelm Holzbauer Kurt Hlaweniczka, Harry Glück, Hannes Lintl, Georg Lippert
22.**24**	Housing Pilotengasse	1989	Adolf Krischanitz, Herzog & de Meuron, Otto Steidle & Partners
18.**5**	Single Family House	1989	Adolf Krischanitz
22.**12**	Housing Kamillenweg	1989	Georg Reinberg, Martin Treberspurg & Erich Raith and Kislinger & Trudak
19.**5**	Housing Gatterburggasse	1989	Anton Schweighofer
3.**25s**	Barichgasse Office Building	1989	Peter Schweger & Partners with Iwan Zelenka
13.**35s**	Residential Building	1989	Gert M. Mayr-Keber
12.**11**	Public Square Design in Meidling	1989; 1995	Boris Podrecca
10.**10**	Business Park Vienna	1990	Atelier 4 – Peter Erblich, Zachari Vesselinov, Manfred Hirschler, Peter Scheufler
23.**1**	U6 Underground Stations	1990	Johann Georg Gsteu
22.**13**	Pappelweg Residential Building	1990	Roland Hagmüller
1.**39**	Slavik Gallery	1990	Edmund Hoke
22.**6**	Ice Sports Hall	1990	Sepp Müller, Alfred Berger, Werner Krismer
19.**30s**	Hackenberggasse	1990	Günther Oberhofer
20.**6**	Basler Versicherungen Office Building	1990	Boris Podrecca
23.**3**	Dirmhirngasse School	1990	Boris Podrecca

Index	Building	Planned/Start of Construction	Architect
12.**3**	Mandlgasse Apartment Building	1990	Walter Stelzhammer
19.**27s**	House R.	1990	Boris Podrecca
9.**20s**	Fernwärme (District Heating)	1990	Friedensreich Hundertwasser
23.**10**	Housing Traviatagasse	1991	Raimund Abraham (Masterplan), Carl Pruscha, et al.
22.**33s**	Housing	1991	BKK-2, Christoph Lammerhuber, Axel Linemayr, Franz Sumnitsch, Florian Wallnöfer, Johann Winter, Evelyn Wurster
13.**28s**	Office Building	1991	BKK-2, Christoph Lammerhuber, Axel Linemayr, Franz Sumnitsch, Florian Wallnöfer, Johann Winter, Evelyn Wurster
6.**5**	Apartment Building	1991	Margarethe Cufer, Oswald Oberhuber
11.**2**	Rosa Jochmann School	1991	Hermann Czech, Wolfgang Reder
17.**2**	Residential Building Frauenfelderstraße	1991	Dieter Henke, Marta Schreieck
19.**28s**	Offices Grinzinger Allee	1991	Ulrike Janowetz
11.**11**	Schmidgunstgasse	1991	Franz E. Kneissl
22.**22**	Housing Siegesplatz/ Benjowskygasse	1991	Rüdiger Lainer, Gertraud Auer
5.**3**	Zentagasse Residential Building	1991	Günter Lautner, Peter Scheifinger, Rudolf Szedenik
21.**8**	Office Building	1991	Heinz Neumann
1.**7**	Bibelwerk Bookshop	1991	Elsa Prochazka
9.**6**	Apartment of Sigmund Freud	1991	Wolfgang Tschapeller (Library)
22.**28**	Primary School Pastinakweg	1991	Atelier 4 – Klaus Peter Erblich, Zachari Vesselinov, Manfred Hirschler, Peter Scheufler, Gerhard Schweighofer
8.**7**	Korotan Hotel and Students' Hostel	1991	Boris Podrecca
1.**33**	Akademie Hof Karlsplatz	1991	Gustav Peichl, Roland Rainer
22.**25**	Housing Wiethestrasse 84	1991	Helmut Hempel, Franco Fonatti, Georg Baldass, Heinz H. Weiser, Heidulf Gerngroß
1.**100s**	Glass Gallery	1992	Maria Auböck, Janos Karasz
22.**2**	Danube City	1992	Cufer, Delugan, Hollein, Holzbauer, Krischanitz, Loudon, Neumann
10.**17**	Tesarekplatz, Church, School and Crèche	1992	Otto Häuselmayer, Gustav Peichl, Heinz Tesar
22.**15**	Housing Zschokkergasse	1992	Viktor Hufnagl
22.**20**	Eibengasse Secondary School	1992	Martin Kohlbauer
4.**2**	Kunsthalle Vienna	1992	Adolf Krischanitz
16.**8**	Housing Estate	1992	Adolf Krischanitz
19.**26**	Office Building	1992	Neumann & Partners
3.**1**	Bank Austria Customer Service Centre	1992	Artur Perotti, Günther Domenig
16.**9**	Konrad Lorenz Institute for Behavioural Research	1992	Anton Schweighofer
10.**23s**	Twin Primary School Jagdgasse	1992	Manfred Nehrer, Reinhard Medek
21.**15**	Primary School, Music School Schumpeterweg	1992	Stefan Hübner, Peter Leibetseder
15.**4**	Special School for Children with Visual Disabilities Zinkgasse	1992	Georg Driendl, Gerhard Steixner
1.**85**	"Figarohaus" Wolfgang Amadeus Mozart Gedenkstätte	1992	Elsa Prochazka
3.**23s**	Residential Building	1992	Günther Oberhofer
13.**27**	Hietzinger Hauptstrasse School	1992	Elsa Prochazka
4.**6**	EA Generali Foundation	1992	Andras Pálffy, Christian Jabornegg, Georg Schönfeld
10.**19**	Students' Hostel	1992	Anton Schweighofer
3.**24s**	Shopping Mall	1992	Ernst Hoffmann
S.D.**3**	Evangelical Church Klosterneuburg	1992	Heinz Tesar
22.**17**	Housing Wulzendorf (West)	1993	Ablinger-Vedral, Walter Stelzhammer, Margarethe Cufer

Index	Building	Planned/Start of Construction	Architect
14.**3**	Residential Building Matznergasse	1993	BKK-2, Christoph Lammerhuber, Axel Linemayr, Franz Sumnitsch, Florian Wallnöfer, Johann Winter, Evelyn Wurster
21.**20s**	Housing Anton-Böck Gasse	1993	Eva Ceska, Friedrich Priesner
1.**91**	MAK Café	1993	Hermann Czech
9.**17s**	Management Book Service	1993	Eichinger oder Knechtl
20.**7**	Housing Wexstraße	1993	Otto Häuselmayer
1.**30**	Ringstrasse Galleries	1993	Wilhelm Holzbauer et al.
22.**3**	Andromeda High-rise	1993	Wilhelm Holzbauer
23.**8**	Thermal Power Station	1993	Martin Kohlbauer
12.**7**	Apartment Building	1993	Rüdiger Lainer, Gertraud Auer
12.**9**	Rohrwassergasse School	1993	Manfred Nehrer and Reinhard Medek
16.**2**	Laboratory Building	1993	Manfred Nehrer and Reinhard Medek
3.**8**	Burgtheater Rehearsal Stage	1993	Gustav Peichl
22.**16**	Housing Tamariskengasse	1993	Roland Rainer
22.**18**	Housing Wulzendorf (East)	1993	August Sarnitz, Reinhard Haselwanter, Ernst Linsberger, Helmut Wimmer, Markus Spiegelfeld, Günther Holnsteiner
22.**17**	Housing	1993	Walter Stelzhammer
21.**12**	Housing	1993	Martin Treberspurg, Georg W. Reinberg, Erich Raith
21.**6**	Housing Brünner Strasse	1993	Helmut Wimmer, Eva Reichl et al.
22.**31s**	Primary School Viktor Wittner Gasse	1993	Sepp Frank
22.**23**	Secondary School Simonsgasse	1993	Günther Domenig
21.**19**	Primary School Zehdengasse	1993	ARTEC: Bettina Götz/Richard Manahl
21.**22s**	Kindertagesheim der Stadt Wien	1993	Markus Geiswinkler
22.**32s**	House Hinterberger	1993	Andreas and Gerda Gerner
22.**11**	Housing Mühlgrundweg	1993	Walter Stelzhammer, Paul Katzberger, Karin Bily, Theophil Melicher, Georg Schwalm-Theiss, Horst Gressenbauer
14.**17s**	Annex to the Technical Museum (Entrance Hall)	1993	Atelier in der Schönbrunner Straße
22.**37s**	Housing and Shopping Centre	1993	Ernst Hoffmann
16.**10s**	Secondary School Koppstrasse	1994	Atelier 18: Eder, Pal, Weber, Wieden
22.**4**	Residential Towers Wagramerstraße	1994	Coop Himmelblau; Gustav Peichl, Rudolf F. Weber; NFOG
11.**8**	Leberberg Housing Estate (Nord)	1994	Margarethe Cufer, Otmar Hasler, Walter Stelzhammer, et al.
1.**111s**	Unger & Klein Wine Store	1994	Eichinger oder Knechtl
1.**80**	Ron con Soda	1994	Eichinger oder Knechtl
21.**17**	Housing "Intercultural Living"	1994	Kurt Heidecker, Herbert Neuhauser
7.**8s**	Film House	1994	Helmut Heistinger
2.**7**	Neue Welt Kindergarten	1994	Adolf Krischanitz
1.**89**	General Post Office	1994	Adolf Krischanitz, Heinz Neumann
10.**5**	Secondary School Absberggasse	1994	Rüdiger Lainer and Gertraud Auer
22.**10**	Housing Heinrich Lefler Gasse	1994	Michael Loudon
19.**29s**	Grinzinger Allee Office Building	1994	Heinz Neumann
6.**6s**	Mariahilfer Strasse Office Building	1994	Heinz Neumann
22.**36s**	Primary School	1994	Nigst, Fonatti, Ostertag, Gaisrucker (NFOG)
21.**16**	Housing	1994	Jean Nouvel
21.**14**	Primary and Secondary School Hanreitergasse	1994	Gustav Peichl, Rudolf F. Weber
22.**19**	Housing Erzherzog Karl Stadt	1994	Gustav Peichl, Martin Kohlbauer, Peter Nigst, Paul Katzberger, Karin Bily, Michael Loudon, ARCA (Franco Fonatti, et al.)
8.**8**	Folk Museum	1994	Elsa Prochazka

Index	Building	Planned/Start of Construction	Architect
3.**17**	Rennweg Residential Park	1994	Architektengruppe Rennweg: Schweighofer,Rainer, Nehrer and Medek
14.**6**	Waidhausenstraße/Kinkplatz School	1994	Helmut Richter
12.**13**	Altmannsdorf Garden Hotel	1994	Michael Schluder and Hanns Kastner
21.**18**	Frauen-Werk-Stadt	1994	Franziska Ullmann, Lieselotte Peretti, Gisela Podreka, Elsa Prochazka, Maria Auböck
11.**10**	Svetelskystrasse Primary and Secondary School	1994	Dieter Henke, Marta Schreieck
8.**5**	Branch Office of the Erste Österreichische Spar-Casse	1994	Boris Podrecca
11.**9**	Leberberg Housing Estate (South)	1994	Markus Spiegelfeld, Günther Holnsteiner, Ulrike Janowetz, Michael Wagner, August Sarnitz, Claudio Blazica, Laura Spinadel, Kurt Heidecker, Herbert Neuhauser, Christine Zwingl
20.**5**	Housing Handelskai	1994	Heinz Neumann, Eric Steiner
21.**13**	Housing Ocwirkgasse	1994	Theophil Melicher, Georg Schwalm-Theiss, Horst Gressenbauer
21.**5**	Loftsiedlung Vienna-Floridsdorf	1994	Heidulf Gerngroß, Werkstatt Wien
19.**32s**	House	1994	Ernst Hoffmann
21.**13**	Church	1994	Otto Häuselmayer
22.**29s**	Housing Estate Süssenbrunn	1995	Otto Häuselmayer
1.**95s**	Lichtforum Vienna	1995	Hans Hollein
7.**9s**	Apartment Building	1995	Günther Holnsteiner
10.**20s**	Städtisches Ökohaus	1995	Günther Lautner, Peter Scheifinger, Rudolf Szedenik, Cornelia Schindler
1.**55**	Office Refurbishment of the ÖBV (Civil Service Insurance Company)	1995	Walter Stelzhammer
2.**12s**	Kai 302 Housing Complex	1995	Albert Wimmer
1.**27**	Jewish Museum of Vienna (Renovation)	1995	Eichinger oder Knechtl/Franz Sam
15.**14s**	Bezirksgericht Fünfhaus (District Courts)	1995	Günther Oberhofer
14.**15s**	Hackingersteg (Footbridge)	1995	D. Henke, M. Schreieck, W. Ziesel
22.**34s**	Job Centre	1996	Bernhard Denkinger
1.**101s**	Helmut Lang Boutique	1996	Gustav Pichelmann
3.**3**	Kiang III	1997	Helmut Richter

General Bibliography

Dehio-Handbuch, Die Kunstdenkmäler Österreichs, Band Wien, Ed. Bundesdenkmalamt, Wien-München

Achleitner, Friedrich, *Österreichische Architektur im 20. Jahrhundert*, 4 Vols., Salzburg/Wien 1980–1995

Österreichische Architektur 1960 bis 1970, ed. by Österreichische Gesellschaft für Architektur, Wien 1969

Becker, Steiner, Wang (Eds.), *Österreich-Architektur im 20. Jahrhundert*, München 1995

Architektur in Wien, ed. by Magistrat der Stadt Wien, Wien 1984, 1990

Baujahre. Österreichische Architektur 1967–1991, ed. by Zentralvereinigung der Architekten Österreichs, Wien/Köln/Weimar 1992

Bobek, Hans; Lichtenberger, Elisabeth, *Wien. Bauliche Gestalt und Entwicklung seit der Mitte des 19. Jahrhunderts*, Wien 1966

Gmeiner, Astrid; Pirhofer, Gottfried, *Der österreichische Werkbund*, Salzburg/Wien 1985

Haiko, Peter, *Wien 1850–1930. Architektur*, Wien 1992

Hautmann, Hans; Hautmann, Rudolf, *Die Gemeindebauten des Roten Wien 1919–34*, Wien 1980

Kapfinger, Otto; Kneissl, Franz E., *Dichte Packung. Architektur aus Wien*, Salzburg/Wien 1989

Noever, Peter (Ed.), *Wiener Bauplätze. Verschollene Träume – Angewandte Programme. Wien um 1986*, Wien 1986

Steiner, Dietmar (Ed.), *Werkstatt Metropole Wien. Die Kultur des Wohnens*, Wien 1988

Tabor, Jan (Ed.), *Kunst und Diktatur. Architektur, Bildhauerei und Malerei in Österreich. Deutschland. Italien und der Sowjetunion 1922–1956*, 2 Vols., Baden 1994

Posch, Wilfried, *Die Wiener Gartenstadtbewegung. Reformversuch zwischen Erster und Zweiter Gründerzeit*, Wien, 1981

Wien. Architektur – Der Stand der Dinge, Stadtplanung Wien (Ed.), Wien 1995

Peichl, Gustav (Ed.), *Wiener Wohnbau Beispiele*, Wien 1985

Peichl, Gustav; Steiner, Dietmar (Eds), *Neuer Wiener Wohnbau*, Wien 1986

Weihsmann, Helmut, *Das Rote Wien. Sozialdemokratische Architektur und Kommunalpolitik 1919–1934*, Wien 1985

Monographs on architects

Graf, Otto Antonia, *Otto Wagner. Das Werk des Architekten*, 5 Vols., Wien/Köln/Graz 1982

Sekler, Eduard F., *Josef Hoffmann. Das architektonische Werk*, Salzburg/Wien 1982

Rukschcio, Burkhard; Schachel, Roland, *Adolf Loos. Leben und Werk*, Salzburg/Wien 1982

Spalt, Johannes; Czech, Hermann (Eds.), *Josef Frank 1885–1967*, Wien 1981

Krischanitz, Adolf; Kapfinger, Otto, *Die Wiener Werkbundsiedlung. Dokumentation einer Erneuerung*, Wien 1985

Sarnitz, August, *Lois Welzenbacher: Architekt 1889–1955*, Salzburg/Wien 1989

Sarnitz, August, *Ernst Lichtblau. Architekt 1883–1963. Gestell und Gestalt im Raum. Reflexionen über ein Paradigma der modernen Architektur*, Wien/Köln/Weimar 1994

Roland Rainer: Arbeiten aus 65 Jahren, Salzburg/Wien 1990

Wilhelm Holzbauer, Bauten und Projekte 1985–90, ed. by Hochschule für angewandte Kunst, Wien 1990

Gustav Peichl, Bauten und Projekte, ed. by Kunst-und Ausstellungshalle der Bundesrepublik Deutschland, Stuttgart 1992

Hans Hollein, ed. by Historisches Museum der Stadt Wien, Wien 1995

Coop Himmelblau, *Die Faszination der Stadt*, Darmstadt 1988

Waechter-Böhm, Liesbeth, *Heinz Tesar*, Basel 1995

Austrian journals on architecture

Der Architekt, 1 (1895) – 24 (1921/22)

architektur aktuell, 1 (1967) –

Architektur und Bauforum, 23 (1990)

Der Aufbau, 1 (1946) – 43 (1988) since under the titel: *Perspektiven*

Der Bau, 1 (1946) – 26 (1971)

Bauforum, 1 (1967/68) – 22 (1989) since under the titel: *Architektur und Bauforum*

Österreichs Bau- und Werkkunst, 1 (1924–25) – 8 (1932) Successor: *Profil*

Perspektiven 44 (1989)

UM BAU, 1 (1979) –

Wettbewerbe, 1 (1977)

List of illustrations and photo credits

Akademie der bildenden Künste, Kupferstichkabinett, Wien 353

Driendl, Steixner, Archives 174 b.

Mischa Erben, Wien 202 b.l., b.r., 255, 281 b., 355, 359, 363 t.

Hans Hollein, Archives 71, 78 b., 281, 364

Werner Kaligofsky, Wien 163 t.

Robert Kiermayer, Wien Frontispiece t, 70 b., 71 t., 72 t., 73 b., 74 t., b, 77 b., 78 t., b, 79 t., b., 81 t., m.l., m.r., b.r., 82 b.l, 83, 84 t., b., 85 t., 87, 88 b., 89 t., t.l., 90 t., b., 91 t., b., 92 t., b., 98 t.l., t., 99, 100 b., 101 t., b., 102 t., b.l., 103, 104 t., 106 t., b., 107 b., 108 t., 110 b., 113 t., b., 114 t., 116 b., 118 b., 119, 120 t., 121, 122 t., 126 t., b., 127 m.l., 128 t.l., b., 129, 138 t., 139, 141 t., 143, 144 t., 145 t., 147 b., 149, 152 b., 153, 154 t., b., 155, 156, 161, 162 t., 163 b., 164 b., 165 t., 168 t.r., b., 169 b., 174 t., 176 t., 177 t., 180 t., 181 b., 182 b., 186 b., 188, 192 t., 193 t., b., 194 t., 198 b., b.l., 199, b., 200 t., t.l., 204, 206, 214 b.l., b.r., 215, 224 t., 225 b., 226, 230 t., b., 231, 234 t., 235, 239 b., 241, 247 b., 253, 263 m., b., 264 t., b., 266 b., 267 t., b., 268, 270 b., 271, 272 t., 273 b., 275, 276, 277 t.r., b., 282 t., 290 t., 292 t.l., b., 295 t., b., 297 t., 301 t., 302, 303, 308, 309 t., 310 t., b., 312, 316 t., 317 t., m., 318 b., 319 t., 320 t., 321 t., 322 t., b., 323 t., b., 324 t., b., 326, 330 t., 331, 332, 334, 338 t., b., 339 t., b., 340 t., b., 341 t., b., 342 t., b., 344 b., 345, 346 t., b., 356 t., 357 t., b., 358, 362 b.

Österreichische Donaukraftwerke AG, Archives 142 b.

Gustav Peichl, Archives 297 b.

Boris Podrecca, Archives 225 t., t.l., 179 t.

Roland Rainer, Archives 243 t.

Georg Riha, Wien 32–64

Margherita Spiluttini, Wien Frontispiece b., 70 t., 72 b., 73 t., 75, 76, 77, 80, 81 m.l., b.l., 82 t., b., 85 b., 86 t., b., 88 t., 93, 94, 95, 96, 97 t.,98 b., 100 t., 102 b., 104 b., 105 t., b., 107 t., 108 t., 109 t., b., 110 t., 111, 112 t., b., 114 b., 115, 116 t., 117, 118 t., 120 b., 122 b., 123, 124 t., b., 125, 127 t., b., 128 t., 130 b., 131, 136 t., b., 137, 138 b., 140, 141 b., 142 t., 144 b., 145 b., 146 t., b., 147 t., 148, 150 t., b., 151, 152 t., 160 t., b., 162 b., 164 t., 165 b., 166 t., b., 167 t., b., 168 t.l., 169 t., 170 t., b., 171, 172 t., b., 173 t., b., 175 t., b., 176 b., 177 b., 178 b., 179 b., 180 b., 181 t., 182 t., 183, 184 t., b., 185 t., b., 186 t., 187 t., b., 192 b., 194 b., 195, 196 t., b., 197, 198, 199 t., 200 b., 201 t., b., 202 t., 203, 205, 210 t., b., 211 t., b., 212 t., b., 213, 214 t., 216, 220 t., b., 221 b., 222 t., b., 223 t., b., 224 b., 232 t., b., 233 t., b., 234 b., 236, 237, 238 t., b., 239 t., 240 t., b., 242 t., b., 243 b., 244, 245, 246 t., b., 247 t., 252 t., b., 254 t., b., 256 t., b., 257, 258, 262, 263 t., 264 t., 265 t., b., 266 t., 269, 270 t., 272 b., 273 t., m., 274 t., b., 277 t.l., 278 t., b., 279, 280 t., b., 282 b., 283, 284, 288 t., b., 289 t., b., 290 b., 291, 292 t., 293, 294 t., b., 296 t., b., 298 t., b., 299, 300, 301, 309 b., 316 t., 317 b., 318 t., 319 b., 320 b., 321 b., 325, 333, 335, 336 t., b., 337, 343, 344 t., 347, 356 b., 362 t., 363 b., 364 t.

Gerald Zugmann, Wien 97 b., 130 t., 178 t., 311, 354

Plans – Drawings:

Renate Banik-Schweitzer 10, 11, 20, 21

Otto Antonia Graf; Otto Wagner, Das Werk des Architekten, Böhlau, Wien-Köln-Graz 1986. 117

Eduard F. Sekler; Josef Hoffmann, Das architektonische Werk, Residenz, Salzburg-Wien, 1982. 235, 300

Burkhardt Rukschcio, Roland Schachel; Adolf Loos, Residenz, Salzburg-Wien, 1982. 75, 79, 87, 175, 279

Johannes Spalt, Hermann Czech; Josef Frank, Wien, 1981. 237, 276, 289, 291

Österreichischer Ingenieur-und Architekten-Verein (Ed.); Wien am Anfang des XX. Jahrhunderts, Wien, 1906, all historical ground-plans.

When not from the archives of the authors themselves, all illustrations and photos have been kindly made available by the architects.

SpringerArchitecture

Daniela Hammer-Tugendhat, Wolf Tegethoff (eds.)

Ludwig Mies van der Rohe. The Tugendhat House

1998. Approx. 140 partly coloured figures. Approx. 220 pages.
Format: 21 x 30 cm
Cloth approx. DM 78,–, öS 546,–. ISBN 3-211-83065-0
German Edition:
Ludwig Mies van der Rohe. Das Haus Tugendhat
Gebunden etwa DM 78,–, öS 546,–. ISBN 3-211-83096-0

The Tugendhat House in Brno (Czech Republic) was planned and built by Mies van der Rohe from 1929–1930, and is universally regarded not only as one of his masterpieces, but also as one of the most important buildings of European Modern architecture.

What makes this monograph particularly fascinating is the fact that it presents previously unpublished photographs belonging to the Tugendhat family. These show the house as it was when it was first lived in. A representative collection of plans and drawings from Mies van der Rohe's atelier can also be seen for the first time. Carefully produced photographs of the original furniture in the family's possession, much of which has never been shown, are also included.

Essays by Wolf Tegethoff, Franz Schulze, and Ivo Hammer give a detailed analysis of the significance of the Tugendhat House in the context of Mies van der Rohe's architecture as a whole, as well as the living concepts of Modern architecture, to which Mies made such a decisive contribution.

Daniela Hammer-Tugendhat applies herself to the key question as to how habitable the Tugendhat House was, based on her personal recollections and texts written by her parents.

SpringerWienNewYork

Sachsenplatz 4–6, P.O.Box 89, A-1201 Wien, Fax +43-1-330 24 26
e-mail: order@springer.at, Internet: http://www.springer.at
New York, NY 10010, 175 Fifth Avenue • D-14197 Berlin, Heidelberger Platz 3
Tokyo 113, 3-13, Hongo 3-chome, Bunkyo-ku

SpringerArchitecture

Otto Kapfinger

Klaus Kada

Portraits österreichischer Architekten,
Portraits of Austrian Architects, Vol. 4

1998. Approx. 310 partly coloured figures. Approx. 200 pages.
Format: 32,5 x 23,5 cm
Cloth approx. DM 98,–, öS 686,–
ISBN 3-211-83070-7
Text: German/English

Klaus Kada is today one of the most renowned Austrian architects of international repute. His buildings are a continuation of both precise contextual analysis and dynamic spatial concepts, technological innovation and poetic detail. His work includes such diverse assignments as the Glas Museum in Bärnbach, the Institute of Plant Physiology in Graz, the new Festival Hall in St. Pölten, the European Academy in Bolzano, as well as outstanding industrial buildings, housing estates and villas.
Lucidity of plan structure, space and movement, extending beyond a purely technical transparency, is his maxim. The path that led him out of the sphere of the so-called "Grazer Schule" is documented here for the first time in a comprehensive analysis of his work.

Sachsenplatz 4–6, P.O.Box 89, A-1201 Wien, Fax +43-1-330 24 26
e-mail: order@springer.at, Internet: http://www.springer.at
New York, NY 10010, 175 Fifth Avenue • D-14197 Berlin, Heidelberger Platz 3
Tokyo 113, 3-13, Hongo 3-chome, Bunkyo-ku

SpringerArchitecture

Allan S. Janik, Hans Veigl

Wittgenstein in Vienna

A Biographical Excursion Through the City and its History

1998. Approx. 33 figures. Approx. 200 pages.
Format: 14 x 23,5 cm
Soft cover DM 39,–, öS 275,–. ISBN 3-211-83077-4
German Edition:
Wittgenstein in Wien
Ein biographischer Streifzug durch die Stadt und ihre Geschichte
Broschiert DM 39,–, öS 275,–. ISBN 3-211-83076-6

"Wittgenstein in Vienna" documents Wittgenstein's life in Vienna: the places he, his family and those with whom he was in contact lived, worked and entertained themselves. The book should enrich the experiences of cultural tourists in Vienna. It provides walks in the city and environs.
Its authors are not only profound authorities on Wittgenstein's philosophy but also on Viennese popular culture, especially on the coffee house culture.

Sachsenplatz 4–6, P.O.Box 89, A-1201 Wien, Fax +43-1-330 24 26
e-mail: order@springer.at, Internet: http://www.springer.at
New York, NY 10010, 175 Fifth Avenue • D-14197 Berlin, Heidelberger Platz 3
Tokyo 113, 3-13, Hongo 3-chome, Bunkyo-ku

Springer-Verlag and the Environment

WE AT SPRINGER-VERLAG FIRMLY BELIEVE THAT AN international science publisher has a special obligation to the environment, and our corporate policies consistently reflect this conviction.

WE ALSO EXPECT OUR BUSINESS PARTNERS – PRINTERS, paper mills, packaging manufacturers, etc. – to commit themselves to using environmentally friendly materials and production processes.

THE PAPER IN THIS BOOK IS MADE FROM NO-CHLORINE pulp and is acid free, in conformance with international standards for paper permanency.

Notes